CRITICAL SURVEY OF POETRY

Romantic Poets

Editor

Rosemary M. Canfield Reisman
Charleston Southern University

SALEM PRESS
A Division of EBSCO Publishing, Ipswich, Massachusetts

Cover photo:
John Keats (© Lebrecht Music & Arts/Corbis)

ISBN: 978-1-42983-655-5

CONTENTS

CONTRIBUTORS

Lowell A. Bangerter
University of Wyoming

David Barratt
Montreat College

Todd K. Bender
*University of Wisconsin-
Madison*

Diane D'Amico
Allegheny College

Desiree Dreeuws
Sunland, California

Donald P. Haase
Wayne State University

Irma M. Kashuba
Chestnut Hill College

Frederick Kirchhoff
Fort Wayne, Indiana

Rebecca Kuzins
Pasadena, California

Richard E. Matlak
College of the Holy Cross

Richard E. Meyer
*Western Oregon State
College*

Leslie B. Mittleman
*California State University,
Long Beach*

Joseph Natoli
Irvine, California

Sylvie L. F. Richards
*Northwest Missouri State
University*

Samuel J. Rogal
Illinois State University

Jean M. Snook
*Memorial University of
Newfoundland*

Robert Lance Snyder
*Georgia Institute of
Technology*

ROMANTIC POETS

Between 1780 and 1830, British poetry took a radically new turn. This is commonly known as the Romantic Revolution. It is best to see this change as part of a much wider movement across all the arts and covering much of Western Europe and the United States, the earliest manifestations perhaps going back as far as 1740, and continuing right into the twentieth century. Generically, this very wide-embracing movement is known as Romanticism.

Between 1780 and 1830, there were parallel radical and even revolutionary movements to this cultural and artistic one, including the American and French Revolutions. There were also revolutions in agriculture, which in Britain changed the face of the landscape and the lifestyle of its inhabitants. Even more profound was the Industrial Revolution, which began in Britain, with its rapid urbanization and concomitant social problems. Industrialization was then followed by colonization throughout the nineteenth century, and a vast increase in wealth. Writers such as C. S. Lewis have claimed that this machine age was the biggest cultural shift since medieval times. The links between the Romantic Revolution and these other revolutionary developments are complex and widely debated, but lie outside the focus of this discussion.

ROMANTICISM DEFINED

The related terms "Romantic," "Romance," and "Romanticism" are often used very loosely, and need some definition. First, the terms are used with a capital letter, to distinguish them from "romance" and "romantic," terms that are usually applied to love stories or erotically heightened situations. Although Romances often contain a love interest, that is not what defines them. Likewise, Romantic poets deal with the whole gamut of human experience, not just love affairs or the experience of being in love.

The British Romantic poets of this period never used the term "Romantics" to describe themselves. It was the next generation, the Victorians, who applied the term to them. They used, in certain situations, the term "Romance," to designate a certain traditional genre of literature that can be traced back to medieval times. This genre deals with tales of wonder and adventure, often involving the marvellous and the supernatural. It can be written as either prose fiction or as verse. Samuel Taylor Coleridge (1772-1834) wrote his famous poem *The Rime of the Ancient Mariner* (1798) as such a Romance, part of a long tradition of magical voyages.

However, it is best to set this genre aside in thinking of the terms "Romantic" and "Romanticism." Although generalizations are difficult, the best way to come to an understanding of the terms is by seeing how Romanticism differs from the cultural movement against which it reacted in the first place, and the cultural movement that succeeded it, in which contemporary poetry finds its place.

ROMANTIC VS. CLASSICAL

The cultural movement that preceded Romanticism is known by a variety of names. At its widest, it can be called the Enlightenment, which can be seen as an artistic, philosophical, and scientific movement that privileges the human reason, seeing humankind as self-sufficient in its ability to discover truth of whatever sort. The supernatural is either banished altogether as "superstition" or put into the background as no longer necessary. Thus, Christianity became Deism or atheism. Excessive shows of emotion were seen as antirational and to be suppressed. Intuition, the feminine, and the spiritual were demoted to the second rank of worthwhileness in human study and endeavor.

In terms of literature, the expression of this cultural movement was usually termed classical or neoclassical, since its models went back to Greek and Roman literature. The study of Roman and Greek language, culture, and literature has always been known as studying the classics. In the history of English literature, sometimes the term "Augustan" is used to denote the particular period of the Roman emperor Augustus as the peak of classical civilization.

Romanticism, by contrast, sought to privilege the imaginative and the intuitive as ways to truth. The term "imaginative truth" was coined, and this truth was claimed to be of equal worth to scientific and philosophical truth, or even higher. Poets were seen as truth tellers and prophets to their generation, often taking on a quasi-religious role as members of a new priesthood. Percy Bysshe Shelley (1792-1822) and other anti-Christian Romantics in fact claimed poetry had taken over religion, as did the Victorian Romantic, Matthew Arnold (1822-1888).

This does not mean that all Romantic poets were antireligious or antiscientific, but rather that they downgraded the rational and the logical and valued the intuitive. One manifestation of this was the trust in childhood states of being, of "innocence" as being a form of truth. This goes back to the Greek philosopher, Plato, who held that the human soul comes straight from heaven, entering a baby uncorrupted. Thus, young children are naturally nearer to heaven in their innocence. "Now We Are Seven" and "Ode: Intimations of Immortality from Recollections of Early Childhood," by William Wordsworth (1770-1850) are excellent examples of this, as are the poems in *Songs of Innocence* (1789), by William Blake (1757-1827). By contrast, the Enlightenment philosopher John Locke believed children to be born with nothing, to be "blank slates," and orthodox Christianity believed children to be born already "fallen" and corrupt.

Generally Romantic poets were Platonists, following a long tradition in English poetry that includes the late Elizabethan poet Edmund Spenser, the seventeenth century poet John Milton, and the mystics Henry Vaughan and Thomas Traherne. Classicism tends to build on the thinking of the other great Greek thinker, Aristotle. This Platonism was reinforced by the writings of the eighteenth century French philosopher Jean-Jacques Rousseau, who might well be called the philosopher of childhood. He saw the perfect education as preventing the child's soul from becoming corrupted, which is essentially by contact with society. The ideal education is homeschooling in a country milieu, in nature, a schooling which, by chance, Wordsworth enjoyed in the Lake District of northern England. Rousseau also suggested that in society, the city was more corrupt than the country. This was at odds with neoclassicism, which was basically an urban culture. The Romantics tended to privilege country people, folkways, and primitivism in general as being less corrupt. This led to an interest in remote cultures and poetry.

Neoclassical theory had emphasized the need for a "poetic diction" distinct from everyday speech. In reaction, Wordsworth proposed a vocabulary and speech of ordinary people. He had in mind particularly the speech of the independent small farmers of his native Lake District, who, like their counterparts in Scotland, would have had some education and an oral tradition. This particular part of the Romantic agenda was never fulfilled, and it was left to modernism to embrace demotic speech and ordinary speech rhythms.

ROMANTICISM VS MODERNISM

Generally, the Romantic poets kept to traditional and classical verse forms and genres. Thus, they used sonnets, lyrical verse, odes, epic forms, and especially blank verse and rhymed heroic couplets. They tended to revert to classical imagery, although their concept of Greek and Roman myths was of something dynamic and truth bearing rather than merely ornamental, as it had become in later neoclassical poetry. John Keats (1795-1821) and Shelley, for example, were both fascinated with Greek mythology.

By contrast, twentieth century modernism completed the revolution in speech rhythms and freer verse forms. In modernism, imagery also broke away from either nature imagery or classical mythology. Although Romantic poetry had at first sought engagement with the more sordid aspects of reality, as in Blake's *Songs of Experience*, it quickly withdrew from this, and it was left to modernist poets to reengage with urban, ugly, and sordid scenes and experiences. Romanticism sought to see itself as "uplifting" in its idealism and views on the perfectability of human beings.

In political dimensions, Romantic poets had embraced revolutionary and radical stances. To some extent, these were actually born out of the Enlightenment, with its stress on the dignity of humankind and concepts of human rights. Wordsworth totally embraced the French Revolution at first, as he recounts in his autobiographical long poem *The Prelude: Or, The Growth of a Poet's Mind* (1850). Shelley and George Gordon, Lord Byron (1788-1824) supported Greek freedom from the Turks.

After the excesses of the French Revolution, the older generation of Romantic poets became conservative, although Wordsworth never lost certain radical views. However, the younger generation of Romantic poets, as Keats, Shelley, Lord Byron, and Leigh Hunt (1784-1859), held the faith and either went into exile or finished up in prison on sedition charges. Nevertheless, it was left to modernist poets to reengage with radical politics, although the record here has been as patchy as with the Romantics.

EARLY MOVES

Romantic poetry did not suddenly arrive in Britain with the publication of Blake's *Songs of Innocence* or Wordsworth and Coleridge's joint venture, the *Lyrical Ballads* (1798). There had been a growing interest in different types of poetry to do with three topics: nature, heightened feelings, and primitive cultures.

There had been a long tradition of nature poetry in British poetry, some of it in the classical pastoral tradition, but some of it involving more of a nature mysticism, as in the poetry of Vaughan. In the eighteenth century, there was a growing interest in cultivating nature as well as the well-designed garden. *The Seasons* (1730), a long blank-verse poem by James Thompson (1700-1748), marks a high point of such interest.

An example of the poetry of heightened feelings can be seen in the very popular *The Complaint: Or, Night-Thoughts on Life, Death, and Immortality* (1742-1744; commonly known as *Night-Thoughts*), by Edward Young (1683-1748). These were meditations on death and mutability set in a graveyard. Such meditations were to provoke sensations of fear, dread, and also the sublime. There was, in fact, an intense discussion as to the nature of sublimity and how it might be expressed in art and poetry. This ran parallel to discussion on the nature of beauty. Both were conducted in a neoclassical setting but proved central to Romantic poetry.

There was also a growing interest in primitive, especially Celtic, cultures. When a long poem by the Scottish poet and antiquarian James Macpherson (1736-1796), entitled *Ossian*, based on the adventures of Oisín, a legendary Celtic hero, purportedly translated from the ancient Gaelic, was published in 1761, it took the country by storm. The staunch neoclassical poet and critic Samuel Johnson (1709-1784) denounced it as a forgery, and Macpherson was challenged to produce the original documents. A huge furor ensued, giving the poem further publicity. The incident shows the craving for such primitive lost literature. The poem was translated and influenced early German Romanticism, the Storm and Stress movement, as well as German Romantic music. Felix Mendelssohn's *Fingal's Cave* is directly inspired by *Ossian*.

Also catering to this desire were the forgeries by Thomas Chatterton (1752-1770), beginning with a fabricated history of the old Bristol Bridge in 1768 and including *Poems Supposed to Have Been Written at Bristol, by Thomas Rowley, and Others in the Fifteenth Century*, edited by Thomas Tyrwhitt and published in 1777, after Chatterton's death. Even Johnson was impressed by this sixteen-year-old's gifts. Tragically, Chatterton, "the marvellous boy" as the Romantics called him, committed suicide at the age of seventeen, the first in a long list of early deaths that somehow have come to typify the Romantic poet.

WORDSWORTH AND NATURE POETRY

Wordsworth is probably the best-known British Romantic poet. For much of Wordsworth's own lifetime, he had only a small, if admiring, audience. His poetry was eclipsed by that of Sir Walter Scott (1771-1832) and that of Lord Byron in popularity and sales, and he was dependent on gifts, bequests, and government appointments. It took him until 1830, with the help of Coleridge, to gain sufficient recognition to be seen as a major poet, and it was not until nearly before his death, that he received general recognition in his appointment as poet laureate by Queen Victoria's request.

At first, Wordsworth's poetry offended literary taste by seeming too ordinary, even too childish. The *Lyrical Ballads* was a collection of ballad-type poems about country folk who often had suffered some misfortune and it used deliberately simplistic language. Some characters are decrepit, and some are mentally retarded or unbalanced. However, they are survivors and are meant to show how those living close to nature can have moral courage in the face of the worst circumstances.

One poem in *Lyrical Ballads*, which Wordsworth added to the collection at the last moment, was completely different: "Lines Composed a Few Miles Above Tintern Abbey." It spoke of mystical experiences, epiphanies of nature, and the belief that there was a divine spirit working in and through nature. Through memory and meditation, the perceptive receiver would become a better, more moral person. This statement lies at the heart of Wordsworth's Romanticism.

The immediate impact of such beliefs was to replace the static Enlightenment concept of Creation, an ordered, even mechanistic creation of a distant God with a concept of nature as divine force. At times, Wordsworth is explicitly pantheistic, although in midlife he became more orthodoxly Christian. However, this dynamic view of nature has stayed within Western culture. This must be considered the beginning of nature poetry as it is now understood.

Even in his own day, Wordsworth succeeded in opening up the Lake District as a tourist destination, just as the Scottish Highlands were also being opened up by the Scottish Romantics. Of these, the most significant was Robert Burns (1759-1796), who has come to be regarded as Scotland's national poet. From very humble origins, he devised a poetry using local Scottish dialect that was often humorous and often satirical. He also wrote many poems of great lyric beauty or national fervor, such as "Scots, Wha Hae wi' Wallace Bled." His first volume of poetry was published in 1786, with his famous "Tam O'Shanter" coming out in 1792.

Other Scottish Romantics are Scott, whose major works include *Minstrelsy of the Scottish Border* (1802-1803) and *The Lay of the Last Minstrel* (1805), and James Hogg, the "Shepherd of Ettrick" (1770-1835). Both these men knew Wordsworth, having collected traditional ballads of the border area between England and Scotland. Scott's poetry and novels became popular throughout Europe. His *The Lady of the Lake* (1810), with its typical medieval setting, became the direct inspiration for Keats's *Eve of St. Agnes* (1820).

COLERIDGE AND THE SUPERNATURAL

When Wordsworth and Coleridge collaborated on the *Lyrical Ballads*, Coleridge's task was to write tales of the supernatural. This built on an already existing audience for the gothic, stemming partially from *Night-Thoughts*. Coleridge's major contribution was *The Rime of the Ancient Mariner*, which subsequently became one of the most famous long poems in the English language. Again the theme is nature, but this time, nature as a retributive force if it is wantonly destroyed.

Coleridge wrote other mystical poems, including "Kubla Khan" (1816), which was probably written under the influence of opium. He also wrote a number of poems exploring the state of melancholy, a state that has a long history in English literature, from William Shakespeare's melancholic *Hamlet, Prince of Denmark* (pr. c. 1600-1601) to Robert Burton's *Anatomy of Melancholy* (1621). This state is often associated with the Romantic poets, perhaps through the famous novel *Die Leiden des jungen Werthers* (1774; *The Sorrows of Young Werther*, 1779) of the German poet Johann Wolfgang von Goethe (1749-1832) and perhaps through Keats's "Ode on Melancholy" or "Ode to a Nightingale." Such states are often near suicidal, and their exploration was part of the growing interest in extreme states of being in which perceptions are altered. One of Wordsworth's admirers, Thomas de Quincey, wrote *Confessions of an English Opium-Eater* (1821) which examined altered states of consciousness and became a massive best seller.

Later criticism has linked Coleridge's interest in the supernatural with subconscious states of being. However, Coleridge was a Unitarian and later spoke up in defense of Christianity. Rather than developing as a poet, Coleridge became a spokesperson for Romanticism, and in his *Biographia Literaria* (1817) throws out vital clues as to the early thinking of the British Romantic poets, as did Wordsworth's preface to the second edition of the *Lyrical Ballads* (1800). Other Romantics who wrote or lectured to promote Romanticism were Hunt, William Hazlitt (1778-1830), and Charles Lamb (1775-1834).

KEATS AND SHELLEY

Sometimes the British Romantic poets are divided into the older generation of Blake, Wordsworth, and Coleridge and the younger generation of Byron, Shelley and Keats. While the older generation lived long, the second generation died young, in fact before the first generation. The period in which the two generations coincided, 1810-1820, is one of the most productive periods in the whole of British poetry.

The usefulness of setting the younger Romantics apart is that they can be differentiated by some distinctive developments, especially in terms of using classical mythology for inspiration and subject matter. This is nowhere better seen than in the attempt to write an epic poem. Wordsworth's great unfinished epic, *The Recluse* (1888), was to be set domestically in the Lake District and be a meditative poem about the getting of wisdom through nature. What was published in 1888 was a manuscript left at Wordsworth's death, containing the first book of the first part of the epic poem, which was to have three parts and to contain *The Prelude* as an introduction. *The Prelude* is an epic account of Wordsworth's own poetic formation through epiphanies in nature, education, and the experience of living through the French Revolution. Keats called the type of writing the "egotistical sublime." It is the poet as the subject of his own epic statement.

By contrast, Keats and Shelley attempted to rewrite John Milton's great Christian epic, *Paradise Lost* (1667, 1674), using classical mythology. Keats and Shelley were both atheists and so wanted to reconstruct an epic subject in non-Christian terms. Keats tried with *Hyperion: A Fragment* (1820), which he gave up as "too Miltonic." He tried again with *The Fall of Hyperion: A Dream* (1856), but failing health precluded its completion. The topic was the revolution of the Olympian gods over the older Saturnian ones. Shelley's attempt was more successful. *Prometheus Unbound: A Lyrical Drama in Four Acts* (pb. 1820) takes the myth of Prometheus, the bringer of civilization to humanity in the face of the gods, as a statement about throwing off religious beliefs and embracing a new spirit of liberty.

Both poets wrote other longer mythological poems, but are better remembered for shorter, more lyric pieces, such as Keats's odes and his sonnets, and Shelley's "Ode to the West Wind" and *Adonais: An Elegy on the Death of John Keats* (1821), his very fine tribute to Keats, who died a year before he did.

BLAKE, BYRON, AND OTHERS

Both Blake and Lord Byron stand slightly apart from the other Romantic poets. Both were highly eccentric, but that is not relevant. Although Blake's earliest poetry predates *Lyrical Ballads* by a decade, it was self-published and not widely known until the first decade of the nineteenth century. As such, it had no real appreciable influence on the other poets. Apart from the very simply written ballads of *Songs of Innocence and Experience* (1794), most of his other poems are long, some of epic proportions, after his hero, Milton. Many are highly symbolic and set out Blake's own mystic theology, based on his version of Neoplatonic Christianity.

Byron's eccentricity was to do with self-image. Byronism threatened to take over Romanticism at one stage, so popular were his autobiographical heroes in their mock-epic quests for self-discovery or adventure, described in *Childe Harold's Pilgrimage* (1812-1818, 1819) and *Don Juan* (1819-1824, 1826). It can be questioned whether Byron was a Romantic at all. His verse forms are more typically Augustan, as is his mock-heroic satire, and he quite scathingly attacks certain minor Romantic poets, such as Robert Southey (1774-1843).

However, like Shelley, Byron was a revolutionary and an exile, adding to the picture of the Romantic poet as exile or wanderer, ever restless. It could be argued that he developed, with Shelley, what might be called Mediterranean Romanticism, which was carried on by Victorian poet Robert Browning; his wife, Elizabeth Barrett Browning; and a host of painters.

Other forms of Romanticism also developed. Oriental Romanticism became as interesting as Celtic Romanticism. *Lalla Rookh* (1817), a long poem by Thomas Moore (1779-1852), represents a first step in the newly developing colonial literature of the nineteenth century. Moore was an Irishman, and he exploited Irish folksong, as Hogg (*Scottish Pastorals*, 1801; *The Mountain Bard*, 1807), and Scott had done for Scottish folk songs.

Less well-known poets wrote of the English countryside, such as George Crabbe (1754-1832), whose *The Borough: A Poem, in Twenty-four Letters* (1810) inspired Benjamin Britten's most famous opera, *Peter Grimes* (pr. 1945), and John Clare (1793-1864), whose *The Village Minstrel, and Other Poems* appeared in 1821.

WOMEN WRITERS

Efforts have been made to set up a school of female Romantic poets. Volumes such as Jennifer Breen's *Women Romantic Poets, 1785-1832: An Anthology* (1992) are typical of this enterprise. Certainly, there were a great many women poets of the period, including some quite famous writers such as Hannah Moore, the social reformer. However, whether these writers were really Romantic, or whether they have been suppressed in a male-dominated canon is open to debate.

Wordsworth's sister, Dorothy Wordsworth (1771-1855), might seem an obvious candidate, as her brother actually published some of her poems in his collections. Her *Grasmere Journals* has become rightly famous as an important Romantic document, although it was not published until 1987, but her other poetry, much like that of many of the other women, is somewhat domestic.

Considering the fact that female novelists, such as Fanny Burney and Jane Austen, had no difficulty winning recognition, if not immediately, then not too long after their deaths, then it is difficult to substantiate a male plot of suppression against female poets. However, barring discovery of a yet-unknown female Romantic, it seems best to conclude that the great female Romantic poets appeared a generation later, with the emergence of Emily Brontë, to be followed by Emily Dickinson, Elizabeth Barrett Browning, and Christina Rossetti.

LEGACY

Romanticism between 1780-1830 was not confined to Britain or even to literature. German Romanticism pre-dates it, having occurred in the Storm and Stress period, which included the early Goethe, and Romantic artists John Constable and William Turner revolutionized British painting as much as the poets did poetry.

In Victorian times, Byron and Scott reigned supreme in popular taste, with a solid recognition of Wordsworth, Coleridge, and Shelley. Keats needed some rehabilitation, as did Blake. Tennyson and Browning took various aspects of Romanticism and worked within that, as did other Victorian poets.

The Georgian poets of the first decade of the twentieth century represent a last sentimental flowing of Romanticism before modernism captured the center ground of British poetry. The one colossus representing "the last of the Romantics" was the Irishman, William Butler Yeats, who developed Romantic poetry in significant new ways and made it workable for twentieth century poets.

BIBLIOGRAPHY

Abrams M. H. *Natural Supernaturalism: Tradition and Revolution in Romantic Literature.* New York: W. W. Norton, 1971. A groundbreaking study of the Romantic revolution set against its critical fortunes.

Butler, Marilyn. *Romantics, Rebels, and Reactionaries: English Literature and Its Background, 1760-1830.* New York: Oxford University Press, 1981. Attempts to account for the rise of Romanticism in the light of its historical and cultural context.

McLane, Maureen N., and James Chandler, eds. *The Cambridge Companion to British Romantic Poetry.* New York: Cambridge University Press, 2008. This volume is part of the Cambridge Companions to Literature series, with specially commissioned essays on a wide range of topics and authors.

O'Neill, Michael, ed. *Literature of the Romantic Period: A Bibliographical Guide.* New York: Oxford University Press, 1998. The definitive bibliographical guide to the period.

Wu, Duncan. *Romantic Poetry.* New York: Wiley-Blackwell, 2002. Perhaps the best introductory guide to Romantic poetry, giving full extracts from the major poets and an overview of Romantic poetry.

David Barratt

WILLIAM BLAKE

Born: London, England; November 28, 1757
Died: London, England; August 12, 1827

OTHER LITERARY FORMS

William Blake's prose includes *An Island in the Moon* (1987), *To the Public: Prospectus* (1793), *A Descriptive Catalogue* (1809), marginalia, and letters. It is almost a given with Blake scholarship and criticism that the interrelation of poetry and design is vital. David V. Erdman's *The Illuminated Blake* (1975) includes all of Blake's illuminated works, text, and design, with a plate-by-plate commentary.

ACHIEVEMENTS

William Blake's reputation during his lifetime was not a fraction of what it is today. He worked hard at his trade, that of engraving, but his style was not in fashion, and his commissions were few. His poverty and the laborious process of producing his own illuminated books for sale prevented him from producing more than two hundred copies of his own work in his lifetime. Even the *Songs of Innocence and of Experience*, which

William Blake
(Library of Congress)

he sold sporadically throughout his career, remained virtually unnoticed by his contemporaries. What little reputation he had among his contemporaries was as an artist, ingenious but no doubt mad.

In 1863, Alexander Gilchrist's biography of Blake did much to establish Blake's reputation as an artist and a poet. The Yeats-Ellis edition of Blake (1893) further enhanced his fame, not as a forgotten painter and poet, but as a purveyor of esoteric lore. Accurate transcription of Blake's texts began only in the twentieth century with the work of Geoffrey Keynes. Modern critical work was pioneered by S. Foster Damon in 1924, but it was not until Northrop Frye's *Fearful Symmetry* in 1947 that Blake's work was treated as a comprehensible, symmetrical whole.

A poet-artist who imaginatively remolds his own age and its traditions and then produces poetry, engravings, and paintings within that re-created world is a poet-artist who will attract a wide variety of readers. Blake's profound understanding of the ways in which humans deal with the warring contraries within their minds has become a fertile source for modern psychology. Carl Jung referred to Blake as a visionary poet who had achieved contact with the potent wellspring of the unconscious. Blake's devotion to a humanistic apocalypse created through the display of exuberant energies and expanded imaginative perceptions has been an inspiration to two generations of twentieth century writers: first D. H. Lawrence, E. M. Forster, William Butler Yeats, and Aldous Huxley, and later, Norman O. Brown, Allen Ginsberg, Theodore Roszak, Colin Wilson, and John Gardner, among others. If a poet can be judged by the quality and quantity of the attention he receives, Blake certainly rose in the twentieth century from a vague precursor of Romanticism to one of the six major English Romantic poets.

BIOGRAPHY

William Blake was born in Carnaby Market, London, on November 28, 1757. By the age of four, he was having visions: God put his head through the window to look at him, angels walked among the haymakers, and a tree was starred with angels. The visionary child was spared the rigors of formal schooling and learned to read and write at home. He attended a drawing school for four years and in 1772 began a seven-year apprenticeship to James Basire, engraver. He had already begun three years before to write the lyrics that were later printed in *Poetical Sketches*. It was not as a poet, however, that he would make his living but as an engraver who also could do original designs. The Gothic style of engraving that he learned from Basire was unfortunately somewhat passé. In later years, Blake had to sit back and watch other engravers receive commissions to execute his own designs.

At the age of twenty-two, Blake became a student of the Royal Academy, which meant that he could draw from models, living and antique, and attend lectures and exhibitions for six years. The politics of the day, as well as a spreading evangelical fervor, infused his life as an artist-poet. Blake was part of the 1780 Gordon Riots and was present at the burning of Newgate Prison. He was a vehement supporter of the French Revolution and attended radical gatherings that included William Godwin, Thomas Paine, Mary Wollstonecraft Shelley, and Joseph Priestley. Through John Flaxman, Blake developed an interest in Swedenborgianism. The doctrines of Emanuel Swedenborg seemed both to attract and to repel Blake. *The Marriage of Heaven and Hell* launched an attack on this movement.

In 1782, Blake married Catherine Boucher, whose life apparently became one with his. He tried his hand at running a print shop, but in 1785 it failed. He continued to make a meager living on commissions for designs and engravings, but these were the works of others. In 1800, he moved to Felpham near Chichester at the invitation of William Hayley, a minor poet, who attempted for the next three years to guide Blake's life into a financially lucrative mold. Blake returned as impoverished as ever to London in 1803, never to leave it again. In 1804, he was tried for sedition and was acquitted. It is ironic that Blake was not being tried for his pervasive iconoclasm, thoughts expressed in his unpublished work that would have set the eighteenth century on its head, but because a drunk had falsely accused him. In 1809, he had his one and only exhibition of sixteen paintings, an exhibition ignored by everyone except one reviewer, who attacked it viciously.

If the political and religious spirit of this period inspired Blake, it also worked against his prosperity as an engraver. Few in England during the Napoleonic wars could afford the luxury of commissioning the work of an engraver. In the last ten years of his life, Blake attracted the attention of a group of young painters whose admiration doubtless enriched this period of increasing poverty. On August 12, 1827, Blake died singing of the glories he saw in heaven.

ANALYSIS

William Blake's focus is primarily on inner states; the drama of the later books has been called a *psychomachia*, a drama of the divided psyche. In Blake's world, humankind was once integrated but suffered a Fall when reason sought to dominate the other faculties. The disequilibrium of the psyche, its reduced perception, is the creator of the natural world as it is now known.

CONTRARIES

The notion of "contraries" as defined and developed in *The Marriage of Heaven and Hell* provides a dialectical basis for the regeneration of this psyche. Contraries are to be understood as psychic or mental opposites that exist in a regenerated state, a redeemed paradisiacal state of unlimited energy and unbounded perception. Blake has in his total work depicted the progress to regeneration based on a conflict between contraries. Once contraries are accepted, energy is created, progress is inevitable, and reintegration occurs.

Blake's paradisiacal man differs from fallen man only in that he is aware of his divinity. Paradisiacal man perceives the majesty of the imagination, the passions, the reason, and the senses. The imagination in the redeemed state is called Urthona, and after the Fall, Los. Urthona represents that fourfold, unbounded vision that is the normal attribute of the redeemed man. Such vision is not bound by the particulars it produces through contraction, nor is it bound by the unity it perceives when it expands. Blake, in the imagination's true and saving role as poet, envisions the external world with a fourfold vision. Luvah, the passions or love, is represented after the Fall by Jesus, who puts on the robes of love to preserve some hint of divine love in the fallen world. Urizen, the zoa of reason, is the necessary boundary of energy, the wisdom that supplied form to the energies released by the other contraries. In the fallen world, he is the primary usurper of the dominion of other faculties. Tharmas, the zoa of the senses, has, in his paradisiacal form, unrestrained capacity to expand or contract his senses. In the fallen state, these senses remain but in an enervated condition. Sexuality, the sense of touch shared by two, is a means by which fallen man can regain his paradisiacal stature, but it is unfortunately a suppressed sense. The Blakean Fall that all the personified contraries suffer is a Fall from the divine state to the blind state, to the state in which none of their powers are free to express themselves beyond the severe limitations of excessive reason. Each of the contraries has his allotted place in the Fall; each sins either through commission or omission.

Contraries remain a concern of Blake from *The Marriage of Heaven and Hell* to the later prophecies: *The Four Zoas, Milton*, and *Jerusalem*. The metaphysic of contraries, the theoretical doctrine, is never denied. The opposition of energy to reason, however, dramatized in the Orc cycle, is no longer Blake's "main act" in the later books. From Night IX in *The Four Zoas* onward, Los, who embodies something akin to the Romantic concept of the sympathetic imagination, becomes the agent of regeneration. It is he who can project himself into the existence of his polar opposite and can accept the existence of that contrary in the act of self-annihilation and consequently forgive. Thus, the theory of contraries has not altered; any contrary can assume a selfhood in conflict with dialectic progression itself. Los preserves the dialectic while Orc maintains a hierarchy.

INNOCENCE AND EXPERIENCE

Blake's concern with the earthly states of Innocence and Experience, with a fallen body and its contraries, has been associated with religious apocalypse. Blake's apocalypse involves a progression from Innocence to Experience and an acceptance of the contraries in those states. An acceptance of contraries would lead to the destruction of false perception and disequilibrium and eventually to a complete resurrection of the fallen body. Humanity would again possess divine proportions through a progressive development of its own nature rather than through obedience to the supposed laws of an external deity. Through the faculty of imagination, Blake intuits the divinity of humankind, the falseness of society, and the falseness of laws based on societal behavior. He perceives the spiritual essence of humans, displaying therefore a spiritual rather than a rational brand of humanism. Blake's assumption that the human is a fallen god makes his psychology more than a psychology; and it makes his humanism an apocalyptic humanism. His diagnosis of the divided psyche becomes a revelation, and his therapy, an apocalypse. Blake himself dons the mantle of a prophet.

Able to see God and his angels at the age of four, Blake gave precedence in his life to vision over the natural world. He would continue to see through and not with the eye, and what he saw he would draw in bold outline as ineluctable truth. Ultimately, even the heterodoxy of Swedenborgianism was an encroachment on the supremacy of his own contact with the spiritual world. Early inspired by the revolutionary spirit of the times, he continued throughout his life to advocate a psychic revolution within each person that would lead to regeneration.

ARCHETYPAL THEMES

Blake's mission throughout his work is always apocalyptic, although he creates a political terrain in the Lambeth books (*The [First] Book of Urizen, The Book of Ahania, The Book of Los*, and *The Song of Los*) and a psychological one in his later prophecies

(*The Four Zoas*, *Milton*, and *Jerusalem*). His focus moves from a political-societal revolution of apocalyptic proportions to a psychic, perceptual regeneration of each individual person. It is the regenerated person who can perceive both a unity beyond all diversity and a diversity within that unity.

Songs of Innocence and of Experience demonstrates Blake's concern for individual human life, in particular its course from innocence to experience. What are the destructive forces operating early on humans, on their childhoods, which ultimately imprison them and lead to "mind-forged manacles"? In *Songs of Innocence*, a glimpse of energies is uncircumscribed, of what humans were and again could be if they rightly freed themselves from a limited perception and repressed energies.

The later poems, *The Four Zoas*, *Milton*, and *Jerusalem*, are large-scale epics whose focus is a particularly Romantic one—epistemological and ontological transformation. Los, hero of the imagination, is not a hero who affirms the values of a culture, nor are his strengths and virtues uniformly admired by that culture. Like traditional epics, Blake's epics begin in medias res, but because the natural world is usually seen unclearly, it is worthless to speak of its beginning, middle, or end. The reader who enters the world of Blake's epics enters a psychic world, becomes a "mental traveller," and in his purest states reaches heights traditionally reserved for deity in the Judeo-Christian tradition and deities in the epics of Homer and Vergil.

Blake's work is not unconnected with the natural world, but he attempts to bracket out all but the irreducible elements of the archetypal, individual human life. Paradoxically, Blake's work is characterized by less structural context than that of any poet of whom one could readily think; yet that work is such a dramatic reaction to the eighteenth century and such a dramatic revelation of the new Romanticism that it is unrivaled as an intense portrait of both sensibilities.

HUMANS IMAGINING

In reaction to John Locke's view that the perceiver is separated from the world because of his (or her) incapacity to do more than apprehend the secondary qualities of objects, Blake asserted the supremacy of individual perception. A human perceiving is a human imagining, an act that encompasses the totality of an individual's energies and personality. What is perceived depends on the imaginative act. The world can be construed only imaginatively. Humanity, Blake held, can apprehend the infinity within only through imagination. The London of Blake's poem of that name is a pitiable place because human imagination, human poetic genius, is repressed. London is at every moment available for imaginative transformation; so is every object in the natural world. In this view of imagination, Blake foreshadows Samuel Taylor Coleridge and especially Percy Bysshe Shelley and attacks the rationalism of the eighteenth century. The metaphysics of Francis Bacon, Isaac Newton, and Locke were despicable because they elevated rationality and denied imagination, thus standing in the way of regeneration.

Besides disagreeing with the philosophy and psychology of his own day, Blake criticized traditional religious and aesthetic views. Humanity's fallen perception created the world, not in seven days, but in what became a moment in time. Jesus was a man of revitalized perceptions, and he was fully conscious of his unlimited energies. Jesus was thus a supranatural man, one who had achieved the kind of regeneration that Blake felt it was in every person's power to achieve. In art, Blake applauded the firm outline of Michelangelo and Raphael and despised the indeterminacy of Rubens and Titian. The artist who apprehended with strong imagination drew boldly because the truth was clearly perceived. Socially and politically, Blake, unlike Coleridge and William Wordsworth, remained unreconciled to the status quo. Blake's revolutionary zeal, most pronounced in the Lambeth books, remained undiminished, urging him to portray error so that it could be cast out. Only Shelley equals Blake's faith in poetic genius to transform the very nature of humanity and thus the very nature of the world humans perceive.

SONGS OF INNOCENCE AND OF EXPERIENCE

Songs of Innocence and of Experience shows "the two contrary states of the human soul." The contraries cited in *The Marriage of Heaven and Hell* are "Attraction and Repulsion, Reason and Energy, Love and Hate. . . ." However, because these songs are not sung outside either Innocence or Experience but from within those states, the contraries are not fully presented in their ideal forms. The songs are from corrupted states and portray disproportionate contraries. Theoretically, each contrary state acts as a corrective to the other, and contraries in the *Songs of Innocence and of Experience* are suggested either in the text of the poem or in the accompanying design.

The introduction song to *Songs of Innocence and of Experience* is a good example not only of Blake's view of the role of Innocence and Experience in regeneration but also of the complexity of these seemingly simple songs. This song manages in its twenty lines to present a transition from absolute sensuous Innocence to a recognition of Experience and finally a transition to a higher state. The first stanza presents an almost complete picture of absolute carefree innocence. The adjective "wild" may imply a condemnation of an aspect of absolute Innocence. Because Blake believed that Experience brings an indispensable consciousness of one's actions so that choice becomes possible, the essential flaw in the state of Innocence is that it does not provide the child with alternatives.

The second stanza of this lyric presents the image of the lamb, a symbol of Christ. The lamb, while creating the image of the Innocence of Christ, also exhibits the equally true image of Christ crucified. It is this symbol of Experience that brings tears to the child, and on a psychological level, the child is emerging from a "wild" unconscious realm to a realm of consciousness, of Experience.

The third stanza presents two interesting additions: The pipe is replaced by human song and the child weeps with joy. The pipe had first produced laughter and then tears, but it is the human voice that elicits the oxymoronic reaction of joyful weeping. It is only in the human form that the attributes of the two contrary states of Innocence and Experience can exist harmoniously. "Piping down the valley wild" had brought unconstrained laughter, while the figure of the Christ-lamb had brought a more tearful vision of Experience; yet in stanza 3, such contrary reactions exist, unresolved but coexistent, as do the contrary states that foster them.

The fourth stanza alludes to the loss of childhood through the disappearance of the child of the poem and implies that the elemental properties of Innocence remain after the departure of the physical state of childhood. By plucking the hollow reed, Blake, the piper and singer, reveals a move toward creation that is fully realized in the last stanza. From the vision of Experience of stanza 2, and the acceptance of the necessary contrary states of Innocence and Experience through their inherent qualities, laughter and tears, presented in stanza 3, Blake has reached the higher plateau of conscious selflessness described in stanzas four and five. Through the act of creation, the conscious selfless act, which intends to give joy to every child, the conscious selflessness of Blake's paradisiacal reintegrated state is achieved.

THE BOOK OF THEL

In *The Book of Thel*, a young girl in Innocence named Thel is fearful of advancing to a state of Experience. Lily, Cloud, Clay, and Worm, symbols of innocence and experience, try to allay her fears. Experience may contain key contraries in extreme form; it may be the wrath of the father and the restraint of morality and the curtailment of vision, but it is a state that provides Thel her only opportunity of advancement, of completion and eventual salvation. Experience is a necessary step to the "peace and raptures holy" described by the Cloud. Thel, however, surveys the traditional misfortune of Experience—mortality. She finds no meaningful comfort in the Lily's belief that from Experience, from death, one flourishes "in eternal vales." Thel laments the consciousness that is hers when she takes a trial step into Experience. She finds morality, which represses sexual energy, unbearable. Thus, in spite of the eventual "peace and raptures holy" that Thel can proceed to from a state of Experience, her first look at that state proves too much for her. She flees Experience and consciousness to the vales of Har, the land of superannuated children, described in the poem *Tiriel*; it is a land of unfulfilled innocents who have refused to graduate into the world of Experience. A *Songs of Innocence* poem, "The Lamb," and a *Songs of Experience* poem, "The Tyger," depict the nature of perception in those states and the contraries that abide in each state. The poems may be viewed as "contrary poems."

The questions of the child in "The Lamb" are not the reason's questions but imagination's—questions he can answer because he has perceived the identity of himself, the lamb, and God. The equation is formed thus: The lamb is Christ the lamb; the child is Christ as a child; and the lamb and child are therefore joined by their mutual identity with Christ. In Innocence, all life is perceived as one and holy. Because there are two contrary states of the human soul and "The Lamb" is a product of only one, Innocence, it is not possible to conclude that this poem depicts Blake's paradisiacal state. The vines in the design are twisting about the sapling on both sides of the engraving, indicating in traditional symbolism the importance of going beyond childhood into Experience. If the child-speaker can see all life as one, can imaginatively perceive the whole, he cannot perceive the particularity, the diversity, which makes up that unity, which Experience's reason so meticulously numbers and analyzes. Even as the adult speaker of "The Tyger" can see only a fragmented world that his imagination is too weak to unify, so the child-speaker cannot see the fragments that comprise the world.

The spontaneity and carefree abandon of the lamb in Innocence can in Experience no longer be perceived in the form of a lamb. The perceiver in Experience fears the energy of Innocence and therefore shapes it into a form that his reason has deemed frightening—that of a tiger. This form that the tiger of the poem "The Tyger" possesses is symmetrical, its symmetry lying in its perfect relationship with the energy it contains. It is a "fearful symmetry" only to the perceiver in Experience, who is riddled with the prejudices of Experience, prejudices regarding what is good and what is evil, what is rational and what is irrational, or wild. The moral hierarchy of Experience—good is good and evil is evil—does not permit the perceiver in Experience to perceive a Keatsian "fineness" in the tiger, a marvelous interrelationship of form and energy.

The reader goes back and forth in this poem from a vision of the energies of the unconscious mind to a perception of the boundaries of those energies. It is the mixture of energy and boundary that the speaker-perceiver finds disturbing. The tiger in the first stanza is seen as a burning figure in the night, perhaps symbolizing the burning vibrant passions repressed in the darkened areas of the mind. The tiger perceived by the speaker can live only in the dark because both reason and moral hierarchy have relegated it to that realm. The tiger is, in its energies, in its fire, too great for the conscious mind to accept; yet, like a recurrent nightmare, the tiger burns brightly and cannot be altogether denied. The tiger cannot be quietly integrated into the personality of the speaker-perceiver without doing severe damage to the structure of self carefully fabricated by reason and moral hierarchy. Rather than transform himself, question himself, the speaker-perceiver questions the tiger's creator. What creator could possibly give form to such uncontrollable energy? How can such energy be satisfactorily bounded? The perceiver in Experience assumes that such energy as the tiger represents can be denied only through repression. It cannot be given necessary form; it must be perceived as having a fearful rather than a fine form. This speaker turns questioner and by his questioning reveals his subservience to analytical reason.

The questioner proceeds under the assumption that no creation can be greater than its creator, that in some way the dangerous, fearful energies of the tiger are amenable to that creator, are somehow part of that creator. Where is such a creator to be found? More specifically, where are those burning energies to be found in the spiritual realm? The questioner is already convinced that the creation of the tiger is a presumptuous act and he therefore concludes that Satan is the great presumer. This tiger is, therefore, in the questioner-perceiver's mind, Satan's work, a hellish creation forged in the fires not of Blake's Hell but of a traditional Hell.

The final questions to be asked are merely rhetorical. The questioner has decided that his creator could never have created the tiger. The creator involved here has dared to create the tiger. There exists here a Manichaean split, a desperate attempt to answer the problem of the existence of evil. Part of humanity has been made by God and that part is good, while Satan has made the evil part of humanity, the part symbolized by the tiger. The only symbol of energy that the questioner-perceiver is prepared to face is that of the lamb. However, while the lamb sufficed in Innocence as representative of certain energies, it is no longer indicative of the growth of energy that is a mature person's in Experience. The tiger of Experience expresses the symbolic balance of energy and reason, fire and form; however, only a perceiver whose energies are brought from Innocence and matured in Experience under the guidance of reason in necessary proportions can perceive that balance. This uncorrupted perceiver can see the child lying down with the tiger, as in "A Little Girl Found." That tiger is the perfect symbol of the balance of contraries and is perceived as such; the tiger of "The Tyger" is also a perfect symbol but improperly perceived.

THE MARRIAGE OF HEAVEN AND HELL

The raison d'être of the incorporation of all contraries as they are perceived in the two contrary states, Innocence and Experience, is provided in *The Marriage of Heaven and Hell*. It fulfills more than a mere metaphysical role. It is the foundation of Blake's prophecy, the basis not of extended system but of vision. *The Marriage of Heaven and Hell* preserves the whole body of contraries by a relentless attack on all divisive factors. Dualism in all areas is negated and the suppressed half of the fallen body, represented by the suppressed division of contraries, is supported and affirmed in opposition to the deadening voices of the "Angels."

The framework of *The Marriage of Heaven and Hell* is traditional Judeo-Christian religion and morality. Blake completely alters and destroys this traditional structure and replaces it with an equal acceptance of the two contrary states of the human soul and their inherent contraries. Energies that are indigenous to childhood must take their place alongside the necessary contraries of Experience—reason, repulsion, and hate. The traditional moral hierarchy of good over evil allows one state and its contraries to have ascendancy over the other. Blake boldly adopts the standard nomenclature and marries good and evil as true opposites, essential contraries. Both the passive and active traits of humankind's nature are assumed. Rather than an exclusive emphasis on good, as in the Judeo-Christian ethic, or evil, as in sadism, Blake seeks the reintegration of the unity of humans through the opposition of these strategic contraries. Once Blake's doctrine of contraries as presented in *The Marriage of Heaven and Hell* is understood, it becomes clearer what *Songs of Innocence and of Experience* is describing, what the basis of Orc's battle on behalf of energy in the Lambeth books is, and in what way Los preserves the contraries in the later books.

The Marriage of Heaven and Hell is a theoretical base for Blake's vision; however, the form of the work is by no means expository. It presents a dialectic of contraries in dialectical form. Blake's dialectic is not a system of reason in the Hegelian sense, not a system leading to an external synthesis and to the creation of new contraries. Blake's dialectic is composed of contraries immanent in the human personality, contraries that do not change but that generate increasing energy.

In the "Argument" section, "keeping the perilous path" refers to primal unity, Blakean primal unity, and means maintaining all contraries. The man in the vale maintains the dialectic between the conscious and unconscious mind. In Blake's view, once the "path is planted," once the Fall has occurred, man must journey forward, through Innocence and Experience to reintegration.

In Plate 3, Blake declares the immanence of contraries within the human personality and denies the moral dualism of the Judeo-Christian ethic. These contraries are not illusory; their opposition is real, but one contrary does not subsume or upset another. No hierarchy is imposed. The energies that are traditionally classified as "good" are not superior to the energies traditionally classified as "evil." Neither is the reverse true, because Blake is no disciple of the Marquis de Sade. In Blake's view, the hierarchy of morality is particularly insidious because it prevents man from espousing contraries and achieving the progression resulting from that act.

In Plate 4, Blake indicates that the contraries transcend the dualism of body and soul. It is the Devil who proclaims the body as the only portion of the soul, and thus Blake's Devil is his hero, his spokesman. This identification of the soul with the observable, physical body, when combined with Blake's notion of progression based on a dialectic of contraries, implies that although the body is a mere portion of the soul, its most debased portion, it is the only medium available to man by which an amplified body, a spiritual body or soul, can be reached. Contraries existing within the body that are perceived in this fallen world are accepted in pursuit of "ideal" or amplified contraries. In Blake's view, the body and its contraries are sacred.

In Plates 5 and 6, Blake's Devil says that energies are too often repressed. The person who represses his energies in turn suppresses the energies of others. Plate 5 begins the "Proverbs of Hell" section. The proverbs are designed to strengthen the imagination of the reader so that the dynamic of contraries is perceived. Once the reader perceives imaginatively the reality of this dynamic, the dynamic is maintained and energy ensues. Ever-increasing energy leads to ever-expanding perception, and perception, for Blake, ultimately determines ontology. The Proverbs of Hell are pithy "consciousness raisers," each demonstrating the dynamic or dialectic of contraries in both content and form.

Plate 11 continues Blake's assault on the priesthood. In Plates 12 and 13, Blake allies himself with the prophets, Isaiah and Ezekiel—voices of "firm persuasion" and "honest indignation." In Plates 14 and 15, Blake describes the creative process that produced *The Marriage of Heaven and Hell.* He further defines the psychic terrain in Plate 16 by presenting two groups, "Prolific" and "Devourer," that can be seen as personified categories incorporating all dichotomies previously discussed in *The Marriage of Heaven and Hell;* Devil-Evil-Energy-Hell are subsumed by the Prolific, and Angel-Good-Reason-Heaven are subsumed by the Devourer. Plates 17 to 20 contain Blake's "fantastic" satirical drama between an Angel and Blake, as Devil. Limited or bounded perception creates a world and an end for itself that a liberated, diabolical perception can alter in the twinkling of an eye. The Angel perceives such a world of error because he has no sense of the dynamic interplay of contraries, no idea that "Opposition is true Friendship."

THE FRENCH REVOLUTION

Some of the political implications of Blake's doctrines in *The Marriage of Heaven and Hell* are evident in *The French Revolution.* This poem of twenty pages, posthumously published, has no accompanying designs and was written for the radical publisher Joseph Johnson. It is conjectured that by 1791 it was dangerous for an Englishman to express a revolutionary enthusiasm inspired by the French Revolution. In this poem, Blake's own political radicalism is not couched in symbolic terms, and therefore, he may have had second thoughts about printing it and risking imprisonment. Blake chronicles, with ample poetic license, the period in France from June 19 to July 15, when the king's troops were dispersed. Louis XVI and his nobles debate their course of action in the light of the growing revolution outside, and they finally decide to remove the troops surrounding Paris. In Blake's telling, this decision represents a renewed perception on the part of the king and his nobles. The Bastille, a symbol of political repression, consequently falls. In actuality, the Bastille fell before the decision was made to remove the king's troops.

AMERICA

There is more of what will become Blake's completed mythology in *America* than there is in *The French Revolution.* Besides historical characters such as George Washington, Benjamin Franklin, and Thomas Paine, Blake here introduces Orc and Urizen, personifications of revolutionary energy and reason. In a preludium or preface, Vala, the shadowy female who symbolizes North America, is in chains. Her liberation occurs through her sexual relations with the fiery Orc. To Blake, therefore, a successful American revolution is not only political but also sexual. George III is the Angel of Albion (England) who worships Urizen and Urizen's law of the Ten Commandments. These two attempt to saturate America with their own diseases by sending a plague across the

Atlantic to America. However, the plague is countered by the revolutionary zeal of Orc, who replaces the oppressions of Urizen with genuine political and sexual freedom. All Europe is affected by this revolution, but England, seeking the protection of Urizen, hurries to rebuild the gates of repression, the gates of moral good and evil and a dominant rationality.

Blake's Orc, revolutionary energy, successfully counters Urizen ("your reason") just as the French Revolution countered the Ancient Regime. However, the French Revolution lost its revolutionary energy in the tyranny of Napoleonic France. It became obvious to Blake that historical, political solutions—revolutions—could not effect a break in the historical cycle, a break that would be an apocalypse. Thus, in *The Four Zoas*, Orc becomes a destructive force in nature, an opponent of reason totally oblivious to reason's importance on a regenerated scale. Orc becomes as tied to the natural, unregenerated cycle as Vala, the embodiment of the natural process itself.

Although Urizen is easily defeated by Orc in *America*, he remains an important character in Blake's myth. He is at once Nobodaddy, a comical, ridiculous father figure, and the Ancient of Days, depicted with grandeur in the frontispiece to *Europe: A Prophecy*. Urizen represents the urge to structure and systematize, to reduce all to rational terms. In the language of our own day, he recognizes only what can be quantified and, like a good logical positivist, seeks empirical referents to instill meaning in words.

EUROPE

Europe can be viewed as a continuation of *America* in which revolutionary zeal has been replaced by a repressive conservatism that binds both energies and perceptions. The time is the birth of Jesus, a time of possible regeneration through his example. This possibility is not realized and the world falls into a long sleep, an eighteen-hundred-year sleep of Nature. Los, the poetic genius, naïvely rejoices in a promise of peace while Urizen is attempting to rule outside his own domain; and Los's female counterpart, Enitharmon, is a victim of Urizen's dominion and seeks to bind sexual love with moral law. Urizen solidifies his rule, his brazen book of law that ignores imagination, forgiveness, and the necessity of self-annihilation. Edmund Burke and William Pitt, represented by the characters Palamabron and Rintrah, are also under the dominion of Urizen and Enitharmon. The revolutionary spirit of the youth of England is doomed. Pitt-Rintrah three times attempts to lead England to war, into total devastation. In Blake's view, however, Sir Isaac Newton and his system are the real beginning of devastation in England. Newton's blast on the trumpet does not lead to glorious apocalypse but to death-in-life. Enitharmon wakes and calls her perverted children to her—materialism, delusion, hypocrisy, sensualism, and seduction. The poem ends with Orc inspiring the French Revolution, the spirit of which will be challenged by a Urizenic England. Los, the poetic genius, summons his sons to the coming strife, but it is as yet unclear what his precise role will be. That role is defined in *The Four Zoas*, *Milton*, and *Jerusalem*.

The [First] Book of Urizen and The Book of Los

In *The [First] Book of Urizen* and *The Book of Los*, Blake does not present a cryptic intermingling of history and myth but rather a first attempt at describing his cosmogony and theogony. *The Book of Los* tells the story of the Fall from Los's point of view and *The [First] Book of Urizen* from Urizen's point of view. Thus, the texts interconnect and gloss each other. The Fall is a fall into creation, one precipitated by Urizen's desire for painless joy, for laws binding everything, for "One King, one God, one Law." Urizen's usurpation of power is clearly an act of the Selfhood, a condition in which the legitimacy and importance of other energies are not recognized.

Los, as imagination, is the epistemological faculty by which truth or error is perceived. Urizen's revolt on behalf of reason skews perception and plunges Los into the Fall. The world of time and space, the Natural World, is formed by Los, and both Los and Urizen, fallen, are bound to this Natural World. A fall into sexuality follows the fall into materiality. Sexuality is subject to moral constraints. Science is a woven "woof," which is created to hide the void. Orc is born but his youthful exuberance is bound by the perversions of the Net of Religion, a direct product of the perverted dream of Reason. Urizen explores the dens of the material world and observes the shrunken nature of a humanity that has completely forgotten its eternal life.

The Song of Los

The Song of Los can be viewed as the mythological framework for *America* and *Europe*. The first part of Los's song, "Africa," recounts history leading up to George III—Guardian Prince of Albion's war against the Americans, as depicted in *America*. What exists here is also a historical counterpart to the mythology presented in *The [First] Book of Urizen* and *The Book of Los*. Dark delusion was given Moses on Sinai; abstract law to Pythagoras, Socrates, and Plato; a wretched gospel to Jesus; and the reprehensible Philosophy of the Five Senses to Newton and Locke. The second section, "Asia," is a continuation of *Europe*; it does not speak of events but of the psychological-physiological consequences of Urizen's reign. King, Priest, and Counsellor can only restrain, dismay, and ruin humanity in the service of Urizen. Orc rages over France, but the earth seems too shrunken, humankind too imprisoned to heed. Again, Orc himself, as revolutionary energy, is a questionable savior as he is described as a serpent. The energy of the French Revolution had become debased, and although Blake hoped for a renewal of its original energies, he was already too skeptical of revolution to present Orc as a hero.

The Book of Ahania

The Book of Ahania takes its name from Urizen's female counterpart or emanation, who comes into existence when Fuzon, an Orc-like figure, battles Urizen. Urizen immediately calls Ahania sin, hides her, and suffers jealousy. Ahania becomes the "mother of Pestilence," the kind of pestilence that is a result of a sexuality restrained by the moral law. Urizen's mind, totally victimized by a repressive rationality and the resulting morality, breeds monsters. From the blood of one of these monsters, Urizen forms a bow and shoots a rock at Fuzon, killing him. Fuzon is pictured as a revolutionary who has assumed the seat of tyranny previously occupied by Urizen. Urizen nails Fuzon to a tree, an act that imitates the death of Christ, Christ as rebel. Fuzon dies because he has not broken the material cycle and is thus vulnerable to the repressive laws of the material world. In the same fashion, the creators of the French Revolution failed to achieve a significant ontological and epistemological revolution and therefore became ensnared once again in nets of mystery that led to the Reign of Terror. Fuzon and the French Revolutionaries achieve no true revolution and fall victim to the "black rock" formed by a mind whose energies are repressed in the name of reason and its countless offshoots.

VISIONS OF THE DAUGHTERS OF ALBION

One of the ways to Blakean regeneration is through sexuality, specifically through a reassimilation of the female emanation and the re-creation of the Edenic androgynous body. In *Visions of the Daughters of Albion*, Oothoon is a female emanation; Theotormon is her male counterpart and a victim of a repressive moral code; Bromion is a spokesman of that code. Sexually, Oothoon represents the Prolific; the Devourer equivalent, the opposing sexual nature, must be created in Experience. Jerusalem, in the poem *Jerusalem*, becomes that female emanation cognizant of the nature of the regenerated, androgynous body, and she has gained that knowledge in Experience.

Oothoon is raped by Bromion, and Theotormon treats her like a harlot because she has been raped. Oothoon's imagination gives her a vision of her intrinsic sexual nature. Her vision is of the body, the sexual body no less, a body that is not distinct from the soul. In her newfound identity, Oothoon tries to bring Theotormon to the same vision, tries to bring him beyond the moral categories; but Theotormon demands a rational proof for all living things. Why, he asks implicitly, should he believe Oothoon is pure when the moral code clearly states that she is not pure? Bromion declares that only what can be perceived by the five senses has merit. Oothoon attacks priests and their restraining moral ethic but finally gives up trying to win Theotormon to her newly liberated vision. Her comprehension of the warped picture of sexuality in Experience as demonstrated by Theotormon and Bromion causes her to conclude that Experience has nothing to offer. Although she is not blinded regarding her own sexual nature, she is unable to reunite with Theotormon, male sexuality, and is denied a vision of sexuality based on energies of both Innocence and Experience. Thus, sexual relations, androgyny, and regeneration are denied both Oothoon and Theotormon.

THE FOUR ZOAS

The Four Zoas is an unengraved poem written in two overlapping stages. The main characters, Luvah, Urizen, Tharmas, and Urthona, are the "zoas" of the human personality, each representing an inherent, indivisible quality of the human personality. However, these characters are true characters and not mere allegorical representations. *The Four Zoas* is Blake's account of a split in the Edenic personality of Man, called Albion, of a Fall into the cycle of the natural world, and of the labors of Los, the imagination, to reunite and regenerate the four zoas. This poem is both a historical drama inevitably unfolded in time and space and a psychological drama, one in which time and space have no validity. As a historical drama, the poem lends itself to the kinds of historical connections made in *Europe* or *America*, but this is not a consistent base from which to read the poem, nor will expectations of a conventional narrative structure be at all fruitful.

The poem begins when Luvah and Vala rush from the loins and into the heart and on to the brain, where they replace Urizen's ordering of the body's life with their own cyclical, generative ordering. This sleeping man, Albion, who has within him the whole world—the powers to contract and expand—wakes up in Night VIII of the poem. Albion was asleep because he was in repose in Beulah, a state of threefold perception between Eden (fourfold perception) and Generation (twofold perception). To be in Beulah is to be at rest from the dynamic interplay of contraries of Eden, Blake's paradisiacal state. The aura of Eden pervades Beulah but the threat of the lower state, Generation, is always present. A fall into a reduced perception is always imminent. In *The Four Zoas*, that fall occurs. The fall into Generation is a fall into the natural world; it is Blake's version of the biblical Fall.

In the state of Generation, Urizen declares himself God; the "mundane shell," the material world, is built, and Jesus appears and is sacrificed so that regeneration can become possible. Jesus is identified with Luvah, love; with Orc, revolutionary energy battling Urizen in the Lambeth Books; and with Albion, Universal Man. Under Jesus's inspiration, Los perceives the errors of the Fall and begins to build Jerusalem, a spiritual freedom in which regeneration is possible. From Night IX in *The Four Zoas* onward into *Milton* and *Jerusalem*, Los, who embodies something akin to the Romantic concept of sympathetic imagination, becomes the agent of regeneration. It is Los who can project himself into the existence of his contrary, can accept the existence of that contrary in the act of "self-annihilation," and can consequently forgive. Thus, in the later books, the theory of contraries is not altered; any contrary can assume a selfhood in conflict with dialectical progression itself. Los preserves the dialectic, while Orc maintains a hierarchy——"saviour" and "villain."

MILTON

The historical John Milton is revived in Blake's *Milton* so that he can experience a personal self-annihilation that leads to the incorporation of his Spectre, Satan. Blake's Milton is a Milton of energy and imagination, a Milton determined to correct his view (expressed in *Paradise Lost*, 1667, 1674) that love "hath his seat in Reason." Through self-annihilation, Blake's Milton acknowledges the validity of Reason, his Spectre.

Once Milton is united with his Spectre, he can preach effectively to the public. The repression of the reasoning power is peculiar only to the Blakean "heroes," such as Blake's Milton. Outside this Blakean world, in the world of Innocence and Experience, the reasoning power is not repressed but assumes the role of usurper, a faculty of mind that has overridden the powers of all other faculties. Reason as Blake perceived it in the eighteenth century was in complete control. It is this unrepressed, dominant, reasoning power that Milton calls a "Negation." The reasoning power that Blake's Milton finally accepts is reason as Spectre, not as Negation, reason in its Edenic proportions.

An act of self-annihilation also precipitates the union of female emanation and the fallen male principle. Blake's Milton is reconciled with his emanation, Ololon. What Blake's Milton undergoes here becomes a precedent for what Los and other contraries will undergo. In annihilating his Selfhood, the Los-Blake-Devil Selfhood, Blake's Milton shows that reason is a necessary contrary, that man is not ruled by energies alone. The Spectre as reason has been accepted and Blake's Milton attains an expanded perception. His emanation perceives her power fade. In "delighting in his delight," they are again one in sexuality.

Blake's Milton enables the contraries to be saved, enables a dynamic interplay of contraries once again to take place. In contrast, Orc's obdurate maintenance of his own Selfhood and his denial of Urizen's reality in any proportions did not preserve Edenic contraries and could not therefore lead to regeneration. Blake's Milton achieves self-annihilation through forgiveness, itself based on the imagination. It is Los, the imagination, who perceives the dialectic of contraries and recognizes the message of continued forgiveness. It is Los, the imagination, who is employed by each contrary in recognition of its polar opposite.

JERUSALEM

In *Jerusalem*, Los and the Spectre of Urthona take center stage. Los addresses his Spectre as "my Pride & Self-righteousness," indicating that the Spectre's presence tends to affirm Los's obdurate Selfhood. Throughout *Jerusalem*, the reader witnesses a "compensatory" relationship between the Spectre and Los, although the Spectre seems to be "watching his time with glowing eyes to leap upon his prey." In Chapter IV, Los ends this struggle with his Spectre by accepting it. Once Los, identified here with Blake, becomes one with his Spectre, he appears to Albion, fallen humankind, in the form of Jesus and preaches forgiveness based on imaginative identification and self-annihilation. Jesus-Los annihilates himself before Albion and thus points to the necessary destruction of the Selfhood. Overwhelmed by this act, imaginatively caught in Jesus-Los's sacrifice, the albatross drops from Albion's neck, and it is the Selfhood. This is the apocalyptic moment when Albion, like the phoenix, descends to the flames and rises anew. Regeneration is intimately connected with self-annihilation, as it was in *Milton*.

Albion's emanation, Jerusalem, is also spiritual freedom. A reassimilation of Jerusalem generates a climate of freedom in which contraries can interact. Jerusalem as an emanation is beyond morality. She represents the whole of life, but a fallen Albion applies "one law" to her. Because of this application of a rigid "one law," a rigid hierarchical ethic, Jerusalem is separated from Albion. A female emanation repressed becomes a tyrant. Blake gives readers a close view of this "proud Virgin-Harlot," whom he calls Vala. The Vala whom Blake presents is corrupt, since she stands for restraint in all areas, especially moral, as opposed to Jerusalem-as-liberty. The Vala figure, advocate of a repressive morality, both tempts and lures, and also upholds the sense of sin. She thus becomes woman-as-tyrant. She is the femme fatale who incites desire but never acts. Such a morality turns love into prostitution, the free lover into a prostitute.

Again, Los, the imagination, perceives the validity of Jesus's word to Jerusalem regarding forgiveness, annihilation, and regeneration. Los applies what he has learned, unites with his own Spectre, and sends him forth to preach the methods of regeneration—forgiveness and self-annihilation. Albion regains his Jerusalem; spiritual freedom once again exists; and England itself has apocalyptically become Jerusalem, the city of God.

OTHER MAJOR WORKS

LONG FICTION: _To the Public: Prospectus_, 1793; _An Island in the Moon_, 1987 (wr. c. 1784).

NONFICTION: _A Descriptive Catalogue_, 1809.

ILLUSTRATIONS AND ENGRAVINGS: _The Complaint and the Consolation: Or, Night Thoughts, by Edward Young_, 1797; _Blair's Grave_, 1808; _The Prologue and Characters of Chaucer's Pilgrims_, 1812; _The Pastorals of Virgil_, 1821; _Illustrations of the Book of Job_, 1825; _Illustrations of Dante_, 1827.

BIBLIOGRAPHY

Ackroyd, Peter. _Blake: A Biography_. New York: Alfred A. Knopf, 1996. A penetrating biography of the poet.

Beer, John. _William Blake: A Literary Life_. New York: Palgrave Macmillan, 2005. This biography traces Blake's life, offering commentary on his religious background and painting a clear picture of the complexity of his poetry as well as his visual artistry.

Bloom, Harold, ed. _William Blake_. New York: Chelsea House, 2008. A collection of essays on Blake that examine his poetry, including _Jerusalem, Milton_, and _The Four Zoas_.

Bruder, Helen P. _William Blake and the Daughters of Albion_. New York: St. Martin's Press, 1997. Bruder's overt concern is with issues of "women, sexuality, gender, and sexual difference," but her book is perhaps better regarded as a reassessment of Blake's relation to popular culture. Bruder presents a thorough and astute reception history. Includes a bibliography and an index.

_____, ed. *Women Reading William Blake*. New York: Palgrave Macmillan, 2007. A collection of critical essays analyzing Blake's poetry from a feminist criticism perspective.

Frye, Northrop. *Fearful Symmetry: A Study of William Blake*. Princeton, N.J.: Princeton University Press, 1947. Frye interprets Blake's myth in terms of archetypal symbolic structures, which he also finds underlying much Western literature and mythology. Almost all later writers have been indebted to Frye, although some contemporary Blake critics are wary of being too captured by his ideas.

Lindsay, David W. *Blake: Songs of Innocence and Experience*. London: Macmillan, 1989. A very informative, if brief, introduction that examines a range of critical approaches to *Songs of Innocence and of Experience*. Lindsay's impartial discussions of different interpretations of selected poems will be useful for readers who want a concise survey of the field. The second part of the book gives attention to eight *Songs of Experience* in the context of Blake's other works. Includes bibliography.

Percival, Milton O. *William Blake's Circle of Destiny*. 1938. Reprint. New York: Octagon Books, 1977. This introduction to Blake's prophetic books has stood the test of time. Percival demonstrates that Blake's myth was firmly rooted in a traditional body of thought that included Neoplatonism, Kabala, alchemy, Gnosticism, and individual thinkers such as Jakob Böhme, Paracelsus, Emanuel Swedenborg, and Plotinus.

Roberts, Jonathan. *William Blake's Poetry: A Reader's Guide*. New York: Continuum, 2007. Provides keys to understanding the meaning of Blake's poetry and the complex images therein.

Joseph Natoli

EMILY BRONTË

Born: Thornton, Yorkshire, England; July 30, 1818
Died: Haworth, Yorkshire, England; December 19, 1848
Also known as: Ellis Bell

<small>PRINCIPAL POETRY</small>

Poems by Currer, Ellis, and Acton Bell, 1846 (with Charlotte and Anne Brontë)
The Complete Poems of Emily Jane Brontë, 1941 (C. W. Hatfield, editor)
Gondal's Queen: A Novel in Verse by Emily Jane Brontë, 1955 (Fannie E. Ratchford, editor)

<small>OTHER LITERARY FORMS</small>

Although Emily Brontë (BRAHNT-ee) published only one novel, *Wuthering Heights*, it is this work for which she is best known. When the novel was published in 1847, it won some praise for its originality and power, but in general, reviewers found its violence disturbing and its dominant character, Heathcliff, excessively brutal. *Wuthering Heights* did not offer the charm and optimism that many readers wanted to find in a work of fiction. As is often the case with original work, it took time for the world to appreciate it fully; today, however, *Wuthering Heights* is given a prominent place among the significant novels of the nineteenth century and is often discussed for its elaborate narrative structure, its intricate patterns of imagery, and its powerful themes of the soul's anguish and longing.

By the time Brontë began *Wuthering Heights*, she had long been using her imagination to create stories full of passionate intrigue and romance. First, as a young child she participated in a series of family games called Young Men's Plays, tales of military and political adventures primarily directed and recorded by the older children, her sister Charlotte and her brother Branwell. After Charlotte left for school in 1831, Emily and her younger sister Anne began their own creation, a long saga of an island they called Gondal, placed in the north Pacific yet very much resembling their own Yorkshire environment. They peopled this island-world with strong, passionate characters. Unfortunately, nothing remains of their prose chronicle of Gondal. Two journal fragments and two of the birthday notes that she and Anne were in the habit of exchanging make mention of this land. These notes also offer some insight into the everyday world of the Brontë household and are of great interest for this reason. The only other extant prose, besides a few unrevealing letters, is a group of five essays which she wrote in French as homework assignments while a student in Brussels. This material has since been translated by Lorine White Nagel and published under the title *Five Essays Written in French* (1948). Some similarities can be seen between the destructive and powerful descriptions of nature and human character discussed in these essays and the world of Brontë's poetry and fiction.

Emily Brontë
(Library of Congress)

ACHIEVEMENTS

Emily Brontë did not at first desire public recognition for her poetry. In fact, when her sister Charlotte accidentally discovered a notebook of her poems, it took time for Emily to accept this discovery, even though Charlotte found the poems impressive and uncommon. More time was required for Charlotte to persuade this very private poet to join with her and Anne in a small publishing venture. Once persuaded, Emily did contribute twenty-one of her poems to the slim, privately printed volume *Poems by Currer, Ellis, and Acton Bell*. To disguise her sex, each sister chose a pseudonym corresponding to the first letter of her name. This disguise also protected Emily's privacy, which she very much desired to keep; she resented Charlotte's later unintentional disclosure of Ellis Bell's true identity. This disclosure occurred after the three sisters had all published novels under the name of Bell, arousing considerable curiosity in the literary world. Unfortunately, their collection of poems sold only two copies. Later, after Emily's death, Charlotte, convinced of her sister's talent, tried to keep her poetic reputation alive by including eighteen previously unpublished poems in a second edition of *Wuthering Heights* and Anne's first novel, *Agnes Grey* (1847); however, despite her efforts, it was not until the twentieth century that Emily Brontë's poems received any serious critical attention.

Interest in the poetry began as biographers sought to piece together the life of the Brontë family. It increased when the fantasyland of Gondal was discovered. Attempts were made to reconstruct the story from the poems, for it became clear that Emily had written many of her poems as part of that world of passion and guilt. Further attention was given to the poetry as *Wuthering Heights* gained in recognition, although readers were inclined to interpret the poems merely as an apprenticeship to a more masterful novel. Only since the mid-twentieth century has criticism begun to focus on the poems for their own sake.

Because of the seeming quietness of Brontë's life and because she was never part of a literary circle beyond that of her own home, there is a temptation to see her as an example of the isolated genius, sculpturing her forms in an instinctive style. On the contrary, Brontë was a skillful poet working within the traditions of her Romantic predecessors, handling standard poetic forms with subtle and effective variations. Although the dramatic extremes she found in the works of Sir Walter Scott and Lord Byron led her at times to employ conventional phrases and touches of melodrama, at her best she was able to embody in controlled verse an intensity of genuine feeling that sprang from a love of nature and a worship of the imagination. In her poems of the night winds and the whirling snowstorms of the moors, she distinguishes herself as a poet of nature's starkly vital powers. In her poems of the imagination, she places herself in the visionary company of William Wordsworth and William Blake. Throughout her poetry she expresses the desire of the soul to transcend the mortal limitations of time and space to merge with a larger presence, the source of all energy and life. She was an artist faithful to her visions, whose poems attest the strength of the individual soul.

BIOGRAPHY

Emily Jane Brontë was one of six children, five girls and a boy, born to an Anglican clergyman of Irish descent, Patrick Brontë, and his Cornish wife, Maria Branwell. When Emily was two years old, the family moved to Haworth, where her father had accepted a permanent curacy. Haworth, a place now often associated with the Brontë name, is a village on the moors of West Riding, Yorkshire, in the north of England. In Emily's day, this rural spot was quite removed from the changing events of city life. The parsonage itself is an isolated building of gray stone near an old cemetery with its slanting worn tombstones. In this somber-looking house, in this quiet village, Emily spent most of her life.

The people filling this world were few in number. As a parson's children, Emily and her brother and sisters were not encouraged to associate with the village children, who were regarded as lower in social status. Their father seems to have valued his privacy, often keeping to himself, even dining alone, although there is no reason to doubt his affection for his children. As a result of these social limitations, the children provided their own entertainment, which often consisted of acting out imaginative games and later writing them down. Their education was in part provided by their aunt, Elizabeth Branwell, who came to care for them after their mother died in September, 1821, shortly after their arrival in Haworth. Tutors in art and music were occasionally hired for the children, and at least two libraries were available to them: their father's, and that of the Keighley Mechanics' Institute.

Emily left Haworth few times in her life. When she did, it was usually to continue her education or to gain employment. At the age of six, she and three of her sisters—Maria, Elizabeth, and Charlotte—were sent to the Clergyman Daughters' School at Cowan Bridge. Their stay was brief, for when the two older sisters, Maria and Elizabeth, were stricken with tuberculosis, from which they later died, their father had all his daughters sent home. Several years later, in 1835, Emily attended school for a few months at Roe Head with Charlotte. Their plan was to prepare themselves better for one of the few occupations open to them, that of governess. While at Roe Head, Emily became extremely distressed with her situation. In later years, after her death, Charlotte indicated that she believed the cause to have been intense homesickness. Shortly after this rather unsuccessful venture from home, Emily did leave again, this time to take a position as a teacher at a large school near Halifax called Law Hill, but again her stay was brief. She returned home, obviously unhappy with her life as a teacher. One last trip from Haworth was taken in 1842, when she accompanied Charlotte to Brussels to attend Madame Héger's school. The sisters wanted to increase their knowledge of German and French to become better qualified to open their own school, a project that was to remain only in the dreaming and planning stages. While in Brussels it again became clear that Emily was not comfortable in an environment strange to her, and when the sisters returned home in November, 1842, for their aunt's funeral, Emily remained, seemingly content to do so. Thereafter, she stayed at the parsonage, helping with the household chores. Her family accepted this choice and considered her contribution to the running of the household a valuable one. In September, 1848, Emily caught a cold while attending her brother's funeral. It developed into an inflammation of the lungs from which she never recovered. Her death was perhaps hastened by her refusal to seek medical attention until the very end.

Much consideration has been given to Brontë's inability to adjust to life away from Haworth. Emphasis has been placed on her love of the moors, which was so intense that she could not long be away from the heather and open fields. It is true that her work indicates an abiding—at times compelling—love for their somber beauty; however, some attention should also be given to the fact that all these journeys from home required adjusting to a structured world, one perhaps hostile to the private world of her imagination. It is clear that the powers of the imagination played a dominant role in Brontë's emotional life from her childhood on. Apparently, at home in the parsonage, she found an environment that suited the needs of her imagination and its creative powers.

As the fame of the Brontë family increased, Emily Brontë herself became a figure of legend. She was described as a passionate genius of almost mythic proportions, possessing supreme will and strength. This interpretation was encouraged very early by Charlotte, whose respect for her sister increased greatly during the last months of her life: In Charlotte's eyes, her seemingly unobtrusive sister had become a solitary being, towering above others, heroically hastening her death. So long has this view been presented that it is now inextricably woven with Emily Brontë's name and image. She herself left so few biographical clues that perhaps the actual woman must always be seen from a distance; however, in her work there is indeed evidence of a poet of original, imaginative power, who, having chosen her God of Visions, was able to give poetic expression to the essential emotions of the human soul.

ANALYSIS

When interpreting Emily Brontë's poetry, one must first confront the Gondal problem: What is the significance of that exotic world of emotional drama that so occupied her imagination? Some readers argue that this imaginary world of rebellion and punishment, death and lost love, permeated all her work; others maintain that her finer poems were composed outside its dramatic, at times melodramatic, influences. Brontë's own division of the poems into two notebooks, one titled "Gondal Poems," the other left untitled, would suggest a clear separation; yet a subjective lyrical voice can be heard in many of the Gondal poems, and echoes of the Gondal drama can be heard in non-Gondal material. Because the original prose saga has been lost, perhaps no completely satisfactory solution can be found; nevertheless, a thematic approach to Brontë's poetry does provide a unifying interpretation.

Many of her Gondal characters are isolated figures who yearn for a time of love or freedom now lost. In the non-Gondal poems, the same voice of longing can be heard: The speakers of such poems as "The Philosopher" and "To Imagination" desire a time of union and harmony, or, as in "O Thy Bright Eyes Must Answer Now," a time of freedom from the restraints of reason and earthly cares. The Gondal characters, with their exotic-sounding names (such as Augusta Geraldine Almeda and Julius Brenzaida), are not beings separate and distinct from the poet herself; they are masks through which Brontë speaks. Therefore, although Brontë often uses the dramatic forms of direct address, inquiry, and dialogue, none of her poems can be adequately analyzed as if it were a dramatic monologue prefiguring the work of Robert Browning. She does not attempt to delineate a character through the subtleties of his speech in a particular time and place. The desperate situations in which she places her dramatic figures merely provide appropriate circumstances in which to express the emotional and at times mystical experiences of her own private world. Continually, her poems emphasize the creative power of the individual spirit as it struggles to define itself in relation to the "Invisible," the unseen source of all existence. This struggle in all its intensity is the predominant theme of her poetry, whether it is set in a Gondal prison or on a Yorkshire moor.

Intensity is one of Brontë's distinguishing characteristics. Her poetry gives the impression of having been cut as close to the center of feeling as possible. The portrayal of such passionate intensity can easily lead to excessive exclamations in which meaning is scattered, if not lost; in Brontë's case, however, her skillful handling of form provides the needed restraint. She achieves this control over her subject through such structuring devices as simple metrical patterns (she was especially fond of tetrameter and trimeter), strong monosyllabic rhymes, parallel phrasing, repetition of key words, and appropriately placed pauses. Her use of these devices allows her to shape the intensity into ordered movements appropriate to the subject, whether it be a mournful one or one of joyous celebration.

"ROSINA ALCONA TO JULIUS BRENZAIDA"

One of the best examples of Brontë's use of these structuring techniques to control feeling can be found in her best-known love poem, "Rosina Alcona to Julius Brenzaida," one of her Gondal poems often anthologized under the title "Remembrance." Rosina Alcona is addressing her lover Julius, now dead for fifteen years. She asks to be forgiven for going on with her own life after losing him. The anguish the speaker feels is captured in the wavelike rhythms established in the first stanza through the use of pauses and parallel phrasing: "Cold in the earth, and the deep snow piled above thee!/ Far, far removed, cold in the dreary grave!" Monosyllabic rhyme and the repetition of significant words also aid in embodying the emotional quality of a yearning that is held in check.

Brontë often achieves control through repetition of a key word, one that is repeated but with varying connotations. In the beginning lines of the poem, the word "cold" presents two aspects of the literal circumstances: The lover lies cold in the grave, and the coldness of winter is upon the land. As the poem progresses, "cold" evolves in meaning to encompass the life of the speaker as well. Without her lover, the warmth and light of her life are gone. He was both the sun and stars, and without him the heavens are now dark. Her life through the fifteen years following Julius's death has been winter, continually as barren as the snow-covered land, and to endure such barrenness, she herself has had to become "cold." She has had to "check the tears of useless passion" and to chill the "burning wish" to follow him to the grave. Moreover, losing him to death has taught her one of the "cold" realities of life: "existence can be cherished" even after all love and joy are gone from one's own life.

This expanded definition of the word "cold" is underscored by Brontë's use of antithesis, another technique typical of her style. In stanza 3, Brontë juxtaposes the image of the lover lying cold and still in his grave and the wild movements of the weather that will ultimately lead to the warmth of spring. In the final stanza, she returns to the same pair of opposites: stillness and movement. The speaker refuses to indulge too much in "Memory's rapturous pain," her wild feelings of love and sorrow, for fear that she could not then face the "empty world again," the still frozen world of her own life. With this last description of the "empty world," Brontë returns to the image of coldness with which she began, and the tolling, elegiac poem is brought to rest, although with the phrase "rapturous pain" she points to the restless, unreconciled feelings of the speaker. These conflicting desires between the longing to remember lost love and the need to forget point in turn to the paradoxical nature of the whole poem: The speaker tells of the necessity of forgetting her lover, and yet the poem itself attests to her loving memory of him.

"THE PHILOSOPHER"

In the non-Gondal poem "The Philosopher" there is a description of "warring gods" within the "little frame" of the speaker's physical self. This image could easily serve as a metaphor for much of Brontë's poetry: Within the confines of poetic structure, she attempts to hold conflicting forces and their related images. "Oh Thy Bright Eyes Must Answer Now" is a significant poem in the Brontë canon, for it clearly sets forth the dimensions of these conflicts. The first half of the poem presents the conflict between imagination and reason, between spiritual needs and earthly cares. The speaker turns to the "bright eyes" of the "radiant angel" of her vision, to summon it to speak and defend her choice to worship its power, rejecting the demands of Reason, who in "forms of gloom" with a "scornful brow" judges and mocks her "overthrow." By the world's standards, she has been overthrown, for she has failed to achieve wealth and glory. She has shunned the "common path" and chosen the "strange road."

The second half of the poem examines the inner conflict regarding her relationship to the overseeing "radiant angel" of this strange road. In stanza 5, she addresses this angel as "Thee, ever present, phantom thing—/ My slave, my comrade, and my King!" The speaker controls the influence, good or ill, of this angel. Consequently, he is her slave, and yet he is a comrade, an equal who is always with her, bringing her "intimate delight," and finally—seeming to contradict completely these two roles of slave and comrade—he is her King, directing and dictating. In these lines, Brontë is expressing the conflicting desires within the soul itself: a desire to remain free without being isolated, and a desire to maintain individual identity while simultaneously merging with a larger and more powerful being.

The last stanza of this poem points to the troublesome question underlying the complicated life of Brontë's visions: Is she wrong to choose a faith that allows her own soul to grant her prayers? In a very real way, her own imagination has conjured up the angel who will defeat Reason. It is characteristic of Brontë to place such emphasis on individual power and will. Although this emphasis prefigures the work of later writers in which the self creates its own reality and its own gods, the unorthodox road that Brontë chose to follow did not lead her to this extreme conclusion. The last two lines of "Oh Thy Bright Eyes Must Answer Now" return to her "God of Visions": He must "plead" for her. Her power was expressed in her choice to worship him, and now he must come to defend her.

GOD OF VISIONS AND NATURE

Throughout Brontë's work there remains an emphasis on an outside power that could and would exist whether she herself existed or not. One of the last written and most famous of her poems, "No Coward Soul Is Mine," is a ringing affirmation of her faith in her choice of visions. Her soul stands sure in its relationship to the "Being and Breath" that "can never be destroyed." When suns and universes are gone, it will still remain.

Many of Brontë's poems describing nature also concern this prevailing spirit, and occasionally they seem to present a pantheistic vision; however, although the natural world clearly had the power to stir and inspire her, nature and her God of Visions are not synonymous. Primarily, Brontë uses nature to parallel a state of mind or soul, as she does in "Remembrance," where the cold snow-covered hills objectify the restrained feelings of the speaker. Often the open moors and the movement of the winds are used to embody the wild, free feelings of the human soul. In "Aye, There It Is! It Wakes To-night," Brontë uses the powerful and violent images of the storm to describe a person being transformed into pure spirit as her soul awakens to knowledge of some supreme spiritual power. Like lightning, her "feeling's fires flash," her gaze is "kindled," a "glorious wind" sweeps all memory of this mortal world from her mind, and she becomes "the essence of the Tempest's roaring." The last stanza concludes that this visionary experience prefigures the life of the soul after death, when, free from the prison of the body, it shall rise: "The dungeon mingle with the mould—/ The captive with the skies." In these last two lines, Brontë plays on a rather conventional simile of the body as prisonhouse of the soul to create an original effect. First, she unexpectedly and suddenly introduces the word "mould" to represent the process of the body's decay and the dust to which it returns, and second, she compares the action of the soul after death to this process of decay: The body will "mingle" with the earth; the soul with the skies. There is in this last line a sense of triumphant release, effectively represented in the long vowel sound of "skies" that sharply contrasts with the earlier mournful sounds of "cold" and "mould." Throughout the poem, Brontë has again controlled an intensely emotional subject through antithesis, simple monosyllabic rhymes, and terse metrical patterns.

"JULIAN M. TO A. G. ROCHELLE"

Perhaps the most famous of Brontë's poems depicting this visionary experience is the lengthy fragment of the Gondal poem "Julian M. to A. G. Rochelle," which Brontë published under the title "The Prisoner." The fragment consists of lines 13-44 and lines 65-92 of the original with four new lines added at the end to provide an appropriate conclusion. This slightly revised excerpt, although beginning with the voice of Julian telling of his decision to wander rather casually through the family dungeons, primarily concerns the mystical experiences of one of the prisoners. When she speaks, she displays a spirit undefeated by her imprisonment. Her body is able to endure the chains, for her soul is open to a nightly "messenger" who offers her the hope of "eternal liberty." Her response to this messenger occurs in a series of stages. First, she experiences a mingling of pain and pleasure as visions rise before her. Then she loses all awareness of her earthly self; the world and the body are forgotten. She then is able to experience an "unuttered harmony." Her outward senses and conscious mind have become numb so that the "inward essence" can be released. In the final stage, this inward essence—in one burst of energy, as if leaping—attempts to merge with the "Invisible," the "Unseen," which she also describes as a "home" and a "harbour." At this point, because she cannot completely escape the body and still live, she suddenly and painfully returns to a knowledge of her earthly self and its prison, the literal prison in which she finds herself and the prison of her own body. Only after death can she finally and permanently join with the "Unseen," and so she looks forward to Death as heralding the complete and lasting union with the source of these nightly divine visions.

Brontë's decision to excerpt these particular stanzas from one of her Gondal poems, and the fact that once excerpted they still function as a unified whole, again suggest that Gondal merely provided the stage and the costumes for a drama that was actually taking place in Brontë's own self. In fact, in this case the poem benefits from the cutting of the frame stanzas that are full of conventional descriptions of stone dungeons and Lord Julian's somewhat expected romantic response to the fair prisoner. Obviously, Brontë's interest and poetic talent lay in examining and capturing the visionary experience.

OTHER MAJOR WORKS

LONG FICTION: *Wuthering Heights*, 1847.

NONFICTION: *Five Essays Written in French*, 1948 (Lorine White Nagel, translator); *The Brontë Letters*, 1954 (Muriel Spark, editor).

BIBLIOGRAPHY

Barnard, Robert. *Emily Brontë*. New York: Oxford University Press, 2000. An overview of Brontë's life and work. Bibliography, maps, illustrations, index.

Barnard, Robert, and Louise Barnard. *A Brontë Encyclopedia*. Malden, Mass.: Blackwell, 2007. An alphabetical treatment of the life and writings of the Brontë family.

Davies, Stevie. *Emily Brontë: Heretic*. London: Women's Press, 1994. Examination of the complex personality that produced *Wuthering Heights* and a collection of haunting Romantic poetry.

Frank, Katherine. *A Chainless Soul: A Life of Emily Brontë*. Boston: Houghton Mifflin, 1990. Biographical study demonstrating the complex relationships between Emily Brontë and her family members.

Gezari, Janet. *Last Things: Emily Brontë's Poems*. New York: Oxford University Press, 2007. Although most works on Emily Brontë focus on her novel, this one provides critical analysis of her poetry.

Miller, Lucasta. *The Brontë Myth*. London: Jonathan Cape, 2001. Biography of the Brontë sisters, explaining how previous biographers have shaped readers' understanding of the three novelists' major works.

Pykett, Lyn. *Emily Brontë*. Savage, Md.: Barnes & Noble, 1989. Feminist assessment of Brontë's work.

Rollyson, Carl, and Lisa Paddock. *The Brontës A to Z: The Essential Reference to Their Lives and Work*. New York: Facts On File, 2003. Takes an encyclopedic approach to the family, including ill-starred brother Branwell. Includes discussions of even many of the lesser known poems, as well as details of the lives of the authors.

Vine, Steve. *Emily Brontë*. New York: Twayne, 1998. Biography and critical analysis of *Wuthering Heights* and Brontë's poetry, intended as an introduction for general readers.

Winnifrith, Tom, and Edward Chitham. *Charlotte and Emily Brontë: Literary Lives*. New York: St. Martin's Press, 1989. Brief assessment of the impact the two sisters had on each other's writing.

Diane D'Amico

LORD BYRON
George Gordon

Born: London, England; January 22, 1788
Died: Missolonghi, Greece; April 19, 1824

PRINCIPAL POETRY

Fugitive Pieces, 1806
Hours of Idleness, 1807
Poems on Various Occasions, 1807
Poems Original and Translated, 1808
English Bards and Scotch Reviewers, 1809
Hints from Horace, 1811
The Curse of Minerva, 1812
Childe Harold's Pilgrimage, 1812-1818 (cantos 1-4), 1819 (the 4 cantos together)
The Bride of Abydos, 1813
The Giaour, 1813
Waltz: An Apostrophic Hymn, 1813
The Corsair, 1814
Lara, 1814
Ode to Napoleon Buonaparte, 1814
Hebrew Melodies Ancient and Modern, 1815
Monody on the Death of the Right Honourable R. B. Sheridan, 1816
Parisina, 1816
Poems, 1816
The Prisoner of Chillon, and Other Poems, 1816
The Siege of Corinth, 1816
The Lament of Tasso, 1817
Beppo: A Venetian Story, 1818
Mazeppa, 1819
Don Juan, 1819-1824 (cantos 1-16), 1826 (the 16 cantos together)
The Prophecy of Dante, 1821
The Vision of Judgment, 1822
The Age of Bronze, 1823
The Island, 1823
The Complete Poetical Works of Byron, 1980-1986 (5 volumes)

OTHER LITERARY FORMS

It should be noted that the titles of Lord Byron's principal poetic works include dramatic as well as lyrical and narrative works. Byron wrote eight plays in all, most of which focused on either speculative or historical subjects and were never intended for the stage. He designated them "mental theatre," or closet drama modeled after classical principles, and clearly regarded the plays as among his most important productions. Complementing Byron's extraordinarily prolific and diverse career as a poet is his versatility as a writer of epistolary prose. During his lifetime Byron composed more than twenty-nine hundred letters, which have been scrupulously edited by Leslie A. Marchand and published between 1973 and 1982 in twelve volumes under the title *Byron's Letters and Journals*. The sheer immensity of this correspondence is matched only by the unlimited range and immediacy of Byron's voice as he speaks without reserve on a variety of topics. In addition to these private documents, along with John Keats's letters the most revealing correspondence of the British Romantic poets, Byron also published the combative *Letter to [John Murray] on the Rev. W. L. Bowles' Strictures on the Life and Writings of Pope* (1821) and, in the first number of Leigh Hunt's *The Liberal* (1822), "A Letter to the Editor of 'My Grandmother's Review.'" *The Parliamentary Speeches of Lord Byron*, comprising three addresses he made while a member of the House of Lords, was issued in 1824, well after he had grown disillusioned with what he called "Parliamentary mummeries."

ACHIEVEMENTS

If poets can be judged by the intellectual and cultural myths which they inspire, then Lord Byron must be deemed the most broadly influential of the Romantic writers. Through his creation of a brooding and defiant persona known as the Byronic Hero—according to Peter L. Thorslev, Jr., a composite blend of the attributes of Cain, Ahasuerus, Satan, Prometheus, Rousseau's Child of Nature, the Man of Feeling, the Gloomy Egoist, the Gothic Villain, and the Noble Outlaw—Byron exerted a profound impact on the entire nineteenth century and its conception of the archetypal Romantic sensibility. The essential trait that came to be associated with Byronism is what Bertrand Russell, in his *History of Western Philosophy* (1945), identifies as "Titanic cosmic self-assertion." Signifying less a specific stance than a generalized attitude, the phrase denotes a proud, often despairing, rebellion against any institutional or moral system that threatens to rob the self of its autonomy, centrality, and independence. Something of the extent to which this outlook captured the imagination of the age can be gauged from a brief list of artists and thinkers whose works reflect Byron's influence: in Germany, Johann Wolfgang von Goethe, Heinrich Heine, Ludwig van Beethoven, and Friedrich Nietzsche; in France, Honoré de Balzac, Stendhal, Hector Berlioz, and Eugène Delacroix; in Russia, Alexander Pushkin and Fyodor Dostoevski; and in America, Herman Melville. Even Matthew Arnold, that most Wordsworthian of Victorian

Lord Byron
(Library of Congress)

critics, admitted in his 1850 poem "Memorial Verses" that the collective English soul "Had *felt* him like the thunder's roll." Thirty-one years later, Arnold's view had not changed: "The power of Byron's personality," he wrote, approvingly quoting Algernon Charles Swinburne, "lies in . . . '*the excellence of sincerity and strength.*'"

What fascinated nineteenth century audiences about Byron was not simply the larger-than-life character of the man transmuted into art but also the flinty integrity of his mind that penetrated all deception and constantly tested the limits of skepticism. In this respect Byron seems peculiarly modern. Although often considered a Romantic paradox because of various antitheses in his nature (he led the Romantic revolution toward "expression" in poetry, for example, but was thoroughly Augustan in his literary ideals and a lifelong admirer of Alexander Pope), he rarely succumbs to the temptation of believing his own fictions and always examines his experience with obsessive honesty. In conversations with his friend and confidante Lady Blessington, Byron thus confessed to being "so changeable . . . such a strange *mèlange* of good and evil, that it would be difficult to describe me," but he goes on to say: "There are but two sentiments to which I am constant—a strong love of liberty, and a detestation of cant." These last qualities undoubtedly explain why the vein of satire was so congenial to him as a poet. In both the barbed heroic couplets of *English Bards and Scotch Reviewers*, the scathing burlesque that launched his career, and the seriocomic use of ottava rima in *Don Juan*, the epic satire that he did not live to complete, Byron sought to expose the smug complacencies and absurd pretensions of his time and, if possible, to restore to it the ability to see itself objectively. The dark *Weltschmerz* of poems such as *Childe Harold's Pilgrimage* may attest his personal despair over whether that goal could ever be accomplished, but in all his variegated moods he writes with energetic conviction born of "sincerity and strength." Byron's seminal achievement, therefore, may be his capacity for embodying the strivings of a deeply restless age, for articulating those longings and doing what all great poets do—namely, to return the imagination to the world.

Biography

George Gordon, the sixth Lord Byron, was born with a clubbed right foot, a deformity that caused him considerable suffering throughout his life and did much to shape his later character. He was descended from two aristocratic and colorful families: His father, who died when Byron was three years old, was Captain John ("Mad Jack") Byron, a rake and fortune hunter who traced his ancestry back to the time of William the Conqueror; his mother, Catherine Gordon of Gight, was the irascible and outspoken heiress who liked to boast of her lineal connection to James I of Scotland. After her husband squandered the Gordon inheritance, Catherine moved to Aberdeen, where she reared her son under straitened financial circumstances and the Calvinistic creed of Scottish Presbyterianism. With the death of his great-uncle in 1798, the ten-year-old Byron became a titled English peer and took up residence at the patrimonial estate of Newstead Abbey in Nottingham. During this period the precocious young lord fell in love with two cousins named Mary Duff and Margaret Parker, was initiated into premature sexual dalliance by a nurse, and began his zealous regimen of swimming, boxing, fencing, and horsemanship to compensate for his physical lameness.

While at Harrow (1801-1805) and subsequently at Cambridge (1805-1807), Byron started to develop some of the strong attachments and habits that remained with him into adulthood. Though he little relished formal schooling, he periodically immersed himself in reading, became infatuated with Mary Chaworth, and cultivated lasting friendships with his half sister Augusta Leigh as well as with John Cam Hobhouse, Scrope Davies, Francis Hodgson, and others. He also incurred sizable debts for his extravagant revelries at Newstead during college vacations, and, simultaneously, he was entering the arena of literary authorship. His first few volumes of juvenilia, *Fugitive Pieces* and *Poems on Various Occasions*, were privately printed and circulated; *Hours of Idleness*, however, his ensuing venture into the public domain, prompted caustic notice by Henry Brougham, which in turn fueled the retaliatory satire of *English Bards and Scotch Reviewers*. Shortly thereafter, tiring of his life of routine dissipation, Byron prepared to leave England.

The next seven years were momentous ones in Byron's life. Before committing himself to what he thought might eventually be a Parliamentary career, he determined to broaden his education by visiting other lands and peoples. Accordingly, in 1809 he embarked with Hobhouse on an exhilarating tour through Portugal, Spain, Malta, Albania, Greece, and Asia Minor. The vivid scenes and experiences of this two-year excursion provided Byron with the materials for cantos 1-2 of his autobiographical travelogue *Childe Harold's Pilgrimage* and his several Eastern tales in verse. Eight months after his return to England in 1811, part of *Childe Harold's Pilgrimage* was published and Byron became an overnight celebrity: "I awoke one morning," wrote the nobleman-poet, "and found myself famous." Because Byron was readily identified with the melancholic, jaded, and quasi-erotic hero of his poem, he was besieged by ladies of fashion and lionized by the beau monde of Regency London. Foremost among those giddily vying for the attentions of the handsome and aristocratic young author was Lady Caroline Lamb, a flamboyant, decidedly eccentric woman who to her delight discovered Byron to be "mad—bad—and dangerous to know." Perhaps as much to escape such frenzied pursuit as for any other reason, Byron in early 1815 married Annabella Milbanke, a demure and somewhat priggish "bluestocking" whom Byron dubbed "my Princess of Parallelograms." The ill-fated marriage dissolved a year later, after the birth of a daughter, Augusta Ada, when Lady Byron learned of her husband's incestuous relations with his half sister. Socially ostracized by all but his close friends and beset by creditors, Byron left England on April 25, 1816, never to return.

The legendary final phase of Byron's career, which saw his full maturation as a poet, was crowded with events that ensured his lasting renown. Journeying through France to Switzerland, he spent his first summer in exile near Geneva, where he met two other expatriates, Percy Bysshe Shelley and Mary Shelley, with whom he enjoyed many evenings of intellectual conversation. While there, Byron also completed canto 3 of *Childe Harold's Pilgrimage*, began *Manfred* (pb. 1817), and tried unsuccessfully to stay uninvolved with Mary Shelley's persistent stepsister Claire Clairmont. In January, 1817, Clairmont and Byron had a child, a daughter they named Allegra. By the spring of that year Byron had established himself in Venice, "the greenest isle" of his imagination, where he diverted himself with numerous affairs while periodically exploring the antiquities of Florence and Rome.

The atmosphere of Italy did much to stimulate his literary creativity in new directions. By the end of 1817 he finished canto 4 of *Childe Harold's Pilgrimage*, an elegiac canto signaling Byron's decisive break with the past, and, influenced by John Hookham Frere's *Whistlecraft* (1817), a mock-heroic satirical poem in the flexible form of ottava rima, he completed the experimental *Beppo*, which looks forward to the narrative style of *Don Juan*. The period from 1818 to 1822 brought additional changes. Wearying of his promiscuous debaucheries on the Grand Canal in Venice, Byron met Countess Teresa Guiccioli of Ravenna, then nineteen years old, and soon became her devoted *cavalier servente*. This attachment, in turn, drew him into the revolutionary Carbonari struggle against Austrian rule in northern Italy, an interest reflected in his political dramas (*Marino Faliero, Doge of Venice*, pr., pb. 1821; *The Two Foscari*, pb. 1821; and *Sardanapalus*, pb. 1821). With the defeat of the Carbonari movement in 1821, Byron followed the Gambas, Teresa's family, to Pisa, where he again joined the Shelley circle, which now included Edward John Trelawny and Thomas Medwin, and composed his devastating satire *The Vision of Judgment*. News of Shelley's drowning in July, 1822, however, stunned and sobered Byron. Shortly thereafter, he left for Genoa with Countess Guiccioli, but found his thoughts increasingly preoccupied with the Greek War of Independence. The final chapter of his life, always dominated by the trait that Lady Blessington called "mobility," forms a fitting memorial to Byron's restless spirit. Elected a member of the London Greek Committee, a Philhellene organization, the poet felt obligated to translate his political convictions into action. Despite skepticism concerning various Greek leaders' loyalty to the cause and despite a sense of his own imminent death, Byron set forth to do what he could. Sailing for Missolonghi in late December, 1823, he devoted his personal fortune and energy to forming a united front against the Turks. Four months later he died of a fever; to this day he is hailed as a national hero by the Greek people.

Analysis

The history of the poetic development of Lord Byron intersects at every stage with the saga of his life; yet it is only one of many paradoxes that he valued the writing of poetry primarily for the opportunity it afforded him to escape what he termed "my own wretched identity." More than anything else, poetry for Byron was a means both of sublimation and, ultimately, of self-realization. In his letters he thus suggests the former function when he speaks of poetry as "the lava of the imagination whose eruption prevents an earthquake," the volcanic metaphor signifying the cathartic release that the process of writing afforded him. The precise way in which it fulfilled the second function, however, is less obvious. Through the dynamics of self-projection, of investing much of his own multifaceted character in his personae, Byron strives to transcend the narrow limits of "personality" and achieve a more comprehensive perspective on himself and his experience. The essential goal of this artistic quest, which constitutes a progressive ontology, is delineated in canto 3 of *Childe Harold's Pilgrimage*: "'Tis to create, and in creating live/ A being more intense." To trace Byron's growth as a poet, therefore, is to witness him reaching beyond subjectivism and attempting to realize that intensity of being that comes about through the continuous act of self-creation.

Hours of Idleness

Any account of Byron's achievement must begin with the poems collected in *Hours of Idleness* and the early satires. In the preface to the 1807 miscellany, the nineteen-year-old Byron calls attention to himself by posing as an unlikely author (one "accustomed, in my younger days, to rove a careless mountaineer on the Highlands of Scotland"), by minimizing the merits of his literary endeavor ("to divert the dull moments of indisposition, or the monotony of a vacant hour, urged me 'to his sin'"), and by passing preemptive judgment on his work ("little can be expected from so unpromising a muse"). Such ingenuous posturing is clearly meant to invite, under the guise of dismissing, public recognition and acclaim. Despite the transparency of the subterfuge, the poems within *Hours of Idleness* form a revealing self-portrait in which Byron, while paraphrasing past idioms in poetry and exploiting eighteenth century literary conventions, obliquely seeks to discover a mythologized pattern for his emerging sense of himself. The one theme sounded repeatedly is what Robert F. Gleckner designates "the ruins of paradise," or the fall from youthful innocence. As he explores the experience of spiritual loss and shattered illusions, Byron can be seen moving toward this latter belief that "the great object of life is Sensation—to feel that we exist—even though in pain."

Admittedly imitative in style, often to the point of mannerism, *Hours of Idleness* revolves around several episodes of separation and disenchantment that, for the speaker, spell the end of an idealized, prelapsarian past. The short poem "Remembrance," composed in 1806 but not published until 1832, epitomizes both the tone and outlook of the volume as a whole:

> My days of happiness are few:
> Chill'd by misfortune's wintry blast,
> My dawn of life is overcast,
> Love, Hope, and Joy, alike adieu!—
> Would I could add Remembrance too!

Although the lines verge on doggerel, the same mood of melancholic nostalgia informs such other generally more successful poems as "On Leaving Newstead Abbey," "The First Kiss of Love," "On a Distant View of the Village and School of Harrow on the Hill," and "Lachin y Gair." In all these works Byron cannot disown the power of memory because, though denounced as a curse, it alone provides glimpses of what in "Childish Recollections" he refers to as "the progress of my youthful dream," the foundation for his concept of self. This tension gives rise in other lyrics to a plangent wish to escape the "dark'ning shades" of maturity, regaining the uncompromised or "freeborn soul." Knowing the fatuity of the desire, however, the poet resorts at last to a kind of protective cynicism. In "To Romance," for example, abandoning what he derides as the "motley court" of "Affectation" and "sickly Sensibility," he admits that "'tis hard to quit the dreams,/ Which haunt the unsuspicious soul" but abjures the past as illusory and refuses any longer to be the dupe of his romantic fancy. Embittered by his early discovery, as Byron was later to write in canto 3 of *Childe Harold's Pilgrimage*, that "life's enchanted cup but sparkles near the brim," the poet in *Hours of Idleness* fluctuates between moments of elegiac regret and tenacious hope, the ambivalent response itself prefiguring the skeptical idealist of the major poems to follow.

POETIC ACRIMONY

The Popean satires, which were composed shortly after the 1807 collection, disclose Byron's reaction to his disillusionment and punctured faith. In *English Bards and Scotch Reviewers*, *Hints from Horace*, and *The Curse of Minerva*—all written during the next four years—Byron lashes out at various individuals whom he regarded as typifying the literary and moral shortcomings of his age. The motto of "these degenerate days," he announces in *English Bards and Scotch Reviewers*, is "Care not for feeling," and so in arraigning nearly all his contemporaries except Samuel Rogers and Thomas Campbell he poses as the hardened realist determined to expose error on every hand: "But now, so callous grown, so changed since youth,/ I've learned to think, and sternly speak the truth." In the diatribe Byron often vents his anger indiscriminately, but the acrimony of his attack stems from a keen sense of embarrassment and outrage at the reception accorded *Hours of Idleness* by such critics as Henry Brougham in the *Edinburgh Review*. Thus, before indicating all those "afflicted," as his preface charges, "with the present prevalent and distressing *rabies* for rhyming," Byron debunks himself as well:

> I, too, can scrawl, and once upon a time
> I poured along the town a flood of rhyme,
> A school-boy freak, unworthy praise or blame;
> I printed—older children do the same.
> 'Tis pleasant, sure, to see one's name in print;
> A Book's a Book, altho' there's nothing in't.

The same irreverent or iconoclastic spirit pervades *Hints from Horace*, a mocking jab at contemporary literary practice from the vantage point of Horace's *Ars Poetica* (13-8 B.C.E., *The Art of Poetry*), and *The Curse of Minerva*, a Swiftian condemnation of Lord Elgin for his despoiling Greek sculpture. In these strident satires Byron alters his earlier poetic stance through two mechanisms: by adopting the voice of savage indignation and by spurning the accepted standards of his age. The detachment that he tries to win through both devices is another step toward his large aesthetic goal of self-realization.

INTERTWINED MODALITIES

A crucial phase in that ongoing process involves the composition, spanning the period from 1809 to 1817, of *Childe Harold's Pilgrimage* and, to a lesser extent, of the exotic Oriental tales that include *The Giaour*, *The Bride of Abydos*, *The Corsair*, and *Lara*. These verse narratives are significant because in them two sides of Byron's complexity as an artist are counterbalanced—the usually antithetical modes that Keats, in his letters, conceptualizes as the "egotistical sublime" and "the camelion [sic] Poet." Though Keats associated the first quality with William Wordsworth, the element of the "egotistical sublime" in Byron reveals itself in the highly developed reflexivity of his semiautobiographical poems and in his tendency to concentrate on his own immediate thoughts and emotions. At the same time, however, there emerges an equal but opposite impulse that reflects Byron's essentially centrifugal rather than centripetal habit of mind. This is his characteristic propensity for employing a gamut of masks or personae through which he endeavors to escape the restrictive confines of self-consciousness, especially as molded by memory, and to achieve the intensity of being that comes with self-transcendence. Together, these intertwined modalities, the "egotistical" and the "chameleonic," make up the unique "strength" of Byron's imagination.

Readers of the time were nevertheless inclined to recognize only the former tendency in his works and so to find him guilty of facile exhibitionism. Certainly when Byronism was rampant, no one impersonated Byron better than Byron himself; yet, if one allows for this susceptibility, the earnestness with which the poet responded to his detractors is instructive. Echoing the well-known protest lodged in his 1820 "Reply to Blackwood's *Edinburgh Magazine*," he expostulated a year later to Thomas Moore that "a man's poetry is a distinct faculty, or soul, and has no more to do with the every-day individual than the Inspiration with the Pythoness when removed from her tripod." Similarly, in the privacy of his journal for 1813, while writing the very poems that incurred the charge, he remarks: "To withdraw *myself* from *myself* (oh that cursed selfishness!) has ever been my sole, my entire, my sincere motive in scribbling at all; and publishing is also the continuance of the same object, by the action it affords to the mind, which else recoils upon itself." The vehemence of these statements should not be allowed to obscure Byron's clear point regarding the psychology of composition. The vicarious world of poetry, as he views it, makes possible a release from the concentricity of the mind that otherwise, to borrow two of his favorite images in *Childe Harold's Pilgrimage*, would sting itself to death like the scorpion ringed by fire or consume its scabbard like a rusting sword.

CHILDE HAROLD'S PILGRIMAGE

Byron first expands upon this aesthetic in cantos 3-4 of *Childe Harold's Pilgrimage*, but some attention to the earlier cantos is prerequisite to understanding the later two. When he began the travelogue in 1809 while touring Europe and the Levant, Byron conceived of a work in Spenserian stanza form which would depict, in the eighteenth century tradition of topographical or "locodescriptive" poetry, his vivid impressions of the scenes and peoples he visited, intermixed with meditative reflections. "For the sake of giving some connection to the piece," which otherwise, according to the preface, "makes no pretension to regularity," Byron introduces the "fictitious character" of Harold, who serves as the nominal hero-protagonist, although this syntactical function is about all that can be claimed for him. Out of "the fulness [*sic*] of satiety," it is true, Harold "resolve[s]" to leave England behind, having run through "Sin's long labyrinth"; yet in his wandering pilgrimage through Spain, Portugal, Albania, and Greece he remains a curiously static, one-dimensional figure and is little more than a partial projection of

Byron's darker moods (for example, misanthropy, remorse, cynicism, and forced stoicism). As such, he adumbrates the explicit theme of cantos 1-2: that is, "Consciousness awaking to her woes." Neither Harold nor Byron, however, has yet learned "what he might be, or he ought," and it is somehow fitting that canto 2 should close in a Greece stripped of its ancient grandeur and heroes.

Throughout this half of the poem, Byron's protagonist bears a marked resemblance to the poet himself, but it is well not to overlook the punning assertion made in the 1812 preface that Harold is "the child of imagination." Shortly before the publication of cantos 1-2, in a letter to Robert Charles Dallas, Byron reinforces the distinction between himself and his central character: "If in parts I may be thought to have drawn from myself, believe me it is but in parts, and I shall not own even to that . . . I would not be such a fellow as I have made my hero for all the world." The disclaimer has not won wide acceptance, largely because in the holograph copy of the poem Byron initially christened his protagonist "Childe Burun"; yet the first two cantos themselves substantiate the dissociation which Byron's comment to Dallas emphasizes. On one hand, they dramatize the alienated figure of Harold, who, like the tortured hero of *Lara*, is portrayed as "a stranger in this breathing world,/ An erring spirit from another hurled;/ A thing of dark imaginings"; on the other hand, they are mediated by a separate narrator who, distanced from the foreground, objectively recognizes that "the blight of life" that overtakes men like Harold is "the demon Thought," or the canker of self-consciousness. In actuality, both entities are Byron, and through the dichotomy he seeks to plumb his own contradictory nature.

By the time that Byron came to write canto 3, however, life had paradoxically imitated art: Exiled from England by public vilification for his alleged cruelty toward his wife, the poet became that which before he had only imagined. This turn of events contributed to a new coalescence or ironic similarity between the author and his persona. Byron still does not identify himself completely with his titular hero, but he is now able to assimilate Harold as an exponent of himself without capitulating to the kind of Haroldian angst that suffuses cantos 1-2. He seems to register this altered orientation in the following lines: "Yet am I changed; though still enough the same/ In strength to bear what time can not abate,/ And feed on bitter fruits without accusing Fate." Implicit in the passage, with its allusion to John Milton's *Paradise Lost* (1667, 1674), is an undertone of confidence that even despair can be transformed into a source of stimulation and proof of his endurance. Byron now is speaking *in propria persona*. No longer rhapsodizing as in canto 1 "a youth,/ Who ne in virtue's ways did take delight," he is instead dealing with himself as a social and moral pariah—"the wandering outlaw of his own dark mind." The full assurance that he can avoid entrapment from within remains to be found, but the seeds of spiritual recovery are before him.

The groundwork is laid at the start of canto 3 when, after the framing device of an apostrophe to his daughter, Byron declares his artistic manifesto for the work: "'Tis to create, and in creating live/ A being more intense, that we endow/ With form our fancy, gaining as we give/ The life we image, even as I do now." Reflecting Shelley's influence on Byron in 1816, the passage continues and reveals that the poet now views his quotidian identity as "Nothing," as a hollow fiction, while the project of art discloses to him an ideal "other" or truer self which he will appropriate through the act of creating. The poem itself, in short, becomes the vehicle for self-discovery. Thus, although Harold continues to be much the same character as he was in cantos 1-2, what has changed greatly is Byron's positioning of himself as artist vis-à-vis the poem. He no longer depends on his protagonist as a surrogate or alter ego; even though the disease of self-consciousness has not been expunged, his faith has been restored in the imagination's ability to locate new horizons of meaning in an otherwise entropic world.

Both the third and fourth cantos of *Childe Harold's Pilgrimage* contain clear evidence of his shift in outlook. The two major scenes visited in canto 3 are Waterloo and the Swiss Alps, locales which by their historical associations stand symbolically opposed. In the former, Byron finds only the tragic vanity of life and the futility of worldly ambition; in the latter, he surveys the benign sublimity and undisturbed repose of nature. Initially, it would seem that he is elevating one sphere above the other, idealizing the serenity of "throned Eternity" in contrast to the agitation of "earth-born jars." He is, to some extent, but in a unique manner. Rather than treating these landscapes as discrete alternatives, Byron exploits them as provisional constructs for raising questions and defining some of his own misgivings about the human condition. Thus, if at Waterloo he rejects the "wretched interchange of wrong for wrong" within society, in the Alps he sees nothing "to loathe in nature, save to be/ A link reluctant in a fleshly chain."

In much the same way, he responds ambivalently to the fallen figureheads of each domain—Napoleon Bonaparte and Jean-Jacques Rousseau—whom he envisions as variants of himself. Both the Napoleon who was "conqueror and captive of the earth" and the "inspired" Rousseau whose oracles "set the world in flame" were men of unbounded energy, yet each was responsible for the shambles of the French Revolution and each was subverted by "a fever at the core,/ Fatal to him who bears, to all who ever bore." Byron recognizes their failure as potentially his own as well: "And *there* hath been thy bane," he proclaims. The stanza's rhetoric reverberates with his affinity for these individuals and suggests that Byron, as Jerome J. McGann observes in *Fiery Dust* (1968), is coming to the realization that "to 'know oneself' one must submit to immediate and partial acts of perception." Within canto 3 of *Childe Harold's Pilgrimage*, therefore, the poet moves further toward the understanding that to be human means to be a pilgrim, but a pilgrim ever in the process of redefining himself and the world that he inherits.

Canto 4 continues the archetypal pattern of the journey, in this case one extending from Venice to Rome, but broadens at the end to reveal a significantly matured Byron arriving at the genuine goal or embodiment of his questing spirit. Centered around the elegiac motif or *sic transit gloria mundi*, the last canto weighs the respective claims of both art and nature to permanence as Byron tries to decipher the enigma of humanity's existence. "The moral of all human tales," he postulates, is the inevitability of ruin and unfulfilled hopes, such that "History, with all her volumes vast,/ Hath but *one* page." This stark lesson occasionally moves the poet to invective, as when he declares that "Our life is a false nature—'tis not in/ The harmony of things." Nevertheless, in the poetry of Torquato Tasso, the sculpture of Venice, and the Colosseum in Rome, he discerns a grandeur and genius which transcend the melancholy attrition of time. That discovery, in turn, rekindles conviction as to the vitality of his own essential self, a realization heightened when Byron finds that he has outgrown the fictive prop of Harold:

> But where is he, the Pilgrim of my song,
> The being who upheld it through the past?
>
> . . . .
>
> He is no more—these breathings are his last;
> His wanderings done, his visions ebbing fast,
> And he himself as nothing. . . .

In the poem's concluding apostrophe to the sea near Albano, conceived as a "glorious mirror" and thalassic "image of Eternity," Byron achieves the true goal toward which he has been tending all along. Awesome in its untrammeled energy, the ocean becomes the symbol of the creating self that the poet has reclaimed. "My Pilgrim's shrine is won," writes Byron, for "I am not now/ That which I have been." With that declaration, Byron enters upon the last great phase of his poetic career.

DON JUAN

The monumental epic *Don Juan* forms the inspired climax to Byron's evolution as an artist, but to understand how this is so requires brief attention to a disturbing undercurrent in *Childe Harold's Pilgrimage*. Despite the general movement toward self-apprehension in that work, there yet occur moments when the inadequacy of language to articulate "all I seek,/ Bear, know, feel" subverts the poet's faith in his enterprise. Thus, although in canto 3 he would willingly believe that "there may be/ Words which are things," he has not found them; nor is he able to disguise from himself the knowledge that language is part of the disintegrated syntax of a fallen world. Along the same lines, after pondering in canto 4 the disappointed ideals of such poets as Dante and Petrarch, he ruefully admits that "what we have of feeling most intense/ Outstrips our faint expression." The intransigence of language, its inherent circularity as an instrument of meditation, was for Byron tied to the kind of Metaphysical despair dramatized in *Manfred* and *Cain* (pb. 1821), and by way of overcoming those quandaries he adopts in *Don Juan* a more radically versatile poetics.

The chief difference between *Childe Harold's Pilgrimage* and his later "epic of negation," as Brian Wilke describes *Don Juan* in *Romantic Poets and Epic Tradition* (1965), lies in Byron's refusal any longer to be controlled by "the stubborn heart." After opening with the farce of Juan's sexual initiation, before which he pauses to berate Plato as a charlatan, Byron makes his new outlook resoundingly clear:

> No more—no more—Oh! never more, my heart,
> Canst thou be my sole world, my universe!
> . . . .
> The illusion's gone for ever, and thou art
> Insensible, I trust, but none the worse,
> And in thy stead I've got a good deal of judgment,
> Though heaven knows how it ever found a lodgement.

Cognizant of the fictiveness of all experience, he plans to make his rambling medley of a poem mirror the manifold delusions and deceptions that man allows to impose upon his right of thought. In the face of such knowledge "Imagination droops her pinion," turning "what was once romantic to burlesque"—lines aptly capturing the shift from his stance in *Childe Harold's Pilgrimage*. In composing his "versified Aurora Borealis," however, Byron obviously sensed a creative exhilaration linked to his complete separation of himself from his hero. His letters written during the work's early stages reveal an exuberant confidence in the undertaking which, as he told Thomas Moore, was "meant to be a little quitely facetious upon every thing." Thus, addressing his old friend Douglas Kinnaird in 1819, he expressed a typically high-spirited opinion of his achievement: "As to 'Don Juan'—confess—confess—you dog—and be candid—that it is the sublime of *that there* sort of writing—it may be bawdy . . . but it is not *life*, is it not *the thing*?—Could any man have written it—who has not lived in the world?"

Byron's governing purpose in *Don Juan* is to "show things really as they are,/ Not as they ought to be." Toward that end he does not forbear lampooning all the assorted follies and philistine pretenses of "that microcosm on stilts,/ Yclept the Great World," for he sees its attachment to illusion as the root cause of men's inability to recognize or accept the truth about themselves. Byron's attack is all the more effective because he exempts neither himself as poet nor the function of language from his skeptical scrutiny. Overturning all conventional notions of structure and voice in poetry, he is intent upon making his "nondescript and ever-varying rhyme" demystify itself at every turn. Both serious and cynical, he consequently avers that compared to the epic myths of Vergil and Homer "this story's actually true," then later reminds his audience that his work "is only fiction,/ And that I sing of neither mine nor me." Nearly every stanza of *Don Juan* unmasks itself in similar fashion through the whimsical freedom of Byron's style. Fearless of incongruities in a world permeated by fraud, the poem's narrator defends his fluid cynicism in the name of verisimilitude (his aim is to "show things existent") while simultaneously debunking traditional concepts of authorial integrity: "If people contradict themselves, can I/ Help contradicting them, and everybody,/ Even my veracious self?" True "sincerity" in these terms is equated with inconsistency, paradox, and radical doubt, an outlook anticipated as early as 1813 when Byron, with uncanny self-knowledge and prescience, remarked in his journal that "if I am sincere with myself (but I fear one lies more to one's self than to any one else), every page should confute, refute, and utterly abjure its predecessor." By constantly deflating the artifices on which his own poem is built, Byron seeks to generate a self-critical model for exposing the larger abuses of his society.

Don Juan is, as William Hazlitt was quick to note in *The Spirit of the Age* (1825), a "poem written about itself," but foremost among the vices it satirizes are the contemporary prevalence of cant and the moral blindness or hypocrisy which it fosters. Both traits are first encountered in the character of Donna Inez, Juan's mother, in canto 1. A prodigy of memory whose brain is filled with "serious sayings darken'd to sublimity," she is walking homily—"Morality's prim personification"—who sees to it that her son is taught from only the most carefully expurgated classics. Unable to find anything to censure or amend in her own conduct, Donna Inez nevertheless carries on a clandestine affair with Don Alfonso, the husband of her close friend Julia, and later writes in fulsome praise of Catherine the Great's "maternal" attentions to Juan. Such self-deceiving and myopic piety moves Byron to wish for "a *forty-parson power* to chant/ Thy praise, Hypocrisy," the vice that he regards as endemic to his age and culture at all levels.

On a larger scale, Byron dramatizes the disastrous consequences of cant and its ability to obscure human realities in the Siege of Ismail episode beginning in canto 7. Here his target is in part the gazettes and their debased glorification of war, particularly as they promote "the lust of notoriety" within modern civilization. Spurred on by the hope of being immortalized in the newspapers or war dispatches, a polyglot collection of soldiers join with the Russians in devastating the Turkish fortress. Before recounting scene after scene of the mindless butchery, in which thirty thousand are slain on both sides, Byron reflects on whether "a man's name in a *bulletin*/ May make up for a *bullet in* his body." The final irony is that the gazettes, preoccupied with trivial gossip of the beau monde at home, generally garble the names of the dead and thoroughly distort the facts of the campaign. Determined to unriddle "Glory's dream," Byron shows that it is founded on nothing more than an abject appetite for fame and conquest. His greatest ire is reserved for someone such as the Russian leader Aleksandr Suwarrow, who, in a dispatch to Catherine after the slaughter, can glibly write, "'Glory to *God* and to the Empress!' (*Powers/ Eternal! such names mingled!*) 'Ismail's our's.'" The same purblind insensitivity, he charges, makes it possible for Wordsworth to speak of carnage as "God's daughter." In all these instances, Byron shows how language is a ready instrument for the perversion of thought and action.

His own aesthetic in *Don Juan* thus bases itself on an unswerving respect for truth, "the grand desideratum" in a society glutted with cant and equivocation. Early in the poem he comments that his is "the age of oddities let loose," such that "You'd best begin with truth, and when you've lost your/ Labour, there's sure market for imposture." The lines also echo his mocking dedication of the work to Robert Southey, who succeeded Henry James Pye as poet laureate in 1813, and his arraignment there of the other so-called Lake Poets. Having disowned the radical politics of their youth, they are depicted as comprising a "nest of tuneful persons" who now warble sycophantic praise for the Tory regime of King George III. Their apostasy in Byron's eyes is all the more reprehensible because they have, in effect, become the hirelings of the "intellectual eunuch Castlereagh," a master of oratorical "trash of phrase/ Ineffably—legitimately vile." To counteract this mounting Tower of Babel in his age, Byron persistently explodes the enchantment of words and their tendency to falsify reality. There is, accordingly, an underlying method to his chameleonic *mobilité* and digressiveness in the poem, for he demonstrates that only by doubting the language-based constructs, which people impose upon experience, can he, like the poet himself, avoid the pitfall of "universal egotism." Viewed in this light, the whole of *Don Juan* becomes an open-ended experiment in linguistic improvisation, a poem that demythologizes the very act by which it comes into being.

Because Byron's mock-epic attempts to encompass no less than "life's infinite variety," any synopsis of its innumerable subjects and themes is doomed to failure. From the opening line in which the narrator declaims "I want a hero" and then seems arbitrarily to settle on "our ancient friend Don Juan," it is evident that the ensuing comedy will follow few established conventions or patterns. This impression is reinforced later, in canto 14, when Byron points out his technique in composing *Don Juan*: "I write what's uppermost, without delay." The stated casualness in approach, however, belies the artistic integrity of the satire. Jerome J. McGann, in *Don Juan in Context* (1976), convincingly shows that the poem is "both a critique and an apotheosis of High Romanticism," primarily because it implicitly denies that any imaginative system can be an end unto itself while also endeavoring to reinsert the poetic imagination back into the context of a fallen world. If there is one crux around which the entire mosaic turns, it is that of the fundamental opposition between nature and civilization. After Juan's idyllic love affair with Haidée, "Nature's bride," is destroyed by her jealous father in canto 4, Byron suggests that the Fall is humanity's permanent condition; he conducts his hero into slavery at Constantinople in canto 5, into the bloodbath of the Siege of Ismail in cantos 7-8, into the lustful tyranny of the Russian empress in cantos 9-10, and finally into the fashionable corruptions of English society in cantos 11-17. Not all, however, is moral cannibalism. By the introduction of such unspoiled figures as Haidée at the start and Aurora Raby at the end, Byron ascribes a certain redemptive value to natural innocence that offsets, even if it does not quite counterbalance, the ruling vices of society. *Don Juan* thus immerses itself in all the unflattering details of "life's infinite variety," but always with the purpose of embodying the human realities with which the artist must deal. Byron distills the complexity of the matter in a few words: "I write the world."

LEGACY

Byron has often been criticized as a poet for his many supposed failures—for not projecting a coherent metaphysic, for not developing a consistent attitude to life, for not resisting the Siren call of egotism, for not paying sufficient attention to style, and for not, in short, being more like Wordsworth, Samuel Taylor Coleridge, Keats, and Shelley. Because he did not adopt the vatic stance of his contemporaries or espouse their belief in organicism, he has been labeled the leading exemplar of Negative Romanticism. Common to such estimates, however, is a reluctance to recognize or concede Byron's uniqueness as a poet. Although he did not share with others of his time an exalted conception of the imagination as being equivalent, in Keats's metaphor, to "Adam's dream," he was able ultimately to do what the other four poets generally could not—namely, to accept the mixed quality of human experience. Through his ironic detachment and comic vision he permanently enlarged the domain of poetry and made it meaningful in a fresh way. This he accomplished through his skeptical idealism and his acceptance of his own paradoxes as a man and poet. "I am quicksilver," he wrote to a friend in 1810, "and say nothing positively." Therein lies perhaps the essence of his "sincerity" and "strength," traits that continue to make him an enduring cultural force.

OTHER MAJOR WORKS

PLAYS: *Manfred*, pb. 1817 (verse play); *Cain: A Mystery*, pb. 1821 (verse play); *Marino Faliero, Doge of Venice*, pr., pb. 1821 (verse play); *Sardanapalus*, pb. 1821 (verse play); *The Two Foscari*, pb. 1821 (verse play); *Heaven and Earth*, pb. 1822 (fragment; verse play); *Werner: Or, The Inheritance*, pb. 1823 (verse play); *The Deformed Transformed*, pb. 1824 (fragment; verse play).

NONFICTION: *Letter to [John Murray] on the Rev. W. L. Bowles' Strictures on the Life and Writings of Pope*, 1821; "A Letter to the Editor of 'My Grandmother's Review,'" 1822; *The Blues: A Literary Eclogue*, 1823; *The Parliamentary Speeches of Lord Byron*, 1824; *Byron's Letters and Journals*, 1973-1982 (12 volumes; Leslie A. Marchand, editor).

BIBLIOGRAPHY

Brewer, William D., ed. *Contemporary Studies on Lord Byron*. Lewiston, N.Y.: Edwin Mellen Press, 2001. A collection of essays. Bibliography and index.

Crane, David. *The Kindness of Sisters*. New York: Alfred A. Knopf, 2003. A study of Byron's reputation after his death, exploring bitter and conflicting accounts by the woman he divorced and the half sister he seduced.

Eisler, Benita. *Byron: Child of Passion, Fool of Fame*. New York: Alfred A. Knopf, 1999. A narrative biography that does justice to the love affairs that made Byron notorious while giving ample coverage of the reasons Byron is an influential and important poet. Includes bibliographic references.

Franklin, Caroline. *Byron: A Literary Life.* New York: St. Martin's Press, 2000. A study of Byron's career, examining both his poetry and plays.

MacCarthy, Fiona. *Byron: Life and Legend.* New York: Farrar, Straus and Giroux, 2003. A biography that reexamines the life of the poet in the light of MacCarthy's assertion that Byron was bisexual, a victim of early abuse by his nurse.

Marchand, Leslie A. *Byron: A Portrait.* Chicago: University of Chicago Press, 1970. The best biography for the general reader. It is based on Marchand's definitive three-volume biography published in 1957 but includes research done in the 1960's. Marchand's portrait of Byron is balanced and free of bias. Includes fifty-six illustrations, genealogical tables, and two maps showing Byron's travels from 1809 to 1811, and Byron's Greece.

Martin, Philip. *Byron: A Poet Before His Public.* New York: Cambridge University Press, 1982. This biographical-historical analysis of Byron's works places Byron's work within the context of his contemporaries of the second generation of Romantic poets. Contains a number of illustrations and a complete bibliography.

O'Brien, Edna. *Byron in Love: A Short, Daring Life.* New York: W. W. Norton, 2009. Distinguished Irish writer O'Brien provides a biography of Byron that is perceptive and well written. O'Brien approaches the artist as a character rather than as a subject, producing a novelistic portrait of the poet.

Peters, Catherine. *Byron.* Stroud, Gloucestershire, England: Sutton, 2000. A concise biography of Byron that covers his life and works. Bibliography.

Wilson, Frances. *Byromania: Portraits of the Artist in Nineteenth- and Twentieth-Century Culture.* New York: St. Martin's Press, 1999. These eleven essays shed light on the scandalous nature of Byron's fame, including his carefully wrought self-presentation, as well as the extraordinary popularity of his work and persona. The poet is viewed through multiple, if sometimes contradictory, perspectives, the essays varying in tone from academic to humorous.

Robert Lance Snyder

SAMUEL TAYLOR COLERIDGE

Born: Ottery St. Mary, Devonshire, England; October 21, 1772
Died: Highgate, London, England; July 25, 1834

PRINCIPAL POETRY

Poems on Various Subjects, 1796, 1797 (with Charles Lamb and Charles Lloyd)
A Sheet of Sonnets, 1796 (with W. L. Bowles, Robert Southey, and others)
Lyrical Ballads, 1798 (with William Wordsworth)
The Rime of the Ancient Mariner, 1798
Christabel, 1816
Sibylline Leaves, 1817
The Complete Poetical Works of Samuel Taylor Coleridge, 1912 (2 volumes;
    Ernest Hartley Coleridge, editor)

OTHER LITERARY FORMS

The original verse dramas of Samuel Taylor Coleridge (KOHL-rihj, also KOH-luh-rihj)—*The Fall of Robespierre* (pb. 1794, with Robert Southey), *Remorse* (pr., pb. 1813, originally *Osorio*), and *Zapolya* (pb. 1817)—are of particular interest to readers of his poetry, as is *Wallenstein* (1800), his translation of two dramas by Friedrich Schiller. His major prose includes the contents of two periodicals, *The Watchman* (1796) and *The Friend* (1809-1810, 1818), two lay Sermons, "The Statesman's Manual" (1816) and "A Lay Sermon" (1817), the *Biographia Literaria* (1817), "Treatise on Method," originally published in *The Encyclopaedia Metropolitana* (1818), and a series of metaphysical aphorisms, *Aids to Reflection* (1825). His lectures on politics, religion, literature, and philosophy have been collected in various editions, as have other short essays, unpublished manuscripts, letters, records of conversations, notebooks, and marginalia. These prose works share common interests with his poetry and suggest the philosophical context in which it should be read. Coleridge's literary criticism is particularly relevant to his poetry.

ACHIEVEMENTS

It is ironic that Samuel Taylor Coleridge has come to be known to the general reader primarily as a poet, for poetry was not his own primary interest and the poems with which his name is most strongly linked—*The Rime of the Ancient Mariner*, "Kubla Khan," and *Christabel*—were products of a few months in a long literary career. He did not suffer a decline in poetic creativity; he simply turned his attention to political, metaphysical, and theological issues that were best treated in prose. That Coleridge is counted among the major poets of British Romanticism is, for this reason, all the more

Samuel Taylor Coleridge
(Library of Congress)

remarkable. For most poets, the handful of commonly anthologized poems is a scant representation of their output; for Coleridge, it is, in many instances, the sum of his accomplishment. His minor verse is often conventional and uninspired. His major poems, in contrast, speak with singular emotional and intellectual intensity in a surprising range of forms—from the symbolic fantasy of *The Rime of the Ancient Mariner* (which first appeared in *Lyrical Ballads*) to the autobiographical sincerity of the conversation poems—exerting an influence on subsequent poets far beyond what Coleridge himself anticipated.

BIOGRAPHY

Samuel Taylor Coleridge was born October 21, 1772, in the Devonshire town of Ottery St. Mary, the youngest of ten children. His father, a clergyman and teacher, died in October, 1781, and the next year Coleridge was sent to school at Christ's Hospital, London. His friends at school included Charles Lamb, two years his junior, whose essay "Christ's Hospital Five-and-Thirty Years Ago" (1820) describes the two sides of Coleridge—the "poor friendless boy," far from his home, "alone among six hundred playmates"; the precocious scholar, "Logician, Metaphysician, Bard!," holding his auditors "entranced with imagination." Both characteristics—a deep sense of isolation and the effort to use learning and eloquence to overcome it—remained with Coleridge throughout his life.

He entered Cambridge in 1791 but never completed work for his university degree. Depressed by debts, he fled the university in December, 1793, and enlisted in the Light Dragoons under the name Silas Tompkyn Comberbache. Rescued by his brothers, he returned to Cambridge in April and resumed his studies. Two months later, he met Robert Southey, with whom he soon made plans to establish a utopian community ("Pantisocracy") in the United States. Southey was engaged to marry Edith Fricker, and so it seemed appropriate for Coleridge to engage himself to her sister Sara. The project failed, but Coleridge, through his own sense of duty and Southey's insistence, married a woman he had never loved and with whom his relationship was soon to become strained.

As a married man, Coleridge had to leave the university and make a living for his wife and, in time, children—Hartley (1796-1849), Berkeley (1798-1799), Derwent (b. 1800), and Sara (1802-1852). Economic survival was, it turned out, possible only with the support of friends such as Thomas Poole and the publisher Joseph Cottle and, in 1798, a life annuity from Josiah and Tom Wedgwood. The early years of Coleridge's married life, in which he lived with his family at Nether Stowey, were the period of his closest relationship with the poet William Wordsworth. Inspired by Wordsworth, whom he in turn inspired, Coleridge wrote most of his major poetry. Together, the two men published *Lyrical Ballads* in 1798, the proceeds of which enabled them, along with Wordsworth's sister Dorothy, to spend the winter in Germany, where Coleridge studied metaphysics at the University of Göttingen.

Returning to England the following year, Coleridge met and fell deeply in love with Sara Hutchinson, a friend of Dorothy who later became Wordsworth's sister-in-law. This passion, which remained strong for many years, furthered Coleridge's estrangement from his wife, with whom he moved to Keswick in the Lake District of England, in July, 1800, to be near the Wordsworths at Grasmere. Coleridge's health had always been poor, and he had become addicted to opium, which, according to standard medical practice at the time, he had originally taken to relieve pain. Seeking a change of climate, he traveled to Malta and then Italy in 1804 to 1806. On his return, he and his wife "*determined* to part absolutely and finally," leaving Coleridge in custody of his sons Hartley and Derwent (Berkeley had died in 1799).

In 1808, Coleridge gave his first public lectures and in the next two years published the twenty-seven issues of *The Friend*. By now, he was a figure of national standing, but his private life remained in disarray. Sara Hutchinson, who had assisted him in preparing copy for *The Friend*, separated herself from him, and in 1810, he quarreled decisively with Wordsworth. (They were later reconciled, but the period of close friendship was over.) Six years later, after various unsuccessful attempts to cure himself of opium addiction and set his affairs in order, he put himself in the care of James Gillman, a physician living at Highgate, a northern suburb of London. Under Gillman's roof, Coleridge was once again able to work. He wrote the two lay Sermons, "The Statesman's Manual" and "A Lay Sermon"; completed the *Biographia Literaria*, originally planned as an autobiographical introduction to *Sibylline Leaves* but ultimately two volumes in its own right; and revised the essays he had written for *The Friend*, including among them a version of the "Treatise on Method," which he had composed for the first volume of *The Encyclopaedia Metropolitana*. He also resumed his public lectures on philosophy and literature and in time became a London celebrity, enthralling visitors with his conversation and gradually attracting a circle of disciples. Meanwhile, he worked at the magnum opus that was to synthesize his metaphysical and theological thought in a single intellectual system. This project, however, remained incomplete when Coleridge died at Highgate, July 25, 1834.

ANALYSIS

Samuel Taylor Coleridge's major poems turn on problems of self-esteem and identity. Exploring states of isolation and ineffectuality, they test strategies to overcome weakness without asserting its antithesis—a powerful self, secure in its own thoughts and utterances, the potency and independence of which Coleridge feared would only exacerbate his loneliness. His reluctance to assert his own abilities is evident in his habitual deprecation of his own poetry and hyperbolic praise of William Wordsworth's. It is evident as well in his best verse, which either is written in an unpretentious "conversational" tone or, when it is not, is carefully dissociated from his own voice and identity. By means of these strategies, however, he is often able to assert indirectly or vicariously the strong self he otherwise repressed.

"THE EOLIAN HARP"

Writing to John Thelwall in 1796, Coleridge called the first of the conversation poems, "The Eolian Harp" (written in 1795), the "favorite of *my* poems." He originally published it, in 1796, with the indication "Composed August 20th, 1795, At Clevedon, Somersetshire," which dates at least some version of the text six weeks before his marriage to Sara Fricker. Since Sara plays a role in the poem, the exact date is crucial. "The Eolian Harp" is not, as it has been called, a "honeymoon" poem; rather, it anticipates a future in which Coleridge and Sara will sit together by their "Cot o'ergrown/ With white-flower'd Jasmin." Significantly, Sara remains silent throughout the poem; her only contribution is the "mild reproof" that "darts" from her "more serious eye," quelling the poet's intellectual daring. However, this reproof is as imaginary as Sara's presence itself. At the climax of the poem, meditative thought gives way to the need for human response; tellingly, the response he imagines and therefore, one must assume, desires, is reproof.

"The Eolian Harp" establishes a structural pattern for the conversation poems as a group. Coleridge is, in effect, alone, "and the world *so* hush'd!/ The stilly murmur of the distant Sea/ Tells us of silence." The eolian harp in the window sounds in the breeze and reminds him of "the one Life within us and abroad,/ Which meets all motion and becomes its soul." This observation leads to the central question of the poem:

> And what if all of animated nature
> Be but organic Harps diversely fram'd,
> That tremble into thought, as o'er them sweeps
> Plastic and vast, one intellectual breeze,
> At once the Soul of each, and God of all?

Sara's glance dispels "These shapings of the unregenerate mind," but, of course, it is too late, since they have already been expressed in the poem. (Indeed, the letter to Thelwall makes it clear that it was this expression of pantheism, not its retraction, that made the poem dear to Coleridge.) For this reason, the conflict between two sides of Coleridge's thought—metaphysical speculation and orthodox Christianity—remains unresolved. If the poem is in any way disquieting, it is not because it exemplifies a failure of nerve, but because of the identifications it suggests between metaphysical speculation and the isolated self, religious orthodoxy and the conventions—down to the vines covering the cottage—of married life. Coleridge, in other words, does not imagine a wife who will love him all the more for his intellectual daring. Instead, he imagines one who will chastise him for the very qualities that make him an original thinker. To "possess/ Peace, and this Cot, and thee, heart-honour'd Maid!," Coleridge must acknowledge himself "A sinful and most miserable man,/ Wilder'd and dark." Happiness, as well as poetic closure, depends on this acceptance of diminished self-esteem. Even so, by embedding an expression of intellectual strength within the context of domestic conventionality, Coleridge is able to achieve a degree of poetic authority otherwise absent in the final lines of the poem. The ability to renounce a powerful self is itself a gesture of power: The acceptance of loss becomes—as in other Romantic poems—a form of strength.

The structure of "The Eolian Harp" can be summarized as follows: A state of isolation (the more isolated for the presence of an unresponsive companion) gives way to meditation, which leads to the possibility of a self powerful through its association with an all-powerful force. This state of mind gives place to the acknowledgment of a human relationship dependent on the poet's recognition of his own inadequacy, the reward for which is a poetic voice with the authority to close the poem.

"THIS LIME-TREE BOWER MY PRISON"

This pattern recurs in "This Lime-Tree Bower My Prison" (1797). The poem is addressed to Charles Lamb, but the "gentle-hearted Charles" of the text is really a surrogate for the figure of Wordsworth, whose loss Coleridge is unwilling to face head-on. Incapacitated by a burn—appropriately, his wife's fault—Coleridge is left alone seated in a clump of lime trees while his friends—Lamb and William and Dorothy Wordsworth—set off on a long walk through the countryside. They are, like Sara in "The Eolian Harp," there and yet not there: Their presence in the poem intensifies Coleridge's sense of isolation. He follows them in his imagination, and the gesture itself becomes a means of connecting himself with them. Natural images of weakness, enclosure, and solitude give way to those of strength, expansion, and connection, and the tone of the poem shifts from speculation to assertion. In a climactic moment, he imagines his friends "gazing round/ On the wide landscape" until it achieves the transcendence of "such hues/ As veil the Almighty Spirit, when yet he makes/ Spirits perceive his presence."

As in "The Eolian Harp," the perception of an omnipotent force pervading the universe returns Coleridge to his present state, but with a new sense of his own being and his relationship with the friends to whom he addresses the poem. His own isolation is now seen as an end in itself. "Sometimes/ 'Tis well to be bereft of promised good," Coleridge argues, "That we may lift the soul, and contemplate/ With lively joy the joys we cannot share."

"FROST AT MIDNIGHT"

"Frost at Midnight," the finest of the conversation poems, replaces silent wife or absent friends with a sleeping child (Hartley—although he is not named in the text). Summer is replaced by winter; isolation is now a function of seasonal change itself. In this zero-world, "The Frost performs its secret ministry,/ Unhelped by any wind." The force that moved the eolian harp into sound is gone. The natural surroundings of the poem drift into nonexistence: "Sea, and hill, and wood,/ With all the numberless goings-on of life,/ Inaudible as dreams!" This is the nadir of self from which the poet reconstructs his being—first by perception of "dim sympathies" with the "low-burnt fire" before him; then by a process of recollection and predication. The "film" on the grate reminds Coleridge of his childhood at Christ's Hospital, where a similar image conveyed hopes of seeing someone from home and therefore a renewal of the conditions of his earlier life in Ottery St. Mary. Even in recollection, however, the bells of his "sweet birth-place" are most expressive not as a voice of the present moment, but as "articulate sounds of things to come!" The spell of the past was, in fact, a spell of the imagined future. The visitor he longed for turns out to be a version of the self of the poet, his "sister more beloved/ My play-mate when we both were clothed alike." The condition of loss that opens the poem cannot be filled by the presence of another human being; it is a fundamental emptiness in the self, which, Coleridge suggests, can never be filled, but only recognized as a necessary condition of adulthood. However, this recognition of incompleteness is the poet's means of experiencing a sense of identity missing in the opening lines of the poem.

"Frost at Midnight" locates this sense of identity in Coleridge's own life. It is not a matter of metaphysical or religious belief, as it is in "The Eolian Harp" or "This Lime-Tree Bower My Prison," but a function of the self that recognizes its own coherence in time. This recognition enables him to speak to the "Dear Babe" who had been there all along, but had remained a piece of the setting and not a living human being. Like the friends of "This Lime-Tree Bower My Prison," who are projected exploring a landscape, the boy Hartley is imagined wandering "like a breeze/ By lakes and sandy shores." The static existence of the poet in the present moment is contrasted with the movement of a surrogate. This movement, however, is itself subordinated to the voice of the poet who can promise his son a happiness he himself has not known.

In all three poems, Coleridge achieves a voice that entails the recognition of his own loss—in acknowledging Sara's reproof or losing himself in the empathic construction of the experience of friend or son. The act entails a defeat of the self, but also a vicarious participation in powerful forces that reveal themselves in the working of the universe, and through this participation a partial triumph of the self over its own sense of inadequacy. In "Frost at Midnight," the surrogate figure of his son not only embodies a loco-motor power denied the static speaker, but also, in his capacity to read the "language" uttered by God in the form of landscape, is associated with absolute power itself.

THE RIME OF THE ANCIENT MARINER

Although written in a very different mode, *The Rime of the Ancient Mariner* centers on a similar experience of participation in supernatural power. At the core of the poem is, of course, the story of the Mariner who shoots the albatross and endures complete and devastating isolation from his fellow man. The poem, however, is not a direct narrative of these events; rather, it is a narrative of the Mariner's narrating them. The result of the extraordinary experience he has undergone is to make him an itinerant storyteller. It has given him a voice, but a voice grounded on his own incompleteness of self. He has returned to land but remains homeless and without permanent human relationships. In this respect, *The Rime of the Ancient Mariner* is Coleridge's nightmare alternative to the conversation poem. As "conversations," they suggest the possibility of a relationship with his audience that can in part compensate for the inadequate human relationships described in the poem. The Mariner's story is a kind of conversation. He tells it to the Wedding-Guest he has singled out for that purpose, but the relationship between speaker and audience can scarcely be said to compensate for the Mariner's lack of human relationships. The Wedding-Guest is compelled to listen by the hypnotic power of the Mariner's "glittering eye." He "beats his breast" at the thought of the wedding from which he is being detained and repeatedly expresses his fear of the Mariner. In the end, he registers no compassion for the man whose story he has just heard. He is too "stunned" for that—and the Mariner has left the stage without asking for applause. His audience is changed by the story—"A sadder and a wiser man,/ He rose the morrow morn"—but of this the Mariner can know nothing. Thus, the power of the Mariner's story to captivate and transform its audience simply furthers his alienation from his fellow human beings.

Structurally, the poem follows the three-stage pattern of the conversation poems. A state of isolation and immobility is succeeded by one in which the Mariner becomes the object of (and is thus associated with) powerful supernatural agencies, and this leads to the moralizing voice of the conclusion. Unlike the conversation poems, *The Rime of the Ancient Mariner* prefaces individual isolation with social isolation. The Mariner and his shipmates, in what has become one of the most familiar narratives in English literature, sail from Europe toward Cape Horn, where they are surrounded by a polar ice jam. An albatross appears and accepts food from the sailors; a fair wind springs up, and they are able to resume their journey northward into the Pacific Ocean; the albatross follows them, "And every day, for food or play,/ Came to the mariner's hollo!"—until the Mariner, seemingly without reason, shoots the bird with his crossbow. Coleridge warned readers against allegorizing the poem, and it is fruitless to search for a specific identification for the albatross. What is important is the bird's gratuitous arrival and the Mariner's equally gratuitous crossbow shot. The polar ice that threatens the ship is nature at its most alien. Seen against that backdrop, the albatross seems relatively human; the mariners, accordingly, "hailed it in God's name"; "As if it had been a Christian soul." Like the "film" in "Frost at Midnight"—a poem in which crucial events are also set against a wintry backdrop—the bird offers them a means of bridging the gap between humans and nature, self and nonself, through projecting human characteristics on a creature of the natural world. By shooting the albatross, the Mariner blocks this projection and thus traps both himself and his shipmates in a state of isolation.

The Mariner's act has no explicit motive because it is a function of human nature itself, but it is not merely a sign of original sin or congenital perversity. His narrative has until now been characterized by a remarkable passivity. Events simply happen. Even the ship's progress is characterized not by its own movement but by the changing position of the sun in the sky. The ice that surrounds the ship is only one element of a natural world that dominates the fate of the ship and its crew, and it is against this overwhelming dominance that the Mariner takes his crossbow shot. The gesture is an assertion of the human spirit against an essentially inhuman universe, aimed at the harmless albatross.

He is punished for this self-assertion—first, by the crewmen who blame him for the calm that follows and tie the albatross around his neck as a sign of guilt. It is only after this occurs that the Mariner, thirsty and guilt-ridden, perceives events that are explicitly supernatural, and the second stage of his punishment begins. However, the Mariner's isolation, even after his shipmates have died and left him alone on the becalmed ship, remains a consequence of his assertion of self against the natural world, and the turning point of the poem is equally his own doing. In the midst of the calm, the water had seemed abhorrently ugly: "slimy things did crawl with legs/ Upon the slimy sea," while "the water, like a witch's oils,/ Burnt green, and blue and white." Now, "bemocked" by moonlight, the same creatures are beautiful: "Blue, glossy green, and velvet black,/ They coiled and swam; and every track/ Was a flash of golden fire." In this perception of beauty, the Mariner explains, "A spring of love gushed from my heart,/ And I blessed them unaware." At the same moment, he is once again able to pray, and the albatross falls from his neck into the sea. Prayer—the ability to voice his mind and feelings and, in so doing, relate them to a higher order of being—is a function of love, and love is a function of the apprehension of beauty. In blessing the water snakes, it should be noted, the Mariner has not returned to the viewpoint of his shipmates when they attributed human characteristics to the albatross. When he conceives of the snakes as "happy living things," he acknowledges a bond between all forms of organic life, but their beauty does not depend on human projection.

However, achieving this chastened vision does not end the Mariner's suffering. Not only must he endure an extension of his shipboard isolation, but also when, eventually, he returns to his native land, he is not granted reintegration into its society. The Hermit from whom he asks absolution demands quick answer to his own question, "What manner of man art thou?" In response, the Mariner experiences a spasm of physical agony that forces him to tell the story of his adventures. The tale told, he is left free of pain—until such time as "That agony returns" and he is compelled to repeat the narrative: "That moment that his face I see,/ I know the man that must hear me:/ To him my tale I teach." The Mariner has become a poet—like Coleridge, a poet gifted with "strange power of speech" and plagued with somatic pain, with power to fix his auditors' attention and transform them into "sadder and wiser" men. However, the price of this power is enormous. It entails not only the shipboard suffering of the Mariner but also perpetual alienation from his fellow human beings. Telling his story is the only relationship allowed him, and he does not even fully understand the meaning of his narration. In the concluding lines of the poem, he attempts to draw a moral—

> He prayeth best, who loveth best
> All things both great and small;
> For the dear God who loveth us,
> He made and loveth all.

These words are not without bearing on the poem, but they overlook the extraordinary disproportion between the Mariner's crime and its punishment. Readers of the poem—as well as, one supposes, the Wedding-Guest—are more likely to question the benevolence of the "dear God who loveth us" than to perceive the Mariner's story as an illustration of God's love. Thus, the voice of moral authority that gave the conversation poems a means of closure is itself called into question. The soul that acknowledges its essential isolation in the universe can never hope for reintegration into society. The poet whose song is the tale of his own suffering can "stun" his reader but can never achieve a lasting human relationship. His experience can be given the aesthetic coherence of narrative, but he can never connect the expressive significance of that narrative with his life as a whole.

It is in part the medium of the poem that allows Coleridge to face these bleak possibilities. Its ballad stanza and archaic diction, along with the marginal glosses added from 1815 to 1816, dissociate the text from its modern poet. Freed from an explicit identification with the Mariner, Coleridge is able both to explore implications of the poet's role that would have been difficult to face directly and to write about experiences for which there was no precedent in conventional meditative verse.

"KUBLA KHAN"

A similar strategy is associated with "Kubla Khan," which can be read as an alternative to *The Rime of the Ancient Mariner*. The poem, which was not published until 1816, nearly two decades after it was written, is Coleridge's most daring account of poetic inspiration and the special nature of the poet. In the poem, the poet's isolation is perceived not as weakness but strength. Even in 1816, the gesture of self-assertion was difficult for Coleridge, and he prefaced the poem with an account designed to diminish its significance. "Kubla Khan" was, he explained, "a psychological curiosity," the fragment of a longer poem he had composed in an opium-induced sleep, "if that indeed can be called composition in which all the images rose up before him as *things*, with a parallel production of the correspondent expressions, without any sensation or consciousness of effort." Waking, he began to write out the verses he had in this manner "composed" but was interrupted by a visitor, after whose departure he found he could no longer remember more than "the general purport of the vision" and a few "scattered lines and images."

The problem with this explanation is that "Kubla Khan" does not strike readers as a fragment. It is, as it stands, an entirely satisfactory whole. Moreover, the facts of Coleridge's preface have themselves been called into question.

Just what was Coleridge trying to hide? The poem turns on an analogy between the act of an emperor and the act of a poet. Kubla Khan's "pleasure-dome" in Xanadu is more than a monarch's self-indulgence; symbolically, it attempts to arrest the process of life itself. His walls encircle "twice five miles of fertile ground," in the midst of which flows "Alph," the sacred river of life, but they control neither the source of the river nor its conclusion in the "lifeless ocean" to which it runs. The source is a "deep romantic chasm" that Coleridge associates with the violence of natural process, with human sexuality, and with the libidinal origins of poetry in the song of a "woman wailing for her demon lover." Kubla's pleasure-dome is "a miracle of rare device," but it can exert no lasting influence. The achievement of the most powerful Oriental despot is limited by the conditions of life, and even his attempt to order a limited space evokes "Ancestral voices prophesying war!"

In contrast, the achievement of the poet is not bounded by space and time and partakes of the dangerous potency of natural creativity itself. The nature of inspiration is tricky, however. The speaker of the poem recollects a visionary "Abyssinian maid" playing a dulcimer, and it is the possibility of reviving "within me/ Her symphony and song" that holds out the hope of a corresponding creativity: "To such a deep delight 'twould win me,/ . . . I would build that dome in air, . . ." The poet's act is always secondary, never primary creativity. Even so, to re-create in poetry Kubla's achievement— without its liabilities—is to become a dangerous being. Like the Mariner, the inspired poet has "flashing eyes" that can cast a spell over his audience. His special nature may be the sign of an incomplete self—for inspiration depends on the possibility of recovering a lost recollection; nevertheless, it is a special nature that threatens to re-create the world in its own image.

CHRISTABEL

Nowhere else is Coleridge so confident about his powers as a poet or writer. *Christabel*, written in the same period as *The Rime of the Ancient Mariner* and "Kubla Khan," remains a fascinating fragment. Like "Kubla Khan," it was not published until 1816. By then, the verse romances of Sir Walter Scott and Lord Byron had caught the public's attention, and among Coleridge's motives in publishing his poem was to lay claim to a poetic form he believed he had originated. More important, though, his decision to publish two parts of an incomplete narrative almost two decades after he had begun the poem was also a means of acknowledging that *Christabel* was and would remain unfinished.

To attribute its incompletion to Coleridge's procrastination evades the real question: Why did the poem itself preclude development? Various answers have been offered; the most convincing argue a conflict between the metaphysical or religious significance of Christabel—whose name conflates Christ and Abel—with the exigencies of the narrative structure in which she is placed. As Walter Jackson Bate explains it, the "problem of finding motives and actions for Christabel . . . had imposed an insupportable psychological burden on Coleridge." The problem that Coleridge fails to solve is the problem of depicting credible innocence. Christabel, the virgin who finds the mysterious Lady Geraldine in the forest and brings her home to the castle of her father, Sir Leoline, only to fall victim to Geraldine's sinister spell, is either hopelessly passive and merely a victim, or, if active, something less than entirely innocent. At the same time, Geraldine, who approaches her prey with "a stricken look," is potentially the more interesting character. Christabel is too much like the albatross in *The Rime of the Ancient Mariner*; Geraldine, too much like the Mariner himself, whose guilt changes him from a simple seaman to an archetype of human isolation and suffering. Christabel's name suggests that Coleridge had intended for her to play a sacrificial role, but by promising to reunite Sir Leoline with his childhood friend, Roland de Vaux of Tryermaine, whom she claims as her father, Geraldine, too, has a potentially positive function in the narrative.

Whether or not her claim is true, it nevertheless initiates action that may lead to a reconciliation, not only between two long-separated friends but also between Sir Leoline's death-obsessed maturity and the time in his youth when he was able to experience friendship. There is, therefore, a suggestion that Geraldine is able to effect the link between childhood and maturity, innocence and experience, of particular concern to Coleridge—and to other Romantic poets as well. If Christabel and Geraldine represent the passive and active sides of Coleridge, then his failure to complete the narrative is yet another example of his inability to synthesize his personality—or to allow one side to win out at the expense of the other.

A few other poems from 1797 to 1798 deserve mention. "The Nightingale" (1798), although less interesting than the other titles in the group, conforms to the general structure of the conversation poems and so confirms its importance. "Fears in Solitude" (1798) is at once a conversation poem and something more. Like the others, it begins in a state of isolation and ends with social reintegration; its median state of self-assertion, however, takes the form of a public political statement. The voice of the statement is often strident, but this quality is understandable in a poem written at a time when invasion by France was daily rumored. "Fears in Solitude" attacks British militarism, materialism, and patriotism; however, it is itself deeply patriotic. "There lives nor form nor feeling in my soul," Coleridge acknowledges, "Unborrowed from my country," and for this reason the poem is not a series of topical criticism but an expression of the dilemma of a poet divided between moral judgment of and personal identification with his native land.

"DEJECTION"

When Coleridge returned from Germany in the summer of 1799, his period of intense poetic creativity was over. The poems that he wrote in the remaining years of his life were written by a man who no longer thought of himself as a poet and who therefore treated poetry as a mode of expression rather than a calling. "Dejection: An Ode," which Coleridge dated April 4, 1802, offers a rationale for this change and seems to have been written as a formal farewell to the possibility of a career as a poet. The poem's epigraph from the *Ballad of Sir Patrick Spence* and its concern with perception link it with *The Rime of the Ancient Mariner*; its use of the image of the eolian harp links it with the poem by that name and, by extension, with the free-associational style of the conversation poems as a group. Its tone and manner are also close to those of the conversation poems, but its designation as an ode suggests an effort to elevate it to the level of formal statement. At the same time, its recurrent addresses to an unnamed "Lady" (Sara Hutchinson) suggest that the poem was primarily intended for a specific rather than a general audience, for a reader with a special interest in the poet who will not expect the poem to describe a universal human experience. Thus, the poem is at once closely related to Coleridge's earlier verse and significantly different from it.

In keeping with the conversation-poem structure, "Dejection" begins in a mood of solitary contemplation. The poet ponders the moon and "the dull sobbing draft that moans and rakes/ Upon the strings of this Aeolian lute." Together, they portend a storm in the offing, and Coleridge hopes that the violence of the "slant night shower" may startle him from his depression. His state, he explains, is not merely grief; it is "A stifled, drowsy, unimpassioned grief,/ Which finds no natural outlet, no relief,/ In word, or sign, or tear." All modes of emotional expression are blocked: He is able to "see" the beauty of the natural world, but he cannot "feel" it, and thereby use it as a symbol for his own inner state. He has lost the ability to invest the "outward forms" of nature with passion and life because, by his account, his inner source of passion and life has dried up. This ability he calls "Joy"—"the spirit and the power,/ Which wedding Nature to us gives in dower/ A new Earth and new Heaven." The language of apocalypse identifies "Joy" with religious faith; the notion of language suggests a more general identification with the expressive mode of his earlier poetry and its ability to transform an ordinary situation into an especially meaningful event. To have no "outlet . . ./ In word" is to have lost the voice of that poetry; to make the observation within a poetic text is to suggest one more difference between "Dejection" and Coleridge's earlier poetry.

"Dejection" may seem like a restatement of the notion of a possible harmony—now lost—between nature and the human that was expressed in the earlier poetry. In fact, "Dejection" denies the grounds of the harmony advanced in the earlier poems. In "Frost at Midnight," for example, the "shapes and sounds" of the natural world are perceived as an "eternal language, which thy/ God utters." In "The Eolian Harp," man is conceptualized (tentatively) as only one of the media through which the eternal force expresses itself. "Dejection," in contrast, identifies the source of "Joy" in man himself. In feeling the beauty of nature, "we in ourselves rejoice." Although the earlier poems toyed with pantheism, this focus on the state of mind of the individual soul is squarely orthodox, but the religious conservatism of "Dejection" does not in itself explain the termination of Coleridge's poetic career.

Coleridge himself attributes this termination to his own self-consciousness. As he explains in "Dejection," he had sought "by abstruse research to seal/ From my own nature all the natural man." This scientific analysis of the self got the better of him, however, and now his conscious mind is compelled to subject the whole of experience to its analytic scrutiny. Nothing now escapes the dominance of reason, and insofar as the power of Coleridge's greatest poetry lay in its capacity to dramatize or at least imagine a universe imbued with supernatural meaning, the power is lost. Theologically, this capacity can be associated with pantheism or the vaguely heterodox natural theology of the conversation poems; psychologically, its potency, derived from primal narcissism, is related to the animism given explicit form in the spirits who supervise the action in *The Rime of the Ancient Mariner*. The power of this poetry, it can be argued, lies in its ability to recapture a primitive human experience of the world.

The psychological awareness that Coleridge gained by his own self-analysis made this primitive naïveté impossible. "Dejection" is thus potentially a poem celebrating the maturity of the intellect—its recognition that its earlier powerful experience of nature, even when attributed to a Christian deity, was a matter of projection and therefore a function of his need to associate himself with an objective expression of his own potency. If the poem is not celebratory, it is because the consequences of this recognition amount to an admission of the importance of his individual self at odds with Coleridge's need for social acceptance. At the same time, it deprives him of that powerful confirmation of self derived from the illusionary sense of harmony with the animistic forces of the natural world. "Dejection" should have been a poem about Coleridge's internalization of these forces and triumphant recognition of his own strength of mind. Instead, he acknowledges the illusion of animism without being able to internalize the psychic energy invested in the animistic vision.

In disavowing belief in a transcendental power inherent in nature, Coleridge disavows the power of his own earlier poetry. "Dejection" lacks the ease and confidence of the conversation poems, and its structure is noticeably mechanical. The storm that ends "Dejection" replaces the voice of authority that defined their closure, but, despite being anticipated by the opening stanzas, it is a deus ex machina without organic connection with the poet. For reasons that the poem itself makes clear, it can effect no fundamental transformation of his being. Hence, it is simply unimportant, and to expect it to have greater effect is, in the words of "The Picture" (1802), to be a "Gentle Lunatic."

LATER POETRY

Having forgone "Gentle Lunacy," the best of Coleridge's later poetry speaks with an intense but entirely naturalistic sincerity. In poems such as "The Blossoming of the Solitary Date-Tree" (1805), "The Pains of Sleep" (1815), and "Work Without Hope" (1826), Coleridge makes no attempt to transform his poetic self into the vehicle for universal truth. He simply presents his feelings and thoughts to the reader. He complains about his condition, but there is no sense that the act of complaint, beyond getting something off his chest for the time being, can effect any significant alteration of the self. Other poems lack even this concern for the limited audience whom he might have expected to be concerned with his personal problems. Poems such as "Limbo" (1817) and "Ne Plus Ultra" (1826?) are notebook exercises in conceiving the inconceivable—in this case, the states of minimal being, in which even the Kantian categories of space and time are reduced to uncertain conceptions, and absolute negation, "The one permitted opposite of God!" With other poems written for a similar private purpose, they are remarkable for the expressive power of their condensed imagery and their capacity to actualize philosophical thought. Coleridge's mastery of language never deserted him.

The greatness of the half dozen or so poems on which his reputation is based derives, however, from more than mastery of language. It derives from a confidence in the power of language that Coleridge, for legitimate reasons, came to doubt. Those half dozen or so poems assume that Coleridge is not a great poet, but that the grounding medium of poetry, like the "eternal language" of nature, is itself great. The very fact of his achievement from 1797 to 1798 presented to him the possibility that it was Coleridge and not poetry in which greatness lay; and, given that possibility, Coleridge could no longer conceive of himself as a poet. He would continue to write, but in media in which it was the thought behind the prose, and not the thinker, that gave meaning to language.

OTHER MAJOR WORKS

PLAYS: *The Fall of Robespierre*, pb. 1794 (with Robert Southey); *Remorse*, pr., pb. 1813 (originally *Osorio*); *Zapolya*, pb. 1817.

NONFICTION: *The Watchman*, 1796; *The Friend*, 1809-1810, 1818; "The States-man's Manual," 1816; *Biographia Literaria*, 1817; "A Lay Sermon," 1817; "Treatise on Method," 1818; *Aids to Reflection*, 1825; *On the Constitution of the Church and State, According to the Idea of Each: With Aids Toward a Right Judgment on the Late Catholic Bill*, 1830; *Specimens of the Table Talk of the Late Samuel Taylor Coleridge*, 1835; *Letters, Conversations, and Recollections of S. T. Coleridge*, 1836; *Letters of Samuel Taylor Coleridge*, 1855 (2 volumes; Ernest Hartley Coleridge, editor); *Coleridge's Shakespearean Criticism*, 1930; *Coleridge's Miscellaneous Criticism*, 1936; *Notebooks*, 1957-1986 (4 volumes).

TRANSLATION: *Wallenstein*, 1800 (of Friedrich Schiller's plays *Die Piccolomini* and *Wallensteins Tod*).

MISCELLANEOUS: *The Collected Works of Samuel Taylor Coleridge*, 1969-2001 (13 volumes; Kathleen Coburn et al., editors).

BIBLIOGRAPHY

Alexander, Caroline. *The Way to Xanadu*. New York: Knopf, 1994. The author relates her travels to the places that inspired Coleridge's "Kubla Khan" and describes the texts that inspired Coleridge.

Ashton, Rosemary. *The Life of Samuel Taylor Coleridge: A Critical Biography*. Cambridge, Mass.: Blackwell, 1996. Examines Coleridge's complex personality, from poet, critic, and thinker to feckless husband and guilt-ridden opium addict. Coleridge's life is placed within the context of both British and German Romanticism.

Blades, John. *Wordsworth and Coleridge: "Lyrical Ballads."* New York: Palgrave Macmillan, 2004. Detailed analysis of the poems in the literary and historical contexts in which *Lyrical Ballads* was first conceived and created. Documents the revisions made for the second edition and traces the literary criticism of the work in the following decades.

Bloom, Harold, ed. *Samuel Taylor Coleridge*. New York: Chelsea House, 2009. A collection of essays that provide literary criticism of the works of Coleridge.

Christie, William. *Samuel Taylor Coleridge: A Literary Life*. New York: Palgrave Macmillan, 2006. Part biography, part literary criticism, this text provides readers with an in-depth account of Coleridge's personal life and his progression as a writer. Christie helps readers understand Coleridge's works by placing them into the context of his life and providing their publication history. Drawing on the author's notebooks and letters, Christie presents his own interpretation of Coleridge's writing, and discusses other critics' texts, as well.

Holmes, Richard. *Coleridge: Early Visions, 1772-1804*. New York: Viking Press, 1990. The first volume of a two-volume biography. Covers Coleridge's life up to his departure for Malta in 1804. This splendid book is virtually everything a biography should be: well researched, lively, full of insight, and sympathetic to its subject without ignoring other points of view. Fully captures Coleridge's brilliant, flawed, fascinating personality.

————. *Coleridge: Darker Reflections, 1804-1834*. London: HarperCollins, 1998. In this second, concluding volume of his biography of Coleridge, Holmes traces the tragedies and triumphs of the poet's later career.

Perry, Seamus. *Samuel Taylor Coleridge*. New York: Oxford University Press, 2003. This biography of Coleridge traces his life from its early beginnings through the end of his life. Examines his friendships with Southey and Wordsworth and his numerous careers.

Sisman, Adam. *The Friendship: Wordsworth and Coleridge*. New York: Viking, 2007. An intimate examination of their friendship and its deterioration.

Vigus, James, and Jane Wright, eds. *Coleridge's Afterlives*. New York: Palgrave Macmillan, 2008. Thirteen essays that examine the influence of Coleridge's writings on imagination, narrative structure, and other topics.

Frederick Kirchhoff

GEORGE CRABBE

Born: Aldeburgh, Suffolk, England; December 24, 1754
Died: Trowbridge, Wiltshire, England; February 3, 1832

PRINCIPAL POETRY
Inebriety, 1775
The Candidate, 1780
The Library, 1781
The Village, 1783
The News-Paper, 1785
Poems, 1807
The Borough: A Poem, in Twenty-four Letters, 1810
Tales in Verse, 1812
Tales of the Hall, 1819
Poetical Works, 1834 (8 volumes)

OTHER LITERARY FORMS

Little has survived of the nonverse writings of George Crabbe (krab). Extant are critical prose prefaces to various of his published verse collections, a treatise on "The Natural History of the Vale of Belvoir" that appeared in 1795, an autobiographical sketch published anonymously in *The New Monthly Magazine* in 1816, a selection of his sermons published posthumously in 1850, and certain of his letters, journals, and notebook entries that have been published in varying formats throughout the years since his death. With the exception of several of the critical prefaces, particularly that which accompanies *Tales in Verse*, and portions of the letters and journal entries, these do not shed significant light on Crabbe's poetic accomplishments. In 1801-1802, Crabbe is known to have written and subsequently burned three novels and an extensive prose treatise on botany.

ACHIEVEMENTS

The problem of assessing George Crabbe's achievements as a poet has proved a difficult one from the start. It vexed Crabbe's contemporaries and continues in some measure to vex scholars today. To a large extent this may be caused by the difficulties in classification. His works bridge the gap between neoclassicism and Romanticism and on separate occasions—or even simultaneously—display characteristics of both movements. As the bewildering variety of labels that have been applied to Crabbe indicate, the multifaceted nature of his canon defies easy categorization. He has been termed a realist, a naturalist, an Augustan, a Romantic, a sociological novelist in verse, a psychological dramatist, a social critic, a poetic practitioner of the scientific method, a didactic moralist, a social historian, a "Dutch painter," and a human camera. Such labels, often supportable when applied to selected portions of Crabbe's work, do not appear useful in describing his total achievement. Nevertheless, it is on such restricted interpretations that estimations of Crabbe have frequently been built. While attesting to his artistic versatility and providing a focal point for isolated instances of detailed analysis and appreciation, the result has been in large part detrimental to the establishment of a sound critical tradition with respect to Crabbe, for readers of all types—and especially the critics—are most often reluctant to give serious consideration to an artist who cannot be conveniently classified.

Crabbe's earliest literary productions were clearly derivative, most often fashionable satires and other forms in the Augustan mode, but after the appearance of *The Village* one begins to find such terms as "original," "unique," and "inventive" being consistently applied to him. Samuel Johnson, who read *The Village* in manuscript, praised it as "original, vigorous, and elegant." The sensation surrounding the publication of *The Village* proved to be a mixed blessing, for while it won Crabbe many admirers, it also served to fix him in the popular imagination as an antipastoralist and as the "poet of the poor," tags that are misleading and inaccurate when applied to a large part of his work. Crabbe's art showed consistent development throughout his long writing career, particularly in the progressively sophisticated manner in which he articulated his main form, narrative verse. He experimented frequently with narrative techniques and with innovative framing concepts for his collections of verse tales and is often credited with having influenced such writers of prose fiction as Jane Austen and Thomas Hardy. On the other hand, he remained doggedly faithful to that stalwart of eighteenth century prosody, the heroic couplet, departing from it only rarely in his more than sixty-five thousand lines of published verse. Following the appearance of *The Village*, Crabbe's reputation continued to grow, despite a twenty-two-year hiatus in his publishing career, finally declining in his later years largely as a result of the predominant influence of Romantic literary tastes. In his time, he was praised highly by Johnson; Sir Walter Scott; Lord Byron, and even William Wordsworth, with whom he had little in common in either taste or technique; his most consistent and eloquent champion, however, was Francis Jeffrey, the formidable critic of *Edinburgh Review*. His harshest critics, on the other hand, were Samuel Taylor Coleridge and William Hazlitt, both of whom found him significantly deficient in "imagination" (as the Romantics were prone to define that term) owing to his meticulous attention to realistic detail. The high estimation of Crabbe's achievements drifted slowly downward throughout the course of the nineteenth century but began to revive in the twentieth century with largely favorable critical reassessments by such figures as E. M. Forster, F. L. Lucas, and F. R. Leavis. His work has been the subject of several extended critical studies, and although it is doubtful that he will ever be awarded a place among the highest ranking English poets, it appears certain that he is again being accorded some of the critical and popular esteem in which he once was held.

BIOGRAPHY

George Crabbe was born on Christmas Eve in 1754 in Aldeburgh (or, as it was then known, Aldborough), Suffolk, the eldest son of the local collector of salt duties, who early recognized the intellectual potential of his son and endeavored to provide educational opportunities for him beyond those normally accessible to one in his station. Once a busy and prosperous seaport, Aldeburgh had dwindled in size and importance by the middle of the eighteenth century and contained a populace whose general poverty, ignorance, and ill-nature was matched by the isolated, inhospitable conditions of a seacoast plagued by tempestuous weather and surrounded by a dreary countryside consisting largely of salt marshes, heaths, and tidal flats. Crabbe's early experiences in this setting left a lasting impression: Throughout his life, Aldeburgh retained a strong hold on his imagination. This strange mixture of fascination and repugnance formed the basis for a large number of the characters and settings that are possibly the most striking features of his poetry.

Between the ages of eight and thirteen, Crabbe's father arranged for him to attend grammar schools in Bungay and Stowmarket, both in Norfolk, where he received the foundations of a classical education and is known to have made his first attempts at composing doggerel verse. Unable to continue financing his son's education and having determined that the field of medicine would be the most suitable to his son's talents and inclinations, the elder Crabbe in 1768 engaged for George to be bound as an apprentice to an apothecary and surgeon at Wickhambrook, near Bury St. Edmund's, in Suffolk. Used more as a farmhand than as a surgical apprentice, young Crabbe was exceedingly unhappy there and, in 1771, was removed by his father to a more favorable situation in Woodbridge, Suffolk. These were to prove relatively happy years, for though he seems to have shown no great interest in his medical studies, life in Woodbridge was an agreeable contrast to what he had known in Aldeburgh and Wickhambrook. It was also during this period that he met and courted his future wife, Sarah Elmy, and saw his first poem of any consequence, *Inebriety*, appear in print in 1775.

In the summer of that year, his apprenticeship over, Crabbe returned to Aldeburgh, and after a period of uncertainty during which he worked as a common laborer on the docks (much to the dismay of his father), he finally began to practice his profession late in the year. The next four years were particularly frustrating and unhappy ones for the young doctor: It is clear that he never had any real confidence in his abilities as a physician and that he felt himself to be surrounded by people who did not appreciate him and to whom he felt in every way superior. His practice was unsuccessful, and his continuing poverty made it appear doubtful whether he would ever find himself in a position financially stable enough to marry his beloved Sarah. Thus, in early 1780, he abandoned his practice, borrowed five pounds from a local philanthropist, and journeyed to London to take his chances as a poet. Although he would never again return to the profession of medicine, the years spent in training and practice were not entirely wasted ones, for they are undoubtedly responsible for such often-noted features of his poetry as his minute attention to detail and his fascination with aberrant psychological states.

London did not treat Crabbe kindly. Although he did manage to publish *The Candidate*, a dull, unreadable poem, his attempts to secure patronage were singularly unsuccessful, and his increasingly desperate financial state brought him to the point where, by early 1781, he was threatened with debtors' prison. At this propitious moment, he found the patron he had been seeking, the influential statesman Edmund Burke, who eased his financial straits, helped him find publishers for his poetry, and introduced him to such eminent figures of the day as Sir Joshua Reynolds, Charles James Fox, and Johnson. It was Burke also who convinced Crabbe to take holy orders in the Anglican Church and who used his influence to get the young poet ordained, which occurred in 1782. Burke then secured for him a position that allowed him to pursue his duties as a clergyman while at the same time leaving sufficient leisure to write poetry.

His financial worries finally over, his career set, Crabbe entered a largely productive and happy phase in his life. He and Sarah were married in 1783, and over the years, Crabbe was assigned to various livings in Suffolk and Leicestershire. In the early 1790's, the deaths of several of their children affected Sarah's mental state in a way that would become progressively more desperate until her death in 1813. At about the same time, Crabbe began to suffer from vertigo and digestive ailments. Opium was prescribed, and he continued to use the drug for the remainder of his life. For these and perhaps other reasons, he published no poetry for a period of twenty-two years, though he is known to have continued writing poems and other literary works, the majority of which he ultimately destroyed. Crabbe's literary reemergence in 1807 marked the beginning of his most significant period of poetic production, culminating in the 1819 publication of *Tales of the Hall*. Following Sarah's death, he assumed the livings at Trowbridge, in Wiltshire, where he passed the remaining years of his life as a celebrated member of his community, taking occasional trips to London and Suffolk to visit old friends. Though he never remarried, he maintained a lively correspondence with admiring female readers in several parts of the British Isles. Crabbe died in the rectory at Trowbridge on February 3, 1832.

ANALYSIS

No critical assessment of George Crabbe's work has ever isolated his essence more precisely than do the words he himself provided in the concluding lines of letter 1 of *The Borough*:

> Of sea or river, of a quay or street,
> The best description must be incomplete;
> But when a happier theme succeeds, and when
> Men are our subjects and the deeds of men;
> Then may we find the Muse in happier style,
> And we may sometimes sigh and sometimes smile.

Any reader who has generously sampled Crabbe's work would likely agree with the point suggested here: It is indeed people and their actions that form the central focus in the majority of his poems. Crabbe was, above all else, a narrative poet, and in the estimation of some critics second only to Geoffrey Chaucer. Paradoxically, however, his reputation in his own day (and to some extent even in the present) was not primarily based on that fact. Rather, he was seen as a painter in words—a master of highly particularized visual imagery who conjured up vivid landscapes and interior settings, most often for the purpose of emphasizing the sordid and brutal elements of existence. Though people might be present in these scenes, they were generally seen as little more than corollary features to the inanimate components dominating the whole (such as the famous description of the aged shepherd in the poorhouse found in book 1 of *The Village*). Hence, Sir Walter Scott's well-known epithet, "nature's sternest poet" ("nature" in the nineteenth century sense of the term), has come to epitomize the predominant attitude toward Crabbe as a poet. That view is indeed unfortunate, for the narrowness of its emphasis ignores the very features of Crabbe's work on which his surest claim to significance might be built. Missing in this approach, for example, is any notion of the richness and diversity of Crabbe's humor, surely one of his most delightful features. Furthermore, such a limited view fails to note the increasingly optimistic tone of Crabbe's work, in its progress from *The Village* to *Tales of the Hall*. Most important, however, the opinion reverses what surely must be the proper emphasis when considering Crabbe's poetry as a whole: People, rather than merely serving to enhance Crabbe's realistic descriptions, are in fact the subject and center of his concern. Nature and external detail, while present to a significant degree in his poetry, exist primarily to illuminate his fascination with character.

If any one reason might be cited for the disproportionate emphasis given to Crabbe's descriptive and pessimistic qualities, it would most likely be the influence of *The Village*. This poem, a sensation in its own day and still the most consistently anthologized of Crabbe's works, paints an unrelentingly bleak picture of human existence in a manner that is essentially descriptive and makes extensive use of external detail. These same concerns and techniques may also be seen to operate in large portions of Crabbe's next two major works, *The Parish Register* (which appeared in *Poems*) and *The Borough*. In all these, the influence of Crabbe's early life, and especially his perceptions of his native town of Aldeburgh, form the controlling focus. At the same time, however, as early as *The Village* itself and certainly in the works that follow it, the perceptive reader can note Crabbe's increasing interest in character and narration. By the time *Tales in Verse* was published, the mode had become completely narrative and continued to be so throughout the poet's writing career.

Moreover, a concomitant softening of the hard lines presented in Crabbe's early poetry becomes increasingly evident as he moved more and more in the direction of a psychological and sociological examination of the factors necessary for successful human interaction. True, social criticism, human suffering, and the stultifying effects of an inhospitable environment are factors that never disappear entirely from Crabbe's writings. As time goes on, however, they retreat significantly from their earlier position of predominance and assume no more than their proportionate role in what Jeffrey referred to as "the pattern of Crabbe's arabesque."

With a canon as large as Crabbe's, it is perhaps to be expected that a remarkably large and diverse array of themes and motifs may be cataloged when examining his work as a whole. Nevertheless, certain patterns recur frequently enough in dynamic variation so as to be considered dominant. Proceeding, as they invariably do, from an intense interest in character and in human interaction, they are all rich in psychological and sociological insights. Chief among them are the problems of moral isolation, of the influence of relatives on young minds, of success and failure in matters of love, courtship and marriage, and of the search for reconciliation as an antidote to bitterness and estrangement. To watch these thematic concerns grow in texture and complexity as Crabbe explores them in a succession of tales is one of the pleasures of reading a generous and representative selection of his works. Of no less interest is the process of experimentation and refinement by which Crabbe first discovers and then seeks to perfect the stylistic and structural mechanisms best suited to his characteristic narrative voice.

THE VILLAGE

From the moment of its first appearance in 1783 to the present, the most immediate response of critics and general readers alike has been to see *The Village* as a poem written in response to Oliver Goldsmith's *The Deserted Village* (1770), published thirteen years earlier. This is certainly understandable. The respective titles invite such comparison, and Crabbe himself explicitly alludes to Goldsmith's poem on several occasions. Furthermore, it is apparent to even the most casual reader that Crabbe's Aldeburgh (for most assuredly it is Aldeburgh that forms the model for *The Village*) is in every conceivable way the very antithesis of Goldsmith's Auburn. Although all this is true, the notion of Crabbe's poem as a simple rebuttal of Goldsmith is far too limiting; rather, it should be seen as a poem that constitutes in large part a reaction against the entire eighteenth century literary convention that governs Goldsmith's poem. The term antipastoral is a convenient label to use here, but only if one keeps in mind the fact that Crabbe's bias against the pastoral mode is somewhat specialized. It is not classical pastoralism or even its manifestations in earlier English poetry to which Crabbe objects, but rather the manner in which, in the eighteenth century, poets and public alike had irrationally come to accept the conventions of pastoral description as constituting accurate and useful representations of rural life. If it is somewhat difficult to understand the tone of outrage that underlies the cutting edge of Crabbe's realism in this poem, it is perhaps because most modern readers, unlike Crabbe, have been spared the effusions of countless minor poets, most of them deservedly now forgotten, whose celebrations of the joys of pastoral rusticity filled the "poet's corner" of many a fashionable eighteenth century magazine. He speaks to them when he says: "Yes, thus the Muses sing of happy swains,/ Because the Muses never knew their pains." Crabbe knew their pains; he had felt many of them himself, perhaps too many to assure his own objectivity. For, whatever the merits of seeing *The Village* as a realistic rejoinder to an artificial and decadent literary tradition, one must always remember that Crabbe's brand of realism may at times in itself be somewhat suspect by virtue of the conscious and unconscious prejudices he bears toward his subject matter.

The Village consists of two parts—books 1 and 2—but it is book 1 that has always commanded the greatest interest. This portion of the poem is dominated by a number of descriptive set pieces, perhaps the most frequently quoted passages in all of Crabbe's works. The first of these, and the one that perhaps best epitomizes the poem's uncompromisingly harsh view of rural life, concerns the countryside that surrounds the village—the coastline and adjoining heaths. It is a bleak, barren, forbidding prospect that Crabbe presents, a landscape inhospitable to people and barely capable of sustaining life of any sort. Images of decay and sickness, of despair, of almost anthropomorphic hostility pervade the descriptions, chiefly of vegetation, of this isolated sector of the East Anglian seacoast. Almost imperceptibly, Crabbe moves from this dominant sense of place to his initial, tentative descriptions of the inhabitants, the first of many instances in his poetry in which people and physical setting are juxtaposed in meaningful counterpoint.

The next of the famous set pieces in the poem is a description of the village poorhouse, the vividness and intensity of which so struck Crabbe's contemporaries that the language they frequently used to discuss it is of a sort most generally reserved for discussions of painting. Several modern commentators have argued that, in this section of the poem, Crabbe is functioning primarily as a social critic, calling into question, among other things, the prevailing Poor Laws and their administration in local parishes. This may be so; nevertheless, it is again the pure descriptive vividness of this scene that remains its most memorable feature. The details relating to the exterior and interior of the building form a backdrop to the cataloging of its miserable inhabitants. Again, the predominant images are of decay, oppressiveness, and despair. Amid these scenes of not-so-quiet desperation, Crabbe gives particular attention to one inhabitant of the poorhouse, an old shepherd, worn out, useless, lodged there to pine away his days in loneliness and frustration. Perhaps nowhere else in the poem does Crabbe so brutally and cynically mock the pastoral ideal. Book 1 ends with vicious satirical portraits of the doctor and priest who, paid by the parish to attend to the needs of the inhabitants of the poorhouse, openly and contemptuously neglect their duties.

Book 2 is considerably less successful in its execution, primarily owing to a lack of consistency in tone and format. Crabbe begins by intimating that he wishes to soften his harsh picture of village life by showing some of its gentler moments; soon, however, this degenerates into a description and condemnation of the drunkenness of the villagers, a subject that he had previously explored in the youthful *Inebriety*. Even more disturbing, however, is the poem's conclusion, which takes the form of an unrelated and lengthy eulogy on Lord Robert Manners, late younger brother of the duke of Rutland, the man whom Crabbe was currently serving as private chaplain.

Although it is probably his best-known work and contains some of his finest descriptive writing, *The Village* is hardly Crabbe's most representative poem. In his treatment of the aged shepherd, in the satiric portraits of the doctor and priest, one may sense the embryonic forms of the distinctive narrative voice that would ultimately come to dominate his poetry; before this manifested itself, however, a number of years had intervened.

POEMS

With the exception of *The News-Paper*, a lukewarm satire on the periodical press very much in the Augustan mode, Crabbe published no poetry in the period between the appearance of *The Village* in 1783 and the release of the collection, *Poems*, in 1807. That he was not artistically inactive during this period, however, is evidenced by the vigor and diversity of the poems found in the 1807 volume, and there is ample reason to lament the many efforts in manuscript he is known to have destroyed at this time. In addition to his previously published works, the 1807 *Poems* contained a number of commendable new efforts, including "The Birth of Flattery," "The Hall of Justice," and the provocative "Sir Eustace Grey." All these works show Crabbe experimenting with various narrative techniques. The star attraction of the new collection, however, was a much longer poem entitled *The Parish Register*.

THE PARISH REGISTER

Readers who enjoyed the angry, debunking tone of Crabbe's antipastoralism in *The Village* were probably delighted by the first several hundred lines of *The Parish Register*, which seem to signal a continuation of the same interests. "Since vice the world subdued and waters drown'd,/ Auburn and Eden can no more be found," Crabbe notes wryly and then proceeds to unveil a number of highly particularized descriptions, the most memorable of which outlines in vivid and often disgusting detail the vice and squalor of a poor village street. If anything, Crabbe appears to be well on his way to outdoing his previous efforts in this vein. At this point, however, the poem suddenly takes a new tack and begins to present a series of narratives that in the aggregate constitute its dominant feature.

The plan of *The Parish Register* is, in essence, simple and ingenious. A narrative voice is created by Crabbe; it is that of the parish priest of a small village who, at year's end, reviews the records in his church register and comments in varying fashion on the real-life stories that lie behind the cold names and dates. The poem has three divisions—"Baptisms," "Marriages," and "Burials"—and in each the loquacious speaker presents a number of narratives ranging in length and complexity from simple vignettes of a few lines to more ambitious efforts resembling full-blown tales. Generally, the best narratives are found in "Baptisms" and "Burials," particularly in the latter. Two stories of chief interest in the "Baptisms" section are that of Lucy, the daughter of a proud and wealthy miller, who conceives a child out of wedlock, is ostracized by her father and the community, and slowly goes mad, and that of Richard Monday, a foundling brought up and abused in the village poorhouse, who leaves the village to become an enormous success in the world and on his deathbed leaves only a pittance to his native town. "Burials" contains a number of memorable portraits, including those of the prudent, matriarchal Widow Goe and of old Sexton Dibble, who managed to outlive the five parsons he successively served. The most interesting, however, are the stories of Robin Dingley and Roger Cuff. In the first of these, Robin, a poor but contented man, becomes the victim of a clever attorney who leads him to place all his hopes on the possibility of a rich inheritance; when these are dashed, the loss drives him crazy and makes him a wanderer for life. The acuteness of Crabbe's psychological perceptions are noteworthy in this story, one of the first of a number of tales in which he explores the bases of aberrant behavior. Borrowing certain motifs from older folk tales, the story of Roger Cuff tells of a young man who has a falling out with his kin, goes off to sea, and years later, having made his fortune, returns disguised as a beggar to test the moral fiber of the surviving members of his family. Refused by the closest of them, he shares his wealth with an unpretentious distant relative who lives as a reclusive hermit in the forest. Years later, in "The Family of Love," one of the stories from his posthumous collection of tales, Crabbe returned to this theme but with significant alterations.

In *The Parish Register*, one can observe Crabbe in the process of discovering his considerable talents as a writer of narrative verse. His experimentations with frame, point of view, dialogue and character interaction, and a host of other practical and thematic considerations, point the way toward more sophisticated efforts yet to come. Even as he was finishing this poem, he was hard at work on a far more ambitious undertaking, *The Borough*.

THE BOROUGH

One of Crabbe's longest poems—approximately eight thousand lines—*The Borough* is also one of his most perplexing and in many ways his least successful effort when considered as a whole. Within its vast scope, however, there are isolated instances of writing that rank among the poet's best. As in *The Village* and *The Parish Register*, the subject of Crabbe's third major poem is once again a thinly disguised Aldeburgh. This time, however, the scale is much more ambitious, for, as he makes clear in his lengthy prose preface and in the opening section of the poem, the aim of *The Borough* is nothing less than complete description: All aspects of the town, its buildings, trades and professions, public institutions, social activities, and inhabitants are to be revealed. Naturally, the scheme is so grandiose as to preclude its complete achievement, but the efforts that Crabbe makes in pursuing it are in themselves somewhat remarkable. The result, unfortunately, sometimes seems more akin to social history than to poetry. In structure, the poem is epistolary, consisting of a series of twenty-four verse letters written by a resident of the borough to a friend in a far distant part of the country who has requested a description of the place. Among them are some of the dullest pieces of writing in Crabbe's entire canon, including the letters on "Elections," "The Hospital and Governors," and "Schools." Paradoxically, however, this same ponderous framework yields some of Crabbe's finest narrative pieces.

Letters 19 to 22, collectively entitled "The Poor of the Borough," provide the most fully developed narratives found in Crabbe's work to this point. They are, in essence, short stories in verse, each one focusing on a different character type and probing the psychological dimensions of motivation and consequence. "Ellen Orford" (letter 20), a story in which Crabbe broadens his narrative technique by having Ellen tell a large part of her own history, is an account of cumulative personal tragedy, borne stoically by a woman whose essential goodness and faith in God enable her to rise above what Hamlet termed "the slings and arrows of outrageous fortune." No such inspirational note is provided in "Abel Keene" (letter 21), in which a pious man is seduced into abandoning his faith, the process ending in despair and suicide. A fascinating study of self-deception and its disastrous results is presented in "The Parish Clerk" (letter 19), which tells the story of Jachin, the spiritually proud clerk of the parish who feels he is above sin and alienates everyone with his smug sanctimony. Tempted by his poverty and secure in the rationalizations he has constructed for his conduct as well as in the foolproof method he has devised for its implementation, Jachin begins to steal from the collection plate during services. Eventually caught and publicly disgraced, he goes the way of many of Crabbe's moral outcasts, retreating from the society of men to blend into the bleakness of the surrounding countryside, where his mental and physical energies are gradually dissipated and death comes as a welcome relief.

By most accounts, the finest story in *The Borough*, perhaps the best in all Crabbe's canon, is "Peter Grimes" (letter 22), on which Benjamin Britten based his well-known opera. The tale has so many remarkable features—its implicit attack on the abuses of the apprentice system, its subtle articulation of the notion that the ultimate responsibility for deviant behavior may rest within the society that fosters it, its powerful juxtapositions of external description and interior states of mind, and its surprisingly modern probing of the psychological bases of child abuse—that it is difficult to isolate any one of them as the key factor in assessing the impact it has had on most readers. A misanthropic fisherman who lives on the fringes of his community, Peter Grimes emerged from a childhood in which he irrationally hated the father who loved him. As an adult, he acquires and successively destroys three young orphans from London who are bound to him as apprentices. The townspeople, aware of what is occurring, turn their backs on what they view as none of their business ("Grimes is at his exercise," they say when the cries of his victims are heard in the town's streets), until the death of the third boy proves to be more than they can ignore. Although they cannot legally punish him—nothing can be proved conclusively—Grimes is forbidden to take any more apprentices and is ostracized by the community. He withdraws into the desolation of the tidal flats and salt marshes surrounding his village, and there, brooding alone under the hot sun, he becomes possessed by wild and persistent visions of his father and the murdered apprentices, who dance on the waters and beckon him to join them in their element. His mind shattered, he sinks to death in an agony of terror and desperation. "Peter Grimes" is a story of considerable power, owing in large part to Crabbe's masterful conception of the title character, who, like William Shakespeare's Iago and Herman Melville's Claggart, taxes the limits of critical understanding.

Despite the ponderous framing device employed by Crabbe in *The Borough*, it is possible in the narrative portions of that poem to see him working toward the use of a narrator who is to a certain degree effaced, as well as toward an occasional reliance on multiple points of view. In *Tales in Verse*, which appeared in 1812, he continued those trends and abandoned, temporarily, the use of any sort of framing device. Here, in his first collection of poetry devoted entirely to narrative themes, Crabbe presents a series of twenty-one discrete verse tales in which, as he notes in his preface

> the attempt at union therefore has been relinquished, and these relations are submitted to the public, connected by no other circumstance than their being the productions of the same author, and devoted to the same purpose, the entertainment of his readers.

Ironically, what Crabbe himself half-apologetically presented as a loose compendium of disparate elements may, in fact, be his most thoroughly integrated work, for there is one factor that the vast majority of the individual tales share in common: They are, in large part, variations from every conceivable point of view on the themes of love, courtship, and marriage.

TALES IN VERSE

In the collection *Tales in Verse*, Crabbe presents a number of his most memorable stories. One useful method of approaching the collection is to distinguish between those tales in which two persons have successfully found the basis for compatibility, avoiding the numerous pitfalls that at any point in the love-courtship-marriage continuum can destroy the entire process, and those in which the reverse has occurred. Thus, in the latter category may be grouped such tales as "Procrastination" (4), "The Patron" (5), "The Mother" (8), "Squire Thomas: Or, The Precipitate Choice" (12), and "Resentment" (17), while the former is represented by "The Parting Hour" (2), "The Frank Courtship" (6), "The Widow's Tale" (7), "Arabella" (9), "The Lover's Journey" (10), "Jesse and Colin" (13), "The Confidant" (16), and "The Wager" (18). Myriad influences may affect the delicate balance of the relationships explored in these tales, ensuring their ultimate success or failure, but two situations recur in a variety of forms. In the first of them, Crabbe explores the power, for better or for worse, that a third person may exert on a couple's life. The influence may range from a healthy one, as in the case of the emancipated aunt in "The Frank Courtship," to that which is destructive, as in "The Mother." In other situations, the influence may present an obstacle that must be overcome and resolved so that the relationship may achieve its true potential, as is demonstrated in "The Confidant." The other recurring situation, one that came to be a dominant motif in Crabbe's remaining work, is the need to seek out and establish the compassionate basis of understanding that must ultimately be the cornerstone of any successful, lasting human relationship. Frequently, this is seen in the context of a major disrupting incident in a couple's life that tests the ability of one of them to display the qualities of forgiveness and understanding necessary to keep the relationship alive. The opposite effects of this type of situation are presented, respectively, in "Resentment" and "The Confidant," as well as in certain other of the tales.

Beyond its thematic articulations, which are at once perceptive and sophisticated, "The Frank Courtship" is a tale that commands attention by virtue of its tone and stylistic qualities. Perhaps nowhere else in Crabbe's poetry is dialogue used to such delightful effect as in the courting scene between Sybil and her young suitor, Josiah; it is a piece of dramatic interchange that in the sharpness and vivacity of language reminds one of the best of Shakespeare's romantic comedies. Further, the optimistic, at times almost playful, tone of this composition may be cited as one of several memorable instances in Crabbe's poetry that serve to balance the elements of somberness and pessimism most frequently ascribed to him.

TALES OF THE HALL

In _Tales in Verse_, while not abandoning his interests in individual psychological observation, Crabbe moved strongly in the direction of exploring the dynamics of social interaction between people. This interest carried over into his next major production, _Tales of the Hall_. One of the features most immediately apparent in _Tales of the Hall_ is the author's return to the use of a comprehensive framing device for the presentation of a number of separate tales. Crabbe has integrated within the controlling frame of his new collection the same sort of thematic cohesiveness that serves to connect the individual narratives of _Tales in Verse_. Again, the great majority of the various tales (here called "books") represent diverse angles of vision from which to observe the many features inherent in the love-courtship-marriage syndrome. As if to emphasize his desire to pursue these studies from as many angles as possible, Crabbe further complicates his design by experimenting freely with multiple points of view and with other structural complexities in certain of the tales.

The frame itself is of considerable interest and, in its complex pattern of development, has led more than one critic to the conclusion that *Tales of the Hall* may justifiably be termed a novel in verse. As outlined in "The Hall" (1) and the several books that immediately succeed it, the collection is bound by the story of two half brothers, George and Richard, who after a long separation have come together on a somewhat experimental basis to see what, if anything, they might have in common. Here, on the elder brother George's recently purchased estate (the Hall), they spend some weeks together, gradually wearing away the reserve and potential misunderstandings that at various points threaten to disturb the growing bond between their vastly differing personalities. In the course of this process, they tell tales of various sorts, some concerning themselves, others about people they have known in the past or have recently met in the surrounding area, and are frequently joined by a third companion and narrator, the local vicar. As the various tales unfold, the story of George and Richard itself develops in texture and complexity, resolving itself amicably, if somewhat flatly, in the final book. If the overall form of *Tales of the Hall* may be compared to that of the novel, however, it also bears certain affinities in substance to the type of long autobiographical poem that was proving increasingly popular among poets during this period (as, for example, those of Wordsworth and Byron). A convincing case might be made for seeing George and Richard—and to a certain extent even Jacques, the vicar—as varying projections of Crabbe's own conceptualized self-image.

The quality of the individual stories of *Tales of the Hall* is perhaps more uneven than that of *Tales in Verse*. The best of the stories, however, are definitely of a very high order. One is "Smugglers and Poachers" (21), an intricately plotted tale that, in addition to evidencing Crabbe's ongoing concern with social injustices, provides, in its depiction of the enmity between the brothers James and Robert, a bitter and dramatic counterpoint to the happier circumstances of the brothers found in the frame tale. Estrangement and failure in matters of love continue to find expression, as in the powerfully tragic "Ruth" (5) or the more philosophical "Lady Barbara: Or, The Ghost" (16); but on the whole, the tone of this collection is more consistently optimistic than in any of Crabbe's previous efforts and the note of forgiveness and reconciliation that dominates a number of the tales continues a trend first noticed in *Tales in Verse*. Two tales that illustrate this rather well are "William Bailey" (19) and the structurally complex "Sir Owen Dale" (12), both of which feature central characters who ultimately come to realize that the errors of the past cannot be allowed to poison the present forever. If there is a moral lesson to be drawn from the essentially nondidactic poetry of the later Crabbe, it is surely this point.

Two years after Crabbe's death, there appeared the most complete edition of his poetry available up to that time. Edited by his son and including as its final volume the highly readable biographical account of his father's life, the *Poetical Works* of 1834 featured a number of poems never published by Crabbe during his lifetime, many of which were obviously still in a state of manuscript revision at the time of his death. Of chief interest among them is the group known collectively as *Posthumous Tales*.

POSTHUMOUS TALES

Actually, the twenty-two tales that constitute this final collection of narrative verse fall into two groups. Tales 6 through 22 represent what may be described as draft versions of a new collection of poems that Crabbe had tentatively entitled *The Farewell and Return*. Crabbe's organizing principle in the collection posits a situation in which a young man leaves his native town and returns many years later to find it immensely changed. Each tale is divided into two basic parts, the first of which provides a description of a person or thing at the time of the narrator's departure, while the second involves an updating on the part of a friend whom the narrator encounters on his return. The concept, while ingenious in nature and serving to demonstrate Crabbe's continuing preoccupation with the problem of narrative frames, is far from successful; the individual tales often resolve themselves into a depressingly predictable series of variations on the theme of destructive mutability. These evident shortcomings should not be judged too harshly, however, since it is reasonable to assume that, given the chance for suitable revision, Crabbe would ultimately have rendered the collection consistent with the quality of his previous work. One tale from *The Farewell and Return* group, "The Boat Race" (18), is deserving of special mention, if only by virtue of its splendidly effective description of a sudden storm on the river and its disastrous effects.

In some respects, the best narratives in the *Posthumous Tales* are found in the five unrelated tales that begin the collection, including the delightful "Silford Hall: Or, The Happy Day" (1), a highly autobiographical account of an impressionable young lad's sense of wonder and delight on receiving a guided tour of an aristocrat's palatial estate. Also of significant interest is "The Family of Love" (2), a tale in many ways reminiscent of the account of Roger Cuff found in *The Parish Register*, but with the significant difference that the central character of this later narrative finds it within himself to forgive his erring kin, reestablishing the bond of human understanding he could so easily and irrevocably destroy. In this contrasting treatment of an earlier theme, one can again gauge the distance that Crabbe has traveled in his attitude toward the potential for social fulfillment.

In the last analysis, one cannot escape the conclusion that there is a certain amount of unevenness in Crabbe's work, perhaps enough to justify his exclusion from the first rank of English poets. His occasional difficulty in blending new characters into a narrative, his sometimes annoying penchant for wordy digressiveness, his periodic lapses in tone and in the handling of dialogue, even those infrequent examples of "bad lines" that his nineteenth century detractors so loved to quote—all these and perhaps others as well might be charged to him as observable defects in technique. To dwell too long and too hard on these factors, however, is to miss the true essence of Crabbe and to a large degree his power. In his relentless scrutiny of psychological and sociological themes, from the dark, brooding malevolence of "Peter Grimes" to the delicate social harmonies of "The Frank Courtship" and the frame of *Tales of the Hall*, one can clearly see the elements that link him securely to such widely divergent masters of English storytelling as

Emily Brontë and Jane Austen. A later commentator on Crabbe, Oliver Sigworth, strikes the proper balance when he notes that "we may wish for various perfections which Crabbe did not attain, but, unique as he is, some may be happy in those which he possessed."

OTHER MAJOR WORKS

NONFICTION: "The Natural History of the Vale of Belvoir," 1795; *Selected Letters and Journals of George Crabbe*, 1985 (Thomas C. Faulkner, editor).

BIBLIOGRAPHY

Bareham, Tony. *George Crabbe*. New York: Barnes & Noble, 1977. Examines how Crabbe's poetry reflects contemporary ideas on religion, politics, psychology, and aesthetics. Emphasizes that Crabbe was a "proper spokesman" for mainstream English thought. The 245-page text includes an index and a chronology of major events in Crabbe's career.

Crabbe, George. *The Life of George Crabbe by His Son*. 1834. Reprint. London: Cresset, 1947. This standard biography, written from the unique perspective of the poet's son, offers a benign yet candid glimpse into the poet's personality. An introduction by Edmund Blunden provides further criticism of Crabbe's poetry, including an interesting discussion on the influence that Crabbe's training as a physician and clergyman had on his writing.

Edwards, Gavin. *George Crabbe's Poetry on Border Land*. Lewiston, N.Y.: E. Mellen Press, 1990. This critical work, organized by subject, takes a social historical approach to Crabbe's poems, dealing with Crabbe's ability to reflect his time accurately. It thoroughly discusses the concept of Crabbe as a realist, suggesting his poetry has a more complex relationship to history than just simple realism.

Hatch, Ronald B. *Crabbe's Arabesque: Social Drama in the Poetry of George Crabbe*. Montreal: McGill-Queen's University Press, 1976. Attempts to show how Crabbe grew beyond being simply a social critic by focusing on his handling of social issues in his poetry. Suggests that Crabbe's development can be seen in the way his poems' dramatic structures handle conflicting questions that either clash or are reconciled. Includes a chronology of Crabbe's life, a selected bibliography, and index.

Mahood, M. M. *The Poet as Botanist*. New York: Cambridge University Press, 2008. Contains a chapter looking at the descriptions of plants in Crabbe's poetry.

Pollard, Arthur, ed. *Crabbe: The Critical Heritage*. London: Routledge & Kegan Paul, 1972. An interesting compilation of criticism of Crabbe's writings by his contemporaries, including William Hazlitt, William Wordsworth, and Samuel Taylor Coleridge, along with later commentary. Arranged by individual works, the book also contains an informative introduction on Crabbe and his writing and indexes to names, works, characteristics, and periodicals.

Powell, Neil. *George Crabbe: An English Life, 1754-1832*. London: Pimlico, 2004. A readable biography of the poet that draws largely on the biography of his son and namesake.

Whitehead, Frank S. *George Crabbe: A Reappraisal*. Cranbury, N.J.: Associated University Presses, 1995. A critical assessment of Crabbe's work with bibliographical references and an index.

Richard E. Meyer

JOHANN WOLFGANG VON GOETHE

Born: Frankfurt am Main (now in Germany); August 28, 1749
Died: Weimar, Saxe-Weimar-Eisenbach (now in Germany); March 22, 1832

OTHER LITERARY FORMS

The unique significance of the contribution to German letters made by Johann Wolfgang von Goethe (GUR-tuh) lies in the fact that his best creations provided models that influenced, stimulated, and gave direction to the subsequent evolution of literary endeavor in virtually every genre. Among more than twenty plays that he wrote throughout his career, several have special meaning for the history of German theater. *Götz von Berlichingen mit der eisernen Hand* (pb. 1773; *Götz von Berlichingen with the Iron Hand*, 1799) was a key production of the Storm and Stress movement, mediating especially the influence of William Shakespeare on later German dramatic form and substance. With *Iphigenie auf Tauris* (first version pr. 1779, second version pb. 1787; *Iphigenia in Tauris*, 1793), Goethe illustrated profoundly the ideals of perfected form and style, beauty of language, and humanistic education that characterized German literature of the classical period. His famous masterpiece *Faust: Eine Tragödie* (pb. 1808, 1833; *The Tragedy of Faust*, 1823, 1838), with its carefully programmed depiction of the spiritual polarities that torment the individual, rapidly became the ultimate paradigm for the portrayal of modern humanity's fragmented nature.

Goethe's major narratives, including *Die Leiden des jungen Werthers* (1774; *The Sorrows of Young Werther*, 1779), *Wilhelm Meisters Lehrjahre* (1795-1796; *Wilhelm Meister's Apprenticeship*, 1825), *Die Wahlverwandtschaften* (1809; *Elective Affinities*, 1849), and *Wilhelm Meisters Wanderjahre: Oder, Die Entsagenden* (1821, 1829; *Wil-*

Johann Wolfgang von Goethe
(Library of Congress)

helm Meister's Travels, 1827), are powerful illuminations of fundamental human problems. The monumental saga of Wilhelm Meister established the pattern for the German bildungsroman of the nineteenth century, and it also had a substantial impact on Romantic novel theory.

A large portion of Goethe's oeuvre is nonfiction. He completed more than fourteen volumes of scientific and technical writings, the most important of which are *Versuch die Metamorphose der Pflanzen zu erklären* (1790; *Essays on the Metamorphosis of Plants*, 1863) and *Zur Farbenlehre* (1810; *Theory of Colors*, 1840). His historical accounts, specifically *Campagne in Frankreich, 1792* (1822; *Campaign in France in the Year 1792*, 1849) and *Die Belagerung von Mainz, 1793* (1822; *The Siege of Mainz in the Year 1793*, 1849), are vividly readable reports of firsthand experience. Writings that reveal a great deal about Goethe himself and his perception of his artistic calling are his autobiography, *Aus meinem Leben: Dichtung und Wahrheit* (1811-1814; *The Autobiography of Goethe*, 1824; better known as *Poetry and Truth from My Own Life*), and the many published volumes of his correspondence.

ACHIEVEMENTS

Johann Wolfgang von Goethe's overwhelming success as a lyricist was primarily the result of an extraordinary ability to interpret and transform direct, intimate experience and perception into vibrant imagery and symbols with universal import. In the process of overcoming the artificiality of Rococo literary tendencies, he created, for the first time in modern German literature, lyrics that were at once deeply personal, dynamically vital, and universally valid in what they communicated to the reader. Beginning with the poems written to Friederike Brion, and continuing through the infinitely passionate affirmations of life composed in his old age, Goethe consistently employed his art in a manner that brushed away the superficial trappings and facades of existence to lay bare the essential spirit of humankind.

In his own time, Goethe became a world figure, although his immediate acclaim derived more from his early prose and dramatic works than from his lyrical writings. Even after the turn of the nineteenth century, he was still recognized most commonly as the author of *The Sorrows of Young Werther*, the novel that had made him instantly famous throughout Europe. Nevertheless, the simple power, clear, appealing language, and compelling melodiousness of his verse moved it inexorably into the canon of the German literary heritage. Much of his poetry was set to music by the great composers of his own and subsequent generations, and the continuing popularity of such creations as "Mailied" ("Maysong") and "Heidenröslein" ("Little Rose of the Heath") is attributable at least in part to the musical interpretations of Franz Schubert and others.

The real importance of Goethe's lyric legacy is perhaps best measured in terms of what it taught other writers. Goethe established new patterns and perspectives, opened new avenues of expression, set uncommon standards of artistic and aesthetic achievement, assimilated impulses from other traditions, and mastered diverse meters, techniques, and styles as had no other German poet before him. His influence was made productive by figures as different as Heinrich Heine and Eduard Mörike, Friedrich Hölderlin and Hugo von Hofmannsthal, Stefan George and Rainer Maria Rilke. As a mediator and motivator of the literary and intellectual currents of his time, as a creator of timeless poetic archetypes, as an interpreter of humanity within its living context, Goethe has earned an undisputed place among the greatest poets of world literature.

BIOGRAPHY

Three aspects of Johann Wolfgang von Goethe's childhood contributed substantially to his development as a literary artist. A sheltered existence, in which he spent long hours completely alone, fostered the growth of an active imagination. A complicated attachment to his sister Cornelia colored his perceptions of male-female relationships in ways that had a profound impact on the kinds of experience from which his works were generated. Finally, contrasts between his parents in temperament and cultural attitudes gave him an early awareness of the stark polarities of life on which the central tensions of his major literary creations are based.

While studying law in Leipzig between 1765 and 1768, Goethe began to write poems and simple plays in the prevailing Anacreontic style. Although some of these productions relate to his infatuation with Kätchen Schönkopf, an innkeeper's daughter, they are more the product of his desire to become a part of the contemporary intellectual establishment than a direct outpouring of his own inner concerns. Among the important figures who influenced his education and thinking during this period were Christoph Martin Wieland, Christian Fürchtegott Gellert, and Adam Friedrich Oeser.

The experiences that resulted in Goethe's breakthrough to a distinctly individual and characteristic literary approach began when he entered the University of Strasbourg in 1770. Encounters with two very different people during the winter of 1770-1771 sharply changed his life. Johann Gottfried Herder introduced him to the concepts and ideals of the Storm and Stress movement, providing him with new models in Homer and Shakespeare and moving him in the direction of less artificial modes of expression. Of equal consequence for the immediate evolution of his lyrics was an idyllic love affair with Friederike Brion that ended in a parting, the emotional implications of which marked his writings long afterward.

On his return to Frankfurt in 1771, Goethe was admitted to the bar. During the next five years, he fell in love with at least three different women. A painful involvement with Charlotte Buff, the fiancé of his friend Johann Christian Kestner, was followed by a brief attraction to Maximiliane Laroche. In April, 1775, he became engaged to Lili Schönemann, the daughter of a wealthy Frankfurt banker. Of the three relationships, only the interlude with Maximiliane Laroche failed to have a significant impact on his art. *The Sorrows of Young Werther* derived much of its substance from Goethe's experiences with Charlotte Buff, while the powerful internal conflicts generated by his feelings for Lili gave rise to a small group of very interesting poems.

When the engagement to Lili became intolerable because of its demands and restrictions, Goethe went to Weimar, where he settled permanently in 1776. For the next ten years, he served as adviser to Carl August, duke of Weimar, whom he had met in Frankfurt in 1774. A broad variety of political and administrative responsibilities, ranging from supervision of road construction to irrigation, from military administration to direction of the court theater, left Goethe little time for serious literary endeavor. The resulting lack of personal fulfillment coupled with the prolonged frustrations of an unhappy platonic love affair with Charlotte von Stein caused him to flee to Italy in search of artistic and spiritual rejuvenation. While there, he perfected some of his most significant dramatic works.

The combination of exposure to Roman antiquity, classical Italian literature, and a uniquely satisfying love alliance with the simple, uneducated Christiane Vulpius formed the basis for renewed poetic productivity when Goethe returned to Weimar. In *Roman Elegies*, he glorified his intimate involvement with Christiane in imagery of the Eternal City. A second, more disappointing trip to Italy in 1790 provided the stimulus for the less well known *Venetian Epigrams*.

In 1794, Goethe accepted Friedrich Schiller's invitation to collaborate in the publication of a new journal. There followed one of the most fruitful creative friendships in the history of German letters. Among the famous lyrical compositions that emerged from their relationship were the terse, pointed forms of the epigram war that they waged against their critics in 1796, and the masterful ballads that were written in friendly competition in 1797. Goethe regarded Schiller's death, in 1805, as one of the major personal tragedies of his own life.

The two specific experiences of later years that provided the direction for Goethe's last great productive period were exposure to the works of the fourteenth century Persian poet Hafiz and a journey to the places of his own childhood. While in Frankfurt in 1814, Goethe fell in love with Marianne von Willemer, the wife of a friend. The Hafiz-like dialogue of their intense spiritual communion is the focus of *West-Eastern Divan*, in which Goethe reached the culmination of his career as a lyricist. After it was published, only the final work on his immortal masterpiece *Faust* remained as a substantial task to be completed before his death.

ANALYSIS

In his famous letter to Johann Wolfgang von Goethe of August 23, 1794, Schiller identified the addressee as a writer who sought to derive the essence of an individual manifestation from the totality of natural phenomena. More particularly, he saw Goethe's goal as the literary definition of humankind in terms of the organization of the living cosmos to which it belongs. Only to the extent that Goethe viewed himself as representative of humanity in general does Schiller's assessment offer a valid approach to the understanding of his friend's lyric poetry. The focus of Goethe's verse is less humankind in the abstract than it is Goethe himself as a distinct, feeling, suffering, loving, sorrowing, longing being. From the very beginning, his works assumed the character of subjective poetic interpretations of his specific place in society, the implications of direct encounters with nature and culture, and the significance of concrete interpersonal relationships. He later described his creative writings as elements of a grand confession, pinpointing the fact that a major key to them lay in the penetration of his own existence.

Goethe's development as a lyric poet is clearly a continuum in which internal and external events and circumstances contribute to sometimes subtle, sometimes obvious modifications in approach, technique, and style. It is nevertheless possible to recognize a number of well-defined stages in his career that correspond to important changes in his outward situation and his connections with specific individuals. The predominant tendency of his growth was in the direction of a poetry that reaches outward to encompass an ever-broader spectrum of universal experience.

The Anacreontic creations of Goethe's student years in Leipzig are, for the most part, time-bound, occasional verse in which realistic emotion, feeling, and perception are subordinated to the artificial conventions and devices of the time. Typical motifs and themes of the collection *New Poems* are wine, Rococo eroticism, the game of love with its hidden dangers, stylized pastoral representations of nature, and a peculiarly playful association of love and death. Individual poems often move on the border between sensuality and morality, mirroring the prevailing social patterns. Especially characteristic is the employment of language that magnifies the separation of the world of the poem from experienced reality. In their affirmation of the elegant facades, the deliberate aloofness, the uncommitted playfulness of Rococo culture, these lyrics document Goethe's early artistic attitudes, even though they reveal little of his unique poetic gift.

STRASBOURG PERIOD

Under the influence of Herder in Strasbourg, Goethe began to move from the Decadent artificiality of his Leipzig songs. A new appreciation for the value of originality, immediacy of feeling, unmediated involvement in nature, and directness of approach is apparent in creations that are notable for their vivid imagery, plastic presentation of substance, force of expression, and power of language and rhythm.

Two types of utterance dominate the verse of this period. Highly personal outpourings of the soul, in which the representation of love is more passionate, serious, and captivating than in the Leipzig productions, are couched in formal stanzas that arose from Goethe's fondness for Friederike Brion. Free-verse poems that focus on Storm and Stress ideals of individuality, genius, and creativity reflect the lyrical influence of Pindar and the dramatic legacy of Shakespeare in their form and tone. In what they reveal of Goethe's worldview, the love poetry and the philosophical reflections are deeply intertwined. Without love, Goethe's perception of life is empty; without the depth of awareness of individual responsibility in creation, love loses its strength and vitality. Love forms the basis for the experience of nature, while the external surroundings with their beauties, tensions, conflicts, and potential for joy give full meaning to love.

The most important new feature of the Strasbourg poetry is the visible emphasis on existential polarities in the description of the poet's relationship to people and things. Love and suffering, defiance and submission, danger and ecstasy are juxtaposed in the portrayal of a world of change, growth, and struggle. In endless variation, Goethe offers the intimate revelation of loneliness, longing, and lack of final fulfillment that are the fundamental ingredients of life viewed as a pattern of restless wanderings. The very acts of searching, striving, creating, and loving are communicated with an energy and a spiritual intensity that carries the reader along in a rush of emotional participation in universal experience.

THE LILI POEMS

Among Goethe's most interesting early works are the sometimes tender, often intensely painful lyric documents of his courtship of Lili Schönemann. Few in number, these writings illustrate the poet's cathartic use of his talent in a process of self-analysis and clarification of his position with respect to external events. At the same time, they underscore a growing tendency to come to grips with and master life through his art. Consisting of occasional pieces that are connected by recurring themes related to the tension between the attractions of love and the devastating torments of an accompanying loss of freedom, the Lili poems combine visions of joy with ironically biting yet dismal portraits of despair. A gem of the period is the famous "Auf dem See" ("On the Lake"), a vivid projection of both physical and spiritual flight from oppressive love, written in Switzerland, where Goethe had taken temporary refuge from the demands of life with Lili.

WEIMAR PERIOD

During Goethe's first years in Weimar, the frustrations of an unsatisfying association with Charlotte von Stein, the all-consuming responsibilities of the court, and his own inability to overcome completely the break with Lili contributed to his lyrics a new preoccupation with themes of melancholy resignation and self-denial. The heavy moods that characterize his works of this period inform short meditative poems as well as longer philosophical reflections, mournful love songs, and a few haunting ballads. Especially profound are two eight-line stanzas, each titled "Wanderers Nachtlied" ("Wanderer's Night Song"), in which the poet longs for and admonishes himself to courage, comfort, hope, belief, and patience. "Warum gabst du uns die tiefen Blicke?" ("Why Did You Give Us the Deep Glances ?"), the most powerful of his poems to Charlotte von Stein, presents love as a mystical mystery. The two dramatic ballads, "Erlkönig" ("Elf King") and "Der Fischer" ("The Fisherman"), emphasize humanity's psychological subjection to the demonic power of its own impressions of nature.

ITALIAN JOURNEY

The experience of Italy completely changed Goethe's poetry. Among the most important developments that the journey inspired were the abandonment of suggestion and tone in favor of pure image, the transition from lyrical song to epic description, and the replacement of extended elaboration of worldview with terse epigrams and short didactic verse. During Goethe's classical period, his ballads achieved perfected form, while his depictions of nature attained their final goal in brightness and joyful plasticity. Where earlier poems feature colors that flow softly together, or points of color that invoke mood and an impression of the whole, the works created after 1790 are dominated by structure and the placement of objects in space. Ideas are presented in classical meters, especially hexameter, and as a result confessional poetry loses much of its melody.

ELEGIES, EPIGRAMS, AND BALLADS

Three groups of poems are particularly representative of the new directions in Goethe's lyrics: *Roman Elegies*, the epigrams, and the classical ballads. In their rich mural presentation of the poet's life in Rome, the *Roman Elegies* document the author's increasing tendency to circumscribe his own existence in verse, while their form, style, and combination of classical dignity with inner lightheartedness reflect the direct influence of Ovid, Catullus, and Propertius. The poems of *Venetian Epigrams* were similarly motivated by direct exposure to elements of classical Italian culture. They are especially notable for their rich imagery and their realism in depicting the emotional intensity of the poet's longing for Germany. In structure and style, they were models for the more famous epigrams written by Goethe and Schiller in 1796. Unlike the elegies and epigrams, Goethe's powerful ballads of 1797 arose out of materials that he had carried within him for a long time. The lyrical and melodic aspects that are absent from the other forms remain strong in rhythmic creations that emphasize passion and excitement while developing themes related to the classical ideal of pure humanity. Goethe viewed the ballad as an archetypal lyric form. His "Die Braut von Korinth" ("The Bride of Corinth") and "Der Gott und die Bajadere" ("The God and the Bayadere") are among the greatest German ballads ever written.

Poetry of later years

The erotic poetry of Goethe's old age had its beginnings in a group of sonnets that he wrote to Minchen Herzlieb in 1807. During the seven years that followed their creation, he wrote verse only occasionally. At last, however, the combination of stimuli from the deeply meaningful love affair with Marianne von Willemer and exposure to the works of Hafiz moved him to compose his greatest poetic accomplishment, *West-Eastern Divan*. In the framework of a fantasy journey of rejuvenation, Goethe entered a friendly competition with Hafiz while simultaneously declaring his own newly regained inner freedom. The central themes of the collection include longing for renewal of life, recognition of the need for spiritual transformation, coming to grips with Hafiz as a poet, love, wine, worldly experience, paradise, looking upward to God, and looking downward to the human condition. In some of the poems, Goethe returned to a kind of Anacreontic love poetry. In the heart of the cycle, he made of Hatem and Suleika timeless archetypal models for man and woman bound in the love relationship.

After *West-Eastern Divan*, Goethe wrote only a few poems of consequence. Among them, "Uworte, Orphisch" ("Primeval Words, Orphic"), in which he attempted to develop the core problems of human existence in five eight-line stanzas, and "Trilogie der Leidenschaft" ("Trilogy of Passion"), a tragic document of the state of being unfulfilled that was inspired by his final love experience, attained the power and stature of earlier lyrics. In these two creations, Goethe pinpointed once more the essence of his own spiritual struggle between the light and the night of human existence.

"Welcome and Farewell"

While living in Strasbourg and courting Friederike Brion, Goethe created for the first time sensitive love poetry and descriptions of nature that exude the vitality of immediate experience. Perhaps the most characteristic of these works is the famous "Willkommen und Abschied" ("Welcome and Farewell"). The substance of the poem is a night ride through the countryside to Sesenheim and a joyful reunion with Friederike, followed by a painful scene of parting when morning comes. Significant elements include a new and plastic rendering of nature, fresh and captivating imagery, and melodic language that is alive with rhythm and motion. A special power of observation is demonstrated in the poet's representation of that which cannot or can hardly be seen, yet the scenery is not portrayed merely for its own sake; rather, it is symbolic, for the uncanny aspects of the ride through the darkness are overcome by a courageous heart that is driven by love. Landscape and love thus become the two poles of the poem generating an inner tension that culminates in a peculiar equation of the beloved with the world as a whole. The portrayal of Friederike is especially notable for its psychological depth, while the expression of Goethe's own feelings of passion and eventual guilt lends the entire picture qualities of a universal experience of the heart.

"PROMETHEUS" AND "GANYMED"

Deeply personal yet broadly valid content is also typical of the so-called genius poems of Goethe's Storm and Stress period. The intensity of emotional extremes is particularly vivid in the sharply contrasting hymns "Prometheus" and "Ganymed," which reflect the poles of Goethe's own spirit even more strongly than do his dramas. In depicting the two mythological titans, the poet concentrated on the creation of dynamic archetypes. "Prometheus" is a hard, even harsh portrait of modern humanity. The speaker of the lines is loveless and alone. Emphasis is placed on "I"; the focus is inward and limiting. In his defiant rejection of Father Zeus and the attendant process of self-deification, Prometheus champions the value of individuality and independence. Important themes of his declaration of emancipation from gods who are less powerful than humans include faith in self, belief in the power of action, knowledge of the difficulty and questionability of life, and the divinity of humans' creative nature. The tone of "Ganymed" is completely different. In the soft language of a prayer, the title figure proclaims his total submission to the will of the Father and his desire to return to the divine presence. A new side of Goethe's religiosity is revealed in the transformation of his sensitivity to nature into a longing for God's love. The central concern is no longer "I" but "you"; the direction is outward toward the removal of all boundaries in a coming together of deity and humankind. In the manner in which they play off the real world against the ideal realm, "Prometheus" and "Ganymed" are especially representative of the existential polarity lyrics that Goethe wrote during the pre-Weimar years.

ROMAN ELEGIES

Roman Elegies, the major lyrical product of Goethe's first Italian journey, comprises twenty confessional hexameter poems knit tightly together in a cycle that documents the poet's love for a fictitious young widow (Christiane Vulpius in Roman disguise). Two primary thematic configurations dominate creations that are among Goethe's most beautiful, most sensuously erotic works. The story of the tender love affair with Faustine, integrated into the Italian framework, is played off against the problems associated with renewal and adaptation of antiquity by the modern poet. Within this context, love becomes the key that makes entry into the Roman world possible.

Lively, direct reflection of the writer's enthusiasm for Rome sets the tone for the cycle. At the center of the introductory elegy, which forms an overture to the love adventure, there is a longing for the beloved who gives the city its true character. This yearning is followed in the next segment by a cynical glance backward at the boredom of Weimar society, which is in turn contrasted with the first report of the developing amorous relationship. An attempt to idealize the new situation, focusing specifically on the rapidity with which Faustine gives herself, leads to the elaboration of the described experiences in the light of ancient mythological gods. Through the creation of a new goddess, "Opportunity," as a symbol for the woman he loves, Goethe effectively connects the motifs of the sequence with classical themes. The fifth elegy provides the first high point in the poetic chain with its projection of the spirit of the author's existence in Rome as a blend of antiquity, art, and the erotic, which mutually illuminate, intensify, and legitimize each other to yield a true "life of the gods." Other important sections of the cycle touch on questions of jealousy, gossip about the lovers, a Homeric idyll of the hearth, and a variety of encounters with Rome and its traditions, history, and secrets. Elegy thirteen is especially interesting for the tension that it establishes between the demands of lyric art and those of love for Faustine. A dialogue between Amor and the poet develops the idea that the former provides plenty of material for poetry but does not allow enough time for creative activity. Colorful pictures of the joys of love culminate in imagery of the couple's morning awakening together in bed. There is grand irony in the fact that the lament about not having enough time to write becomes a magnificent poem in itself.

Throughout the collection, love is the focus of polar conflicts on several levels. The intense need for unity with Faustine in the physical alliance is juxtaposed to the act of self-denial that provides the quiet enjoyment of pure observation and contemplation in the creative process. Within the social frame, the fulfilled love that is sought and attained cannot be brought into harmony with reality. Fear of discovery necessitates disguise of the beloved, deception of relatives, secret meetings, and isolation from the surrounding world. In the final elegy, however, Goethe is forced to conclude that the beautiful secret of his love cannot remain hidden for long because he himself is incapable of remaining quiet about it. The result is a many-faceted revelation of love as a timeless human situation.

BALLADS

Careful examination of Goethe's most representative ballads reveals a clear progression from verse stories in which humans are at the mercy of a potentially destructive, magically powerful natural world to lyric accounts that proclaim the supremacy of the human spirit over the restrictions of mortal experience. Influenced by the popular pattern established in Gottfried August Bürger's "Lenore," Goethe's early ballads such as "Elf King" and "The Fisherman" describe the fatal resolution of inner conflicts in terms of individual surrender to seductive impressions of external reality. Later, philosophically more complex works ("The Bride of Corinth" and "The God and the Bayadere") portray death as a process of transcendence that purifies the individual while preparing the soul for joyful fulfillment on a higher plane of existence.

"Elf King" is somewhat similar to "Welcome and Farewell" in its representation of a night landscape's malevolent lure as it impresses its terror on the minds of those who encounter it. The substance of the narrative is the homeward night ride of a father and son; the darkness gives uncanny form and life to things that would appear harmless by day. The boy, who is ill with fever, believes that he hears the elf king enticing him, describes what he sees and feels to his father, and dies of fright when the older man's reassurances fail to convince him of the falseness of his delirious vision. Rhythmic language that conveys the beat of the horse's hooves through the countryside, immediacy created by dialogues involving the child, the phantom elf king, and the father, and moods evoked by contrasts between light and shadow, intimate fear and pale comfortings, all contribute to the psychological intensity of a presentation in which the poet attempted to find accurate formulation for the fantastic, indefinite problem of human destiny.

In "The God and the Bayadere," a confrontation with death is handled much differently. The legend of the prostitute who spends a night providing the pleasures of love to the god Siva in human form, only to awaken and find him dead on the bed, is a forceful lyrical statement about the redeeming properties of love. Denied her widow's rights because of her way of life, the bayadere makes good her claim by springing into the flames that arise from the funeral pyre. In response to this act of purification, Siva accepts the woman as his bride. Strong Christian overtones exist in the first stanza's emphasis on the god's humaneness and in the obvious parallels to the relationship between Christ and Mary Magdalene. The poem's thrust is that the divine spark is present even in a degraded individual and that even the lowest human being can be transformed and exalted through the cleansing influence of pure love.

WEST-EASTERN DIVAN

A major key to the literary productions of Goethe's old age is found in the notion of personal fulfillment through direct sensual and spiritual enjoyment of life. The implications of that approach to experience are most thoroughly and splendidly elaborated in *West-Eastern Divan*, a carefully constructed collection of verse that attempts to blend and join the artistic legacies of East and West in a book about love in all its manifestations. Both the pinnacle of Goethe's lyric oeuvre and one of the most difficult of his creative works, *West-Eastern Divan* is a conscious declaration of the validity of humanity's unending search for joy in the world.

As revealed in the opening poem, the focal metaphor of the volume is the Hegira, which Goethe uses as an image for his flight from oppressive circumstances into the ideal realm of foreign art. Two central relationships dominate the twelve sections of his dream journey to the Orient. On one level, the individual poems are portions of a playful fantasy dialogue between Goethe and his Eastern counterpart Hafiz. The object of their interchange is a friendly competition in which the Western poet seeks to match the achievements of a revered predecessor. Conversations between two lovers, Hatem and Suleika, develop the second complex of themes, derived from elements of the love experience shared by Goethe and Marianne von Willemer.

"Buch des Sängers" ("Book of the Singer"), the most important of the first six cycles, sets the tone for the entire work. In the famous poem "Selige Sehnsucht" ("Blessed Longing"), Goethe explored the mystery of how one gains strength through the transformation that occurs as a result of sacrifice. Borrowing from a ghazel by Hafiz the motif of the soul that is consumed in the fire of love like a moth in a candle flame, he created a profound comment on the necessity of metamorphosis to eternal progress. The uniting of two people in love to generate the greatest possible joy is made to stand for the longing of the soul to be freed from the bonds of individuality through union with the infinite. The antithesis of "Blessed Longing" is presented in "Wiederfinden" ("Reunion"), a creation of extremely vivid imagery from "Buch Suleika" ("Book of Suleika"), the eighth and most beautiful section of *West-Eastern Divan*. Based on Goethe's separation from Marianne and their coming together again, the poem develops the idea that parting and rediscovery are the essence of universal existence. In a uniquely powerful projection of creation as division of light from darkness and their recombination in color, Goethe produced new and exciting symbols for love's power, rendered in lines that form a high point in German lyric poetry.

OTHER MAJOR WORKS

LONG FICTION: *Die Leiden des jungen Werthers*, 1774 (*The Sorrows of Young Werther*, 1779); *Wilhelm Meisters Lehrjahre*, 1795-1796 (4 volumes; *Wilhelm Meister's Apprenticeship*, 1825); *Die Wahlverwandtschaften*, 1809 (*Elective Affinities*, 1849); *Wilhelm Meisters Wanderjahre: Oder, Die Entsagenden*, 1821, 1829 (2 volumes; *Wilhelm Meister's Travels*, 1827).

SHORT FICTION: *Unterhaltungen deutscher Ausgewanderten*, 1795 (*Conversations of German Emigrants*, 1854); *Novelle*, 1826 (*Novel*, 1837).

PLAYS: *Götz von Berlichingen mit der eisernen Hand*, pb. 1773 (*Goetz of Berlichingen, with the Iron Hand*, 1799); *Clavigo*, pr., pb. 1774 (English translation, 1798,

1897); *Götter, Helden und Wieland*, pb. 1774; *Erwin und Elmire*, pr., pb. 1775 (libretto; music by Duchess Anna Amalia of Saxe-Weimar); *Claudine von Villa Bella*, pb. 1776 (second version pb. 1788; libretto); *Die Geschwister*, pr. 1776; *Stella*, pr., pb. 1776 (second version pr. 1806; English translation, 1798); *Iphigenie auf Tauris*, pr. 1779 (second version pb. 1787; *Iphigenia in Tauris*, 1793); *Die Laune des Verliebten*, pr. 1779 (wr. 1767; *The Wayward Lover*, 1879); *Jery und Bätely*, pr. 1780 (libretto); *Die Mitschuldigen*, pr. 1780 (first version wr. 1768, second version wr. 1769; *The Fellow-Culprits*, 1879); *Die Fischerin*, pr., pb. 1782 (libretto; music by Corona Schröter; *The Fisherwoman*, 1899); *Scherz, List und Rache*, pr. 1784 (libretto); *Der Triumph der Empfindsamkeit*, pb. 1787; *Egmont*, pb. 1788 (English translation, 1837); *Faust: Ein Fragment*, pb. 1790 (*Faust: A Fragment*, 1980); *Torquato Tasso*, pb. 1790 (English translation, 1827); *Der Gross-Cophta*, pr., pb. 1792; *Der Bürgergeneral*, pr., pb. 1793; *Was wir bringen*, pr., pb. 1802; *Die natürliche Tochter*, pr. 1803 (*The Natural Daughter*, 1885); *Pandora*, pb. 1808; *Faust: Eine Tragödie*, pb. 1808 (*The Tragedy of Faust*, 1823); *Des Epimenides Erwachen*, pb. 1814; *Faust: Eine Tragödie, zweiter Teil*, pb. 1833 (*The Tragedy of Faust, Part Two*, 1838); *Die Wette*, pb. 1837 (wr. 1812).

NONFICTION: *Von deutscher Baukunst*, 1773 (*On German Architecture*, 1921); *Versuch die Metamorphose der Pflanzen zu erklären*, 1790 (*Essays on the Metamorphosis of Plants*, 1863); *Beyträge zur Optik*, 1791, 1792 (2 volumes); *Winckelmann und sein Jahrhundert*, 1805; *Zur Farbenlehre*, 1810 (*Theory of Colors*, 1840); *Aus meinem Leben: Dichtung und Wahrheit*, 1811-1814 (3 volumes; *The Autobiography of Goethe*, 1824; better known as *Poetry and Truth from My Own Life*); *Italienische Reise*, 1816, 1817 (2 volumes; *Travels in Italy*, 1883); *Zur Naturwissenschaft überhaupt, besonders zur Morphologie*, 1817 , 1824 (2 volumes); *Die Belagerung von Mainz, 1793*, 1822 (*The Siege of Mainz in the Year 1793*, 1849); *Campagne in Frankreich, 1792*, 1822 (*Campaign in France in the Year 1792*, 1849); *Essays on Art*, 1845; *Goethe's Literary Essays*, 1921.

MISCELLANEOUS: *Works*, 1848-1890 (14 volumes); *Goethes Werke*, 1887-1919 (133 volumes); *Goethe on Art*, 1980.

BIBLIOGRAPHY

Armstrong, John. *Love, Life, Goethe: Lessons of the Imagination from the Great German Poet*. New York: Farrar, Straus and Giroux, 2007. Goethe's works are analyzed and his life examined in this comprehensive volume. Armstrong discusses a wide range of Goethe's writings, including his lesser known works, and gives a close study of his personal life. Knowing German and English, he provides translations of several key passages, while keeping his writing style plain and clear. This volume offers readers a better understanding of Goethe's writing, and the circumstances that inspired it.

Atkins, Stuart. *Essays on Goethe*. Columbia, S.C.: Camden House, 1995. Essays on the apprentice novelist and other topics, by the preeminent Goethe scholar.

Boyle, Nicholas. *Goethe: The Poet and the Age, Volume I: The Poetry of Desire (1749-1790)*. Oxford, England: Clarendon Press, 1991. A monumental scholarly biography. See the index of Goethe's works.

_____. *Revolution and Renunciation (1790-1803)*. Volume 2 in *Goethe: The Poet and the Age*. New York: Oxford University Press, 2000. This second volume covers only the next thirteen years of Goethe's life. Boyle's extensive discussion of the Wilhelm Meister novels and Goethe's drama *Faust* is set amid a period of radical political and social change, fallout from the French Revolution.

Kerry, Paul E. *Enlightenment Thought in the Writings of Goethe: A Contribution to the History of Ideas*. Rochester, N.Y.: Camden House, 2001. An examination of the philosophy that filled Goethe's writings. Bibliography and index.

Swales, Martin, and Erika Swales. *Reading Goethe: A Critical Introduction to the Literary Work*. Rochester, N.Y.: Camden House, 2002. A critical analysis of Goethe's literary output. Bibliography and index.

Wagner, Irmgard. *Goethe*. New York: Twayne, 1999. An excellent, updated introduction to the author and his works. Includes bibliographical references and an index.

Weisinger, Kenneth D. *The Classical Facade: A Nonclassical Reading of Goethe's Classicism*. University Park: Pennsylvania State University Press, 1988. The works covered by this interesting volume all come from the middle period of Goethe's life. In his analysis, Weisinger searches for a kinship between *Faust* and Goethe's classic works. The author asserts that all these classic works share a nonclassic common theme: the disunity of the modern world.

Williams, John R. *The Life of Goethe: A Critical Biography*. Malden, Mass.: Blackwell, 1998. An extensive examination of the major writings, including lyric poems, drama, and novels. Includes a discussion of epigrams, aphorisms, satires, libretti, and masquerades. Discusses Goethe's personal and literary reactions to historical events in Germany, his relationship with leading public figures of his day, and his influence on contemporary culture. Suggests that Goethe's creative work follows a distinct biographical profile. Includes large bibliography.

Lowell A. Bangerter

HEINRICH HEINE

Born: Düsseldorf, Prussia (now in Germany); December 13, 1797
Died: Paris, France; February 17, 1856
Also known as: Christian Johann Heinrich Heine

PRINCIPAL POETRY

Gedichte, 1822 (*Poems*, 1937)
Tragödien, nebst einem lyrischen Intermezzo, 1823 (*Tragedies, Together with Lyric Intermezzo*, 1905)
Buch der Lieder, 1827 (*Book of Songs*, 1856)
Deutschland: Ein Wintermärchen, 1844 (*Germany: A Winter's Tale*, 1892)
Neue Gedichte, 1844 (8 volumes; *New Poems*, 1858)
Atta Troll, 1847 (English translation, 1876)
Ein Sommernachtstraum, 1847 (*A Midsummer Night's Dream*, 1876)
Romanzero, 1851 (English translation, 1859)
Gedichte, 1851-1857 (4 volumes; *Poems*, 1937)
Letzte Gedichte und Gedanken, 1869 (*Last Poems and Thoughts*, 1937)
Atta Troll, and Other Poems, 1876 (includes *Atta Troll* and *A Midsummer Night's Dream*)
Heinrich Heine: The Poems, 1937
The Complete Poems of Heinrich Heine, 1982

OTHER LITERARY FORMS

Although Heinrich Heine (HI-nuh) is best remembered for his verse, he also made significant contributions to the development of the feuilleton and the political essay in Germany. Experiments with prose accelerated his rise to fame as a writer. Among the most important of his nonfiction works are *Reisebilder* (1826-1831 ; *Pictures of Travel*, 1855), a series of witty essays that are spiced with poetic imagination and penetrating social commentary; *Zur Geschichte der neueren schönen Litteratur in Deutschland* (1833; *Letters Auxiliary to the History of Modern Polite Literature in Germany*, 1836), which was later republished and expanded as *Die romantische Schule* (1836; *The Romantic School*, 1876) and constitutes Heine's personal settlement with German Romanticism; *Französische Zustände* (1833; *French Affairs*, 1889), a collection of sensitive newspaper articles about the contemporary political situation in France; and *Vermischte Schriften* (1854), a group of primarily political essays.

Heine's attempts to create in other genres were unsuccessful. During his student years in Berlin, he began a novel, *Der Rabbi von Bacherach* (1887; *The Rabbi of Bacherach*, 1891), but it remained a fragment. Two dramas, *Almansor* and *William*

Heinrich Heine
(Library of Congress)

Ratliff, published in *Tragedies, Together with Lyric Intermezzo*, failed on the stage, although *William Ratliff* was later employed by Pietro Mascagni as the basis of an opera.

ACHIEVEMENTS

Second only to Johann Wolfgang von Goethe in impact on the history of German lyric poetry in the nineteenth century, Heinrich Heine was unquestionably the most controversial poet of his time. He was a major representative of the post-Romantic literary crisis and became the most renowned love poet in Europe after Petrarch, yet for decades he was more celebrated abroad than in Germany. Anti-Semitism and negative reactions to his biting satire, to his radical inclinations, and to his seemingly unpatriotic love of France combined to prevent any consistent approbation in Heine's homeland. Nevertheless, he became the first Jewish author to break into the mainstream of German literature in modern times.

Heine's poetic reputation is based primarily on *Book of Songs*, which went through twelve editions during his lifetime. The collection achieved immediate popularity with the public and was well received by critics; since 1827, it has been translated into more than fifty languages. Lyrics that became part of the *Book of Songs* were set to music as early as 1822, and within a year after the book appeared, Franz Schubert used six poems from the "Heimkehr" ("Homecoming") section in his famous cycle *Schwanengesang* (1828; "Swan Song"). Robert Schumann's *Dichterliebe* (1840; love poems) features musical settings for sixteen poems from *Tragedies, Together with Lyric Intermezzo.* By 1840, Heine's works had become prime texts for German songs. In all, more than three thousand pieces of music have been written for the creations of Heine's early period.

In 1835, four years after he went into self-imposed exile in France, Heine's works were banned in Germany, along with the writings of the social reform and literary movement Junges Deutschland (Young Germany). The critics rejected him as a bad influence on Germany's youth. His immediate popularity waned as conflicts with government censors increased. In the late nineteenth century, attempts to reclaim his works for German literature touched off riots, yet by then his enchanting lyrics had become so ingrained in German culture that it was impossible to expel them. The measure of Heine's undying significance for German poetry is perhaps the fact that even the Nazis, who formally prohibited his works once again, could not exclude his poems completely from their anthologies of songs.

BIOGRAPHY

Heinrich Heine was born Chaim Harry Heine, the son of a Jewish merchant. He spent his early years working toward goals set for him by his family. His secondary education ended in 1814 when he left the Düsseldorf Lyceum without being graduated. After failing in two apprenticeships in Frankfurt, he was sent to Hamburg to prepare for a career in commerce under the direction of a wealthy uncle. While there, he fell in love with his cousin Amalie. This unfulfilled relationship was a stimulus for verse that the young poet published in a local periodical. In 1818, his uncle set him up in a retailing enterprise, but within a year Harry Heine and Co. was bankrupt. Acknowledging that his nephew was unsuited for business, Uncle Salomon at last agreed to underwrite his further education.

Between 1819 and 1825, Heine studied in Bonn, Berlin, and Göttingen. His university years were very important for his development as a poet. While in Bonn, he attended lectures given by August Wilhelm von Schlegel, whose interest in his work stimulated Heine's creativity. In the fall of 1820, he moved to Göttingen. Besides law, he studied German history and philology until January, 1821, when he challenged another student to a duel and was expelled from the university. He continued his studies in Berlin and was rapidly accepted into prominent literary circles. Included among the writers with whom he associated were Adelbert von Chamisso, Friedrich Schleiermacher, and Christian Dietrich Grabbe. Rahel von Varnhagen helped in the publication of Heine's first collection of poems in 1822, and he quickly became known as a promising talent.

During a visit to Hamburg in 1823, he met Julius Campe, who afterward published all Heine's works except a few commissioned essays that he wrote in Paris. Literary success persuaded him away from the study of law, but at his uncle's request Heine returned to Göttingen to complete work toward his degree. In the summer of 1825, he passed his examinations, though not with distinction. To facilitate a public career, he was baptized a Protestant, at which time he changed his name to Heinrich.

Travel was a significantly formative experience for Heine. Vacations in Cuxhaven and Norderney provided initial powerful impressions of the sea that informed the two North Sea cycles of the *Book of Songs*. Journeys through the Harz Mountains in 1824, to England in 1827, and to Italy the following year provided material for the *Pictures of Travel* series that elevated him to the literary mainstream of his time. Exposure to foreign points of view also aroused his interest in current political questions and led to a brief involvement as coeditor of Johann Friedrich von Cotta's *Politische Annalen* in Munich in 1827 and 1828.

When continued efforts to obtain permission to practice law in Hamburg failed, Heine moved to Paris in 1831, where he began to write articles for French and German newspapers and journals. Heine loved Paris, and during the next few years friendships with Honoré de Balzac, Victor Hugo, George Sand, Giacomo Meyerbeer, and other writers, artists, and composers contributed to his sense of well-being. When the German Federal Diet banned his writings, making it impossible for him to continue contributing to German periodicals, the French government granted him a modest pension.

The 1840's were a stormy period in Heine's life. In 1841, he married Cresence Eugénie Mirat (whom he called Mathilde), his mistress of seven years. Her lack of education and understanding of his writings placed a strain on their relationship and later contributed to the poet's increasing isolation from his friends. After returning from Hamburg in 1843, Heine met Karl Marx. Their association sharpened Heine's political attitudes and increased his aggressive activism. Salomon Heine's death in 1844 unleashed between the writer and his cousins a struggle for the inheritance. Eventually they reached an accommodation that guaranteed an annuity in exchange for Heine's promise not to criticize family members in his writings.

After a collapse in 1848, Heine spent his remaining years in unceasing pain. An apparent venereal disease attacked his nervous system, leaving him paralyzed. Physical infirmities, however, did not stifle his creative spirit, and from the torment and loneliness of his "mattress grave," he wrote some of the best poetry of his career.

ANALYSIS

Unlike many poets, Heinrich Heine never stated a formal theory of poetry that could serve as a basis for interpreting his works and measuring his creative development. For that reason, confusion and critical controversy have clouded the picture of his oeuvre, resulting in misunderstandings of his literary orientation and intentions. The general concept that he was a poet of experience is, at the very least, an oversimplification. To be sure, immediate personal observations of life were a consistent stimulus for Heine's writing, yet his product is not simply a stylized reproduction of individual encounters with reality. Each poem reveals a reflective processing of unique perceptions of people, milieus, and events that transforms seemingly specific descriptions into generally valid representations of humankind's confrontation with the times. The poet's ability to convey, with penetrating exactitude, feelings, existential problems, and elements of the human condition that correspond to the concerns and apperceptions of a broad readership enabled him to generate lyrics that belong more to the poetry of ideas than to the poetry of experience.

A characteristic of Heine's thought and verse is a purposeful poetic tension between the individual and the world. The dissonance between the artistic sensibility and reality is presented in unified constructs that represent qualities that were missing from the poet's era: unity, form, constancy, and continuity. By emphasizing condition rather than event, Heine was able to offer meaningful illustrations in the juxtaposition of antithetical concepts: sunny milieu and melancholy mood, pain and witticism, affirmation and negation, enchantment of feeling and practical wisdom of experience, enthusiasm and pessimism, love and hate, spirit and reality, tradition and anticipation of the future. The magic and power of his verse arise from his ability to clothe these dynamic conflicts in deceptively simple, compact forms, pure melodic sounds and rhythms, and playfully witty treatments of theme, substance, motif, and detail.

More than anything else, Heine was a poet of mood. His greatest strengths were his sensitivity and his capacity to analyze, create, and manipulate feeling. A colorful interchange of disillusionment, scorn, cynicism, rebellion, blasphemy, playful mockery, longing, and melancholy is the essence of his appeal to the reader's spirit. The goal, however, is not the arousal of emotion but rather the intensification of awareness, achieved by drawing the audience into a desired frame of feeling, then shattering the illusion in a breach of mood that typifies Heine's poetry.

Although he was not a true representative of any single German literary movement, Heine wrote poems that reflect clear relationships to definite intellectual and artistic traditions. Both the German Enlightenment and German Romanticism provided him with important models. In matters of form, attitude, and style, he was a child of the Enlightenment. Especially visible are his epigrammatic technique and the tendency toward didactic exemplification and pointed representation. Gotthold Ephraim Lessing was his favorite among Enlightenment authors. Heine combined the technical aspects of Enlightenment literary approach with a pronounced Romantic subjectivity in the handling of substance, theme, and motif, particularly in the examination of self, pain, experience, and condition. The absolute status of the self is a prominent characteristic of his works. In the emancipation of self, however, he carried the thoughtful exploration of personal individuality a step beyond that of the early Romantics and in so doing separated himself from them. Other Romantic traits in his lyrics include a dreamy fantasy of feeling and a pronounced element of irony. Where Friedrich Schlegel employed irony to transcend the restrictive material world and unite humankind with a spiritual cosmos, Heine used it to expand the self to encompass the cosmos. The feature of Romanticism with which Heine most consciously identified was the inclination of Joseph von Eichendorff and others toward simple musical poems modeled on the German folk song. Heine specifically acknowledged the influence of Wilhelm Müller, whose cultivation of pure sound and clear simplicity most closely approximated his own poetic ideal.

In many respects, the polish of language and form that marked Heine's *Book of Songs* was never surpassed in later collections. At most a strengthening of intonation, an increase in wit, a maturing of the intellect subtly and gradually enhanced his writings with the passing years. Nevertheless, his literary career can be divided into four distinct phases with regard to material focus and poetic concern.

EARLY YEARS

Heine's initial creative period encompassed his university years and reached its peak in the mid-1820's. In *Poems*, the cycle of verse in *Tragedies, Together with Lyric Intermezzo*, and, finally, *Book of Songs*, the young poet opened a world of personal subjectivity at the center of which is a self that undergoes unceasing examination. Consciousness of the self, its suffering and loneliness, is the essence of melodic compositions that include poems of unrequited love, lyrical mood pictures, satires, romances, confessions, and parodies. Lines and stanzas deftly reflect Heine's ability to feel his way into nature, the magic of legend, and the spiritual substance of humankind, while the poetic world remains a fragmentary manifestation of the subjective truthfulness of the moment.

THE SELF AS A MIRROR OF THE TIMES

A major change in orientation coincided with Heine's move to Paris. The political upheaval in France and the death of Goethe signaled the end of an artistic era, and Heine looked forward to the possibility of a different literature that would replace the subjectivity of Romanticism with a new stress on life, time, and reality. He was especially attracted to the Saint-Simonian religion, which inspired within him a hope for a modern doctrine that would offer a new balance between Judeo-Christian ideals and those of classical antiquity. The lyrics in *New Poems*, the major document of this period, reveal a shift in emphasis from the self per se to the self as a mirror of the times. Heine's poetry of the 1830's is shallower than his earlier creations, yet it effectively presents the inner turmoil, confusion, and splintering of the era as Heine experienced it. Accompanying a slightly faded reprise of earlier themes is a new view of the poet as a heathen cosmopolitan who affirms material reality and champions the moment as having eternal value.

POLITICAL RADICALIZATION

The third stage in Heine's career is best described as a period of political radicalization. It most visibly affected his poetry during the mid-1840's, the time of his friendship with Marx. In the aggressively satirical epics *Atta Troll* and *Germany: A Winter's Tale*, he paired sharp criticism of contemporary conditions with revelations of his love for Germany, specifically attacking his own critics, radical literature, militant nationalism, student organizations, the German hatred of the French , the fragmented condition of the German nation, and almost everything else that was valued by the establishment.

LAST OF THE ROMANTICS

Profound isolation and intense physical pain provided the catalyst for a final poetic reorientation after Heine's physical collapse in 1848. Some of the poems that he wrote in his "mattress grave" are among his greatest masterpieces; they reflect a new religiosity in spiritual penetration of the self. In *Romanzero* and other late poems, the poet becomes a kind of martyr, experiencing the world's illness in his own heart. The act of suffering generates a poetry of bleak glosses of the human condition, heartrending laments, and songs about death unequaled in German literature.

Although Heine styled himself the last of the Romantics, a significant difference in approach to substance distinguishes his early poems from those of the Romantic movement. Where Clemens Maria Brentano and Eichendorff celebrated existence as it opened itself to them, Heine sang of a life that had closed its doors, shutting him out. The dominant themes of his *Book of Songs* are longing and suffering as aspects of the experience of disappointed love. Combining the sentimental pessimism of Lord Byron with the objective portrayal of tangible reality, he succeeded in exploring love's frustrations and pain more effectively, more impressively, and more imaginatively than any of his forerunners and contemporaries had done. In dream images, songs, romances, and sonnets that employ Romantic materials yet remain suspicious of the feelings that they symbolize, the poet transformed the barrier that he felt existed between himself and the world into deceptively simple, profoundly valid treatments of universal problems.

BOOK OF SONGS

The poems of *Book of Songs* are extraordinarily flexible, self-contained productions that derive their charm from the combination of supple form and seemingly directly experienced and personally felt content. Colorful sketches of lime trees, an ancient bastion, a city pond, a whistling boy, gardens, people, fields, forests, a mill wheel, and an old tower contribute to a world of great fascination and sensual seduction. The verse is often bittersweet, however, focusing not on the sunny summer landscape but on the sadness of the poet who does not participate in a beauty that mocks him. The forceful presentation of the individual's isolation and conflict with the times represented a fresh direction in poetry that contributed greatly to Heine's early popularity. At the same time, the carefully constructed tension between the poet and his surroundings established a pattern that became characteristic of all his works.

An extremely important feature of these early lyrics is the break in mood that typically occurs at several levels, including tone, setting, and the lyricist's subjective interpretation of his situation. The tone frequently shifts from emotional to conversational, from delicate to blunt, while the settings of the imagination are shattered by the banal reality of modern society. As the poet analyzes his position vis-à-vis his milieu, his positive feeling is broken by frustration and defeat, his hope collapses beneath the awareness of his delusion, and his attraction to his beloved is marred by her unthinking cruelty. There is never any resolution of these conflicts, and the poem itself provides the only mediation between the writer and a hostile world.

Among the most exquisite compositions in *Book of Songs* are the rustically simple lyric paintings from "Die Harzreise" ("The Journey to the Harz") and the rhythmically powerful, almost mystical studies from the two cycles of "Die Nordsee" ("The North Sea"). Filled with the fairy-tale atmosphere of the Rhine and the Harz Mountains, "The Journey to the Harz" poems exemplify Heine's ability to capture the compelling musicality and inner tone of the folk song and to combine these elements with an overwhelming power of feeling in the formation of an intense poetry of mood. In "The North Sea," he cultivated a new kind of language, anticipating twentieth century verse in free rhythms that sounded the depths of elemental human experience. Constant motion, changing patterns of light , play of wind, and movement of ships and fish combine as parts of a unified basic form. Heine pinpointed the individuality of the ocean in a given moment, reproducing atmosphere with precision and intensifying impact through mythological or human ornamentation. The rolling flow of impression is a consistent product of Heine's poetic art in its finest form.

NEW POEMS

Two years after moving to Paris, Heine published *Letters Auxiliary to the History of Modern Polite Literature in Germany*, his most significant theoretical treatise on literature and a work that marked his formal break with Romanticism. The major poetic document of this transition to a more realistic brand of expression is *New Poems*, a less integrated collection than *Book of Songs*, containing both echoes of early themes and the first fruits of his increased political commitment of the 1840's. *New Poems* attests strongly a shift in approach and creative concern from poetry as an absolute to the demand for contemporary relevance.

The first cycle of *New Poems*, "Neuer Frühling" ("New Spring"), returns to the motifs that dominate the "Lyric Intermezzo" and "Homecoming" segments of *Book of Songs* yet presents them with greater polish and distance. New variations portray love as a distraction, a nuisance that causes emotional turmoil in the inherent knowledge of its transitoriness. The tone and direction of the entire volume are established in the prologue to "New Spring," in which the poet contrasts his own subjection to the hindering influence of love with the strivings of others in "the great struggle of the times."

Among the other sections of the book, "Verschiedene" ("Variae"), with its short cycles of rather acidic poems about the girls of Paris, its legendary ballad "Der Tannhäuser" ("Tannhäuser"), and its "Schöpfungslieder" ("Songs of Creation"), is the least coherent, most disturbing group of poems that Heine ever wrote. Campe, his publisher, decried the lyricist's creation of what he called "whore and chamber-pot stories" and was extremely reluctant to publish them. Nothing that Heine wrote, however, is without artistic value, and there are nuggets of brilliance even here. Despite its artificiality and seeming inconsistency with Heine's true poetic nature, "Tannhäuser," for example, must be regarded as one of his greatest masterpieces. The deeply psychological rejuvenation of the old folk epic, which served as the stimulus for Richard Wagner's opera, reflects the poet's all-encompassing and penetrating knowledge of the human heart.

"Zeitgedichte" ("Poems of the Times"), the concluding cycle in *New Poems*, sets the pattern for Heine's harsh political satire of the 1840's. Some of the lyrics were written expressly for Karl Marx's newspaper *Vorwärts*. Most of them are informed by homesickness, longing, and the bitter disappointment that Heine felt as the expected dawn of spiritual freedom in Germany failed to materialize in the evolution of a more cosmopolitan relationship with the rest of Europe. Powerful poems directed against cultural, social, and political dilettantes anticipate the incisively masterful tones of his most successful epics of the period, *Atta Troll* and *Germany: A Winter's Tale*; irreverent assaults on cherished institutions, superficial political activism, and his own critics accent his peculiar love-hate relationship with his homeland.

ROMANZERO

Regarded by many critics as Heine's finest collection of poems, *Romanzero* presents his final attempts to come to grips with his own mortality. Rich in their sophistication, more coherent in tone than the lyrics of *New Poems* or even the *Book of Songs*, the romances, laments, and melodies of *Romanzero* reveal the wit, irony, and epigrammatic style for which Heine is famous in the service of a new, peculiarly transparent penetration of the self. Dominant in the poems is the theme of death, which confronts the individual in many forms. A new religiosity is present in the acknowledgment of a personal God with whom the poet quarrels about a divine justice that is out of phase with humankind's needs. Individual creations pass through the spectrum of human and religious history and into the future in the expectation of a new social order. Bitter pessimism unmasks the dreams of life, pointing to the defeat of that which is noble and beautiful and the triumph of the worse human being over the better as the derisive law of the world. Voicing the mourning and bitter resistance of the tormented soul, Heine transforms personal confrontation with suffering and death into a timeless statement of universal experience.

Romanzero is divided into three main parts, each of which projects a substantial array of feeling: seriousness, despair, goodness, compassion, a longing for faith, bitterness, and mature composure. The first section, "Historien" ("Stories"), is composed of discursive, sometimes rambling narrative ballads and romances dealing with the tragedies of kings, heroes, and poets. Some of them process through a temporal distance such typical Heine themes as the yearning for love, clothing them in historical trappings. Others, such as the cruel poem "Vitzliputzli" that ends the cycle, are profound discourses on humans' inhumanity toward their own kind. The poems of "Lamentationen" ("Lamentations"), the second major section, are directly confessional in form: deeply moving cries of anguish, sublime expressions of horror, statements of longing for home. The "Lazarus" poems that conclude this portion of *Romanzero* are especially vivid documents of the poet's individual suffering in a world where God seems to be indifferent. In "Hebräische Melodien" ("Hebrew Melodies"), the last segment of the collection, Heine presented the essence of his reidentification with Judaism. Three long poems explore the broad dimensions of Jewish culture, history, and tradition, ending with an almost sinister medieval disputation between Christian and Jew that evolves into a tragicomic anticlerical satire. Thumbing his nose at irrational action, intolerance, and superstition, the poet offers a dying plea for humanism.

No other volume presents Heine so thoroughly in all his heights and depths, perfection and error, wit and seriousness. Captivating for the directness of despairing and contrite confession, repelling for its boastful, sometimes vicious cynicism, *Romanzero*, as perhaps no other work in the history of German lyric poetry, reveals the hubris of the problematic individual and penetrates the facade of the bright fool's drama that is life.

OTHER MAJOR WORKS

LONG FICTION: *Der Rabbi von Bacherach*, 1887 (*The Rabbi of Bacherach*, 1891).

SHORT FICTION: *Aus den Memoiren des Herrn von Schnabelewopsky*, 1910 (*The Memoirs of Herr von Schnabelewopski*, 1876).

PLAYS: *Almansor*, pb. 1821 (English translation, 1905); *Der Doktor Faust*, pb. 1851 (libretto; *Doktor Faust*, 1952).

NONFICTION: *Briefe aus Berlin*, 1822; *Reisebilder*, 1826-1831 (4 volumes; *Pictures of Travel*, 1855); *Die Bäder von Lucca*, 1829 (*The Baths of Lucca*, 1855); *Französische Zustände*, 1833 (*French Affairs*, 1889); *Zur Geschichte der neueren schönen Literatur in Deutschland*, 1833 (*Letters Auxiliary to the History of Modern Polite Literature in Germany*, 1836); *Der Salon*, 1834-1840 (4 volumes; *The Salon*, 1893); *Zur Geschichte der Religion und Philosophie in Deutschland*, 1835 (*On the History of Religion and Philosophy in Germany*, 1876); *Die romantische Schule*, 1836 (expansion of *Zur Geschichte der Religion und Philosophie in Deutschland*; *The Romantic School*, 1876); *Über die französische Bühne*, 1837 (*Concerning the French Stage*, 1891-1905); *Shakespeares Mädchen und Frauen*, 1838 (*Shakespeare's Maidens and Ladies*, 1891);

Ludwig Börne: Eine Denkschrift von H. Heine, 1840 (*Ludwig Börne: Recollections of a Revolutionist*, 1881); *Les Dieux en exil*, 1853 (*Gods in Exile*, 1962); *Lutetia: Berichte über Politik, Kunst, und Volksleben*, 1854 (*Lutetia: Reports on Politics, Art, and Popular Life*, 1891-1905); *Vermischte Schriften*, 1854 (3 volumes); *De l'Allemagne*, 1855 (2 volumes).

MISCELLANEOUS: *The Works of Heinrich Heine*, 1891-1905 (12 volumes).

BIBLIOGRAPHY

Cook, Roger F., ed. *A Companion to the Works of Heinrich Heine*. Rochester, N.Y.: Camden House, 2002. A collection of essays that examine Heine's work; topics include the eroticism, Jewish culture, mythology, and modernity in his poems.

Heady, Katy. *Literature and Censorship in Restoration Germany: Repression and Rhetoric*. Rochester, N.Y.: Camden House, 2009. This work on the censorship of literature that occurred in Restoration Germany examines how the intellectual and political climate affected Heine.

Hermand, Jost, and Robert C. Holub, eds. *Heinrich Heine's Contested Identities: Politics, Religion, and Nationalism in Nineteenth-Century Germany*. New York: Peter Lang, 1999. A collection of essays concerning Heine's identity, which was formed and reformed, revised and modified, in relationship to the politics, religion, and nationalism of his era. The essays offer an understanding of Heine's predicaments and choices as well as the parameters placed on him by the exigencies of the time.

Justis, Diana Lynn. *The Feminine in Heine's Life and Oeuvre: Self and Other*. New York: Peter Lang, 1997. Heine's literary representations of women and interactions with women vividly demonstrate his position as a marginal German-Jewish writer of the nineteenth century. Heine, like many Jews of that era, internalized the European cultural stereotype of the Jew as "woman," that is, as essentially inferior and marginal.

Pawel, Ernst. *The Poet Dying: Heinrich Heine's Last Years in Paris*. New York: Farrar, Straus and Giroux, 1995. In this biography of Heine, Pawel portrays a poet at the height of his creativity in the last eight years of his life, when he was confined to his bed with a mysterious ailment.

Phelan, Anthony. *Reading Heinrich Heine*. New York: Cambridge University Press, 2007. Examines Heine's poetry from the earliest to his last, and argues that Heine is a major contributor to the articulation of modernity.

Lowell A. Bangerter

VICTOR HUGO

Born: Besançon, France; February 26, 1802
Died: Paris, France; May 22, 1885

OTHER LITERARY FORMS

Besides his rather prolific output in the field of poetry, Victor Hugo (YEW-goh) achieved prominence in two other genres as well. His novels, for which he is best known in the United States, span most of his literary career and include such recognizable titles as *Le Dernier Jour d'un condamné* (1829; *The Last Day of a Condemned*, 1840), *Notre-Dame de Paris* (1831; *The Hunchback of Notre Dame*, 1833), and *Les Misérables* (1862; English translation, 1862). Hugo was a successful playwright in his time, but only *Hernani* (pr., pb. 1830; English translation, 1830) has received sustained attention. The preface to his play *Cromwell* (pb. 1827; English translation, 1896), however, is frequently studied by scholars because of its attack on the three unities, so long observed by French classical writers, and because of Hugo's elaboration on his theory of the union of the grotesque and the sublime. His other plays are a *mise en oeuvre* of the dramatic principles found in the *Cromwell* preface.

Although less well known as an essayist, Hugo did write in the genre. His better-known essay collections include *Le Rhin* (1842; *The Rhine*, 1843), *William Shakespeare* (1864; English translation, 1864), *Choses vues* (1887; *Things Seen*, 1887), and *En voyage: Alpes et Pyrénées* (1890; *The Alps and Pyrenees*, 1898). Hugo also wrote and delivered a number of political speeches in the Chambre des Pairs. Among these are the "Consolidation et défense du littoral," which was delivered in the summer of 1846, "La Famille Bonaparte," which was delivered the following spring, and "Le Pape Pie IX," which was presented in January, 1848.

ACHIEVEMENTS

"Ego Hugo": This was the inscription emblazoned on the Gothic armchair that stood in the dining room in the Hugos' Guernsey home. Dubbed an ancestral chair by the poet, it remained conspicuously empty at mealtime. For Victor Hugo's critics, this motto became a symbol of an oversized ego. For his admirers, the empty chair symbolized the greatness of Hugo the poet, if not Hugo the man. Indeed, his place in literature is unquestioned, and no other French poet since has been able to match his production and influence.

Hugo excelled in a wide variety of verse forms: ode, lyric, epic, satire, and heroic narrative. His versatility in mode was matched by variations in tone, from the eloquence and rhetorical precision found in *Les Châtiments* (the chastisements), for example, to the simplicity and grace of *Les Contemplations*. Conventions that were in vogue at the time, such as the marvelous and the fantastic, the medieval and the Oriental, were translated by Hugo into verse. The poet also found inspiration in the imagery of dreams, spiritualism, and metempsychosis. His poetry set the tone and the style for Romantic verse; his choice of subjects and his novel uses of stylistic devices influenced the Parnassians and the Symbolists.

The sheer volume of Hugo's production would have assured him a place in literary history even if the strength and character of the man had not assured his celebrity. Hugo's resiliency allowed him to overcome personal tragedy and to express his grief in verse. He championed causes such as free, compulsory education, universal suffrage, the right to work, and the abolition of the death penalty, before such political postures were popular. In all, Hugo was a man of deep convictions, of great sensibility, and of tremendous ego whose poetic creation reflected all these aspects of his complex personality.

Victor-Marie Hugo was born at Besançon, the third son of Joseph Léopold Sigisbert Hugo and Sophie Trébuchet. His father, a career military man, served with distinction in the postrevolutionary army. He later became a general and viscount, as well as a close associate of Joseph Bonaparte, Napoleon's brother. Though gifted with military tenacity, the elder Hugo unfortunately was not capable of such steadfastness on the home front. Madame Hugo soon tired of his lusty nature and infidelities, finding relief in the arms of General Victor Fanneau LaHorie, an opponent of Napoleon, who was Victor Hugo's godfather. Shortly after Hugo's birth, Madame Hugo moved her children to Paris to be near LaHorie. After LaHorie became an enemy of Napoleon's regime, she hid him in her quiet house with a large garden in the rue des Feuillantines. During those eighteen months, the gentle "M. le Courlandais" taught the eight-year-old Hugo to read and translate Tacitus, and he impressed the young boy with the ideal of liberty; indeed, Hugo was to have a lifelong sympathy for the oppressed. In later years, he would fondly remember those days spent playing in the garden with his brother and with a girl named Adèle Foucher. Madame Hugo somehow provided a tranquil environment for her children, unembittered by constant marital strife.

Though LaHorie had provided some formal training, the education of the Hugo brothers remained spotty because of the family's frequent moves. The family took two trips to visit the boys' father: to Italy in 1809 and to Spain in 1811-1812. During that last trip, the boys were enrolled at the Collège des Nobles in Madrid. The year in Spain was to provide Hugo with much material for his later works. The Spanish hero Ernani would become the hero of his play, with the Masserano palace as one of its settings; the hunchback Corcova at the seminary would become the inspiration for Quasimodo; the street Ortoleza reappears in the play *Ruy Blas* (pr., pb. 1838; English translation, 1890) .

In 1814, General Hugo insisted that his sons be enrolled at the Pension Cordier, where they spent four years studying the sciences. To relieve the drudgery, the brothers wrote poems and plays during their leisure hours. Soon, this pastime became a successful enterprise. At the age of fifteen, Hugo entered the French Academy's poetry contest, receiving an honorable mention . In 1819, he won two prizes from the Académie des Jeux Floraux of Toulouse. Hugo and his brother Eugène entered law school to please their father but spent most of their efforts in the founding of a magazine called *Le Conservateur littéraire*. Among the early contributors to the venture was Alfred de Vigny, who was to become one of Hugo's closest friends. In this magazine, Hugo published his "Ode sur la mort du duc de Berry" and the first version of what was to become his second novel, *Bug-Jargal* (1826; *The Noble Rival*, 1845). The ode placed Hugo in the favor of the Royalists, among them his idol François-René de Chateaubriand, in whose presence the poet was received shortly after the publication of his ode. Soon, the Hugo brothers were admitted into the Société des Bonnes Lettres, an ultra-Royalist group; by this time, Hugo had adopted his mother's Royalist views.

With the death of his mother in 1821, Hugo entered a period of extreme poverty. He abandoned *Le Conservateur littéraire* and strove to make a living. In 1822, Hugo published the *Odes et poésies diverses*. Conservative and Royalist in content, these odes earned for Hugo a royal pension. He was able to marry his childhood sweetheart, Adèle Foucher, and continue with his literary career.

The years between 1822 and 1828 were filled with creative and literary activities. In 1823, Hugo published the second edition of *Odes et poésies diverses* as well as his first novel, *Han d'Islande* (1823; *Hans of Iceland*, 1845). The following year, Hugo's *Nouvelles Odes* were published. In 1825, Hugo was named, along with Alphonse de Lamartine, to the Legion of Honor "for his noble efforts . . . to sustain the sacred cause of the altar and the throne." The year 1826 saw the publication of Hugo's *Odes et ballades*, as well as his second novel, *The Noble Rival*. The publication the following year of the bold preface to *Cromwell* established Hugo as the spokesperson for the new Romantic school. Hugo's father, Léopold, died in 1828, an event that greatly grieved the poet. Since the death of his mother, Hugo and his father had achieved a rapprochement. This friendship rendered the poet more sympathetic to the Bonapartist cause and served to counterbalance the Royalist fervor that he had received from his mother. In that same year, Hugo's play *Amy Robsart* (pr. 1828; English translation, 1895) was presented.

During these years, the Hugo home had become the focal point for the gathering of literary young men caught up in the Romantic revolution against the formalism of the seventeenth and eighteenth centuries, men such as Charles Augustin Sainte-Beuve, Alfred de Vigny, Alfred de Musset, Théophile Gautier, Gérard de Nerval, and Émile and Antoine Deschamps. This group, which became known as the *cénacle*, sought to break the bonds of the dramatic unities, of poetic versification, and of the choice of subject matter, and rallied to expand the imaginative and aesthetic field. Hugo was the unquestioned head of the group. From his ideas and from the discussions that took place in his home during those years sprang new branches of Romanticism, including the Parnassian school.

The next few years were emotionally difficult ones for Hugo. Though he continued to receive acclaim for his new collection of poems *Les Orientales*, striking because of their exoticism; for his play *Hernani*, which heralded a decisive victory for Romantic drama; and for *The Hunchback of Notre Dame*, which established Hugo as a great writer of the historical novel, the security of his home life had begun to crumble. In 1829, Hugo's best friend, Sainte-Beuve, had revealed to the poet his love for Hugo's wife, Adèle. In spite of this revelation, Hugo tried to maintain the friendship, made more difficult by Sainte-Beuve's assertion that his love was reciprocated. In his distress, Hugo found comfort in a relationship with an actress, Juliette Drouet. It was an affair that would last fifty years and that was eventually accepted by Adèle Hugo. Drouet was transformed through her love for the poet into a devoted companion who remained virtually cloistered in her quarters, content to read and to copy his books.

These personal afflictions and affections found expression in the poetic works that followed: *Les Feuilles d'automne* (the leaves of autumn), *Songs of Twilight, Les Voix intérieures* (the interior voices), and *Les Rayons et les ombres* (the rays and shadows). These collections contrasted markedly with Hugo's previous poetic works in both tone and style. Unlike the exotic and colorful *Les Orientales*, for example, these poems sought to express the more intimate relationships found in love, childhood, and friendship, as well as in humankind's association with nature. In 1843, two other disasters, the death of his daughter Léopoldine and the failure of his play *Les Burgraves* (pr., pb. 1843; *The Burgraves*, 1896) caused Hugo to put down his pen for some time. As always, tragedy accompanied success in the poet's life.

Meanwhile, Hugo's political involvement intensified. In 1841, he was elected to the French Academy. As his prominence grew, it followed that he should be raised to peerage, and this indeed occurred in 1845. From this position, Hugo addressed the parliament on such matters as capital punishment and the plight of the poor, subjects on which he had already written in *The Last Day of a Condemned* and *Claude Gueux* (1834), and which would be fully exploited in a work already in progress at this time, *Les Misérables*. Because of his concern for the ordinary man and the unfortunates, he was elected a "representative of the people" in 1848 and a year later became a Parisian delegate to the Assemblée Nationale. During the 1848 Revolution, Hugo published his opinions in his journal *L'Événement*, and though he was aligned with no particular political party, the periodical was suppressed. He grew increasingly suspicious of Louis Napoleon's ambitions, and though Hugo had originally supported him for the presidency, he delivered a scathing address before the Assemblée in July of 1851 in which he called the president "Napoleon the Little." As a consequence of this attack, Hugo fled France shortly after the coup d'état of December, 1851. This event marked another change in the poet's political stance: Having been a Royalist and then a Bonapartist, Hugo next became a Republican.

Hugo went first to Belgium, where he stayed only for a short time, then moved to the Channel Islands of Jersey and then Guernsey, where he finally settled with his family and with Juliette Drouet from 1855 to 1870. These were to be very productive years for Hugo. After a long silence, the poet's voice was again heard in 1853 with the publication of *Les Châtiments*, in which he vehemently denounced Louis Napoleon and his empire. In 1856, Hugo published *Les Contemplations*, in which he integrated lyrics, meditative poems on his daughter's death, and more visionary and mystical verses. In large measure, these poems would influence the Symbolists. With the publication of the first *The Legend of the Centuries* in 1859, an extensive epic that detailed humankind's progress from slavery to freedom, Hugo achieved the unquestioned reputation of "poet-seer."

It was as if Hugo's long silence had caused him to relish his renewed literary voice, for his productivity during the 1860's remained substantial. In 1862, his great novel *Les Misérables* appeared, succeeded by *Les Chansons des rues et des bois* (the songs of the streets and the woods) in 1865. These were followed in 1866 by another novel, *Les Travailleurs de la mer* (1866; *The Toilers of the Sea*, 1866). As always, his literary acclaim was accompanied by personal sorrow. Adèle Hugo died in 1868 in Brussels of apoplexy. Her wish had been to be buried beside her daughter Léopoldine. Hugo accompanied her body as far as the French frontier. The following year, Hugo's next novel, *L'Homme qui rit* (1869; *The Man Who Laughs*, 1869), was published. It received little acclaim at the time, and it has been only rarely studied since.

The fall of the Second Empire on September 3, 1870, ended Hugo's long exile from France. He returned during turbulent times: The war with Prussia and the civil war that ensued left Hugo disillusioned. During this time, his son Charles died, his daughter Adèle was confined to an asylum, and his son François became gravely ill. Once more, the poet returned to Guernsey, this time not so much to escape political forces as to seek solace. He recorded his feelings in *L'Année terrible* (terrible year).

Hugo returned to Paris in 1873 after finishing his novel *Quatre-vingt-treize* (1874; *Ninety-three*, 1874), which was published the following year. Then seventy-one years old, he found great consolation in his grandchildren, spending long hours with them and sharing childhood delights. For his age, his productivity was amazingly constant. In 1877, there appeared the second volume of *The Legend of the Centuries*, as well as *L'Art d'être grand-père* (the art of being a grandfather). These were followed by *Le Pape* (the pope), *La Pitié suprême* (the supreme pity), *Religions et religion* (1880), *L'Âne* (the ass) and a play, *Torquemada* (pb. 1882; English translation, 1896). On May 11, 1883, Juliette Drouet died of stomach cancer; her death was a terrible blow to Hugo. He published nothing else during his lifetime except the final volume of *The Legend of the Centuries* in 1883. His health steadily declined, and he died of pneumonia on May 22, 1885. He was buried in the Panthéon beside Voltaire and Jean-Jacques Rousseau.

In 1875, Hugo had written his literary will, which specified that after his death all his manuscripts without exception should be published. This testament was faithfully executed, allowing for the appearance of the following posthumous publications: *Théâtre en liberté* (pb. 1886), *La Fin de Satan* (the end of satan), *Toute la lyre* (all of the lyre), *Dieu* (God), *Les Années funestes* (the fatal years), and *Dernière Gerbe* (last sheaf). A portion of his letters, *Correspondence* (1896-1898), and his travel books, *The Alps and Pyrenees* and *Things Seen*, were also published.

ANALYSIS

Victor Hugo's poetry took many forms, from the lyric to the epic to the elegiac. Along with this variety of form, the range of the poet's ideas expanded during his long career. From poems with political overtones, Hugo's poetry grew to exhibit the tenets of Romanticism. He wrote of more personal and intimate subjects, such as family and love. He also wrote about humankind's relationship with nature and with the Creator. As Hugo matured, his themes became more philosophical and humanitarian, and his self-appointed role became that of a poet-seer attempting to understand the mysteries of life and creation.

ODES ET BALLADES

Hugo's shift toward Romanticism and away from political themes first became apparent in *Odes et ballades*. In this collection, the poet makes copious use of the fantastic, the uncanny, and the horrifying, a popular style of the time, exemplified by the German ballads of Gottfried Burger, Christoph Wieland, and Johann Wolfgang von Goethe. Hugo's inspiration was drawn also from contemporary translations of Spanish, English, and French ballads, a diversity of sources that infused his own ballads with eclecticism.

In the preface to *Odes et ballades*, Hugo compares the sculptured gardens of Versailles with the primitive forests of the New World. The artificiality of the former, Hugo claims, stands in opposition to the laws of nature, whereas in the untouched forests, "everything obeys an invariable law." The true poet, then, must look to nature as his model, forsaking the contrived in favor of the natural. This was the new precept that Hugo sought to follow in this work.

Hugo received praise from his contemporaries for his imaginative use of his subject matter and for his great technical versatility. He used not only the classical Alexandrine but also other forms of versification, such as the octosyllabic line in the poem "La Fiancée du timbalier" ("The Cymbaleer's Bride") and the little-used Renaissance seven-syllable line in "À Trilby." Though original and clever, these poems are devoid of the philosophical intent that characterizes the poet's later work. They were pronounced excellent, however, by a young critic for *Le Globe* by the name of Charles-Augustin Sainte-Beuve.

LES ORIENTALES

Les Orientales marks Hugo's departure from neoclassical rhetorical forms and inaugurates his bolder, more colorful style. Hugo's use of metaphor gains precision and originality; he employs verse forms drawn from the Renaissance Pléiade, to which he had been led by Sainte-Beuve.

The most famous poem of *Les Orientales* is "Les Djinns" ("The Djinns"), which exhibits Hugo's technical virtuosity. There is exoticism in the choice of both subject and form; in this, the poem is representative of the entire collection. The djinns are identified as evil spirits who sweep into a town and leave just as quickly. Their anticipated arrival is marked by a mounting from a two-syllable line to a decasyllabic line, while their departure is signaled by a parallel decrescendo. In this manner, Hugo is able to create an atmosphere of mystery and terror, with a contrasting feeling of relief. The poem won the plaudits not only of Hugo's contemporaries, but also of later poets and critics; Algernon Charles Swinburne was to comment that no other poet had "left a more exquisite piece or one more filled with delicate lyricism."

LES FEUILLES D'AUTOMNE

In *Les Feuilles d'automne*, Hugo's lyrical voice achieves maturity. The central themes are those of childhood, nature, and love. Although the style is less spectacular than that of *Les Orientales*, Hugo achieves a profound poetic effect through greater simplicity. His treatment of domestic themes is reminiscent of William Wordsworth, whose works Hugo may have known through the influence of Sainte-Beuve.

The opening poem is a tribute to the poet's mother's love and devotion. This is followed by a warm acknowledgment of his father, in which Hugo recalls the General's house at Blois and mourns his father's death. These panegyrics to his parents set the tone for the entire collection.

Less than a handful of poems deal with the topic of childhood, yet Hugo was the first to introduce this subject into French verse. The masterpiece of the collection is one such poem, "Lorsque l'enfant paraît" ("Infantile Influence"), touching in its description of the young child whose presence signifies a blessed household. Hugo concludes with a prayer imploring God to preserve family and friends from a home without a child. Such a sentimental ending would not have been found in *Les Orientales*, and it manifests a further development in the poet's style.

Another development, but on a different plane, establishes the poet's concern for the correspondences between people and nature, as in the poem "Ce qu'on entend sur la montagne" ("What Is Heard on the Mountain"). The role of the poet becomes significant in such an interchange; he becomes an interpreter in this dialogue, as Hugo announces in "Pan." These assertions were manifest again in later poetic works.

LES RAYONS ET LES OMBRES

In *Les Rayons et les ombres*, Hugo conceives of a social mission for the poet. The poet becomes a sacred dreamer, an impartial observer of his time, seeking inspiration from humankind, nature, and God. This collection is, therefore, rather diverse in its subject matter. There are love poems, poems devoted to nature, verses inspired by a search for religious significance, childhood memories, and poems with greater social content.

Two celebrated poems are to be found in *Les Rayons et les ombres*. The first is "Tristesse d'Olympio," in which the poet is presented as a keeper of the secrets of the universe. The tone of sadness that pervades the piece is in large measure a reflection of the unhappy events of 1837, the year it was written. Sainte-Beuve had published a story titled "Mme de Pontivy," in which he described a love affair similar to his alleged affair with Adèle Hugo. Hugo's daughter Léopoldine had been seriously ill that year. At the same time, the poet himself had been afflicted with an eye disorder. In that same year also, Hugo's brother Eugène died after spending many years in an asylum, his illness caused in large part by Hugo's marriage with Adèle, whom he had also loved. The inspiration for the poem is, therefore, overwhelmingly personal. The mood of the poem reflects Hugo's disillusionment with the mutability of nature. In striking contrast with poems of this same genre, such as Alphonse de Lamartine's "Le Lac" ("The Lake"), Hugo asserts that, though nature may forget, humankind will not.

The second important poem in this collection is "Oceano Nox." Though it is much shorter and less complicated than "Tristesse d'Olympio," it nevertheless successfully introduces the sea into Hugo's poetic corpus. The poet chose the elegiac form to describe the force of the ocean and the tragedy of men who are engulfed in the sea, remembered only for a short time by their loved ones. The final stanza is powerful in its description of the desperate voices contained in the roar of the sea at night.

"L'EXPIATION"

It was during his stay in Jersey in 1853 that Hugo published *Les Châtiments*, a volume of satiric poetry. The work is a ceaseless diatribe against the Second Empire and Louis Napoleon. Hugo's indignation against the emperor was inexhaustible. He believed Napoleon to be a tyrant, a ruler who had compromised the liberty of the French people. Hugo evokes every imaginable vituperative image in his denunciation of "Napoleon the Dwarf." Though these pages are replete with a succession of ingenious epithets and metaphors, one poem in this collection is particularly noteworthy, "L'Expiation."

The poem combines both epic and satiric styles; its structure is particularly ingenious. Opening with an account of the glorious reign of Napoleon I, it develops the concept of the crime that the poet must expiate: the coup d'état on the *Dix-huit Brumaire* of the revolutionary calendar. Hugo then details the emperor's retreat from Moscow, his army's struggle in the blinding snow, the loss of countless men to the elements. Napoleon wonders at this point whether this is his punishment. A voice replies: *No.*

The second part of the poem recounts the Battle of Waterloo. Hugo describes the conflict at its height. Napoleon witnesses the fall of the French army, and this time he knows that his defeat will be total. Once more the question is asked: Is this the punishment? Once more, the voice answers: *No.*

The third segment of the poem concerns Napoleon's exile on Saint Helena. Hugo ably contrasts the prisoner Napoleon with the formerly glorious emperor. The latter is now preoccupied with the memories of Moscow, with his wife's infidelity, and with the constant surveillance of his jailer, Sir Hudson Lowe. As the fallen emperor lies dying, he once more raises the question: Is this the punishment? This time, the voice replies: *Not yet.*

Thirty years later, Napoleon I is awakened in his tomb by a familiar voice. It is the voice of his nephew, who has debased the name of Napoleon. Now the punishment is clear: The name of Napoleon is to be remembered not in glory but in ignominy.

Though it is known that Hugo researched his subject carefully, the tension and the concentration of events that make this poem so remarkable are his own distinctive contributions. The ingenuity of the threefold intervention of the voice sustains the dramatic movement, while the portrait of Napoleon is a powerful study in contrast.

LES CONTEMPLATIONS

Published in two volumes, titled *Autrefois* (former times) and *Aujourd'hui* (today), *Les Contemplations* has been called by the critic Ferdinand Brunetière "the most lyrical collection in the French language." The dividing line between the two volumes was the death of Hugo's daughter Léopoldine, in 1843. Consequently, the poems in this collection are very personal, yet the poet generalizes his experiences to include the experiences of all people. Central to the work is the relationship of God and humankind, of humankind and external nature, and of life and death.

In this collection, there are two groups of poems that are particularly significant. The first is "Pauca meae," comprising seventeen poems composed between 1841 and 1855. They were inspired by Hugo's daughter, Léopoldine. The best-known poem in this series is "A Villequier," which expresses the poet's deep despair at the loss of his beloved daughter. It treats the poet's attempt to submit to the will of God and to resign himself to a life without his child. Though he is able to achieve the former, complete resignation is something that eludes him. Unable to restrain his emotion, he claims the right to weep. The grief of a father dominates the rest of the poem, which concludes on a note of extreme sadness.

The second important series in *Les Contemplations*, "Au bord de l'infini," comprises twenty-six poems containing a statement of Hugo's philosophical ideas. The poet aspires to penetrate the unknown, perhaps through prayer. His search for truth will be as a winged dreamer or as a startled wise man. The crowning piece of this series, "Ce que dit la bouche d'ombre" ("What the Mouth of the Shadow Says"), deals with such concepts as Pythagoreanism (in particular, the metempsychosis of souls), Platonism, and pantheism.

"What the Mouth of the Shadow Says" is set at the dolmen of Rozel. There the poet meets a specter with whom he discusses the unity of the universe and the essential vitality of all that is in it. Everything in creation has a soul and a consciousness, but how is this universe to be explained? If God is in everything and everything is in God, then how can one reconcile the imperfections of the world with the perfection that is God? It is here that Hugo introduces the notion of evil. If evil is caused by the absence of light, then the resulting darkness and heaviness can only be associated with matter. Because humans are conscious of the difference between darkness and light, then humans choose to do evil by their own free will. Moreover, humans choose their own punishment. An evildoer's soul will be metamorphosed into something degrading; the soul of Judas, for example, is to be found in the spit of men. Ultimately, however, there is hope for humankind, a hope that the dualism between light and darkness, between goodness and evil, will be reconciled. It is on this thought that the poem ends.

THE LEGEND OF THE CENTURIES

Considered by many to be the greatest epic poem since the Middle Ages, *The Legend of the Centuries* differs from other epics in its humanitarian concerns. Hugo states in the preface that he is interested in showing the human profile "from Eve, the mother of men, to the Revolution, the mother of peoples." This is to be accomplished with the notion of progress foremost in his mind. This is not a historical collection, but rather, as Charles Baudelaire put it, a collection of those things that are poetic, that is, legend, myth, and fable, those things that tap the deep reservoirs of humanity.

Among the many subjects presented are the following: "Le Sacre de la femme" ("The Crowning of Women"), which opens the volume and which treats the story of Eve, not from the perspective of Original Sin, but from the perception of idyllic beauty; "La Conscience" ("Conscience"), which is the story of Cain's attempt to flee from the Eye that follows him everywhere, even to his grave; "Booz endormi" ("Boaz Asleep"), which was inspired by the Book of Ruth and in which Hugo attributes to the patriarch Boaz a dream in which he sees a great oak leading from himself to David and finally to Christ; "Le Mariage de Roland," which is considered by critics to be the prototype of the little epic and which presents the four-day struggle between Roland and Olivier, ending with the proposal that Roland marry Olivier's sister; "La Rose de l'infante" ("The Infanta's Rose"), which deals with the destruction in 1588 of the Spanish Armada and describes a great gust of wind that scatters the fleet and simultaneously arrives in the royal garden of Aranjuez, stripping the petals of the rose held by the infanta and scattering them in the nearby fountain; "Le Satyr" ("The Satyr"), which is considered to be the most important philosophical poem of the collection and treats the double nature of humankind, beings at once allied with the gods because of their spirit, but who now have their feet in the mud; and two poems, "Pleine mer" ("Out at Sea") and "Plein ciel" ("Up in the Sky"), which together constitute "Vingtième siècle," contrasting the evils of oldworld war symbolized by the steamship Leviathan with the vision of goodness symbolized by the airship.

LA FIN DE SATAN

Although *La Fin de Satan* was not published until after Hugo's death, it was conceived of during his stay in Guernsey. Hugo's treatment of the fallen angel differs greatly from the Miltonic version. Whereas the fall of Satan in Milton's work is precipitous, in Hugo's version Satan's fall takes thousands of years, while the feathers from his wings fall even more slowly. Furthermore, while Milton's Satan reigns over a host of other devils, Hugo's Satan is alone until he is able to engender a daughter, the veiled Isis-Lilith. It is she who brings evil into the world. After the great Flood, she returns to Earth the three weapons with which Cain had slain Abel: a bronze nail, a wooden club, and a stone. For Hugo, these instruments symbolically represent war, capital punishment, and imprisonment. These thre e representations determine the structure of the work.

In the first section, "Le Glaive," Hugo illustrates the evils of war through the symbolic character of Nimrod. Hugo's Nimrod is arrogant and bellicose, and his attack on the kingdom of God is doomed to failure. The most remarkable section of this first part concerns another Hugoesque creation. One of the feathers from Lucifer's wings had not fallen into the abyss, landing instead on the edge of a precipice. The angel, Liberty, engendered from this feather is a creation of God rather than of Satan, and together with Lilith, she represents the dual nature of Lucifer-Satan.

The second section, centering on an earthly drama, is titled "Le Gibet" ("The Cross"). It is divided into three parts: "La Judée," "Jésus-Christ," and "Le Crucifix." Hugo's attack on capital punishment takes the form of a contrast between the innocent Christ, who is crucified, and the guilty Barabbas, who is set free. Hugo adds an effective scene not found in the biblical narration, wherein Barabbas comes to the foot of the Cross after the Crucifixion.

In the meantime, Liberty beseeches God to allow Lucifer to return to the light. Before putting Lucifer into a peaceful sleep, she receives his blessing to undo the work of Lilith on Earth. The final section of the poem, dealing with imprisonment, was not complete at Hugo's death. Hugo, however, did write a conclusion to the work, titled "Satan pardonnée" ("Satan Pardoned"). Liberty is able to gain the salvation of both humankind and Lucifer.

DIEU

Composed in large part during Hugo's stay in Guernsey in 1855, *Dieu* was left unfinished for many years. Hugo returned to it in 1875, and it was published posthumously in 1891. The poem concerns Hugo's search for God. Twenty-one voices warn the poet of the futility of his search for a complete understanding of God; nevertheless, the poet continues on his journey. He meets a series of symbolic birds, for he himself is winged. These birds are emblems of various understandings of the godhead: atheism, skepticism, Manichaeanism, paganism, Judaism, and Christianity. Finally, the poet achieves the light in "La Lumière" ("The Light"), although he is denied complete understanding, for a veil falls before him. Humankind is to know the secrets of the infinite only in death.

Together with *La Fin de Satan*, *Dieu* represents a synthesis of Hugo's religious and philosophical ideas, revealing the poet as a privileged seeker of truth. Hugo shows himself to be not only a master of versification but also a man consumed by the desire to comprehend the deeper mysteries of existence and of the universe.

OTHER MAJOR WORKS

LONG FICTION: *Han d'Islande*, 1823 (*Hans of Iceland*, 1845); *Bug-Jargal*, 1826 (*The Noble Rival*, 1845); *Le Dernier Jour d'un condamné*, 1829 (*The Last Day of a Condemned*, 1840); *Notre-Dame de Paris*, 1831 (*The Hunchback of Notre Dame*, 1833); *Claude Gueux*, 1834; *Les Misérables*, 1862 (English translation, 1862); *Les Travailleurs de la mer*, 1866 (*The Toilers of the Sea*, 1866); *L'Homme qui rit*, 1869 (*The Man Who Laughs*, 1869); *Quatre-vingt-treize*, 1874 (*Ninety-three*, 1874).

PLAYS: *Cromwell*, pb. 1827 (verse drama; English translation, 1896); *Amy Robsart*, pr. 1828 (English translation, 1895); *Hernani*, pr., pb. 1830 (verse drama; English translation, 1830); *Marion de Lorme*, pr., pb. 1831 (verse drama; English translation, 1895); *Le Roi s'amuse*, pr., pb. 1832 (verse drama; *The King's Fool*, 1842; also known as *The King Amuses Himself*, 1964); *Lucrèce Borgia*, pr., pb. 1833 (*Lucretia Borgia*, 1842); *Marie Tudor*, pr., pb. 1833 (English translation, 1895); *Angelo, tyran de Padoue*, pr., pb. 1835 (*Angelo, Tyrant of Padua*, 1880); *Ruy Blas*, pr., pb. 1838 (verse drama; English translation, 1890); *Les Burgraves*, pr., pb. 1843 (*The Burgraves*, 1896); *Inez de Castro*, pb. 1863 (wr. c. 1818; verse drama); *La Grand-mère*, pb. 1865, pr. 1898; *Mille Francs de Recompense*, pb. 1866; *Les Deux Trouvailles de Gallus*, pb. 1881; *Torquemada*, pb. 1882 (wr. 1869; English translation, 1896); *Théâtre en liberté*, pb. 1886 (includes *Mangeront-ils?*); *The Dramatic Works*, 1887; *The Dramatic Works of Victor Hugo*, 1895-1896 (4 volumes); *Irtamène*, pb. 1934 (wr. 1816; verse drama).

NONFICTION: *La Préface de Cromwell*, 1827 (English translation, 1896); *Littérature et philosophie mêlées*, 1834; *Le Rhin*, 1842 (*The Rhine*, 1843); *Napoléon le petit*, 1852 (*Napoleon the Little*, 1852); *William Shakespeare*, 1864 (English translation, 1864); *Actes et paroles*, 1875-1876; *Histoire d'un crime*, 1877 (*The History of a Crime*, 1877-1878); *Religions et religion*, 1880; *Le Théâtre en liberté*, 1886; *Choses vues*, 1887 (*Things Seen*, 1887); *En voyage: Alpes et Pyrénées*, 1890 (*The Alps and Pyrenees*, 1898); *France et Belgique*, 1892; *Correspondance*, 1896-1898.

MISCELLANEOUS: *Oeuvres complètes*, 1880-1892 (57 volumes); *Victor Hugo's Works*, 1892 (30 volumes); *Works*, 1907 (10 volumes).

BIBLIOGRAPHY

Bloom, Harold, ed. *Victor Hugo*. New York: Chelsea House, 1988. Essays on all aspects of Hugo's career. Includes introduction, chronology, and bibliography.

Frey, John Andrew. *A Victor Hugo Encyclopedia*. Westport , Conn.: Greenwood Press, 1999. A comprehensive guide in English to the works of Victor Hugo. Includes a foreword, a biography, and a bibliography. Frey addresses Hugo as a leading poet, novelist, artist, and religious and revolutionary thinker of France. The balance of the volume contains alphabetically arranged entries discussing his works, characters, and themes as well as historical persons and places. Includes a general bibliography.

Ionesco, Eugène. *Hugoliad: Or, The Grotesque and Tragic Life of Victor Hugo*. New

York: Grove Press, 1987. This uncompleted work of Ionesco's youth—written in the 1930's in Romanian—is a sort of polemical antibiography, intended to dethrone its subject. The reader must take responsibility for separating fact from fiction, to say nothing of judging the aptness of the playwright's cheerless embellishments of anecdotal material. Postscript by Gelu Ionescu.

Ireson, J. C. *Victor Hugo: A Companion Guide to His Poetry.* New York: Clarendon Press, 1997. A detailed critical study dealing with Victor Hugo's verse in its totality, showing how each work was composed, how the themes evolved, and the considerations that dictated the sequence of his publications. Includes bibliographic references.

Maurois, André. *Olympio: The Life of Victor Hugo.* Translated by Gerard Hopkins. New York: Harper & Row, 1956. Originally published in French in 1954. This is probably as close an approach as possible to an ideal one-volume biography dealing with both the life and the work of a monumental figure such as Hugo. Of the sparse illustrations, several are superb; the bibliography, principally of sources in French, provides a sense of Hugo's celebrity and influence, which persisted well into the twentieth century.

_____. *Victor Hugo and His World.* London: Thames & Hudson, 1966. The 1956 English translation of Maurois' text noted above was edited to conform to the format of a series of illustrated books. The result is interesting and intelligible, but rather schematic. In compensation for the vast cuts in text, a chronology and dozens of well-annotated illustrations have been added.

Peyre, Henri. *Victor Hugo: Philosophy and Poetry.* Translated by Roda P. Roberts. University: University of Alabama Press, 1980. A study of Hugo's philosophy as evidenced by his poetry. Contains translations of selected poems with an index and bibliography.

Porter, Laurence M. *Victor Hugo.* New York: Twayne, 1999. A basic biography of Hugo that covers his life and works. Bibliography and index.

Richardson, Joanna. *Victor Hugo.* New York: St. Martin's Press, 1976. A well-written, scholarly biography divided into three sections, "The Man," "The Prophet," "The Legend." With detailed notes and extensive bibliography.

Robb, Graham. *Victor Hugo.* New York: W. W. Norton , 1998. Thorough biography of Victor Hugo reveals many previously unknown aspects of his long life and literary career. Includes detailed notes and bibliography.

Sylvie L. F. Richards

JOHN KEATS

Born: Moorfields, London, England; October 31, 1795
Died: Rome, Papal States (now in Italy); February 23, 1821

<small>PRINCIPAL POETRY</small>
Poems, 1817
Endymion: A Poetic Romance, 1818
"Lamia," "Isabella," "The Eve of St. Agnes," and Other Poems, 1820
Life, Letters, and Literary Remains of John Keats, 1848
The Fall of Hyperion: A Dream, 1856

<small>OTHER LITERARY FORMS</small>

In *The Use of Poetry* (1933), T. S. Eliot referred to the letters of John Keats (keets) as "the most notable and the most important ever written by any English poet," primarily because "there is hardly one statement of Keats about poetry, which . . . will not be found to be true." The letters also offer an important gloss on specific poems and have thus become important for understanding Keats. Besides many passing comments of brilliance, the central concept of the letters is "negative capability." As defined by Keats, it is the capability to remain "in uncertainties, Mysteries, doubts, without any irritable reaching after fact & reason," which implies a disinterestedness that permits even competing ideas full play to reach their potential. In his letters, Keats often carried an idea to its extreme with extraordinary intellectual flexibility; another day, its opposite will surface to be worked out, as all things "end in speculation." The concept is also taken to include Keats's understanding of the poetical character, or the ability to surrender one's personal self to create characters and objects with independent life. Keats believed that the artist's first responsibility was to create beauty, which implies that the artist's personally held ideas and beliefs should be temporarily suspended or treated only partially so as to realize fully the work's aesthetic potential. Through the use of sympathetic imagination, Keats attempted to become the thing he was creating, to intensely identify with its life, not to find his personal life reflected in it. The standard edition of Keats's letters is *The Letters of John Keats, 1814-1821* (2 volumes; 1958, Hyder Edward Rollins, editor). Text citations are to that edition.

<small>ACHIEVEMENTS</small>

Without being facetious, one could identify John Keats's greatest achievement as becoming one of the greatest poets of the English language in twenty-five years, three months, and twenty-three days of life, for Keats died before the age of twenty-six. Douglas Bush has said that no other English poet would rank as high as Keats if he had

John Keats
(Library of Congress)

died as young—not William Shakespeare, John Milton, or Keats's greatest contemporary, William Wordsworth. Whereas other poets, especially his Romantic contemporaries, have gone in and out of critical fashion, Keats's reputation has endured since shortly after his death.

Keats followed the Shakespearean model of impersonality in art; that is, the surrendering of self to the fullest development of character and object, and it is this impersonality, coupled with intensity, that makes his poetry readily accessible to a wide range of modern readers. The reader does not have to re-create Keats's time, empathize with Romantic norms and beliefs, or identify with the poet's unique biographical experiences to appreciate his poetry fully. Keats is sane, honest, and open; his art is varied, intense, and rich in texture and experience. As he said of his poetic model, Shakespeare, Keats was as little of an egotist as it was possible to be, in the Romantic period, at least, in the creation of art.

BIOGRAPHY

Though the events of John Keats's life are meager, his biography has fascinated many. Keats did not have a single physical, social, familial, or educational advantage in life, nothing to prepare for or enhance the development of his genius. Internally, however, he was afire with ambition and the love of beauty. Even at that, he did not discover his poetic vocation until late, given the fact that he died at the age of twenty-five and spent the last eighteen months of his life in a tubercular decline. His career lasted from 1816, when Keats renounced the practice of medicine, to the fall of 1819, when he stopped working on his last great, though incomplete, poem, *The Fall of Hyperion.* One almost has to count the months, they are so few and precious. In fact, in a single month, May, 1819, he wrote four of his great odes—"Ode to a Nightingale," "Ode on a Grecian Urn," "Ode on Melancholy," and ironically, "Ode on Indolence."

This remarkable and courageous poet, the oldest of four children, was born to keepers of a London livery stable. His father was killed in a fall from a horse when John was eight; his mother died from tuberculosis when he was fourteen. His relatives arranged for schooling and apothecary training so that he might make a living, but the year he received his certificate, 1816, he began to devote himself to poetry. He wrote some good, but mostly bad, poetry, or at least poetry that does not add much to his reputation, until the summer of 1818. His reward was a brutal review of his major early work, *Endymion,* in a leading magazine of the day. Keats was criticized so severely that Percy Bysshe Shelley speculated that the review began Keats's physical decline.

Actually, the truth was much worse. Keats was nursing his brother Tom, who was dying from tuberculosis, when the reviews came out. Though he was too strong in character to be deeply affected by criticism, especially when he was a more astute critic of his poetry than his readers, a contagious illness could hardly be thwarted with character. In the fall of 1818, Keats also fell deeply in love with Fanny Brawne. They intended to marry, but his illness soon made their future together impossible. Sadly, the futility of their love and passion offered important inspiration to Keats's poetry. By late fall, 1819, in the same year that he had written "The Eve of St. Agnes," the odes, *Lamia,* and *The Fall of Hyperion,* his illness was severe enough to arouse his deep concern. In July, 1820, his influential volume *"Lamia," "Isabella," "The Eve of St. Agnes," and Other Poems* was published. Keats, however, now separated from Fanny, ill, in desperate need of money, and unable to achieve his major ambition of writing a "few fine Plays" in the manner of Shakespeare, was utterly despondent. He later spent a few months under the care of the Brawnes, but left England for Italy in September, 1820, in an attempt to save his life in the milder Italian weather. Joseph Severn, a dear friend, nursed him until his death in Rome in February, 1821.

Forever thinking aloud in his letters about the central concerns of existence, Keats once found purpose in this earthly life as "a vale of soul-making"; that is, although every human being perhaps contains a spark of divinity called soul, one does not attain an identity until that soul, through the medium of intelligence and emotions, experiences the circumstances of a lifetime. Thus the world has its use not as a vale of tears, but, more positively, as a vale of becoming through those tears. Keats's soul flourished as rapidly as his genius, and the poetry is evidence of both.

ANALYSIS

To love and to work are, psychologists say, the principal concerns of early adulthood. In John Keats's case, they became, as well, the dominant themes of his most important poetry. The work theme includes both the effort and the love of creating beauty and the immortality Keats longed for as recompense. Once, perhaps exaggerating, Keats wrote that "the mere yearning and fondness" he had "for the Beautiful" would keep him writing "even if [his] night's labours should be burnt every morning and no eye ever shine upon them." Not passing, however, was the tenacity of his ambition: "I would sooner fail than not to be among the greatest." Keats's quest for immortality takes several forms: It appears openly, especially in the sonnets and in "Ode on Indolence" and "Ode to Psyche" as the anxieties of ambition—being afforded the time, maintaining the will and energy, and, not least, determining the topic, or territory, for achievement. It includes a metamorphosis fantasy, whereby the young poet becomes deified or capable of immortal poetry through absorption of divinely granted knowledge. The ambition/ work theme also takes a self-conscious turn in *The Fall of Hyperion*, questioning the value to a suffering humankind of the dreamer-poet's life and work.

The love theme explores dreams of heterosexual bliss, but it also moves into the appropriate relationships to be had with art and nature. The imagination is the ally of love's desires; reality and reason are their nemeses. In "The Eve of St. Agnes," a better lover, in *Lamia*, a better place, are dreams that dissipate in the light of reality and reason. "Ode to a Nightingale" attempts a flight from reality through identification with beautiful song rather than through dream, but the result is an intensification of distress. "Ode on Melancholy," "To Autumn," and "Ode on a Grecian Urn," however, suggest perspectives on the human condition, nature, and art that can be maintained with honesty and deeply valued without recourse to dream. One could say that Keats's love theme moves toward the understanding and acceptance of what is.

Concomitant with the maturation of theme and perspective is Keats's stylistic development. Like most poets, Keats went through phases of imitation during which he adapted the styles and themes he loved to his own work and ambitions. Leigh Hunt, Edmund Spenser, John Milton, and always Shakespeare provided inspiration, stylistic direction, and a community of tradition. Regardless of origin, the principal traits of Keats's style are these: a line very rich with sound pattern, as in "with brede/ of marble men and maidens overwrought," which also includes puns on "brede" ("breed") and "overwrought" (as "delicately formed on" and as "overly excited"); synesthetic imagery, or imagery that mingles the senses ("soft incense," "smoothest silence"); deeply empathic imagery ("warmed jewels," "all their limbs/ Locked up like veins of metal, crampt and screwed"); stationing or positioning of characters to represent their dramatic condition (so Saturn after losing his realm, "Upon the sodden ground/ His old right hand lay nerveless, listless, dead,/ Unsceptered; and his realmless eyes were closed"); the use of the past participle in epithets ("purple-stained mouth," "green-recessed woods");

and, of course, as with every great writer, that quality that one can only describe as *Je ne sais quoi*—I know not what—as in the lines from the sonnet "Bright Star": "The moving waters at their priest-like task/ Of pure ablution round earth's human shores."

Themes of ambition and accomplishment inform many of Keats's sonnets. The claiming of territory for achievement is the focus of "How Many Bards Gild the Lapses of Time," "On First Looking into Chapman's Homer," "Great Spirits Now on Earth Are Sojourning," and the great "Ode to Psyche." In "On First Looking into Chapman's Homer," for example, Keats recounts the discovery of Homer's "demesne." The extended metaphor of the sonnet is narrator-reader as traveler, poet as ruler, poem as place. The narrator, much-traveled "in the realms of gold," has heard that Homer rules over "one wide expanse," yet he has never "breath[ed] its pure serene." During the oration of Chapman's translation, however, he is as taken as an astronomer "When a new planet swims into his ken" or as an explorer, such as "stout Cortez," when "He stared at the Pacific—and all his men/ Looked at each other with a wild surmise—/ Silent, upon a peak in Darien." The complementary images of the distant planet and the immense ocean suggest both the distance the narrator is from Homeric achievement and its epic proportions. His reaction, though, represented through the response of Cortez, is heartening: while lesser beings look to each other for cues on what to think, how to react, the greater explorer stares at the challenge, with "eagle eyes," to measure the farthest reaches of this new standard for achievement.

Following the lead of his contemporary William Wordsworth, though with a completely original emphasis, Keats's territory for development and conquest became the interior world of mental landscape and its imaginings. Wordsworth had defined his territory in his "Prospectus" to *The Recluse* (1798) as "the Mind of Man—/ My haunt, and the main region of my song." Whereas Wordsworth believed that mind, "When wedded to this goodly universe/ In love and holy passion," could create a vision of a new heaven and a new earth, Keats initially sought to transcend reality, rather than to transform it, with the power of the imagination to dream. "Ode to Psyche" explores Keats's region and its goddess, who was conceived too late in antiquity for fervid belief. While Wordsworth asserts in "Lines Composed a Few Miles Above Tintern Abbey" (1798) that "something far more deeply interfused" could sanctify our experience with nature, Keats locates days of "holy . . . haunted forest boughs" back in a past that precedes even his goddess of mind. The only region left for her worship must be imagined, interior. As priest, not to nature, but to mind, the poet says he will be Psyche's "choir" to "make delicious moan/ Upon the midnight hours," her voice, lute, pipe, incense, shrine, grove, oracle, her "heat/ Of pale-mouthed prophet" dreaming in "some untrodden region of [his] mind." In the "wide quietness" of this sacred microcosm, "branchèd thoughts, . . ./ Instead of pines shall murmur in the wind"; a "wreathed trellis of working brain" will dress "its rosy sanctuary"; the goddess's "soft delight" will be all that "shadowy thought can win." In keeping with the legend of Cupid as lover of Psyche, a casement will remain open at night "To let the warm Love in!" Keats's topic becomes, then, how the mind is stimulated by desire to create imagined worlds, or dreams, rather than, as in Wordsworth's case, how the mind is moved by love to re-create its perception of the real world.

HYPERION

Besides finding his territory for achievement, Keats struggled as well with the existential issues of the artist's life—developing the talent and maintaining the heart to live up to immense ambitions. It is to be doubted whether poets will ever be able to look to Shakespeare or to Milton as models without living in distress that deepens with every passing work. The "writing of a few fine Plays," meaning Shakespearean drama, remained Keats's greatest ambition to the end. Yet the achievement of *Paradise Lost* (1667, 1674) haunted him as well, and *Hyperion* was an attempt in its mold. Keats became more critical of Milton's achievement during the course of composing *Hyperion*, however, for it was, "though so fine in itself," a "curruption [sic] of our Language," too much in "the vein of art," rather than the "true voice of feeling." In fact, Keats gave up *Hyperion* because Milton's influence weighed so heavily that he could not distinguish the poem's excessively self-conscious artistry from its true beauty derived from accurate feeling.

Aesthetic considerations aside, a recurring theme in Keats's works of epic scope was the fantasy of poetic metamorphosis. The sonnet "On Sitting Down to Read King Lear Once Again" introduces the wish for transformation that will enable the poet to reach Shakespearean achievement. The metaphor is consumption and rebirth through fire, as adapted from the Egyptian legend of the phoenix bird, which was said to immolate itself on a burning pile of aromatic wood every five hundred years to engender a new phoenix from its ashes. The narrator-poet lays down his pen for a day so that he might "burn through" Shakespeare's "fierce dispute/ Betwixt damnation and impassion'd clay." To "burn through" must be read two ways in the light of the phoenix metaphor—as reading passionately through the work and as being burned through that reading. He prays to Shakespeare and the "clouds of Albion" not to let him "wander in a barren dream" when his long romance, *Endymion*, is concluded, but that "when . . . consumed in the fire" of reading *King Lear*, he may be given "new phoenix wings to fly at [his] desire." Out of the self-immolating achievement of reading will arise a poet better empowered to reach his quest.

The transformation theme of *Hyperion* exceeds the passionate wishfulness of "On Sitting Down to Read King Lear Once Again" by stressing the need for "knowledge enormous," as befits the poem's epic ambitions. *Hyperion* is a tale of succession in which the Titans are supplanted by the Olympians as the reigning monarchs of the universe, with focus upon Hyperion the sun god being replaced by Apollo, the new god of poetry and light. It has been suggested that *Hyperion* becomes Keats's allegory for his own relationship with his poetic contemporaries, especially Wordsworth. Keats had said that Wordsworth was Milton's superior in understanding, but this was not owing to "individual greatness of Mind" as much as to "the general and gregarious advance of intellect." *Hyperion* embodies this hypothesis of progress in its succession and transformation themes.

The poem opens with Saturn, who was the supreme god of the Titans, in a position of perfect stasis—the stationing referred to above—stupefied by his loss of power—"His old right hand lay nerveless, listless, dead,/ Unsceptered." Thea, the bewildered wife of the as-yet-undeposed Hyperion, visits to commiserate. She informs Saturn that the new gods are wholly incompetent; Saturn's "sharp lightning in unpracticed hands/ Scorches and burns our once serene domain." The question is: Why, with the world running perfectly, was there a need for change? Saturn, an image of pomposity and egotism, perhaps inspired by Wordsworth's character, knows only of his personal loss:

> I have left
> My strong identity, my real self,
> Somewhere between the throne, and where I sit
> Here on this spot of earth.

"Thea, Thea! Thea!" he moans, "where is Saturn?" Meanwhile, Hyperion is pacing his domain in the region of the sun, wondering: "Saturn is fallen, am I too to fall?" In his anxiety he overreacts, attempting to wield more power than he ever possessed by making the sun rise early. "He might not," which dismays him tremendously. The first book of this unfinished three-book epic ends with Hyperion sailing to earth to be with his fallen peers.

At the same time, Saturn and Thea also reach those "regions of laborious breath" where the gods sit

> Dungeoned in opaque element, . . .
> Without a motion, save of their big hearts
> Heaving in pain, and horribly convulsed
> With . . . boiling gurge of pulse.

The Titans receive their deposed king with mixed response—some groan, some jump to their feet out of old respect, some wail, some weep. Saturn, being unable to satisfy their need to know why and how they have fallen, calls on Oceanus, the former god of the sea, for not only does he "Ponderest high and deep," but he also looks content! Oceanus then reveals a law of succession particularly appropriate for the early nineteenth century: "We fall," he says, "by course of Nature's law, not force/ Of thunder, or of Jove." Blinded by sheer supremacy, Saturn has not realized that, as he was not the first ruler, so he will not be the last. Nature's law is the law of beauty. Just as heaven and earth are more beautiful than chaos and darkness, and the Titans superior in shape and will to heaven and earth, so the new gods signal another significant advance in being; "a fresh perfection treads,/ A power more strong in beauty, born of us/ And fated to excel us," Oceanus explains, "as we pass/ In glory that old Darkness." In short, the eternal law is that "first in beauty should be first in might."

On Apollo's isle, the important transformation is about to begin. Apollo, as a good Keatsian poet, can make stars throb brighter when he empathizes with their glory in his poetry; yet he is inexplicably sad. Mnemosyne the muse seeks to assist her favorite child, who aches with ignorance. She emits what he needs to know and he flushes with

> Names, deeds, gray legends, dire events, rebellions,
> Majesties, sovran voices, agonies
> Creations and destroyings, all at once
> Pour[ing] into the wide hollows of [his] brain.

Apollo shouts, "knowledge enormous makes a God of me" and "wild commotions shook him, and made flush/ All the immortal fairness of his limbs." It is like a death pang, but it is the reverse, a dying into life and immortal power. The poem ends incomplete with Apollo shrieking, Mnemosyne arms in air, and the truncated line—"and lo! from all his limbs/ Celestial * * *." No one has been able to conjecture to the satisfaction of anyone else where the poem might have gone from there, although the result of Apollo's transformation seems inevitable. He would replace Hyperion, effortlessly, in this pre-Darwinian, pre-Freudian, universe where sons, like evolving species, acquire power over the earth without conscious competition with their fathers. As Oceanus indicates, the Titans are like the

> forest-trees, and our fair boughs
> Have bred forth . . .
> . . . eagles golden-feathered, who do tower
> Above us in their beauty, and must reign
> In right thereof.

However timorously, it would follow that Keats, bred on Spenser, Shakespeare, Milton, and Wordsworth, would have to live up to, if not exceed, their accomplishments.

This myth of progress would necessarily still require the superior poem to be written to support its prophetic validity. Keats knew that he needed deeper knowledge to surpass Wordsworth, but there was not much he could do about it. Though it was an attractive imagining, no god was likely to pour knowledge into the wide hollows of his brain. "I am . . . young writing at random—straining at particles of light in the midst of a great darkness," he wrote with characteristic honesty, "without knowing the bearing of any one assertion of any one opinion." Ironically, his dilemma brought out the strength his modern readers prize most highly, his courageous battling with, to use his favorite phrase of Wordsworth's, "the Burthen of the mystery." Caught in this impasse between noble ambition and youthful limitation, Keats's spirit understandably failed in weaker moments. His self-questioning was exacerbated when he reflected on the frailty of earthly achievement. Such is the torment in "On Seeing the Elgin Marbles," the Grecian ruins brought to England by Lord Elgin.

The narrator opens feeling "Like a sick eagle looking at the sky" in the face of the magnificent architectural ruins. Ironically, they are only the "shadow of a magnitude" that once was, an insubstantial image emphasizing how much has been lost rather than how much was once achieved. Human achievement wasted by time brings the narrator a "most dizzy pain" born of tension between body and soul over committing one's life to mortal achievement. In "Ode on Indolence," Keats enjoys a temporary respite from his demons—love, ambition, and poetry—in a state of torpor in which the body temporarily overpowers spirit. One morning the shadows come to him: love the "fair Maid"; "Ambition, pale of cheek,/ And ever watchful with fatiguèd eye"; and, "the demon Poesy." At first he burns to follow and aches for wings, but body prevails: even poetry "has not a joy—/ . . . so sweet as drowsy noons,/ And evenings steeped in honeyed indolence." The victory is transitory outside the poem; within it, a respite from ambition, love, and work is accepted.

THE FALL OF HYPERION

All these issues—the quest for immortality; the region of quest as dream; the transformation essential to achieve the quest; the spiritual weakness inevitably felt in the face of the challenge to be immortal; and, beyond all these, an altruism that seeks to distinguish between the relative value of humanitarian works and poetry in behalf of suffering humanity—are melded in Keats's second quest for epic achievement, *The Fall of Hyperion*. Following a brief introduction, the poem moves to a dream arbor reserved for the dreamer, who "venoms all his days,/ Bearing more woe than all his sins deserve." Remnants of a feast strew the ground; the narrator eats, partakes of a draft of cool juice and is transported through sleep and reawakening to a second dream kingdom. He finds himself this time amid remnants of an ancient religious festival. These dream regions represent Keats's aspirations to romance and epic respectively. Off in the west, he sees a huge image being ministered to by a woman. The image is Saturn; the minister is Moneta, Mnemosyne's surrogate. Moneta's face is curtained to conceal the immense knowledge her eyes can reveal to those worthy of receiving her immortal knowledge. She challenges the narrator to prove himself so worthy by climbing the altar stairs to immortality, or dying on the spot. Cold death begins to mount through his body; in numbness he strives to reach the lowest step—"Slow, heavy, deadly was my pace: the cold/ Grew stifling, suffocating, at the heart;/ And when I clasped my hands I felt them not." At the last moment, he is saved; his "iced feet" touch the lowest step and "life seemed/ To pour in at the toes." He learns that he has been saved because he has felt for the suffering of the world, though he is only a dreamer, without hope for himself or of value to others. True poets, Moneta tells him, pour balm on the world; dreamers increase the vexation of humankind.

Although in his letters Keats gave precedence to "fine doing" over "fine writing" as "the top thing in the world," the poem does not clarify whether humanitarians are above the poets of humankind, though both are unquestionably above the dreamers. The poem then moves to the metamorphosis that will make the dreamer a poet through the acquisition of knowledge. Moneta's bright-blanched face reveals the immortal sorrow she has endured for eons; her eyes hold the narrator enthralled with the promise of the "high tragedy" they contain, for their light and the sorrowful touch of her voice reveal deep knowledge. He begs to know, and she relates the fall of the Titans. The revelation begins the narrator's transformation: "Whereon there grew/ A power within me of enormous ken./ To see as a God sees." His vision opens with the "long awful time" Saturn sat motionless with Thea at his feet. In anguish, the narrator sits on a tree awaiting action, but the pain must be endured, for knowledge does not come easily or quickly, not even in a dream. The narrator curses his prolonged existence, praying that death release him from the vale, until Saturn moves to speak and the narrator witnesses scenes of the beginning of things from Hyperion. The poem continues but this version also ends incomplete, with Hyperion flaring to earth.

It is a poignant fact that Keats never believed that his poetry, his work, had come to anything, his epic endeavors left incomplete, no "few fine Plays" written. Writing to Fanny Brawne in February, 1820, he said that he had frequently regretted not producing one immortal work to make friends proud of his memory. Now frighteningly ill, the thought of this failure and his love for Fanny were the sole two thoughts of his long, anxious nights. Quoting Milton's lines on fame from "Lycidas," Keats wrote to her: "Now you divide with this (may *I* say it) 'last infirmity of noble minds' all my reflection."

Their love had earlier spawned his most important love poems, though he refused his created lovers the bliss of unreflecting love. It would seem unfortunate that dreams do not outlast the act of dreaming, but Keats's romances, "The Eve of St. Agnes" and *Lamia*, approach wish-fulfillment more critically. "The Eve of St. Agnes" permits a love dream to become flesh to provoke a dreamer's response to the contrast between dream and reality, though they are, in person, the same; *Lamia* permits a too-ordinary mortal to enter the love dream of a lovely immortal to elicit the likely response of the nondreamer to the experience of continuous, in this case, carnal, perfection. Together the poems serve to show that lovers cannot have it either way: Either reality will not be good enough for the dreamer, or the dream will not satisfy the extra-romantic desires of the nondreamer.

"THE EVE OF ST. AGNES"

"The Eve of St. Agnes" presents an array of wish-fulfilling mechanisms that seek to alter, control, or purify reality—praying, suffering, drinking, music, ritual, dance, and, at the center, dreaming. This poem with a medieval setting opens with a holy beadsman, "meagre, barefoot, wan," praying to the Virgin in the castle's icy chapel. Though he is fleetingly tempted to walk toward the music dancing down the hall from a party within, he turns to sit among "rough ashes" in recompense for his and others' sins. Among others praying this frigid night is Madeline, who follows the ritual of Saint Agnes: If a maiden refrains from eating, drinking, speaking, listening, looking anywhere, except up to heaven, and lies supine when she retires, she will be rewarded with the vision of her future husband. The irony of the patron saint of virgins inspiring a heterosexual vision is lost on the young girl, panting as she prays for all "the bliss to be before to-morrow morn." Meanwhile, Porphyro, her love, is in reality racing across the moors to worship his Madeline. As Madeline works on her dream, Porphyro will act on his desired reality—getting into Madeline's bedroom closet where "he might see her beauty unespied,/ And win perhaps that night a peerless bride."

The lovers' stratagems provide a weird culmination, though they move in complementary pattern. While Madeline is undergoing her ritualistic deprivations, Porphyro is gathering, through the assistance of her wily old nurse, Angela, a banquet of delights to fulfill deliciously her sensual needs; while she undresses, he gazes, of course, unseen; while she silently sleeps, he pipes in her ear "La belle dame sans merci." When she awakens to find the man of her dream at her side, however, the seemingly perfect solution is shattered. Madeline's dream of Porphyro was better than Porphyro and she tells him so: "How changed thou art! how pallid, chill, and drear!" She implores that he return to her as the dream. Porphyro arises, "Beyond a mortal man impassioned far/ At these voluptuous accents" and

> like a throbbing star
>
> .   .   .   .
>
> Into her dream he melted, as the rose
> Blendeth its odor with the violet—
> Solution sweet.

The moon of Saint Agnes, which has been languishing throughout the poem, sets as Madeline loses her virginity. Madeline, however, comes out of the experience confused; she wanted a dream, not reality, and apparently she could not distinguish between them at their climax. Now bewildered, and feeling betrayed and vulnerable to abandonment, she chides Porphyro for taking advantage. He assures her of his undying devotion and the two flee the sleeping castle into the storm, for he has prepared a home for her in the southern moors. The drunken revelers from the party lie benightmared; Angela soon dies "palsy-twitched"; and the loveless beadsman, after thousands of Aves, sleeps forever among his ashes.

A skeptical reading of the poem has found Porphyro a voyeur and (perhaps) a rapist, Madeline a silly conjurer whose machinations have backfired; an optimistic reading has

Madeline and Porphyro ascending to heaven's bourn. The language, imagery, and structure allow both interpretations, which is the way of complex ironic honesty. The dream experience, for example, has two parts: the first when Madeline awakens to find Porphyro disappointingly imperfect; the second when the two blend into "solution sweet." It would seem that dream and reality have unified in the second part, but the first part is not thereby negated. Rather, the lovers are lost in sensory intensity, which, according to Keats, makes "all disagreeables evaporate." Whether the moment of intensity is worth the necessary conjuration before or the inevitable disillusionment afterward is a judgment on the nature of romance itself, down to this very day.

LAMIA

Lamia provides the nondreamer, Lycius, with much more than the two ordinary lovers of "The Eve of St. Agnes" are permitted; but the question is whether more is better. T. S. Eliot wrote that humankind cannot stand very much reality; Keats suggests in *Lamia* that neither can people bear very much dreaming. Lamia, as imagination incarnate, provides her lover Lycius with a realized dream of carnal perfection that extends continuously until he tires of her adoration. When Lamia, once bound in serpent form, was capable of sending her imagination abroad to mingle among the mortals of Corinth, she saw Lycius in a chariot race and fell in love. After being released from her serpent prison house by another immortal, Hermes, in an exchange of wish fulfillments, she assumes a glorious woman's body to attract Lycius. She is successful, but a series of compromises must be made to win him and satisfy his desires. Those compromises are the record of imagination's degeneration. Because Lycius is so overwhelmed by her beauty, he believes she must be immortal and loses his confidence. She "throws the goddess off" to encourage his masculinity. When he tires of the carnal pleasure she provides in the "purple-lined palace of sweet sin," she begs on her knees that he might preserve the privacy of their dream, for she knows of her vulnerability to reason. The sight of her begging brings out the sadist in Lycius, who "takes delight in her sorrows, soft and new." His passion grown cruel, Lamia plays the complementary masochist, burning, loving the tyranny. She grants his wish that they should be married before all of Corinth, and creates a feast and a vision of palatial splendor for the "gossip rout." The philosopher Apollonius, tutor to Lycius, crashes the party to destroy the dream with his "keen, cruel, perceant, stinging" eye. Apollonius is reason to Lamia's imagination, and in the confrontation between them, Lamia dissipates; Lycius the scholar-lover dies because he is incapable of balancing reason and imagination; and Apollonius is left with a Pyrrhic victory, for he has lost his pupil whom he intended to save.

Ironically, the loss of the dream, the dreamers, and the battle is not even tragic because not one was worthy of salvation. Lycius risks his dream so that his friends will look with admiration, but his friends choke over his good fortune; Lamia concedes to this foolish vanity; and Apollonius, the brilliant sophist, mistakes the whole situation, feeling that Lycius has become the prey of Lamia. More than saying that dreams cannot mix with reality, *Lamia* warns that imagination cannot be prostituted to the pleasure principle. Dreams are pure and sensitive constructs inspired by love, created for the psyche by the imagination. The eye of self-consciousness; participation with others, including loved ones; the dictates of forces less pure than love—all cause dissolution of the ephemeral dream.

"ODE TO A NIGHTINGALE"

"Ode to a Nightingale" leaves the medium of the dream for empathic identification with a natural being that seems to promise transcendence of the human condition. Again, a transcendence of self is fleetingly achieved, leaving the poet, *in propria persona*, more isolated and bewildered thereafter. He opens the poem having returned from identification with the bird's "happiness" that causes and permits it to sing "of summer in full-throated ease." The poet, however, is now drowsy and numb, so far has he sunk from that high experience of unself-conscious joy. He wishes for any wine, human or divine, that might effect a dissolution of consciousness and a return to the bird; for among men, "but to think is to be full of sorrow/ And leaden-eyed despairs." The transience of the physical splendor of beauty, of the psychological heights of love; the tragedy of early death, the indignity of aging to death; participation in human misery—all have thwarted any love or hope he might feel for the human condition.

In the fourth stanza, the poet seems to join the bird, but ambiguously. After exhorting either his imagination or the bird (or both) to fly "Away! away!" where he will reach it on "the viewless wings of Poesy," he seems to achieve the connection: "Already with thee! tender is the night." The eighth and final stanza supports the interpretation of his extended identification, for it has the poet being tolled back from the bird "to my sole self." Before the identification in stanza 4, however, he has qualified the power of those viewless wings to keep him in stable flight, for "the dull brain perplexes and retards." Consequently, throughout the poem, he is neither entirely with the bird, nor entirely in his metaphysical agony, but rather in a state of mixed or split consciousness that leads to the poem's concluding questions: "Was it vision, or a waking dream?/ Fled is that music:—Do I wake or sleep?" In the sixth stanza, for example, as he sits in his "embalmèd darkness" in the arbor, he says, "Darkling I listen; and, for many a time/ I have been half in love with easeful Death." Shortly, he seems to be lost in the ecstasy of the bird's song. Yet immediately he retracts, for common sense tells him that, if he were dead, his ears would be in vain, and "To thy high requiem" of the bird, he would "become a sod."

The seventh stanza distinguishes the immortality of the bird's song from the mortality of the poet, and for another passing moment he seems to experience identification as he slips into empathy with those through time who have also heard the immortal song, especially Ruth of the Old Testament: "Perhaps the self-same song that found a path/ Through the sad heart of Ruth, when, sick for home,/ She stood in tears amid the alien corn." This song that flows through time sparks both the poet's identification with it and his empathy for fellow beings. He is not as explicit as Walt Whitman would be in defining immortality as empathy for all beings and experiences of all times, but his revealed feeling for others is the eternal human counterpart to the song that eternally elicits the feeling. Still, the great divider between the bird and poet is the poet's self consciousness. The bird, unaware of its individuality and coming death, is more a medium of the song of its species than a being in its own right. The poet withdraws completely in the final stanza to his "sole self." The imagination cannot support the identification with a dissimilar being for very long. The bird's song fades until it is metaphorically dead to the poet, "buried deep/ In the next valley glades." The stimulus for experience now fled, the poet recognizes the division he has undergone between empathy and identity, being in and out of self, with neither strain coming to resolution. The bewilderment of the conclusion reflects perfectly the imperfect resolution of his experience.

"ODE ON MELANCHOLY"

The "Ode on Melancholy" offers perhaps the most positive perspective possible to one who appreciates this tragedy of the human condition. Its psychology is a variant of Satan's from *Paradise Lost*: "Evil, be thou my good." The poet advises that when the "melancholy fit shall fall," as fall it must, one should not seek to escape with "poisonous wine," "nightshade," or other agents that would "drown the wakeful anguish of the soul," for that very anguish is the catalyst for more intensely valuing transient beauty, joy, and love. Even the anger of a loved one will reach a value transcending relationship, if one should "Emprison her soft hand, and let her rave,/ And feed deep, deep upon her peerless eyes." The glow fired by her passion, the beauty, joy, and pleasure that accompany love, all must dwindle, die, depart, sour; but if one holds an awareness of their end while indulging in their prime, the triumph of deep inclusive response will reward the sensitive soul with ultimate mortal value. It will be among Melancholy's "cloudy trophies hung," which is to say, the "sadness of her might" will hold him forever sensitive to the richness of transience.

"TO AUTUMN"

In like manner, "To Autumn" offers a perspective on nature in the ultimate richness of its condition. It has always been difficult for poets to look on nature without moralizing its landscape for human edification. The Romantic period especially sought its morality from nature and its processes. Keats, however, describes nature without pressing metaphor out of it; his goal is to offer it as worthy in itself so that one might love it for itself. If there are analogues between human nature and nature, they are not the subject, concern, or purpose of the poem. As several critics have noted, the stanzas move from the late growth of summer to the fulfillment of autumn to the harvested landscape; correspondingly, the imagery moves from tactile to visual to auditory in an ascension from the most grossly physical to the most nonphysical. The sun and the season are in league to load and bless the vines with fruit, and in a string of energetic infinitives, the push of life's fulfillment is represented: "To bend with apples the mossed cottage trees," to "fill all fruit with ripeness to the core," "To swell the gourd, and plump the hazel shells," "to set budding more,/ And still more, later flowers for the bees." An image of surfeited bees, who think summer will never end, their "clammy cells" are so "o'er-brimmed," concludes the first stanza.

Stanza 2 presents the personification of autumn "sitting careless on a granary floor"; sound asleep "Drowsed with the fume of poppies" in the fields; "by a cyder press, with patient look," watching the "last oozings hours by hours." The harvested stubble plains of stanza 3 provoke the poet's question, "Where are the songs of spring?" Even so, the question is raised more to dismiss it as irrelevant than to honor its inevitability. Autumn has its own music and the poem softly presents it: as the stubble plains are covered with the rosy hue of the dying day, the "small gnats mourn," "full-grown lambs loud bleat," "Hedge crickets sing," "with treble soft/ The red-breast whistles from a garden-croft," and "gathering swallows twitter in the skies." The suggestion of animate life singing unconsciously in its joy, while just as unconsciously readying for winter, signals the end of the natural year. Unlike Shelley, however, who in "Ode to the West Wind" looks through the fall and coming winter to spring as an analogue of rebirth for humankind, Keats allows not more than a suggestion of what is to follow, and that only because it belongs to the sound and action of the season. Autumn is accepted for itself, not as an image, sign, or omen of spiritual value. Ripeness is all.

"ODE ON A GRECIAN URN"

As "Ode on Melancholy" and "To Autumn" established perspectives on the human condition and nature, so "Ode on a Grecian Urn" establishes a relationship with art. This ode begins and ends by addressing the urn as object, but the subject-object duality is dissolved in the third of the five stanzas. The experiential movement of the poem is from ignorance through identification to understanding. The poet addresses the urn as a "bride of quietness," "still unravished" by passing generations. It is a "foster child of silence and slow time." Once the child of the artist and his time, the urn belongs not to eternity, for it is vulnerable to destruction, but to the timeless existence of what endures. It is a sylvan historian, containing a narrative relief of the beings and scenes of its surface. The poet asks questions of it as historian; what gods, music, bacchanalian frenzy it images. All is silent; but that is best, we learn, for "Heard melodies are sweet, but those unheard/ Are sweeter," free to become as flawless as imagination can wish. The second stanza finds the poet moving close, addressing the urn's individuals. The "Fair youth" who pipes the song so softly that only the spirit hears, the "Bold lover" who has neared the lips of his maiden, both arouse the poet-lover's empathy.

In the third stanza, the poet participates fully in the urn's existence as he inspires scenery and youths with imaginative fervor. The "happy, happy boughs! that cannot shed/ [their] leaves, nor ever bid the spring adieu"; the "happy melodist, unwearied,/ Forever piping songs forever new"; and, above all, "more happy love! more happy, happy love!/ Forever warm and still to be enjoyed,/ Forever panting, and forever young"—none of it can pass. Nature, art, and love remain in the glow of their promise. The love on the urn arouses a special contrast with "breathing human passion . . ./ That leaves a heart high-sorrowful and cloyed,/ A burning forehead, and a parching tongue." The fourth stanza begins to pull out of intense identification, with questions on the urn's religious scene: "Who are these coming to the sacrifice?" To what "green altar" does the priest lead his sacrificial heifer? What town do they come from that will be emptied of its inhabitants forever? Stanza 5 again addresses the urn as object, but with increased understanding over stanza 1. She is now "Attic shape! Fair Attitude! with brede/ Of marble men and maidens overwrought." The bride, though unravished and wed to quietness, has her breed of beings, themselves passionately in pursuit of experience. She is a "silent form" that "dost tease us out of thought/ As doth eternity: Cold Pastoral!" If her silence provokes participation so that viewers lose self-consciousness in her form, then truly they are teased out of thought, as the poet was in stanza 3. Why, though, is she a "Cold Pastoral!"

Critics have taken this to be the poet's criticism of the urn in her relationship with those who contemplate her; perhaps it is best, however, that the urn remain cold, if she is to encourage and reward the viewers' empathy. Stanza 3 criticized human passion for its torrid intensity in contrast with the urn's image of love "Forever *warm* and [thus] still to be enjoyed." The urn remains a cold object until it is kindled by the viewers' passion. When the mortals of the present generation have been wasted by time, the urn will continue to exist for others, "a friend to man," to whom it (or the poet) has this to say: "Beauty is truth, truth beauty—that is all/ Ye know on earth, and all ye need to know."

Much has been written about these final lines of the "Ode on a Grecian Urn," and the technicalities of this famous problem for criticism must be at least briefly addressed. The difficulty is in determining who is saying what to whom; the issue has a mundane origin in punctuation. According to the text of the *Lamia* volume, the lines should be punctuated with the quotation marks enclosing only the beauty-truth statement: "'Beauty is truth, truth beauty'—that is all. . . ." If the lines are punctuated thus, the urn makes the beauty-truth statement, and the poet himself offers the evaluation of it, either to the urn, to the figures on the urn, or to the reader. Many scholars, however, see the matter differently; they would place the entire aphorism within quotations, based upon manuscript authority: "'Beauty is truth . . . need to know.'" With this punctuation, the urn is talking to man. Both choices lead to problematic interpretations. In the former case, it does not make much sense for the poet to speak to the urn or to its images about "all ye know on earth," as if there were someplace else for the urn to know something. There might be an afterlife where things can be known, but not for the urn. It would be odd for the poet to speak to the reader in that way, too. The inconsistency in tone would be especially awkward. Several lines earlier, he had joined his reader in saying to the urn: "Thou . . . dost tease us out of thought." To refer now to "us" as *ye*, as in "that is all/ Ye know on earth," is out of tone. On the other hand, the argument against the urn speaking the entire aphorism is directed against its sufficiency. It has been argued that human beings need to know a great deal more than "Beauty is truth, truth beauty," no matter how one tries to stretch the meanings of the terms to make them appear all-inclusive. There is no way to resolve this critical problem with confidence, though trying to think through it will provide an exercise in Keatsian specuation at its best.

To agree that the experience the poet undergoes is entirely satisfactory might be enough, though there is not critical unanimity about this, either. Lovers about to kiss, rather than kissing; trees in their springtime promise, rather than in fruition; a song that has to be imagined; a sacrifice still to be made, rather than offered—all can suggest experience short of perfection. Yet, like Keats's dreams that surpass reality, these figures are safely in their imaginative prime. The kiss, after all, may not be as sweet as anticipated; the fruit may be blighted; the song may be tiresome or soon grow so; the sacrifice may be unacceptable.

In fact, a reader comes to Keats's poetry as the poet himself came to the urn. Like all great art, Keats's poetry is evocative; it leads its readers' emotions and thoughts into and then out of its formal beauty to teach and delight. One can stand back and examine its formal perfection; one can ask questions of it about human nature and its desires for being and loving. Yet only through the experience of it can one learn what it has to teach; only after one goes through the empathy of Keats's narrator in stanza 3 can one speak with confidence of its meaning.

OTHER MAJOR WORKS

NONFICTION: *The Letters of John Keats, 1814-1821*, 1958 (2 volumes; Hyder Edward Rollins, editor).

MISCELLANEOUS: *Complete Works*, 1900-1901 (5 volumes; H. B. Forman, editor); *Complete Poems and Selected Letters of John Keats*, 2001.

BIBLIOGRAPHY

Bloom, Harold, ed. *John Keats*. Rev. ed. New York: Chelsea House, 2007. Contains essays on the poetry of Keats. Includes essays on the *Hyperion*s, "La Belle Dame sans Merci," and "The Eve of St. Agnes."

Christensen, Allan C. *The Challenge of Keats: Bicentenary Essays, 1795-1995*. Atlanta: Rodopi, 2000. Contributors to this volume reexamine some of the criticisms and exaltations of Keats to find a new analysis of his achievement. Delivers an appraisal of the historical and cultural contexts of Keats's work and an in-depth discussion of the influences and relationships between Keats and other poets.

Cox, Jeffrey N. *Poetry and Politics in the Cockney School: Keats, Shelley, Hunt, and Their Circle*. New York: Cambridge University Press, 1998. This monograph in the Cambridge Studies in Romanticism series examines the "second generation" of Romantics (those associated with Leigh Hunt) and challenges the common idea that the original Romantics, including Keats, were solitary figures, instead postulating the social nature of their work. An entire chapter, "John Keats, Coterie Poet," is devoted to Keats.

Hebron, Stephen. *John Keats*. New York: Oxford University Press, 2002. A biography of Keats that delves into his life and works.

McFarland, Thomas. *The Masks of Keats: The Endeavour of a Poet*. New York: Oxford University Press, 2000. The well-known scholar of Romantic literature surveys the essence of Keats.

Motion, Andrew. *Keats*. Chicago: University of Chicago Press, 1999. A biography that emphasizes Keats's politics as well as his poetry and personality. Motion won a Whitbread Prize for his biography of Philip Larkin, but *Keats* is his first dealing with the Romantic period. Highlighting the tough side of Keats's character, Motion puts to rest the image of Keats as little more than a sickly dreamer.

Robinson, Jeffrey C. *Reception and Poetics in Keats: My Ended Poet*. New York: St. Martin's Press, 1998. Readings of other poets' poems addressed to or about Keats, followed by an examination of Keats as a precursor to the visionary, open-form poetry of some of the modern age's experimental poets.

Siler, Jack. *Poetic Language and Political Engagement in the Poetry of Keats*. New York: Routledge, 2008. Applies Peter Burger's aesthetic categories in an interpretation of the poetry of Keats.

Sitterson, Joseph C., Jr. *Romantic Poems, Poets, and Narrators*. Kent, Ohio: Kent State University Press, 2000. An examination of narrative and point of view in the poetry of the Romantic poets William Wordsworth, Samuel Taylor Coleridge, William Blake, and Keats. Close readings of the major poems, including *Lamia*, from various critical perspectives. Includes bibliographical references and index.

Whale, John. *John Keats*. New York: Palgrave Macmillan, 2005. Examines the poetry and letters of Keats with an emphasis on gender and sexuality as well as love and desire.

Richard E. Matlak

EDUARD MÖRIKE

Born: Ludwigsburg, Württemberg (now in Germany); September 8, 1804
Died: Stuttgart, Germany; June 4, 1875

Principal poetry
Gedichte, 1838, 1848, 1856, 1867 (*Poems*, 1959)
Idylle vom Bodensee oder Fischer Martin und die Glockendiebe, 1848

Other literary forms
Although Eduard Mörike (MUR-ree-kuh) is famous for his poetry, and many of his poems have been set to music, he was not primarily a poet. His first publication was a three-hundred-page novella in two parts, *Maler Nolten* (1832; *Nolten the Painter: A Novella in Two Parts*, 2005). He also wrote seven shorter works; the most well-known is *Mozart auf der Reise nach Prag* (1855; *Mozart's Journey from Vienna to Prague: A Romance of His Private Life*, 1897). Of particular significance for his poetry are his translations of classical poetry that retain the stanza form of the original. His editorial work attests to his interest in the works of contemporary Swabian poets and novelists, as well as in Greek and Roman poetry.

Achievements
During Eduard Mörike's lifetime, very few German literary awards were being awarded, as most awards were not established until the twentieth century. For that reason, the recognition he received carries all the more weight. In 1847, Mörike won the Tiedge Prize for his *Idylle vom Bodensee oder Fischer Martin und die Glockendiebe*. In 1852, he received an honorary doctorate from the University of Tübingen, and in 1862, the king of Bavaria awarded him the Order of Maximilian for Arts and Sciences. In 1864, Mörike was awarded the Knight's Cross First Class of the Württemberg Order of Friedrich.

Biography
Eduard Mörike spent his entire life in southwest Germany, in what is now the state of Baden-Württemberg. He is sometimes referred to as a Swabian poet, because Swabian is the dialect spoken in that region. The family's standard of living was severely reduced when Mörike's father, a physician, suffered a massive stroke in 1815 and died two years later. Although Mörike was not a good student, an influential uncle arranged for him to attend the theological seminar in Urach and then to study theology in Tübingen. Mörike subsequently served reluctantly as a Protestant clergyman in numerous posts. He was not convinced of the doctrine he was required to preach and was not

appreciated by his parishioners. In 1834, he was appointed pastor in Cleversulzbach and brought his mother and younger sister Klara to live with him there. It was his last position with the church. In 1843, two years after his mother's death, Mörike took early retirement.

The Mörikes were a close-knit family. Eduard Mörike was devastated when his younger brother August died of a stroke in 1824 and commemorated him in the poem "To an Aeolian Harp." Three years later, his older sister Luise died at age twenty-nine, and Mörike had to take several months' leave of absence. His own health was delicate, and he was often overextended financially because he felt obliged to help his siblings. Mörike was apolitical, and was shocked by the interrogation he underwent after his brother Carl was jailed for political protest.

In 1823-1824, during Mörike's student years, he was briefly infatuated with an attractive transient, Maria Meyer. Then, believing she had deceived him, he refused to see her again, a decision that caused him considerable emotional suffering. That relationship is the subject of his five "Peregrina" poems. He was engaged to Luise Rau from 1829 to 1833 but was also working on *Nolten the Painter* at the time, and Rau left him for someone better able to provide for her. Mörike did not marry until he was forty-seven. It is indicative of his open-mindedness in intolerant times that his wife, Margarethe Speeth, was a Roman Catholic. Their two daughters, Fanny and Marie, were born in 1855 and 1857. Mörike supported his family, which still included his sister Klara, by teaching from 1851 to 1866 at the Katharinenstift, a girls' school in Stuttgart.

Throughout Mörike's life, a friend from student days, Wilhelm Hartlaub, was a constant source of companionship and support. Mörike's poem "To Wilhelm Hartlaub" describes how Hartlaub's piano playing could transport him into other worlds. Hartlaub had what Mörike longed for, a sense of fulfillment as a clergyman and a peaceful domestic life. Mörike was estranged from his wife and in financial straits during the last years of his life. He is buried in the Prague Cemetery in Stuttgart.

ANALYSIS

A glance at Eduard Mörike's 225 poems reveals his remarkable versatility as a poet. The influence of Greek and Roman poetry is evident in his sonnets, odes, and idylls, and in his frequent use of iambic hexameter. The Germanic influence is evident in the rhymed quatrains and simple folksongs. However, Mörike was not limited by any form: Some of his poems are just two verses long; others run for pages. In most cases, he uses rhyme, meter, and stanza structures only as artistically necessary. Many of his poems are in free verse. His writing is direct, often conversational in tone. The five "Peregrina" poems are one of only two groups of poems. (The other group, "Pictures from Bebenhausen," has been only partially translated.) Otherwise, each poem stands for itself. Mörike let a friend decide on their order of appearance when his poems were published.

Nothing in Mörike's poetry indicates that he lived in a time of political unrest; nothing indicates that he was a clergyman. Some of his contemporaries criticized him for not mentioning political or historical events, but ironically, it is his refusal to be governed by current events that has made his poetry timeless. Mörike focused on personal issues, everyday life, and the inner peace he experienced in the presence of friends or when beholding a "Beautiful Beech Tree" or an object, as in "On a Lamp." He could capture the moment and infuse it with meaning. Much of his poetry, though, has an undercurrent of dissonance, a dissonance Hugo Wolf transferred well to his musical settings of fifty-seven Mörike poems in the 1880's. Mörike shows that even "At Midnight," one is constantly reminded of the affairs of the day. He was aware of conflicting beliefs, changes brought with the passage of time, and the omnipresence of death.

"PEREGRINA" POEMS

Mörike wrote his five "Peregrina" poems between 1824 and 1828 and included versions of four of them in *Nolten the Painter*. These early poems—some rhymed, some unrhymed, some in regular stanzas, and some in free verse—derive from Mörike's intense love for and then loss of the migrant or peregrine Meyer. The male poetic persona experiences heartbreak because he still loves Peregrina, indeed will always love her, yet feels he had to send her away because of his desire to remain in respectable society.

Mörike portrays a dangerous struggle between emotion and reason, between sexual attraction and societal norms. The temptation is great. In the first poem, the speaker tells Peregrina of her powerful effect on him: "To set us both on fire with wild beguiling:/ Death in the cup of sin you hand me, smiling." The wedding scene in the second poem is far removed from any Christian context. The bride is dressed in explicitly sexual colors, with her black dress and scarlet headscarf, but the reader should remember that black and red are also the colors of traditional Black Forest costumes. The turning point is the third poem, in which the speaker realizes he has been deceived. He sends Peregrina away, but cannot stop thinking of her, and he wonders how he would react if she were to reappear. The fourth poem shows how thoughts of her still intrude and move him to tears in other surroundings. The fifth poem, a sonnet, has him longing for her return, while he remains convinced that she will never come back again.

In *Nolten the Painter*, the Peregrina figure is conflated with the gypsy Elizabeth and is portrayed as truly malign, bringing death to Nolten and any women who are interested in him. This change in her character may be seen as rationalization on the part of the author, making the object of his attraction seem worse than she was to justify his rejection of her.

"ON A CHRISTMAS ROSE"

"On a Christmas Rose," a two-part poem, was written in 1841. Mörike wrote to his friend Hartlaub on October 29 of that year that he and his sister Klara had found the rare flower they had been seeking in a churchyard. Known in English as the Christmas rose, the plant is actually *Helleborus niger*. Mörike describes its delicate fragrance and the green tint in its white petals.

Because he found it blooming on a grave in a churchyard and because of its common name, *Christblume*, Mörike first associates the flower with Christian imagery, mentioning an angel, the Virgin Mary, and the wounds of Christ. However, the purely Christian frame of reference was never adequate for Mörike. In the last stanza of part 1, he draws on the pre-Christian, Germanic belief in spirits of the forest by having an elf tiptoe past the flower. Mörike's poetry is rich in undercurrents because for him, many things could be simultaneously present.

Part 2 is a classic example of Mörike's inclusive vision, a fanciful superimposition of summer on winter. Commenting that a summer butterfly can never feed on the nectar of a Christmas rose that blooms in winter, Mörike then wonders if the butterfly's fragile ghost, drawn by the faint fragrance, may not still be present and hovering around its petals, although invisible to him.

"A Visit to the Charterhouse"

"A Visit to the Charterhouse (epistle to Paul Heyse—1862)," a long idyll in iambic hexameter, was one of Mörike's last poems and was recognized early on as one of his best. It refers to the Carthusian charterhouse or monastery between St. Gallen and Constance that Mörike visited in 1840.

In the poem, the speaker makes a return visit to the charterhouse after fourteen years and finds that the last monks have dispersed and the monastery building is now a brewery. The traveler falls into a reverie about the hospitable prior he met on his previous visit, and by virtue of his vivid description, the prior is present again, in the same way that the butterfly hovers around the Christmas rose.

An object then links the past with the present more tangibly. The traveler recognizes the prior's clock on the mantelpiece, a pewter clock engraved with the Latin memento mori: *Una ex illis ultima* (one of these hours will be your last). The realization that death will put an end to life is one of Mörike's main themes, as in "O Soul, Remember" and "Erinna to Sappho."

In "A Visit to the Charterhouse," thoughts of death are pleasantly interrupted. The local physician entertains the traveler with the story of the clock. The prior bequeathed it to the father steward, and when the father suffered a slight stroke, the clock disappeared. Years later, the brewer's wife found the clock wrapped up behind the chimney stack, with a label bequeathing it to the brewmaster. The poem is a tribute to companionship and conversation, the best means on earth to banish mortal fears.

Other major works

LONG FICTION: *Maler Nolten*, 1832 (*Nolten the Painter: A Novella in Two Parts*, 2005); *Das Stuttgarter Hutzelmännlein*, 1853; *Mozart auf der Reise nach Prag*, 1855

(*Mozart's Journey from Vienna to Prague: A Romance of His Private Life*, 1897); *Die Historie von der Schöen Lau*, 1873 (illustrations by Moritz von Schwind).

TRANSLATION: *Theokritos, Bion und Moschos. Deutsch im Versmasse der Urschrift*, 1855 (with Friedrich Notter).

EDITED TEXTS: *Jahrbuch Schwäbischer Dichter und Novellisten*, 1836 (with Wilhelm Zimmermann); *Classische Blumenlese: Eine Auswahl von Hymnen, Oden, Liedern, Elegien, Idyllen, Gnomen und Epigrammen der Griechen und Römer*, 1840; *Gedichte von Wilhelm Waiblinger*, 1844; *Anakreon und die sogenannten Anakreontischen Lieder: Revision und Erzänzung der J. Fr. Dege'schen Übersetzung mit Erklärungen von E. Mörike*, 1864.

MISCELLANEOUS: *Iris. Eine Sammlungerzählender und dramatischer Dichtungen*, 1839; *Vier Erzählungen*, 1856.

BIBLIOGRAPHY

Adams, Jeffrey. "Eduard Mörike." In *Dictionary of Literary Biography. Nineteenth-Century German Writers to 1840*, edited by James Hardin and Siegfried Mews. Vol. 133. Detroit: Gale, 1993. A chronological overview of Mörike's life and works.

_____, ed. *Mörike's Muses. Critical Essays on Eduard Mörike*. Columbia, S.C.: Camden House, 1990. Of the eleven essays in the anthology, only seven provide English translations of the poems discussed. Mark Lehrer's interesting essay compares Mörike's implicit values with those of his contemporary Karl Marx. Contains Stern's translation of "A Visit to the Charterhouse."

Hölderlin, Friedrich, and Eduard Mörike. *Friedrich Hölderlin, Eduard Mörike. Selected Poems*. Translated by Christopher Middleton. Chicago: University of Chicago Press, 1972. Contains translations of thirty-six of Mörike's poems. Middleton has read all of Mörike's letters and has written an informative introduction and detailed notes about the poems. Includes the five "Peregrina" poems.

Mare, Margaret. *Eduard Mörike. The Man and the Poet*. London: Methuen, 1957. An excellent, classic biography with twenty illustrations consisting of art by Mörike and family portraits. Appendix 1 contains English translations of eight major poems.

Mörike, Eduard. *Mozart's Journey to Prague and a Selection of Poems*. Translated by David Luke. London: Penguin Classics, 2003. Contains translations of forty-three of Mörike's poems, a useful introduction, and notes on the poems.

_____. *Poems by Eduard Mörike*. Translated by Norah K. Cruickshank and Gilbert F. Cunningham. With an introduction by Jethro Bithell. London: Methuen, 1959. Translation includes a useful introduction and brief information about each of the forty translated poems. Includes "On a Christmas Rose."

Oxford German Studies 36, no. 1 (2007). This special issue on Mörike contains two excellent articles on his poetry. "Mörike and the Higher Criticism," by Ritchie Robertson, focuses on Mörike's combination of Christian and pagan elements in the poem

"To a Christmas Rose." "Idyll and Elegy: Mörike's 'Besuch in der Carthause,'" by Ray Ockenden, draws on Mörike's knowledge of classical verse forms to lend deeper understanding to this previously neglected late poem.

Slessarev, Helga. *Eduard Mörike*. New York: Twayne, 1970. The long, well-organized chapter on Mörike's poetry places it in the context of his classical education and the events of his life.

Jean M. Snook

GÉRARD DE NERVAL

Born: Paris, France; May 22, 1808
Died: Paris, France; January 26, 1855

OTHER LITERARY FORMS

Gérard de Nerval (nehr-VAHL) tried his hand at drama, short fiction, and nonfiction. He wrote two dramas in collaboration with Alexandre Dumas, *père*. They are *Piquillo* (pb. 1837) and *Alchimiste* (pb. 1839). His other dramas include *Chariot d'enfant* (1850, with Joseph Méry), *L'Imagier de Harlem* (pr. 1851), and a translation of Johann Wolfgang von Goethe's *Faust: Eine Tragödie* (pb. 1808; *The Tragedy of Faust*, 1823) and *Faust: Eine Tragödie, zweiter Teil* (pb. 1833; *The Tragedy of Faust, Part Two*, 1838) in 1827 and 1840. Among his nonfiction prose works are *Voyage en Orient* (1851; *Journey to the Orient*, 1972); *Les Illuminés* (1852), and *Aurélia* (1855; English translation, 1932). A collection of his stories came out as *Les Filles du feu* (1854; *Daughters of Fire*, 1922).

ACHIEVEMENTS

During his lifetime, Gérard de Nerval was generally regarded as an enthusiastic but harmless eccentric, a writer of some genius whose best and freshest productions were marred by occasional lapses into obscurity. Because of his bouts with madness—both manic-depressive psychosis (or, in modern psychological language, cyclothymic depression) and schizophrenia—he struck most of his contemporaries as an oddity, a poet sometimes pathetic yet never dangerous except to his own well-being. Around him numerous legends accumulated, most of them ludicrous. Some of the more absurd stories were given wider circulation by Jules Champfleury in *Grandes Figures d'hier et d'aujourd'hui: Balzac, Gérard de Nerval, Wagner, Courbet* (1861) and by Arsène Houssaye in *Les Confessions: Souvenirs d'un demi-siècle* (1885, 6 vols.). In part as a result of such droll anecdotes, Nerval's reputation during the first half of the nineteenth century was that of a minor figure: a poet with close affinities with German Romanticism, a distinguished translator of Johann Wolfgang von Goethe's *Faust*, a moderately popular

Gérard de Nerval
(Library of Congress)

playwright and the author of sumptuously exotic travel literature, and a lyricist whose originality and vigor were evident but whose interests were too often attached to the curious and the extravagant. Later during the century, critics compared Nerval with Charles Baudelaire, treating both as psychologists of the aberrant. After the beginning of the twentieth century, commentators judged Nerval favorably in relation to the Symbolists, especially to Stéphane Mallarmé and Arthur Rimbaud. Still later, Nerval was appreciated as a forerunner of Guillaume Apollinaire and modernist experimentation. Since the 1920's, Nerval's achievements have been viewed independently of their connections with other writers or movements. Treated not as a precursor of greater talents but as a towering genius in his own right, Nerval has been examined as a seer, a mystic, a student of Hermetic doctrine and of alchemy, a poet of extraordinary complexit, resonance, and power. His most important works in prose and poetry—*Petits Châteaux de Bohême*, *Aurélia*, and *Daughters of Fire*— are among the glories of French literature.

BIOGRAPHY

Gérard de Nerval was born Gérard Labrunie, the son of Étienne Labrunie, a medical doctor, and of Marie-Antoinette Marguerite Laurent, daughter of a Paris draper. Nerval did not change his name until 1831, when he signed a letter "G. la Brunie de Nerval," taking the name from a property, Le Clos de Nerval, belonging to his mother's family. The name is also an anagram of his mother's maiden name, Laurent. It is known that Nerval hated his father, who served with Napoleon's Grande Armée as a field surgeon and who was, throughout the poet's life, an aloof, insensitive parent. Nerval's mother died when the boy was only two years old, and Nerval was sent to live with his great-uncle, Antoine Boucher, at Mortefontaine. Nerval later described these early years as the happiest of his life. He had free range of a library of occult books and discussed philosophy with his great-uncle, who may have served as a model for Père Dodu in Nerval's short story "Sylvie" (1853; English translation, 1922). When Nerval's father returned from the front in 1814, the boy joined him in Paris. In 1820, Nerval entered the Collège Charlemagne, where he began to exhibit a fondness for literary pursuits and began his lifelong friendship with the poet Théophile Gautier.

In November, 1827, Nerval published his translation of Goethe's *The Tragedy of Faust*, but under the publication date of 1828. This work was well received in Parisian literary circles, and Nerval became a disciple of Victor Hugo and joined his *cénacle romantique*. In the notorious dispute that followed the disruptive theatrical opening (February 25, 1830) of Hugo's play *Hernani* (pr., pb. 1830; English translation, 1830) however, Nerval sided with Gautier, and thereafter Nerval frequented Gautier's *petit cénacle*.

An inheritance from his maternal grandfather in 1834 allowed Nerval to give up his medical studies and pursue a literary career, much to his father's disapproval. In the fall of that year, Nerval visited Italy (Florence, Rome, and Naples), a trip that later proved invaluable to his writing. Upon his return to Paris in 1834, he met and fell in love with the actress Jenny Colon. In May of 1834, he founded the theatrical review *Le Monde dramatique*, dedicated to the glorification of Colon. For a brief time, Nerval enjoyed a life of prosperity, identifying himself with the "Bohème galante." When the review failed in 1836, however, financial difficulties forced Nerval to become a journalist, writing articles for *Le Figaro* and *La Presse*. He visited Belgium with Gautier in 1836 in an effort to forget his personal struggles for a time.

On October 31, 1837, Nerval's play *Piquillo* premiered in Paris with Colon in the lead role as Silvia. The play was a success, and Nerval was encouraged to declare his love for her. On April 11, 1838, however, Colon married the flutist Louis-Gabriel Leplus, an event that left the poet bitterly disillusioned. During the summer of that year, he traveled to Germany with Dumas, *père*, and from that time the two writers began a series of theatrical collaborations.

The next two years were ones of increasing mental instability and depression for

Nerval. Though he published his translation of *The Tragedy of Faust, Part Two* in 1840, the strain of the work took its toll, and Nerval was hospitalized as a result of a nervous breakdown. The death of Colon in 1842 did nothing to restore his ailing spirits. In ill health and overcome with grief, he embarked in 1843 on a trip to Malta, Egypt, Syria, Cyprus, Constantinople, and Naples. He later published an account of his travels in *Journey to the Orient*. Nerval had discovered his psychological need to wander, a theme found in his major works.

Though his mental and physical health continued to deteriorate, Nerval struggled to support himself with his writing. Still hoping to establish himself in the theater, he wrote *Chariot d'enfant* with Méry, a production which premiered on May 13, 1850. In September, 1851, Nerval suffered an accident, followed by a serious nervous breakdown. Nerval believed that he would soon become incurably insane, a realization which made him increase his literary efforts. In 1852, he published *Les Illuminés*, a series of biographies on historical figures interested in mysteries of the occult and of alchemy. In 1853, he published a volume of nostalgic poems recalling a happier youth, *Petits Châteaux de Bohême*. In the summer of that year, Nerval published his best-known story, "Sylvie," followed by two other great works, *Daughters of Fire* and *The Chimeras*, in 1854. *Aurélia*, an account of his madness, appeared in 1855. Alone and destitute, Nerval hanged himself in an alley on January 26, 1855.

ANALYSIS

Gautier, who perhaps appreciated the fine qualities of Gérard de Nerval's character and art more than any other contemporary, once described his friend as an "apodal swallow." To Gautier, Nerval was

> all wings and no feet: At most he had perceptible claws; these enabled him to alight, at least momentarily, just long enough to catch his breath, then go on . . . to soar and move about in fluid realms with the joy and abandon of a being in his element.

Gautier's idealization of Nerval as an ethereal figure—a Percy Bysshe Shelley-like bird in flight who abjured the common terrestrial condition of humanity—is a valid judgment only to a limited degree. To be sure, a reader may approach Nerval on a superficial level as a poet of intense, vivid, direct intuition; a poet of dreams and visions; a creator of myths and fantastic personal symbolic constructs that reach into the archetypal imagination.

Certainly, most of Nerval's poetry, much of his prose poetry, and a portion of his dramatic work can be appreciated according to the qualities of Impressionism. His work has, on a simple level of perception, an evocative, dreamy, otherworldly, melancholy vein that resembles the Impressionism of otherwise dissimilar poets such as Edgar Allan Poe and Paul Verlaine. One can enjoy the seemingly imprecise but hauntingly evocative imagery of a familiar Nerval poem such as "Le Point noir" ("The Dark

Smudge") as though the writer were merely inducing an impression of malign fate. Reading Nerval for his surface characteristics of hauntingly sonorous music, vague but unsettling imagery, and technically perfect mastery of verse forms, one can accept Gautier's early evaluation of the poet as a kind of birdlike spirit—or, to use Baudelaire's image of a poet idealized as an albatross ("L'Albatros"), a creature free in the air but confined and crippled on the crass Earth.

Moreover, a reader who approaches Nerval's basic themes without first investigating their intellectual context is likely to appreciate their surface qualities of authentic feeling and simplicity of expression. Nerval is always concerned with human values, no matter that he may choose exotic subjects or complex methods to express them. His work is nearly always confessional. Although he rarely tends to be self-dramatizing in his poetry, he often places his persona—his other self—at the center of the theme in order to examine the psychological insights of a human life. An early verse, "Épître première" (first epistle), at once expresses his artistic philosophy and predicts his fate; he will, despite madness under the aegis of the moon, serve humanity with a generous desire. In his poems as well as in much of his prose and drama, Nerval appeals directly—without a reader's need for critical exegesis—to the human heart: to its courage, its idealism, its love. Although Nerval's subjects often appear to be odd, exotic, or perverse, the poet treats the flowers of his imagination not as "evil," as does the great poet of the next generation, Baudelaire, but as fragrant symbols of a mysterious, arcane harmony in the universe.

Indeed, Nerval is best appreciated as a mystic and a seer, a poet whose surface qualities of vague dreaminess conceal an interior precision of image and ideas. Reading a popularly anthologized lyric such as "Fantaisie" ("Fantasy"), for example, one tends to dismiss the poem as a piece influenced by German Romanticism, especially by the *Märchen*-like songs of Heinrich Heine or Goethe. A closer reading, however, will show that the seemingly vague images are not merely decorative; they are rendered with precision, although their precise significance as personal symbol is not clear. Nevertheless, the "green slope gilded by the setting sun" and the stone castle are objects, not atmosphere, and the mysterious theme of déjà vu is intended to be psychological truth, not fairy tale.

GERMAN ROMANTICISM

To appreciate Nerval fully, one should understand the poet's relationship to German Romanticism without treating him exclusively as a Romantic—or, indeed, exclusively as a pre-Impressionist, pre-Symbolist, or pre-modernist. Although his affinities to poets such as Heine and Goethe (Romantics), Poe and Verlaine (Impressionists), and Mallarmé and Rimbaud (Symbolists) are obvious—as are his temperamental affinities to Baudelaire—Nerval is best compared to two poets whose productions are similarly visionary and, in some respects, arcane: William Blake and William Butler Yeats. Like Blake, Nerval was a seer who searched into the heart of mysteries to discover the correspondence of opposites; a follower of the eighteenth century mystic Emanuel Sweden-borg; and an originator of complex myths and symbolic systems. Like Yeats, Nerval was a student of theosophy and an adept of the religions of the East. He believed in magic and the occult, communicated with revealers of the spirit world, and—using the phases of the moon and similar cosmic symbols—created a complex system of psychological and historical types of personalities.

ARCHETYPAL IMAGERY

In addition, Nerval cultivated dream visions, experimented with drugs such as hash-ish, and was a student of the Kabbalah, alchemy, ancient mystery religions, Illuminism, Orphism, Sabbean astral worship, and the secrets of the Egyptian pyramids. If his ab-struse researches were merely incidental to his work, much of his thinking might be safely ignored as burdensome, esoteric, or irrelevant. Nerval, however, uses a great deal of his learning in his prose and poetry. An extremely careful writer, he placed layer upon layer of meaning, often mixing different systems that are not related historically into a single new system, within the texture of his poetic prose and his poetry. To ignore these layers of meaning is to neglect as well a great deal of Nerval's subtlety as an artist.

In *Aurélia*, for example, he used archetypal images that appear to emanate from the collective unconscious—among them the image of the *magna mater* (great mother). In-cluded are manifestations of woman as loving, gentle, compassionate, noble-hearted; as vain, dissembling, inconstant; or as the dangerous fury who terrorizes a dreamer; or fi-nally, as the temptress, the coquette. Also he includes, in various manifestations, the fa-ther archetype. In *Journey to the Orient*, the poet transmutes the legend of Solomon and Sheba from a biblical tale into a personal vision centering on the character of Adoniram, a "double" for the artist, the creator. In this book, Nerval exposes themes involving the story of Cain as well as the secrets of Hermetic lore and of the pyramids (Nerval actually visited the site of the Great Pyramid of Khufu, or Cheops, and descended into its depths).

SYMBOLISM AND HERMETICISM

Nerval's poetry is less obviously arcane than much of his symbolic prose; neverthe-less, a careful student should understand that the poet uses language in a very special way. His constant endeavor was to express through symbolic language a unity that he perceived in the spiritual and the material elements of the universe. To grasp this lan-guage, a reader needs to know several concepts basic to Swedenborgian correspon-dence and Hermetic alchemy.

Nerval's research into these abstruse subjects began early in his life, notably from his interest in a tradition of thought known as Illuminism. This tradition affected writers from the middle of the eighteenth century until the end of the nineteenth century. Illuminists were fascinated with ancient Oriental manuscripts and with the tenets of Middle Eastern thinkers. Among the manuscripts that they studied were the *Corpus*

Hermeticum, a collection of forty-two books attributed to Hermes Trismegistus, perhaps the most important source of alchemical knowledge of the period. To these books were added the works of Paracelsus and his disciples.

These doctrines were cultivated by members of various secret societies (Rosicrucians, Freemasons, Martinists) which flourished at the end of the eighteenth century, particularly in France and in Germany. By means of such secret societies, Nerval came to acquire knowledge and appreciation of alchemy, while his visionary application of alchemical principles can be traced to the works of Swedenborg. In his study of the *Corpus Hermeticum* and of the Kabbala, Swedenborg had reached two conclusions that were to have a tremendous influence upon the literary world of the nineteenth century. The first of these conclusions was his idea of correspondence, the notion that every visible phenomenon has a direct opposite—upon which it depends—in the invisible and spiritual world. The second conclusion was his conception of a universal language in which these correspondences can best be expressed.

THE CHIMERAS

Nerval's poetry reveals his obsession with creating a new language, one that will allow for a communication between the visible and the invisible, the sensible and the spiritual. Such a language would permit a correspondence between the two orders. A corollary of this belief is the principle of the identity of contraries or opposites. Thus, in *The Chimeras*, Nerval establishes a syncretism of religious beliefs based upon compatibilities. His object is to demonstrate the oneness of religious thought; to achieve this high purpose, he selects a special language, using the metaphors of alchemy principally but not exclusively, as a vehicle to redeem humanity.

A reader may wonder whether a poet so learned as Nerval actually believed in the esoteric doctrines of alchemy. Certainly he used these doctrines, extracting from their classical and medieval origins a philosophical rather than pseudoscientific content, in order to construct his metaphors. In this sense, Nerval believed in alchemy as Blake believed in his visions and as Yeats believed in the symbolic constructs of his spiritual communicators. Nerval's poetry incorporates four basic alchemical principles: first, the theory of correspondence; second, the act of imagining, which can bring about corporeal transformations; third, meditation, or an inner dialogue with the invisible, which requires a "new language"; and finally, the identity of opposites, whereby every image elicits by definition its contrary. In this complex scheme, Mercury (quicksilver) becomes the symbol of alchemy: liquid metal, or the embodiment of a contradiction.

To appreciate how deeply interfused with the surface dreaminess of Nerval's verse are his symbolic constructs of alchemy, one can examine the cycle of twelve sonnets titled *The Chimeras*. The number twelve is crucial in the alchemical system, since it represents the *coniunctio tetraptiva*, or the dilemma of three and four—the chimera being the archetype of the triad. It should also be noted that the structure of the sonnet itself is representative of the problem of three and four, but in reverse. If the chimera represents the triad in the *coniunctio tetraptiva*, the four symbolizes the union of persons, and this is the underlying matrix of *The Chimeras*. By a process known as *henosis*, a tetrasomia or synthesis of opposites is produced to create a unity.

"EL DESDICHADO"

The first sonnet of *The Chimeras* is probably Nerval's best-known poem, "El desdichado" (the title, meaning "the unhappy one," was borrowed from Sir Walter Scott's *Ivanhoe*, 1819). It focuses upon the descent into the abyss, the *nigredo* of the alchemist, or the opening stage of the process. The images used to describe this phase are all somber: images of death and of caves, and even of Hell (the Achéron and the evocation of Orpheus). More important, however, is Nerval's linking of these dark, demoniac images with traditionally positive images—the union of contraries being the functional principle in such expressions as *soleil noir* ("black sun"). The most powerful character in the poem, one who is there by implication and not by name, is Melusina, the absent-but-present feminine principle. Melusina also embodies the identity of contraries, possessing either the tail of a fish or that of a snake; sometimes she appears only as a snake. Her ability to metamorphose as well as to heal diseases and injuries makes her the feminine counterpart to Mercury. Thus, in "El desdichado," Nerval posits a synthesis of the medieval duality with the Greco-Roman duality, Hermes-Mercury.

"MYRTHO"

In the succeeding sonnet, "Myrtho," Nerval assesses the descent into the abyss. It is in this manner that one can achieve the light. Moreover, it is here that the black is an essential component of the gold: "Aux raisins noirs mêlés avec l'or de ta tresse" ("and black grapes mingled in your golden tresses"). In this descent into the interior world of the light, the poet-seer necessarily meets the sovereign of the underworld, Bacchus-Dionysus-Osiris. The final two lines announce the reconciliation of certain poetic visions: that of Vergil's neopaganism with the Illuminism of the eighteenth century. Like "El desdichado," then, "Myrtho" presents a unification of various systems of thought.

"HORUS"

The sonnet "Horus" concerns the Egyptian deity considered by the syncretists to be a prefiguration of Christ. Horus also symbolizes Hellenistic mysticism, providing a direct link with Hermes and, by association, with Hermes Trismegistus, the alchemist. Isis, Horus's mother, the symbol of nature's mysteries, is identified with Venus in the same manner that Hermes is linked with Osiris, leading to a form of Greco-Egyptian religious syncretism. In this system is to be found the "esprit nouveau," the result of which is a rainbow or the vision of colors, a necessary stage which precedes the appearance of gold in alchemy.

"ANTÉROS"

"Antéros" presents a vision of Hell, with Semitic overtones. To be of the race of Antéros (Antaeus) means to gather strength from the earth from which one has sprouted. This agrarian subtext is consistent with references to Cain, the keeper of the fields, and to Dagon, the Philistine agrarian god. The Satanic aspect is sustained in the mark of Cain and in the thrice-dipping into the Cocyte, one of the rivers of Tartarus. The sonnet projects the archetypal struggle of the vanquished giant who refuses defeat— here represented by the Amalekites, a nomadic tribe which was virtually exterminated by the Israelites during the time of David. These pagans are associated with the race of Satan and Cain. "Antéros" ends with a metaphor of rebirth, that of sowing the dragon's teeth in order to create a new race of giants. In alchemical terms, the sowing of the divine seed (*germinis divi*) provides the continuity necessary for the continual process of transformation which involves death and rebirth, descent and resurrection. The baptism of Hell is the equivalent of the baptism at the holy font.

"DELFICA"

In "Delfica," Nerval includes the trees most often discussed by alchemists as symbols for the human body . Daphne, who was transformed into a tree, is the personification par excellence of the desired synthesis of humanity and nature. The lemons which carry the imprint of her teeth are the natural equivalents in tree code to the metallic gold. Just as the *lapis philosophorum* (the philosopher's stone) holds the key to the mysteries at its center, so too the grotto holds the dragon, sign of the danger of the penetration into the mysteries and also carrier of the all-important seed, or seminal material, which now lies dormant. Ancient beliefs, Nerval suggests, have been overcome by Christianity, yet like the anima of Daphne in the tree, they remain essentially intact, awaiting a revival.

"ARTÉMIS"

"Artémis" begins with an invocation to the mysteries: the number thirteen, an indivisible number, joining the basis of oneness and of the Trinity (which is always One). Thirteen is also the symbol of death in the Tarot (Arcane XIII). The sonnet centers upon the alchemical mystique of the rose; Nerval follows the tradition whereby the rose symbolizes the relationship between king and queen. More important, the rose provides the essential alchemical link with Christ. As such, the rose must be blood-colored in order to be identified with the Redeemer and the Cross. The final line indicates that the descent into the abyss is a necessary step in the making of a saint.

In alchemical writings, the philosopher's stone represents the *homo totus*, which will shed a bloody sweat. In this way, the stone prefigures the agony of Christ. Indeed, the Evangelist Luke says of Christ: "and His sweat was as it were great drops falling down to the ground" (Luke 22:44). It should therefore come as no surprise that Nerval would follow "Artémis" with five sonnets dealing with Christ in the Garden of Gethsemane. In his final hours of agony, Nerval's Christ is truly human, doubting the existence of a supreme power. In the fifth sonnet of the series, he recalls the necessity of descent in order to ascend, the necessity of death in order to give life. Christ's death gives life to a new belief which spells death to the old gods, yet Nerval poses an interesting question: "Quel est ce nouveau dieu qu'on impose à la terre?" ("who is this new god who is being imposed on Earth?"). The answer is reserved for the Almighty, who blessed the children of Adam ("les enfants du limon"). As already noted, the lemon is symbolic of the alchemical gold—that is, the quest for perfection and transcendence that Christ represents.

"VERS DORÉS"

In "Vers dorés" ("Golden Verses"), Nerval not only states his theory of correspondences but also offers his most compact statement concerning the role of alchemy in poetry. A new language is to be found—"À la matière même un verbe est attaché" ("even with matter there's a built-in word")—and a Divine Spirit is present in the darkness, waiting to shed his light. The last two lines describe the poet-seer as having opened his third eye; thus, he is able to strip away the layers of stone (the *lapis*) and finally attain the "gold" of the alchemist. Nerval's *The Chimeras*, therefore, achieves a synthesis of various manifestations of contrary elements, each time through the use of personification. "Vers dorés" symbolizes the achievement of the *coniunctio*, the realization of a new form of poetic inspiration and performance.

OTHER MAJOR WORKS

SHORT FICTION: *Les Illuminés*, 1852; "Sylvie," 1853 (English translation, 1922); *Les Filles du feu*, 1854 (*Daughters of Fire*, 1922).

PLAYS: *Faust*, pb. 1827, 1840 (translation of Johann Wolfgang von Goethe's play); *Piquillo*, pb. 1837 (with Alexandre Dumas, *père*); *Alchimiste*, pb. 1839 (with Dumas, *père*); *Léo Burckart*, pr., pb. 1839 (with Dumas, *père*); *Chariot d'enfant*, pb. 1850 (with Joseph Méry); *L'Imagier de Harlem*, pr. 1851.

NONFICTION: *Voyage en Orient*, 1851 (*Journey to the Orient*, 1972); *Promenades et souvenirs*, 1854-1856; *Aurélia*, 1855 (English translation, 1932).

MISCELLANEOUS: *Selected Writings*, 1957 (Geoffrey Wagner, translator); *Selected Writings*, 1999 (Richard Sieburth, translator).

BIBLIOGRAPHY

Behdad, Ali. "Orientalist Desire, Desire of the Orient." *French Forum* 15, no. 1 (January, 1990): 37-51. Useful background on the psychological implications of Nerval's fascination with the East. The story of Adoniram is discussed in relationship to its context in the storytelling tradition of Constantinople. The veiled women of the East symbolize another aspect of the separation between Nerval and the woman who represents his ideal, and the author sees this concealment as increasing desire.

Dubruck, Alfred. *Gérard de Nerval and the German Heritage.* The Hague, the Netherlands: Mouton, 1965. This study of German influences in Nerval's work cites E. T. A. Hoffmann, Johann Wolfgang von Goethe, and Heinrich Heine.

Ender, Evelyne. "A Case of Nostalgia: Gérard de Nerval." In *Architexts of Memory: Literature, Science, and Autobiography.* Ann Arbor: University of Michigan Press, 2005. In this chapter, Ender argues that the main theme in Nerval's writing is nostalgia, and that his writing predominantly involves memory.

Jones, Robert Emmet. *Gérard de Nerval.* New York: Twayne, 1974. This volume situates Nerval within the Romantic movement in France. Discusses his life and his poetry and prose.

Knapp, Bettina L. *Gérard de Nerval: The Mystic's Dilemma.* Tuscaloosa: University of Alabama Press, 1980. Knapp's study is organized as a biography and looks at mysticism in his works.

Lokke, Kari. *Gérard de Nerval: The Poet as Social Visionary.* Lexington, Ky.: French Forum, 1987. This thematic study uses Nerval's works to define the nature of his hallucinations and his concept of "the other."

MacLennan, George. *Lucid Interval: Subjective Writing and Madness in History.* Rutherford, N.J.: Fairleigh Dickinson University Press, 1992. A history of literature and mental illness with particular attention to the work of Nerval. Includes bibliographical references and index.

Rhodes, S. A. *Gérard de Nerval, 1808-1855: Poet, Traveler, Dreamer.* New York: Philosophical Library, 1951. This biography offers useful background on Jenny Colon and how Nerval linked her to the Queen of Sheba.

Rinsler, Norma. *Gérard de Nerval.* London: Athlone Press, 1973. This volume begins with a brief biography and goes on to cover his works.

Strauss, Jonathan. "Death-Based Subjectivity in the Creation of Nerval's Lyric Self." *Espirit Créateur* 35, no. 4 (Winter, 1995): 83-94. Strauss focuses on Nerval's lyric poetry, specifically his most famous sonnet, "El desdichado," in the context of the influence of Georg Wilhelm Friedrich Hegel. This discussion raises issues of the author's alienation from himself that illuminate the use of doubled characters in the short stories.

_____. *Subjects of Terror: Nerval, Hegel, and the Modern Self.* Stanford, Calif.: Stanford University Press, 1998. Despite the mention of Georg Wilhelm Friedrich Hegel in the title, this is a book about Nerval. The first two chapters deal with Hegel and other influences in order to put Nerval's madness in context in chapter 3, ending with an overview of *Daughters of Fire.* Chapter 4 focuses on "Les Faux Saulniers," an extract from "L'Abbé de Bucquoy" from *Les Illuminés.*

Leslie B. Mittleman

NOVALIS
Friedrich von Hardenberg

Born: Oberwiederstedt, Prussian Saxony (now in Germany); May 2, 1772
Died: Weissenfels, Saxony (now in Germany); March 25, 1801

PRINCIPAL POETRY
Hymnen an die Nacht, 1800 (*Hymns to the Night*, 1897, 1948)
Geistliche Lieder, 1802 (*Devotional Songs*, 1910)

OTHER LITERARY FORMS

The poetry alone does not even hint at the full scope of the literary activity of Novalis (noh-VOL-uhs) or his encyclopedic interest in philosophy, science, politics, religion, and aesthetics. While two seminal collections of aphorisms—*Blütenstaub* (pollen) and *Glauben und Liebe* (faith and love)—were published in 1798, the bulk of his work was published posthumously. Among these writings are six neglected dialogues and a monologue from 1798-1799; the essay *Die Christenheit oder Europa* (*Christianity or Europe*, 1844), written in 1799 but first published fully in 1826; and two fragmentary novels, *Die Lehrlinge zu Sais* (1802; *The Disciples at Sais*, 1903) and *Heinrich von Ofterdingen* (1802; *Henry of Ofterdingen*, 1842), begun in 1798 and 1799 respectively. As prototypes of the German Romantic novel, these two works comprise a variety of literary forms: didactic dialogues, poems, and literary fairy tales. Like so much of Novalis's work, these novels were first published by Ludwig Tieck and Friedrich von Schlegel in the 1802 edition of Novalis's writings. Insights into these literary works and into Novalis's poetics are provided by his theoretical notebooks and other papers, which include his philosophical and scientific studies and outlines and drafts of literary projects, as well as his letters, diaries, and professional scientific reports.

ACHIEVEMENTS

Novalis is perhaps best known as the creator of the "blue flower," the often trivialized symbol of Romantic longing, but his importance has a far more substantial basis than this. Within the German tradition, his Romanticism influenced important writers such as Joseph von Eichendorff, E. T. A. Hoffmann, and Hermann Hesse. As an innovative theorist and practitioner of the Romantic novel, Novalis prepared the way not only for the narrative strategies of Franz Kafka's prose but also for the themes and structures of Thomas Mann's major novels. As the poet of *Hymns to the Night* and as a theorist of poetic language, Novalis set the Orphic tone for German Romantic poetry and the aesthetic agenda for German Symbolists such as Rainer Maria Rilke and Stefan George.

Novalis's impact outside Germany is no less consequential. His evocative imagery, the prose poems included in *Hymns to the Night*, and his view of poetic language as musical and autonomous make him a major precursor of the French Symbolist poets. Among them, Maurice Maeterlinck was especially drawn to Novalis's philosophy of nature, and he translated *The Disciples at Sais* in 1895. Later, Novalis's imaginative poetics not only inspired André Breton, one of the founders of French Surrealism, but also had an impact, less widely known, on Chilean Surrealism via the poets Rosamel del Valle and Humberto Díaz Casanueva. In the English-speaking world, Novalis was first praised in 1829 by Thomas Carlyle, whose enthusiasm spread ultimately to writers as diverse as Ralph Waldo Emerson, George Eliot, Edgar Allan Poe, Joseph Conrad, and George MacDonald.

In the poetry anthology *News of the Universe: Poems of Twofold Consciousness* (1980), the American poet Robert Bly justly lauded Novalis as a prime shaper of modern poetic consciousness. Such an evaluation offers hope that Novalis will continue to gain recognition as an internationally important forerunner of both modern poetry and literary theory, especially as more of his literary and theoretical works become accessible in translation.

BIOGRAPHY

Novalis was born Georg Philipp Friedrich von Hardenberg, the first son of Heinrich Ulrich Erasmus von Hardenberg, a strict member of the pietistic *Herrnhut* sect, and Auguste Bernhardine von Bölzig. Throughout his life, Novalis attempted to reconcile the practical demands of his father with the poetic inspiration he claimed first to have received from his mother. Novalis's acquaintance with the popular poet Gottfried August Bürger in 1789 intensified his early literary aspirations, but encouraged by his father to pursue an administrative career, Novalis began the study of law at the University of Jena in 1790. Although his lyric output during his stay in Jena seems to have abated, he soon found his poetic proclivities rekindled and redirected by the poet Friedrich Schiller, who was then a professor of history at the university. Under Schiller's spell, the young Novalis became more introspective and sought a solid foundation for his life and poetry. With this new outlook, he bowed to paternal pressure and transferred to the University of Leipzig in 1791. His experience there once again only strengthened his literary and philosophical interests, however, for it was in Leipzig that he began his friendship and fruitful intellectual exchange with Schlegel, the brilliant theorist of German Romanticism. Only after taking up studies in Wittenberg did he receive his law degree, in 1794.

After several carefree months with his family in Weissenfels, Novalis was apprenticed by his father to Coelestin August Just, the district director of Thuringia, who lived in Tennstedt. It was during his first months there that Hardenberg came to know the twelve-year-old Sophie von Kühn of nearby Grüningen, who revived his active poetic imagination and became a central figure in his new poetic attempts. Within a year, they were engaged, but Sophie's serious illness led to her death in March, 1797. Sophie's death, followed by the loss of his brother Erasmus in April, shattered Novalis, and he turned inward to come to grips with the experience of death. This experience, certainly the most crucial of his life, helped him to articulate his mission to transcend the dual nature of existence through poetry. His confrontation with death did not weaken his will to live or cause him to flee from life, as is sometimes claimed; rather, it was a catalytic event that enabled him to reorient his life and focus his imaginative powers on the fusion of life and poetry.

With a new, clearly poetic mission before him, Novalis could commit himself to life; it was at this time that he assumed the pen name (meaning "preparer of new land") by which he is known. By the end of 1797, he had resumed his intense study of the Idealist philosophers Immanuel Kant and Johann Gottlieb Fichte. Novalis's interest in science grew also, and in December, he commenced studies at the Freiberg Mining Academy, which would later give him a career. In the next year, he not only published the philosophical aphorisms of *Blütenstaub* and *Glauben und Liebe*, but also attempted to articulate his own philosophical ideas in a novel, *The Disciples of Sais*. By December, 1798, his involvement in life embraced the domestic once again, and he became engaged to Julie von Charpentier.

Novalis had finally reconciled his poetic mission with the practical demands of life and career. During 1799, he not only worked on *Devotional Songs* and *Hymns to the Night*, which had grown out of the crisis of 1797, but also accepted an appointment to the directorate of the Saxon salt mines. Both his career and his literary endeavors flourished. In 1800, he worked on *Henry of Ofterdingen*, conducted a significant geological survey of Saxony, published *Hymns to the Night*, and wrote some of his best poems. However, illness had overpowered Novalis's resolve to live and fulfill his poetic mission. On March 25, 1801, Novalis died in the family home in Weissenfels. A few days before his death, he had said to his brother Carl: "When I am well again, then you will finally learn what poetry is. In my head I have magnificent poems and songs." These died with him.

ANALYSIS

The late eighteenth century in Germany was a time of new beginnings. The gradual change from a feudal to a capitalistic society bestowed a new importance on the individual, as reflected in the philosophy of German Idealism, which emphasized the primacy of the subjective imagination. At the same time, however, the weakening of the Holy Roman Empire gave rise to a new sense of German nationalism. German writers responded to these changes by seeking to initiate a new literary tradition, a new beginning that would free them from the tyranny of foreign taste and example. Understandably, in such a dynamic age, no single, unified movement emerged, and the literary pioneers— writers as diverse as Gotthold Ephraim Lessing, Friedrich Klopstock, and Christoph

Martin Wieland—set out in many different directions. Nevertheless, by the end of the century, Schlegel would proclaim that he lived "not in hope but in the certainty of a new dawn of a new poetry."

Schlegel's optimism was based on his conviction that his contemporaries were on the verge of creating a new mythology, a new Romantic poetry in which the newly emerging self would examine its own depths and discover universal truths, ultimately achieving a synthesis of subject and object. Like the literature of the eighteenth century, the poetry of Novalis moved toward the realization of this Romantic goal. While he experimented with many styles in his early works, betraying his debt to various currents of the Enlightenment, he soon developed a personal Romantic voice and new mode of expression that marked the advent of a new poetic age. This development became more obvious after Sophie's death in 1797, but it is evident even in the poems of his literary apprenticeship (1788-1793). Indeed, many themes that preoccupied Novalis after the crisis of 1797 had already surfaced in his earliest poetry. The theme of death and the dual images of night and darkness, for example, find their initial expression in early poems, although at this stage his poetry was largely imitative. Only after his encounter with Schiller and his relationship with Sophie, which made him more introspective, did Novalis strike out on his own to record his own experiences and the changes that had taken place within himself. He was then able to create a consistent vision, a vision proclaiming the transforming power of love and raising personal experience to the level of mythology. In transforming his subjective experience into universal symbolism, Novalis created the Romantic mythology that Schlegel had proclaimed the *sine qua non* of the new poetic age. In his last poems, which envision the return to paradise brought on by the union of poetry and love, Novalis transcended his personal experience to create symbolic artifacts behind which the poet himself nearly disappears. In his lyric poetry, then, Novalis ultimately reveals himself not only as a pioneer of Romanticism but also as a precursor of Symbolism.

If Novalis's last poems are thematically consistent and anticipate the Symbolist movement, his early poems are endlessly diversified and echo the Enlightenment. In the poets of the eighteenth century, the young writer, searching for a poetic voice, found his models, limited only by his eclectic taste. Besides translations from classical poetry, Novalis composed serious political verse influenced by the work of Friedrich Stolberg and Karl Ramler, and in the bardic tradition of Klopstock; Rococo lyrics under the particular influence of Wieland; elegiac verse echoing Ludwig Christoph Heinrich Hölty and Schiller; and a spate of lyrics in the style of Bürger. The variety of these early attempts, the assorted literary models that they imitate, and the poems showing a young poet experimenting with traditional forms (such as the invented necrologues addressed to living family members) reveal a writer in quest of a suitable mode of expression.

"To a Falling Leaf"

While they do share some common concerns, many of which inform the later writings, the early poems lack the unified vision and unique perspective that would come later with Novalis's Romantic lyrics. Poems that foreshadow later developments also contrast significantly with the more mature poetry. The first version of the poem "An ein fallendes Blatt" ("To a Falling Leaf"), written in 1789, paints a melancholy scene in which the approach of winter storms is compared to the approach of death. The melancholy tone, however, is purposely undercut by a conclusion that affirms death as a joyous experience of the eternal that need not be feared. This view of death hints, perhaps, at the thanatopsis that Novalis would elaborate in *Hymns to the Night*, but it is merely a hint, for here the idea is actually no more than a common poetic cliché, and the poem as a whole lacks the visionary perspective that underlies the later works. This poem's persona, in fact, is barely visible at all, and his emotional response to death's coming at the end of the poem is expressed impersonally: "Oh happy . . ./ One need not then fear the storm/ That forbids us our earthly life." The persona and his climactic emotional exclamation vanish behind the anonymous "one," and death—which had been only indirectly introduced through a comparison—loses not only its sting, as the poet intended, but its poetic bite as well.

"Evening"

The poem "Der Abend" ("Evening"), probably written in the same year as "To a Falling Leaf" but in many ways a more suggestive and complex work, not only has a more directly involved and visible persona but also links death and night in anticipation of *Hymns to the Night*. This poem's persona, who stands in a sympathetic relationship to a thoroughly personified nature, perceives and responds to a serene evening by wishing that "the evening of my life" might be "more peaceful still than this/ Evening of the countryside." The lovely yet decidedly rational comparison of the soul to nature is still far removed from the Romantic identification of self and nature that can be found in Novalis's last poems—for example, in "Der Himmel war umzogen" ("The Heavens Were Covered"). Moreover, despite the reflective mood that nature inspires in the persona, this is not an introspective poem like those found among Novalis's first truly Romantic poems. "Evening" does not yet focus primarily on the poetic self but on the eighteenth century ideal of bucolic harmony. Similarly, the persona's final wish, that his "soul might slumber over to eternal peace" in the same way that the weary farmer "slumbers over" toward the next day, only tentatively prefigures the ideas and vocabulary of *Hymns to the Night*. The link between death and sleep remains, after all, an eighteenth century cliché, and its one-dimensional appearance here only lightly foreshadows Novalis's later and much more complex symbol of the eternal and truly visionary "holy sleep."

This poem, like "To a Falling Leaf," is still controlled by a rationalistic poetic consciousness. Simile, not symbol, is the rhetorical means of linking humanity and nature;

subject and object are linked, not synthesized. This is the overriding technique of the early poems. The transcendent vision based on deep self-reflection and the unifying power of the imagination is not found here. The poet of "Evening" is one step closer to the Romantic poet of *Hymns to the Night* than the poet of "To a Falling Leaf," but the Romantic poet whose feelings, perceptions, and very self are the basis of Romantic expression steps forward only tentatively. Before he could free himself from his Enlightenment models, focus his vision, and become the very subject of his Romantic art, Novalis would first need to know himself.

"ON A SATURDAY EVENING"

The experience of love and death in his relationship with Sophie was the catalyst that would initiate important changes in Novalis's writings, the lens through which he would ultimately bring into sharper focus the themes and images that had been hinted at in the early poems. Initially, however, the experience led to self-examination and the definition of a new, more Romantic voice. Much of the poetry from this period—and there is relatively little—records the changes that the Sophie experience caused in Novalis, and it is, consequently, largely confessional, reflective poetry in which the poet himself becomes the subject.

In the poem "Am Sonnabend Abend" ("On a Saturday Evening"), for example, the persona expresses his astonishment at the transformation that has taken place within himself since his relationship with Sophie: "Am I still the one who yesterday morning/ Sang hymns to the god of frivolity. . . ." This confession suggests not only the changes that had affected a once frivolous university student but also those poetic changes that had occurred in the former poet of lighthearted Anacreontic verse. Earlier, in 1791, Novalis had expressed similar reservations about his lifestyle and youthful verse in "A Youth's Laments," a poem written under the maturing influence of Schiller, but it was only after Novalis had met Sophie that his inner reorientation became complete and the poet could begin anew.

"BEGINNING"

In the poem "Anfang" ("Beginning"), Novalis analyzes the nature of Sophie's effect on him and argues that his new state of mind is not "intoxication" (that is, illusion) but rather "higher consciousness," which Sophie as a mediator had revealed. This aptly titled poem is in several ways profoundly significant for Novalis's development as a Romantic poet. In the first place, its conclusion that higher consciousness not be mistaken for intoxication admits a new Romantic form of perception that is aggressively antirationalistic. Second, the characterization of Sophie, the embodiment of love, as a female mediator between visible and invisible worlds, not only marks the first use of this central Romantic image in Novalis's work but also signals the inception of a Romantic theory of Symbolism, which posits the fusion of the finite with the infinite. Finally, the intensely introspective persona, whose theme is his own consciousness ("the growth of a poet's mind," as William Wordsworth put it), places this poem directly into the Romantic tradition.

In "Beginning," Novalis's new vision, based on the higher consciousness inspired by Sophie, assumes a universal import transcending the initially personal experience. This is manifest in the last lines of the poem, where the private experience of the poet is superseded by a vision of humanity raised to a new level of existence:

> Someday mankind will be what Sophie
> Is to me now—perfected—moral grace—
> Then will its *higher consciousness*
> No longer be confused with the mist of wine.

THE STRANGER

The poems Novalis wrote in 1798 and 1799 in Freiberg after Sophie's death confirm this universalizing tendency. In fact, the relative paucity of poems written in the wake of the experience itself suggests that Novalis was not simply concerned with self-indulgent solipsistic effusions. (The one poem written shortly after Sophie's death in 1797, while Novalis was still in Tennstedt, is a humorous composition commemorating the Just family's purchase of a garden.) Similarly, it has been pointed out that Novalis probably chose the classical verse forms of the Freiberg poems as a more objective medium for his universal themes. One can also point to the objectifying perspective of the several poems that analyze the self from a point of view once removed. In both "Der Fremdling" ("The Stranger"), written in January, 1798, and "Der müde Fremdling ist verschwunden" ("The Weary Stranger Has Disappeared"), a fragment from one year later, Novalis—the stranger—analyzes his initial alienation after Sophie's death and then his self-rediscovery through a persona who "speaks . . . for him." This allows Novalis to remain in the introspective mode, making use of his experience, yet standing at an objective distance. As a consequence, the stranger symbolizes any individual who seeks the return of the paradise he has lost, "that heavenly land."

SELF-KNOWLEDGE

The major poems of the Freiberg period are inhabited by seekers who ultimately find themselves. Introspection leading to self-revelation is the goal and method of these poems, but the path inward does not lead to solipsism. Self-knowledge, as Novalis teaches in "Kenne dich selbst" ("Know Thyself"), results in a deep knowledge of nature's mysteries as well. Moreover, because his own path to self-knowledge, which had been prepared by the guiding spirit of love, led to higher consciousness, Novalis interprets his experience as a symbol. He imbues his introspective poems with a universal significance, as in these lines from "Letzte Liebe" ("Last Love"):

> As the mother wakes her darling from slumber with a kiss,
> As he first sees her and comes to understand himself through her:
> So love with me—through love did I first experience the world,
> Find myself, and become what as a lover one becomes.

What *one*—anyone, not just Novalis—becomes when a lover, is a poet. The successful seeker of love and self-knowledge is called, like the poet addressed in "Der sterbende Genius" ("The Dying Genius"), to "sing the song of return," the myth of the return to paradise.

Having found himself again, Novalis defined for himself a Romantic mission: to transform his personal experience through poetry into a universal vision of love, which would lead others inward along the path to self-knowledge, higher consciousness, and rebirth: "Toward the East sing then the lofty song,/ Until the sun rises and ignites/ And opens for me the gates of the primeval world."

HYMNS TO THE NIGHT

In *Hymns to the Night*, the gates of eternity are opened not by the rising sun—the conventional symbol of rebirth—but by the fall of darkness and night. This poetic work is Novalis's "lofty song," "the song of return," the clearest and most complete fulfillment of his Romantic mission. In it, Novalis transforms his personal experience of Sophie's death—to be precise, his ostensibly mystical experience at her graveside on May 13, 1797—into a universalized vision of death and night as a realm of higher consciousness and eternal love.

Hymns to the Night was not merely an immediate emotional response to Sophie's death. Although he might have begun work on an early version in the fall of 1797, Novalis resumed serious work on the cycle only in late 1799 and early 1800, when he was well over his initial grief and actively involved in life. Moreover, the textual changes that he made between setting down that version in manuscript and publishing a still later prose version in the journal *Athenäum* in 1800 show a conscious effort to rise above personal experience and indicate that his goal was not autobiography but symbolism.

Unlike the fragmentary verse epic of 1789, *Orpheus*, which uses a classical myth to examine the theme of death, *Hymns to the Night* makes personal experience the basis of a broad symbolism utilizing elements of various mythological systems (including the theme of Orpheus). Although the first three hymns describe principally the poet's own experience of "the holy, ineffable, mysterious night"—his own Orphic descent to the realm of death—the work begins significantly with a more universal reference to all living creatures in the world of light. Among these stands "the magnificent stranger" who is man himself. As in the Freiberg poems, the stranger symbolizes the universal seeker of a lost paradise. From this broad context, it becomes clear that the persona, himself a stranger in the rational world of light, is representative and his experience symbolic. This universality is reinforced in the fourth hymn when, for example, the symbol of the Cross, which at first signifies Sophie's death and links her to Christ, is finally called "the victory banner of our race." The fifth hymn continues to broaden the significance of the poet's experience by restating his subjective development toward an understanding of death in terms of humankind's changing relationship to death in history. In the sixth and final hymn, subjective experience coalesces completely with the universal. Not only is the mediating beloved explicitly identified with Christ, but also the poet's individual voice is transformed into a universal "we" singing a communal hymn of praise. The stranger, who in the Freiberg poems had given up his voice to the poet who spoke for him, here lends his voice to the chorus of humankind.

DEVOTIONAL SONGS

Devotional Songs, also written during the years 1799 through 1800, were similarly intended to raise personal experience to the level of universal—if not entirely orthodox—religious symbolism. This is evident not only from the symbols that the poems share with *Hymns to the Night*—for example, the eroticism of Christ the beloved—but also from the shared communal context and implications. Novalis had tentatively planned these songs as part of "a new, spiritual hymnal"; in them, the Sophie experience is so thoroughly transformed by virtue of the pervasive Christian imagery that many have been adopted (and sometimes adapted) for use in hymnals.

The songs, which are sometimes confessional, sometimes exhortative, are all informed by Novalis's self-conscious mission to reveal the role of love in the re-creation of the earth. The ninth song, for example, which proclaims the day of Resurrection to be "a festival of the world's rejuvenation," is more than a profession of religious faith in the coming of God's kingdom; it is a self-conscious profession of faith in the poet's mission to reveal that kingdom in humanity's midst:

> I say to each that he lives
> And has been resurrected
> That he hovers in our midst
> And is with us forever.
> I say to each and each says
> To his friends anon
> That soon everywhere
> The new kingdom of heaven will dawn.

In truly Romantic fashion, the voice of the prophet is first and foremost the voice of a poet, speaking out of his own experience but in the service of a still higher cause and announcing to all humankind the advent of a world renewed by love, which is made manifest in his words.

"THE POEM"

Novalis's last poems are almost exclusively concerned with the renewal of the universe and the return to the Golden Age; their vision is more explicitly secular and aesthetic than that which informs *Hymns to the Night* and *Devotional Songs*. Here, Novalis's belief that poetry itself can transform the world receives full expression, and many of these last works are indeed poems about poems, in which Novalis's personal experience is not the focus.

Such is the case in the significantly titled poem "Das Gedicht" ("The Poem"). The anonymous persona who speaks for humankind in its fallen state relates how "a lost page"—a poetic saga—inspires in the present a vision of the past Golden Age and keeps alive the hope for its return. Because it is able to unite past and future in the present and give form to the spirit of love, the poem itself temporarily re-creates the Golden Age. The paramount concern of "The Poem," then, is precisely what the title announces it to be: the poem—not simply the ancient saga and not even Novalis's poem in itself, but all poems, the poem per se. In its ability to unite subject and object, spirit and matter, every poem becomes a medium of higher consciousness and the salvation of the world.

"TO TIECK"

Once poetry becomes a major theme in Novalis's work, a new poetic voice emerges. The reflective persona that had spoken in the introspective poems of 1794 to 1799 is silenced. In "The Poem," for example, the reflective self is replaced by an essentially impersonal persona. This is no longer a case of a poet reflecting on himself but of poetry reflecting on itself. In the poem "An Tieck" ("To Tieck"), another anonymous persona narrates the tale of a child's discovery of an ancient book and an encounter with Jakob Boehme, which presage the coming of the Golden Age.

Despite the dedicatory title and autobiographical allusions in the poem (Tieck had introduced Novalis to Boehme's writings), the personal significance has been entirely transformed by the symbolism of the poem. The dominance of myth in these last poems precludes the need for a personal voice, as it does in the novel *Henry of Ofterdingen* of the same period. If early poems such as "To a Falling Leaf" resort to an anonymous voice because Novalis lacked experience, then the final poems do so because he succeeded in rising above his personal experience.

AUTONOMOUS LATE POEMS

The appearance of a first-person voice among the late poems does not contradict this conclusion. A number of poems in which the poet speaks in the first person were in fact intended for fictional characters in *Henry of Ofterdingen*. In some of these and in others not intended for the novel, the persona himself becomes part of an integrated mythos. Such poems are distinct from earlier reflective works such as "Beginning" and "Last Love."

Although the late poems also describe the changing consciousness of the persona, they do so in symbolic terms and not in the largely expository or intellectual manner of the earlier poems. Whereas the poet of "Beginning" simply states that Sophie has led him to higher consciousness, the speaker of "Es färbte sich die Wiese grün" ("The Meadow Turned Green") tells the story of his rebirth by narrating his experience of spring and love: During a walk deeper and deeper into the forest, the persona marvels uncomprehendingly at the transformation of nature; he then encounters a young girl and, hidden from the sun in deep shadows, suddenly understands intuitively the changes both in nature and within himself.

One can easily discern the same theme that dominated the Freiberg poems: The spirit of love, embodied by a female mediator, reveals the higher consciousness that leads to knowledge of self and of the external world. In this narrative plot, however, the theme has been thoroughly mythologized. The symbols which Novalis uses here and in all his late poems are autonomous, stripped of all but the most general personal relevance. The forest, the sun, the girl, springtime—all these derive their mythological significance from their shared archetypal context.

"The Meadow Turned Green" is autonomous, too, in that it reflects back upon itself. It is, after all, not merely a description of revelation and the path to higher consciousness; it is both the direct result of the poet's epiphany and the re-creation of it. The poem describes and mythologizes its own creation.

The process of objectifying and imbuing his personal experience with universal meaning that Novalis had begun in the poems of 1794 to 1799 was completed in his last poems, in which he totally transforms experience into myth, into symbols which have no fixed meanings outside themselves. This creation of a reflexive and fully autonomous poetry was a significant landmark on the road to nineteenth century symbolism. To reach this stage and to find his own poetic voice, it was not enough for Novalis that he free himself from Enlightenment models and create a poetry of the self. He also needed to rise above the self and to create a mythological poetry. For this, he needed a poetic voice that not only spoke from the core of his experience but also spoke in the universal language of symbolism. In achieving this goal, Novalis fulfilled the Romantic ideal of becoming like God the Creator, whose creative voice echoes eternally throughout his autonomous creation while he hovers silently above.

OTHER MAJOR WORKS

LONG FICTION: *Die Lehrlinge zu Sais*, 1802 (*The Disciples at Sais*, 1903); *Heinrich von Ofterdingen*, 1802 (*Henry of Ofterdingen*, 1842).

NONFICTION: *Blütenstaub*, 1798; *Glauben und Liebe*, 1798; *Das Allgemeine Brouillon*, 1798-1799 (*Notes for a Romantic Encyclopaedia*, 2007); *Die Christenheit oder Europa*, 1826 (*Christianity or Europe*, 1844); *Philosophical Writings*, 1997; *The Birth of Novalis: Friedrich von Hardenberg's Journal of 1797, with Selected Letters and Documents*, 2007.

MISCELLANEOUS: *Pollen and Fragments: Selected Poetry and Prose of Novalis*, 1989.

BIBLIOGRAPHY

Freeman, Veronica G. *The Poetization of Metaphors in the Work of Novalis*. New York: Peter Lang, 2006. This work examines mysticism and Romanticism in the works of Novalis and his use of metaphors.

Hodkinson, James R. *Women and Writing in the Works of Novalis: Transformation Beyond Measure?* Rochester , N.Y.: Camden House, 2007. Hodkinson examines how Novalis was affected by women, including Sophie von Kühn, and how this is evident in his writing.

Holland, Jocelyn. *German Romanticism and Science: The Procreative Poetics of Goethe, Novalis, and Ritter*. New York: Routledge, 2009. Holland compares and contrasts the works of Novalis, Johann Wolfgang von Goethe, and Johann Wilhelm Ritter, paying particular attention to the idea of procreation.

Kennedy, Clare. *Paradox, Aphorism, and Desire in Novalis and Derrida*. London: Maney, for the Modern Humanities Research Association, 2008. Kennedy examines the themes of desire and paradoxes in the aphorisms of Novalis and philosopher-critic Jacques Derrida.

Molnár, Géza von. *Romantic Vision, Ethical Context: Novalis and Artistic Autonomy*. Minneapolis: University of Minnesota Press, 1987. Highly philosophical approach to the life and work of Novalis. Involves detailed expositions of Novalis's interpretations of Kantian and Fichtean philosophy. Also examines Novalis's relationship with Sophie von Kühn, his novel *Henry of Ofterdingen*, and his *Hymns to the Night*.

Neubauer, John. *Novalis*. Boston: Twayne, 1980. Excellent general introduction to Novalis, tailored to English-speaking readers. Interweaves the life and work to show the relationship between the two and also discusses Novalis both as a visionary and as a logical thinker. Includes discussions of Novalis's contributions to science, philosophy, the novel, poetry, politics, and religion. Includes bibliography and chronology.

Newman, Gail M. *Locating the Romantic Subject*. Detroit: Wayne State University Press, 1997. Complex interpretation of the life and work of Novalis in light of the modern object-relations theory of British psychologist D. W. Winnicott. Particular emphasis on Novalis's novel, *Henry of Ofterdingen*, as a psychoanalytic case study.

O'Brien, William Arctander. *Novalis: Signs of Revolution*. Durham, N.C.: Duke University Press, 1995. Examines both the life and the work of Novalis with the purpose of contradicting "the myth of Novalis" as a dreamy, death-obsessed mystic. Sees Novalis as the quintessential early German Romantic. A chapter called "The Making of Sophie" brings new perspectives to Novalis's profound experience with the young Sophie von Kühn.

Donald P. Haase

ALEXANDER PUSHKIN

Born: Moscow, Russia; June 6, 1799
Died: St. Petersburg, Russia; February 10, 1837

OTHER LITERARY FORMS

Often considered the founder of modern Russian literature, Alexander Pushkin (POOSH-kuhn) was a prolific writer, not only of poetry but also of plays, novels, and short stories. His *malenkiye tragedii*, or "little tragedies"—brief, dramatic episodes in blank verse—include *Skupoy rytsar* (pr. 1852; *The Covetous Knight*, 1925), *Kamyenny gost* (pb. 1839; *The Stone Guest*, 1936), *Motsart i Salyeri* (pr. 1832; *Mozart and Salieri*, 1920), and *Pir vo vryemya chumy* (pb. 1833; *The Feast in Time of the Plague*, 1925).

Boris Godunov (pb. 1831; English translation, 1918) is Pushkin's famous historical tragedy constructed on the Shakespearean ideal that plays should be written "for the people." A story set in late sixteenth century Russia—a period of social and political chaos—it deals with the relationship between the ruling classes and the masses; written for the people, it, not surprisingly, gained universal appeal.

Pushkin's most important prose work, *Kapitanskaya dochka* (1836; *The Captain's Daughter*, 1846), is a historical novel of the Pugachev Rebellion. *Pikovaya dama* (1834; *The Queen of Spades*, 1858) is another well-known prose work, which influenced Fyodor Dostoevski's novels.

Alexander Pushkin
(Library of Congress)

With its emphasis on civic responsibility, Pushkin's works have been translated into most major languages. His letters have been collected and annotated in English by J. Thomas Shaw as *The Letters of Alexander Pushkin* (1963).

ACHIEVEMENTS

Alexander Pushkin was the first poet to write in a purely Russian style. Aleksandr Tvardovsky calls him "the soul of our people." Considered as one of Russia's greatest poets, if not the greatest, he does not hold the same place in foreign countries, because his greatest achievement is in his use of the Russian language, with a flavor impossible to capture in translation. His verses continue to be regarded as the most natural expression of Russian poetry. After a lengthy period of stiff classicism and excessive sentimentality in eighteenth century literature, as seen in Konstantine Batyushkov, Vasily Zhukovsky, and Nikolai Karamzin, Pushkin breathed freshness and spontaneity into Russian poetry. Zhukovsky, the acknowledged dean of Russian letters, recognized this new spirit when, after the publication of *Ruslan and Liudmila* in 1820, he gave Pushkin a portrait of himself with the inscription: "To the victorious pupil from the vanquished master on that most important day on which he completed *Ruslan and Liudmila*."

It was Pushkin who brought the Romantic spirit to Russia, although it is impossible to categorize him as a pure Romantic. Pushkin's Byronic heroes in *The Prisoner of the Caucasus* and Aleko in *The Gypsies* introduced a new type of character, proud, disillusioned, and in conflict with himself and society, which greatly appealed to the Russia of the 1820's. Pushkin also introduced a love for the primitive and the exotic, which he found especially in southern Russia, and a deep and personal appreciation of nature. In the Romantic spirit, Pushkin showed a fond appreciation of Russia's past, her heroes, her folklore, and her people, which Soviet critics saw as *narodnost*.

Pushkin was also a realist who maintained a certain detached objectivity and distance, never quite penetrating beneath the surface of his heroes or completely identifying with them. He documents even his most Romantic poems. Pushkin's last post permitted him access to the imperial archives, a privilege that he deeply cherished. His interest in history led him to works on Peter the Great, on the Pugachev Rebellion, and into his own family history in *Arap Petra velikogo* (1828-1841; *Peter the Great's Negro*, 1896).

Although Pushkin was primarily a lyric poet, he was accomplished in all genres. *Evgeny Onegin* (1825-1832, 1833; *Eugene Onegin*, 1881), the only Russian novel in verse, lacks the richness of plot and social commentary that Honoré de Balzac, Leo Tolstoy, and Fyodor Dostoevski were later to develop, but it does contain humor, satire, and tender lyricism, all presented in poetry of incomparable assurance and grace. The work was acclaimed by the great nineteenth century critic Vissarion Belinsky as "an encyclopedia of Russian life."

Pushkin aimed at revitalizing the Russian theater and saw William Shakespeare as a better model than Jean Racine or Molière. Although his major play *Boris Godunov* falls short of dramatic intensity in its failure to realize the tragic fate of the hero, it is a lyric masterpiece and a profound study of ambition and power. Never a success on the stage, Pushkin's play was the inspiration for operas by Modest Mussorgsky and Sergei Prokofiev. The "little tragedies" are models of concision and true classical concentration. Each highlights one main theme: covetousness (*The Covetous Knight*), envy (*Mozart and Salieri*), passion (*The Stone Guest*, on the Don Juan theme), and pleasure before death (*Feast in Time of the Plague*). These plays rank among Pushkin's finest achievements.

Pushkin's later years were devoted more to prose than to poetry, with the exception of *The Bronze Horseman*, the folktales in verse, and several lyric poems. Pushkin did for Russia what the Brothers Grimm did for Germany in folk literature. Although many of his sources were not specifically Russian, such as *The Tale of the Dead Princess*, Pushkin transformed them into authentic national pieces by his unaffected use of folk expressions, alliteration, and real feeling for the people. In all his work, his effortless rhymes, easy and varied rhythms, natural speech, and true identification with the spirit of his time make him beloved by the Russian people and the founder of all Russian literature.

BIOGRAPHY

Alexander Sergeyevich Pushkin was born in Moscow on June 6, 1799, the second of three children. His mother, Nadezhda Osipovna Hannibal, was of African descent through her grandfather, Abram Hannibal, who was immortalized by Pushkin in *Peter the Great's Negro*. His father, Sergei Lvovich, and his uncle, Vasily Lvovich, were both writers. His father frequently entertained literary friends and had an excellent library of French and Russian classics, in which Pushkin by the age of twelve had read widely but indiscriminately. Pushkin's childhood was marked by the lack of a close relationship with his parents, although he formed lasting ties with his maternal grandmother, Marya Alexeyevna, and his nurse, Arina Rodionovna, who was responsible for his love of folklore. The family could boast of very ancient aristocratic roots but suffered from a lack of money.

In 1811, Pushkin was accepted into the newly founded *lycée* at Tsarskoe Selo, designed by the czar to give a broad liberal education to aristocrats, especially those destined for administrative posts in the government. He remained there until his graduation in 1817, where he distinguished himself less by diligence than by natural ability, especially in French and Russian literature. Always of uneven temperament, he was not the most popular student in his class, but he did form lasting friendships with schoolmates Ivan Pushchin, Wilhelm Küchelbecker and Baron Anton Delvig; he also formed ties with such great literary figures as Zhukovsky and Karamizin, as well as bonds with the hussar officers, notably Pyotr Chaadayev. Pushkin began writing his earliest verses in French but soon turned to Russian.

After completing the *lycée*, Pushkin was appointed to the Ministry of Foreign Affairs in St. Petersburg. From 1817 to 1820, he led a dissipated life in the capital, much like that of Onegin in chapter 1 of *Eugene Onegin*. He became involved in liberal causes, though not as a member of the more revolutionary secret societies, and began to circulate his liberal verses. This alarmed the authorities, who proposed exile in Siberia, but because of the intercession of prominent personalities, among them Zhukovsky and the former principal of the *lycée*, Egor Englehardt, Pushkin was simply transferred to the south under the supervision of the paternal General I. N. Inzov.

Pushkin's first months in the south were spent traveling with the family of General Nikolai Raevsky through the Caucasus and the Crimea. Overwhelmed by the beauty of nature and the simplicity of the people, it was here that he wrote most of his so-called southern poems. The Raevskys introduced him to an appreciation of Lord Byron, which was reflected in his works of this period. Their daughters, especially Marya, were among Pushkin's many passions. Between 1820 and 1823, a productive literary period, he remained mostly in Kishinev. This peaceful existence was to end when Pushkin was transferred to Odessa under the stern General Vorontsov, whose wife, Elisa, became the object of Pushkin's attentions after Amalia Riznich. For this and other offenses, Pushkin was dismissed from the service in 1824 and sent to his mother's estate at Mikhailovskoe near Pskov. Here he was placed under the direct supervision of his father and the local authorities. He quarreled constantly with his family, so that all of them withdrew and left him alone from 1824 to 1826. He had few companions other than the aged nurse Arina Rodionovna. This enforced isolation proved very productive, for it was here that he composed a great deal of *Eugene Onegin*, wrote *Boris Godunov* and many short poems, and drew his inspiration for later *skazki* (tales).

The death of Alexander I in 1825 provoked the Decembrist Revolt on December 26 of the same year. Pushkin's sympathies were with the revolutionaries, but his exile fortunately prevented him from participating. He took the opportunity of the new czar's accession to the throne, however, to make a successful plea for liberation. After 1826, he was permitted to travel to Moscow and, with reservations, to the capital, although his supervisor, Count Benkendorf, was not amenable to his requests. The years between 1826 and 1830 were a period of maturing and searching; they were also rich in literary output, especially of lyric poetry and the "little tragedies."

In 1830, Pushkin became engaged to the Moscow beauty Natalia Nikolayevna Goncharova, whom he married in 1831. It was an unsuccessful match, though not a completely disastrous marriage. Pushkin's wife had no interest in literature and had social aspirations far beyond either her or her husband's means. Four children were born to them, but Natalia's dissipation and Pushkin's jealousy eventually led him to melancholy and resentment. Financial worries and lack of advancement added to his problems. When Baron Georges d'Anthès, a young Alsatian, began paying undue attention to Pushkin's wife and the entire affair became a public scandal, Pushkin challenged d'Anthès to a duel. Pushkin was mortally wounded and died on February 10, 1837.

ANALYSIS

Alexander Pushkin's first verses were written in the style of French classicism and sentimentalism. His models were Voltaire and Evariste Parny, Gavrila Derzhavin, Zhukovsky, and Batyushkov. He wrote light, voluptuous verses, occasional pieces, and epigrams. Even in his early works, of which the most important is *Ruslan and Liudmila*, he shows restrained eroticism, always tempered by his classical training, which led him from the very beginning into excellent craftsmanship, brevity, and simplicity.

WIT, HUMOR, AND SATIRE

The lively wit, humor, and satire that were evident from the first continued to characterize Pushkin's work. *Ruslan and Liudmila* is a mock-epic, and the same strain appears in chapters 1 and 2 of *Eugene Onegin*. *Gabriel*, a parody on the Annunciation, which caused Pushkin a great deal of embarrassment with the authorities, has many witty passages, such as Satan's ensnarement of Adam and Eve by love. Pushkin achieves his humor by the use of parody, not hesitating to use it in dealing with the greatest authors such as Shakespeare and Voltaire, and with his friend and master Zhukovsky. Like Molière, however, he never really offends; his satire and dry irony produce a generally good-natured effect.

POLITICAL POEMS

Pushkin first became known in St. Petersburg as a writer of liberal verses, and this—coupled with charges of atheism—made him a constant target of the imperial censors. His famous "Vol'nost': Oda" ("Ode to Freedom") is severe on Napoleon and condemns the excesses of the French Revolution, yet it reminds monarchs that they must be subservient to the law. In "Derevnya" ("The Countryside"), he longs for the abolition of serfdom, yet looks to the czar for deliverance. Pushkin did not conceal his sympathy for the Decembrists, and in his famous "Vo glubine sibirskikh rud" ("Message to Siberia"), he reminds the exiled revolutionaries that "freedom will once again shine, and brothers give you back your sword." His later poems address more general issues, and in 1831 during the Polish Uprising, he speaks out clearly in favor of the czar in "Klevetnikam Rossii" ("To the Slanderers of Russia"). Finally, *The Bronze Horseman* addresses the very complex theme of the individual in conflict with the state.

HEROINES AND LOVE POETRY

Pushkin knew many passions in his brief lifetime, and several women inspired both his life and poetry. Marya Raevskaya became the model for many of his heroines, from the Circassian girl in *The Prisoner of the Caucasus* to Marya in *Poltava*. Amalia Riznich, destined to die in Italy, reappears in "Dlya beregov otchizny dal'noy" ("Abandoning an Alien Country") in 1830. Elisa Vorontsova, the wife of Pushkin's stern superior in Odessa, was a powerful influence who haunted the poet long after his return to the north. The ring she gave him is immortalized in "Khrani menya, moy talisman" ("Talisman") and "The Burned Letter," where the ashes recall her memory. Anna Kern was the inspiration for the almost mystical "Ya pomnyu chudnoye mgnoven'ye" ("I Remember a Wonderful Moment"). Natalya Goncharova, while still Pushkin's fiancé, likewise assumes a spiritual role in "Madona" ("Madonna"). Pushkin's love poetry, while passionate, is also delicate and sensitive, and even the most voluptuous evocations concentrate on images such as those of eyes and feet.

NATURE

In Romantic fashion, Pushkin was one of the first to introduce nature into his works. First inspired by the trip to the south, where the beauty of the Caucasus overwhelmed him, he sees freedom in the wide expanses and steep mountains. Later, on a second trip—as described in "Kavkazsky" ("The Caucasus")—he evokes the playful rivers, the low clouds and the silver-capped mountains. He feels that the sight of a monastery brings him to the neighborhood of Heaven. The north also has its charms, particularly the Russian winter. There are exquisite verses on winter in the fifth chapter of *Eugene Onegin*, and in his lyrics about the swirling snowstorm in "Zinniy Vecher" ("Winter Evening") or the winter road that symbolizes his sad journey through life. Both city and country come alive in the crisp cold of winter in the prologue to *The Bronze Horseman*.

MELANCHOLY

Despite ever-recurring wit, irony, and gentle sensitivity, Pushkin's poetry is fundamentally melancholy and often tragic. This dichotomy corresponds to the division of his personality: dissipated yet deep. The southern poems all end tragically, his plays are all tragedies, and *Eugene Onegin* ends with the death of Lensky and the irremediable disappointment of Tatyana and Onegin. Pushkin frequently writes of the evil and demoniac forces of nature (as in Tatyana's dream), of madness (Eugene in *The Bronze Horseman*), and of violence (in "Zhenikh," "The Bridegroom"). A melancholy vein permeates his lyrics as well. Like the Romantics, Pushkin speaks frequently of death, perhaps foreseeing his own. The hour of parting from a loved one, a frequent subject of his lyrics, foreshadows death. As early as 1823, in "Telega zhizni" ("The Wagon of Time"), he sees the old man as the one who calmly awaits eternal sleep. Pushkin's tragic vision is complicated by the absence of a Christian worldview with a belief in life after death. Unlike Dostoevski, Pushkin writes of unmitigated, not of redemptive, suffering. S. M. Frank, who does admit a spiritual dimension in Pushkin, compares his work to Mozart's music, which seems gay but is in fact sad. Yet it is this very sadness which puts him in the tradition of Russian literature, anticipating Nikolai Gogol's "laughter through tears."

RUSLAN AND LIUDMILA

Pushkin's first major work, *Ruslan and Liudmila*, was published in 1820. It is now usually placed in a minor category, but it was important at the time as the first expression of the Russian spirit. Witty and ironic, the poem is written in the style of a mock-epic, much in the tradition of Ariosto's *Orlando Furioso* (1516, 1521, 1532; English translation, 1591). It also echoes Voltaire, and the fourth canto parodies Zhukovsky's "Spyaschaya carevna" ("Twelve Sleeping Maidens"). In fact, the whole plot resembles Zhukovsky's projected "Vladimir." It consists of six cantos, a prologue added in 1828, and an epilogue. Pushkin began the poem in 1817 while still in school, and he was already in exile in the south when it was published.

Ruslan and Liudmila, in Walter Vickery's words, transports the reader to the "unreal and delightful poetic world of cheerful unconcern," returning to the legendary days of ancient Kiev, where Prince Vladimir is giving a wedding feast for his daughter

Liudmila. The fortunate bridegroom Ruslan is about to enjoy the moment he has so voluptuously awaited, when a clap of thunder resounds and his bride is snatched away from him by the dwarf enchanter Chernomor. Prince Vladimir promises half of his kingdom and Liudmila as a bride to the man who rescues her. Ruslan sets off with his three rivals, Ratmir, Rogdai, and Farlaf. Ratmir eventually chooses a pastoral life, Rogdai is slain, and Farlaf reappears at the moment when Ruslan is about to return with Liudmila. In true knightly fashion, Ruslan saves Kiev from an attack by the Pechenegs, kills his last rival, and marries the princess.

Pushkin's poem captures many exaggerated scenes from the *byliny* or heroic tales, such as the death of the giant head, and ends with a full-scale epic battle. It is a gentle mockery of chivalry, sorcery, and love. Critics from Zhukovsky to the Soviets hailed it as a true folk-epic in the spirit of *narodnost* (nationalism) although many of Pushkin's contemporaries were shocked at his unfaithfulness to classical antiquity and his trivial subject. The public, however, welcomed it, seeing in it a new inspiration for the times. The prologue, especially, captures the popular spirit with its learned cat on a green oak who recites a folktale when he turns to the left and a song when he moves to the right.

As in all of Pushkin's works, the language is the most important feature, offsetting the many flaws of Pushkin's still immature talent. His choice of vocabulary is very Russian, even popular, and his rhythms and rhymes are graceful and effortless. Henri Troyat refers to him as "a virtuoso of rime" and says that this talent alone announced possibilities for the future.

EUGENE ONEGIN

Eugene Onegin, Pushkin's novel in verse, was begun in 1823 in Kishinev and completed in 1830. It is composed of eight cantos or chapters, as Pushkin preferred to call them. There are projects and fragments for two other parts, including Onegin's journey. Each chapter contains forty to fifty-four stanzas of fourteen lines each, in four-foot iambic, and with a special rhyme scheme called the "Onegin stanza": *AbAbCCddEffEgg* (small letters indicating masculine and capitals feminine rhymes). Pushkin did not return to this stanza form and it has rarely been used since. The novel itself resembles sentimental types such as Jean-Jacques Rousseau's *La Nouvelle Héloïse* (1761; *Julia: Or, The New Eloisa*, 1773) and Benjamin Constant's *Adolphe* (1815; English translation, 1816). It is also a type of bildungsroman or the *éducation sentimentale* of Tatyana and Onegin. It is in reality a combination of several genres: novel, comic-epic, and above all poetry, for it is inseparable from the verse in which it is written.

The first two chapters, the product of Pushkin's youth, show the greatest absence of structure. They abound in digressions and poetic ruminations ranging from the ballet to women's feet. They introduce us to the hero Eugene Onegin, a St. Petersburg dandy, who spends his life in boredom until an inheritance brings him to an equally boring life in the provinces. Here he meets the dreamy poet Lensky, in love with a neighbor, Olga

Larin. It is at this point that the tone of the poem changes, as Olga's older sister, Tatyana, immediately develops an intense passion for Onegin, and in her simplicity reveals her love for him in her famous letter. Onegin politely refuses her and continues his aimless existence, interrupted by a flirtation with Olga, thus provoking a duel with Lensky in which the poet is killed.

Years pass, and Tatyana is married against her will to an elderly and unattractive general. Onegin meets her in Moscow and falls passionately in love with her. He declares his love, but this time it is Tatyana in her mature serenity who informs him: "I love you . . . but I have become another's wife; I shall be true to him through life." Here the poem ends abruptly yet fittingly as Tatyana emerges as the tragic heroine in this tale of twice-rejected love.

The poem maintains an internal unity through the parallel between Onegin's rejection of Tatyana and her refusal of him. *Eugene Onegin* is, however, essentially a lyric poem about the tragic consequences of love rather than a pure novel with a solid substructure. Pushkin draws poetry out of a samovar, the wrinkled nanny who is modeled on Arina Rodionovna, and the broken-hearted resignation of Tatyana. The changing of the seasons indicates the passage of time as Pushkin sings of the beautiful Russian countryside. He likewise enters into his characters, and makes of Onegin a realistic hero and the first of a long line of "superfluous men" to appear in Mikhail Lermontov, Ivan Goncharov, and Ivan Turgenev. Tatyana is perfectly consistent as her youthful naïveté changes into a controlled maturity. She has often been described as the purest figure in the whole of Russian literature, and has become the prototype of Russian womanhood. Pushkin's contemporaries read his poem with enthusiasm, and today it is still one of the great classics of Russian literature. Foreign readers may know it better through Pyotr Ilich Tchaikovsky's opera; again, this results from the fact that it is essentially a poem, defying translation.

Poltava

Pushkin always showed a great deal of interest in Peter the Great, and refers to him in his lyric poetry, in longer poems, and in his prose (*Peter the Great's Negro*). It is in *Poltava* and *The Bronze Horseman* that he reaches his height. *Poltava*, written in three weeks in 1828, has an epic quality but also draws on the ballad, ode, and oral tradition. It recalls Sir Walter Scott's *Marmion* (1808), since it places historical characters in a Romantic background. Lord Byron in *Mazeppa* (1819), drew on the same sources but used instead an apocryphal account of the hero's youth.

The main focus of *Poltava* is the battle of 1709, in which the Russians under Peter the Great defeated the Swedes under Charles XII. Poltava was the turning point in the Russo-Swedish War. Against this historical backdrop is set the romance of the aged Ukrainian Cossack hetman Mazepa with the young and beautiful Marya, daughter of Kochubey, who refuses to allow the marriage. The two marry in spite of him, and

Kochubey seeks revenge by revealing, to Peter, Mazepa's plan of revolt against him. His project miscarries, however, when Peter believes Mazepa's denials. Kochubey is taken prisoner by Mazepa and is about to be executed when Marya learns about her husband's treachery against her father. Arriving too late to save him, she leaves, returning to her husband only briefly as a madwoman before Mazepa's flight with Charles XII after leading an unsuccessful revolt against the victorious Peter.

Although Pushkin has interwoven much historical material into his tale, he has been charged with excessive melodrama by critics from Belinsky to the present day, who see in Mazepa a kind of Gothic villain. Pushkin is likewise charged with unsuccessfully fusing the historical and the Romantic, and more recently, by John Bayley, for the gap "between two kinds of romance, the modern melodrama and the traditional tragic ballad." Mazepa is one of Pushkin's few dark and villainous characters, but Marya has been acknowledged as truly *narodnaya* by Belinsky and Soviet critics. Peter is the all-pervading presence, larger than life, who symbolizes the growing importance of Russia.

THE BRONZE HORSEMAN

In *The Bronze Horseman*, Peter reappears in retrospect. Pushkin wrote *The Bronze Horseman* in 1833 partially in response to the Polish poet Adam Mickiewicz, who had attacked the Russian autocracy. It consists of an introduction and two parts, 481 lines in all, and is rightly considered one of Pushkin's greatest masterpieces. It combines personal lyricism and political, social, and literary themes and raises philosophical questions in paradoxical fashion. The title refers to the equestrian statue of Peter the Great by E. M. Falconet that still stands along the Neva River. The historical incident that inspired the poem was the devastating flood that struck St. Petersburg on November 7, 1824.

In the introduction, Peter the Great stands looking over the Neva, then a deserted swamp with a few ramshackle huts. He plans to build a city there, which will open a window to the West and terrify all his enemies. A hundred years pass, and the young city is the pride of the north, a cold sparkling gem of granite and iron, the scene of royal balls, military reviews, and winter sports. Suddenly, the picture changes as Pushkin begins his sad tale. Eugene, a poor government clerk (whose last name is not important), is making plans to marry Parasha. That very night, the Neva whirls and swirls and rages like an angry beast; the next day Parasha's home is destroyed, and she is lost. Eugene visits the empty spot, and goes mad from the shock. Life continues as usual, but poor Eugene wanders through the city until one day he shakes his angry fist at the Bronze Horseman, who gallops after him down the streets of St. Petersburg. Later, a dilapidated house is washed up on one of the islands; near it Eugene's corpse is found.

Pushkin's poem shows complete mastery of technique. In lines starkly terse yet rich with onomatopoeic sounds, Pushkin conjures up the mighty flood, the proud emperor, and the defenseless Eugene. In the last scene, Peter and Eugene come face to face, and seemingly the emperor wins, yet Pushkin is far from being reconciled to the notion that individual destiny must be sacrificed to historical necessity. Indeed, Eugene is the first of a long line of downtrodden Russian heroes, such as Akakiy Akakyevich and Makar Devushkin, possessing dignity and daring to face authority. Peter is the human hero, contemplating greatness; he is also the impassive face of destiny. The poem itself poses the problem of Pushkin's own troubled existence as well as the ambiguous and cruel fate of all human beings.

OTHER MAJOR WORKS

LONG FICTION: *Evgeny Onegin*, 1825-1832, 1833 (*Eugene Onegin*, 1881); *Arap Petra velikogo*, 1828-1841 (*Peter the Great's Negro*, 1896); *Kirdzhali*, 1834 (English translation, 1896); *Kapitanskaya dochka*, 1836 (*The Captain's Daughter*, 1846); *Dubrovsky*, 1841 (English translation, 1892); *Yegipetskiye nochi*, 1841 (*Egyptian Nights*, 1896); *Istoriya sela Goryukhina*, 1857 (*History of the Village of Goryukhino*, 1966).

SHORT FICTION: *Povesti Belkina*, 1831 (*Russian Romance*, 1875; better known as *The Tales of Belkin*, 1947); *Pikovaya dama*, 1834 (*The Queen of Spades*, 1858).

PLAYS: *Boris Godunov*, pb. 1831 (wr. 1824-1825; English translation, 1918); *Motsart i Salyeri*, pr. 1832 (*Mozart and Salieri*, 1920); *Pir vo vryemya chumy*, pb. 1833 (*The Feast in Time of the Plague*, 1925); *Rusalka*, pb. 1837 (*The Water Nymph*, 1924); *Kamyenny gost*, pb. 1839 (wr. 1830; *The Stone Guest*, 1936); *Skupoy rytsar*, pr. 1852 (wr. 1830; *The Covetous Knight*, 1925); *Stseny iz rytsarskikh vryemen*, pr., pb. 1937 (wr. 1835); *Little Tragedies*, 1946 (includes *The Covetous Knight*, *The Stone Guest*, *Mozart and Salieri*, and *The Feast in Time of the Plague*).

NONFICTION: *Istoriya Pugacheva*, 1834 (*The Pugachev Rebellion*, 1966); *Puteshestviye v Arzrum*, 1836 (*A Journey to Arzrum*, 1974); *Dnevnik, 1833-1835*, 1923; *Pisma*, 1926-1935 (3 volumes); *The Letters of Alexander Pushkin*, 1963 (3 volumes); *Pisma poslednikh let 1834-1837*, 1969.

MISCELLANEOUS: *The Captain's Daughter, and Other Tales*, 1933; *The Poems, Prose, and Plays of Pushkin*, 1936; *The Works of Alexander Pushkin*, 1936; *Polnoye sobraniye sochineniy*, 1937-1959 (17 volumes); *The Complete Prose Tales of Alexander Pushkin*, 1966; *A. S. Pushkin bez tsenzury*, 1972; *Pushkin Threefold*, 1972; *Polnoye sobraniye sochineniy*, 1977-1979 (10 volumes); *Alexander Pushkin: Complete Prose Fiction*, 1983.

BIBLIOGRAPHY

Bethea, David M. *Realizing Metaphors: Alexander Pushkin and the Life of the Poet.* Madison: University of Wisconsin Press, 1998. Bethea illustrates the relation between the art and life of Pushkin and shows how he speaks to modern times.

_____, ed. *The Pushkin Handbook*. Madison: University of Wisconsin Press, 2005.

A collection of essays by Pushkin scholars in the Soviet Union and North America that looks at his life and legacy. Includes essays on his poetic works.

Binyon, T. J. *Pushkin: A Biography*. New York: Knopf, 2004. An extensive biography of Pushkin, Russia's national poet.

Debreczeny, Paul. *Social Functions of Literature: Alexander Pushkin and Russian Culture*. Stanford, Calif.: Stanford University Press, 1997. Debreczeny divides his study into three parts: the first is devoted to selected readers' responses to Pushkin; the second explores the extent to which individual aesthetic responses are conditioned by their environment; and the third concerns the mythic aura that developed around Pushkin's public persona.

Evdokimova, Svetlana. *Pushkin's Historical Imagination*. New Haven, Conn.: Yale University Press, 1999. An examination of the range of Pushkin's fictional and nonfictional works on the subject of history. Evdokimova considers Pushkin's ideas on the relation between chance and necessity, the significance of great individuals, and historical truth.

Feinstein, Elaine. *Pushkin: A Biography*. London: Weidenfeld & Nicolson, 1998. Drawing on newly discovered documents, Feinstein explores the life of one of nineteenth century Russia's greatest writers.

Kahn, Andrew, ed. *The Cambridge Companion to Pushkin*. New York: Cambridge University Press, 2006. Looks at his works and their legacy. Contains several chapters on his poetry.

Ryfa, Juras T., ed. *Collected Essays in Honor of the Bicentennial of Alexander Pushkin's Birth*. Lewiston, N.Y.: Edwin Mellen Press, 2000. A selection of scholarly essays devoted to various works by Pushkin and his influence on his literary descendants.

Shaw, J. Thomas. *Pushkin's Poetics of the Unexpected: The Nonrhymed Lines in the Rhymed Poetry and the Rhymed Lines in the Nonrhymed Poetry*. Columbus, Ohio: Slavica, 1993. This is a highly specialized study of Pushkin's poetic technique that will be of most use to specialists.

Vitale, Serena. *Pushkin's Button*. Translated by Ann Goldstein and Jon Rothschild. New York: Farrar, Straus and Giroux, 1999. A cultural history and narrative of the last months of Pushkin's life before his fatal duel. Vitale brings to life the world of St. Petersburg in the 1830's using her own research with information gleaned from secondary literature and the memoirs and letters of Pushkin's contemporaries.

Irma M. Kashuba

SIR WALTER SCOTT

Born: Edinburgh, Scotland; August 15, 1771
Died: Abbotsford, Scotland; September 21, 1832
Also known as: First Baronet Scott

PRINCIPAL POETRY

The Eve of Saint John: A Border Ballad, 1800
The Lay of the Last Minstrel, 1805
Ballads and Lyrical Pieces, 1806
Marmion: A Tale of Flodden Field, 1808
The Lady of the Lake, 1810
The Vision of Don Roderick, 1811
Rokeby, 1813
The Bridal of Triermain: Or, The Vale of St. John, in Three Cantos, 1813
The Ettrick Garland: Being Two Excellent New Songs, 1815 (with James Hogg)
The Field of Waterloo, 1815
The Lord of the Isles, 1815
Harold the Dauntless, 1817

OTHER LITERARY FORMS

Sir Walter Scott's literary reputation rests firmly on his monumental collection of Waverley novels, the final revision of which was issued, in forty-eight volumes, between 1829 and 1833. The novelist produced those classics on a regular basis during the last eighteen years of his life—beginning with the three-volume *Waverley: Or, 'Tis Sixty Years Since* in 1814 and concluding, shortly before his death, with *Count Robert of Paris* and *Castle Dangerous* (under the collective title *Tales of My Landlord*, fourth series), both in 1831. In addition to the novels, Scott wrote numerous plays, including *Halidon Hill* (pb. 1822), *Macduff's Cross* (pb. 1823), *The House of Aspen* (pb. 1829), *Auchindrane: Or, The Ayrshire Tragedy* (pr., pb. 1830), and *The Doom of Devorgoil* (pb. 1830).

Scott's nonfiction prose includes *Religious Discourses by a Layman* (1828), *The History of Scotland* (1829-1830), and *Letters on Demonology and Witchcraft* (1830). He also produced three biographies of note: *The Life and Works of John Dryden*, first published in 1808 as part of his eighteen-volume edition of that poet's works; *The Memoirs of Jonathan Swift* (1826; originally included in the nineteen-volume *The Life of Jonathan Swift*, 1814); and *The Life of Napoleon Buonaparte: Emperor of the French, with a Preliminary View of the French Revolution* (1827, 9 volumes). In addition, as editor of *Ballantyne's Novelist's Library* 1821-1824 (10 volumes), Scott wrote biographi-

Sir Walter Scott
(Library of Congress)

cal essays on each writer in the series (including Henry Fielding, Tobias Smollett, Samuel Richardson, Ann Radcliffe, Charlotte Smith, and Fanny Burney); he published those sketches separately in 1825 (2 volumes).

Finally, Scott expended considerable energy on a long list of editorial projects carried out between 1799 and 1831: In addition to the works of John Dryden and Jonathan Swift and the *Novelist's Library*, one may note *Minstrelsy of the Scottish Border* (1802-1803, 32 volumes), *A Collection of Scarce and Valuable Tracts* (1809-1815, 13 volumes), and *Chronological Notes of Scottish Affairs from the Diary of Lord Fountainhall* (1822). Various editions of *The Journal of Sir Walter Scott* have appeared, beginning in 1890.

ACHIEVEMENTS

Sir Walter Scott's literary reputation rests on thirty novels. Few twentieth century readers and scholars have been interested in his poetry or have taken the time to examine the distinct stages of his literary career. With the publication of *Waverley* in 1814,

Scott's literary life as a novelist began and his period of intense poetic production terminated. At the outset, then, one is tempted to view the poetry only in the context of its effect on the fiction—or, from another perspective, the effect of Scott the poet on Scott the novelist.

Ample reason exists, however, for studying the poetry on its own merits, for the imaginative power to be found in Scott's metrical romances, lyrics, and ballads. Some contemporary scholars support the claims of their Victorian predecessors, who argued that Scott, among all his "British" contemporaries, emerged as the first writer of the Romantic movement. Indeed, although literary historians correctly offer William Wordsworth's *Lyrical Ballads* (1798)—and its significant preface—as the key to understanding British Romanticism, Scott's *The Lay of the Last Minstrel*, published seven years later, reached a far wider audience (in both England and Scotland) than Wordsworth's collection and achieved a more noticeable impact among the poet's contemporaries than did the earlier work. In fact, no previous English poet had managed to produce a work that reaped such large financial rewards and achieved so much popular acclaim.

Interestingly enough, Scott's poetic achievements came in a form radically different from those qualities that marked the traditional "giants" of his age—Wordsworth, Samuel Taylor Coleridge, John Keats, Percy Bysshe Shelley, and Lord Byron. True, Scott considered, at a variety of levels, the prevalent Romantic themes: the rejection of scientific dogmatism, a return to the glamour of past ages, the discovery of happiness in primitivism rather than in modernity, the enjoyment of emotion, a basic belief in humanitarianism. He rejected, however, the radical sentiments of the Romantic movement. By nature and upbringing a conservative, Scott clung to Tory politics and to the established Church of England rather than rising up in actual or intellectual rebellion against such institutions. He had little or no interest in mysticism, overzealous passion, or the dark unconscious. Scott's poetry is distinguished by its considerable clarity and directness; it is the product of a gentlemanly and reasonably satisfied attitude toward promoting the values of his own social class. He did rush back into an imaginary past to seek out heroes and adventurers whom he found lacking in his own early nineteenth century cultural and artistic environment. Such escapes, however, never really detracted from his belief in the challenge of the present intellectual life and the present world, where, if everything else failed, courage would support the intellectually honest competitor.

Chronologically, Scott belongs with the early Romantics; culturally and intellectually, he occupies a middle ground between Scotland and England, and therein, perhaps, lies his ultimate contribution to poetry in English. He captured, first in the poems and later in his prose fiction, the essence of Scottish national pride; that pride he filtered through the physical image of Scotland, through its varied and conflicting scenery and its traditional romantic lore. The entire area—joined politically to Great Britain in 1707, but still culturally free and theologically independent during Scott's day (as it remains even to this day)—stimulated and intensified his creative genius and supplied the substance first for his poetry, then for his prose fiction. Nevertheless, Scott remained distinctly aware of England and receptive to the demands of the English public—his largest reading audience. For them he translated the picturesqueness of the Highlands and the Lowlands, the islands and the borders. While photographing (or "painting," as his contemporaries maintained), through his imagination, the language and the sentiment of Scotland, Scott gave to his English readers scenes and characters that could be observed as partly English. His poetry has a freshness, a frankness, a geniality, and a shrewdness peculiar to his own Scottish Lowlands. Still, as observers of that part of the world quickly appreciate, there is little difference between a southern Scotsman and a northern Englishman—which, in the end, may also be an apt commentary on Scott's poetry.

BIOGRAPHY

The fourth surviving son of Walter Scott and Anne Rutherford, Walter Scott was born on August 15, 1771, in a house in the College Wynd, Edinburgh. At the age of eighteen months, the infant contracted a fever while teething and, in the end, lost the use of his right leg. The circumstance became noteworthy not only for its effect on Scott's personality and his writing, but also as the first fully authenticated case of infantile paralysis in medical history. After the failure of various attempts to remedy the malady, Scott's father sent him to Sandy Knowe, near Kelso (Roxburgh), to live with his grandfather (Robert Scott) and his uncle (Thomas). Although the five years spent there contributed little or nothing toward curing the boy's lameness, they provided some experiences with lasting influence: subjection to republican and Jacobite prejudices; songs and legends taught to him by his grandmother (Barbara Haliburton); a trip to the spas at Bath, with a stopover at London on the way; sea-bathing at Prestonpans, near Edinburgh (and site of one of the key engagements of the Jacobite uprising of 1745), where he learned of the German wars from an old veteran of Invernahyle, one Captain Dalgetty.

In 1778, the boy returned to his father's house in George's Square, Edinburgh, and later that year entered the high school at Edinburgh. From his principal tutor, a strict Presbyterian named James Mitchell, Scott gained a knowledge of Scottish church history, while his mother encouraged him to read William Shakespeare. His health, however, continued to be a problem, so again the elder Scott sent his son off, this time to Kelso to live with an aunt, Jenny Scott. During his half-year's stay there, he met James Ballantyne and the blind poet Thomas Blacklock; there, also, he read James Macpherson's Ossianic poems, Edmund Spenser's *The Faerie Queene* (1590, 1596), and Thomas Percy's *Reliques of Ancient English Poetry* (1765). Most important, however, he began to collect ballads, a form and a tradition that would remain with him and influence his own literary and cultural directions. By November, 1783, Scott had prepared himself sufficiently to begin studies at Edinburgh University; he pursued only those disciplines, however, that aroused his interest (law, history, romantic legends, and literature). Further illness reduced his stamina, and his education was interrupted once more when he apprenticed himself to his father, copying legal documents. Eventually he did manage to earn a degree in law (1792) and gain admission to the Scottish bar.

Although Scott did indeed practice law and, after a reasonable period as a novice, did manage to earn a fair income from his labors, his interest focused more sharply than ever on literature, ballads, and Scottish folklore. Thus, between 1792 and 1799—first merely as a companion to the sheriff-substitute of Roxburghshire, then as sheriff-deputy of Selkirkshire—he engaged in his "border raids," exploring the country, collecting ballads and tales, and generally enjoying the hospitality of many and various true and traditional Scottish characters. To that activity, he added a deep interest in German literature; he learned the language (but not the formal grammar) well enough to read and to translate, publishing in 1799 an edition of Johann Wolfgang von Goethe's *Goetz von Berlichingen* (1774), one of that writer's earliest heroic creations in which an old knight bows to the forces of decay about him. Scott did not emerge as a public figure, however, until about six years later, when he published *The Lay of the Last Minstrel*. In rather quick succession, he became a partner in and large contributor to James Ballantyne's publishing house, gained a permanent appointment (1806) as clerk of session at Edinburgh, and was a principal founder (along with John Murray the younger) of *Quarterly Review*, the Tory rival to *Edinburgh Review*. In 1813, he declined the honor of being named poet laureate of England in favor of Robert Southey. A year later, his first novel, *Waverley*, was published.

As sheriff of Selkirkshire, Scott went, in 1804, to live at Ashestiel, on the banks of the River Tweed (dividing England and Scotland); there he wrote, between 1805 and 1813, *The Lay of the Last Minstrel, Marmion, The Lady of the Lake, The Vision of Don Roderick, The Bridal of Triermain*, and *Rokeby*. In 1812, he had begun the construction of a baronial mansion at Abbotsford (near Melrose in Roxburghshire)—once known as the little farm of Cartleyhole belonging to the monks of Melrose. After taking up residence there he could, indeed, lay claim to the title of "gentleman." He continued to reap financial benefits from his writing, and in 1820, he received a baronetcy. He would, however, be denied the luxury of lasting contentment. Economic depression swept the British Isles in 1825; a year later, the firm of John Ballantyne and Company collapsed, and Scott found himself being left responsible (morally and actually) for most of the publishing house's debts. Rather than declaring bankruptcy, the poet-novelist pressed forward on a number of literary projects to pay his creditors. To compound the emotional strain and the problems of failing health, Scott's wife, Charlotte Carpentier, died in the same year.

Thus, the last several years of Scott's life were marked by struggle and overwork; he was kept afloat, so to speak, on the strength of his pride and personal integrity. By 1831, his health had declined seriously; an Admiralty frigate carried him on a sea voyage through the Mediterranean; he had been sent off from Abbotsford with a fresh sonnet by

Wordsworth. While on board, he suffered a stroke of apoplexy resulting in paralysis and was forced to return to Abbotsford. There he lingered, from mid-July, 1832, until September 21, when he died quietly in the presence of all his children.

ANALYSIS

Sir Walter Scott's poetry, unlike that of his Romantic contemporaries, is vigorous, high-spirited, and unreflective. Scott delighted in war and pageantry, in the rich traditions of antiquity. As a Scottish poet born among a people who sought action, he was drawn to his heritage, to his connections with the border chieftains and the House of Buccleuch. Thus, his narrative poems and ballads reflect the character of a strong and proud man who, though he was lame, dreamed of the ultimate masculine activities: of chivalry, adventure, the qualities of feudalism, and the military picturesqueness of another age.

BALLADS

Any survey of Scott the poet must consider his interest in the popular ballad, an interest that came naturally because of the love for the old, harsh times. Scott saw in the popular Scottish ballad a contrast to the relative serenity of his own early nineteenth century. He relished the clannish loyalties, the bravery, the cruelty, the revenge, and the superstitions of the old ballads. Thus, he began with "The Chase" and "William and Helen" (1796)—two translations from the German lyric poet (and, coincidentally, lawyer) Gottfried August Burger (1747-1794); next came three strange, almost mystical ballads contributed to Matthew Gregory "Monk" Lewis's *Tales of Wonder* in 1801: "Glenfinlas," "The Eve of St. John," and "The Gray Brother." His interest in the ballad reached its height—a scholarly as well as a poetic pinnacle—with *The Minstrelsy of the Scottish Border*, wherein Scott the editor and poet gathered and polished the best examples of what will always be considered the true literature of Scotland.

The ballad, however, was not to be the end-all for Scott the poet, but rather a springboard to other forms and variations of ballad themes. He turned his poetic attention to a series of complex and ornamental romances wherein, instead of the harshness and rusticity of the border, lords, ladies, and even clerics came forth to expound lofty themes in elevated language. Still, the stuff from which the popular ballads sprang is there. In *The Lay of the Last Minstrel*, for example, romantic love blends easily with magic, dwarfs, and goblins, while in *Marmion*, the early sixteenth century battle at Flodden Field in Northumberland, where the English, in 1513, defeated the Scots under James IV, allowed Scott to develop elaborate descriptions of conflict and chivalry, of the detailed instruments of warfare and the awesomeness of border castles. More important in terms of the ballad influence, *Marmion* draws considerable poetic life from its thoroughly romantic narrative—from intrigue, disguise, and unfaithfulness (both clerical and secular). *The Lady of the Lake* intensifies those actions, featuring Highland clans rushing to battle after being summoned by a fiery cross. Scott carried his readers on a tour of chieftain's lodge and king's court, setting the stage for James Fitz-James to reveal himself as King James and to restore the noble Ellen to her true love, Malcolm Graeme. Although the later poems—*The Vision of Don Roderick*, *Rokeby*, and *Harold the Dauntless*—reveal Scott as more than ready to abandon verse for prose fiction, the worlds of knighthood, sorcery, and the ancient bards and minstrels continued to fascinate him—no matter that the locales and circumstances seemed far removed from that wild terrain north of the River Tweed.

HISTORY AND NARRATIVE

One must not too quickly assume that Scott's poetry contains little beyond historical or romantic re-creations. Although he himself readily admitted that his work did not rise to the levels of Wordsworth or Coleridge, he nevertheless remained a legitimate poet, not simply a compiler and reviser of historical verse tales. Scott fully realized the depth and complexity of human emotions; he chose, however, to portray the manifestations of those emotions within the context of his own historical knowledge and his own historical imagination. Thus, he could set forth value judgments and insights into history rather than simply displaying the past as mere background scenery. Scott knew only too well that he was living in the present—in a world marked by political and social revolution to which the romantic past must, for the sake of reason and order, subordinate itself. Nevertheless, history could continue to instruct the present; it could also amuse and it could momentarily ease the confusion within the minds of the poet's readers. History could help a restless and degenerate age to imagine the heroics of an older time.

With only a few exceptions, the poetry of Scott conveys action and excitement, for the poet had learned at an early age to master the conventions of narrative. But narration alone could not carry the essence of the poem. In *The Lady of the Lake*, he demonstrated the quality of painting lovely scenery, giving it dimension, and fusing it skillfully with the poetry of clan life. Scott opened the gates to the Scottish Highlands for his cultivated readers to the south. For the height of action and excitement, however, those same readers had to turn to *Marmion*, to the strong horse striding over green terrain in the fresh air, its shrill neighing and the sun's rays reverberating and reflecting from the shield and the lance of its rider. In fact, the poet stacked his details one upon the other in almost breathless fashion: "Green, sanguine, purple, red, and blue,/ Broad, narrow, swallow-tailed, and square,/ Scroll, pennon, pensil, brandrol."

CHARACTERS

The major weakness of Scott as a poet is his inability to create believable characters. Margaret of Branksome Hall (in *The Lay of the Last Minstrel*) exudes considerable charm, but she does little beyond fulfilling her function as the typical "fair maid," even amid a fast-paced series of armed encounters and magical spells. Roderick Dhu,

Malcolm Graeme, and Lord James Douglas (*The Lady of the Lake*) appear active enough, but they have little else to do aside from their obvious responsibilities as fierce Highland chieftains, outlawed lords, and young knights. Also acting according to form (and little else) are Roland de Vaux (*The Bridal of Triermain*), Philip of Montham (*Rokeby*), and Edith of Lorn and Lord Ronald (both from *The Lord of the Isles*)—although Edith's disguise as a mute page, as well as the dangers she encounters, allows her some room for depth and variety. There is little doubt that Scott's best poetic characters assume the forms not of romantic heroes but of heroic scoundrels, such as the stately forger Marmion and the pirate Bertram Risingham (*Rokeby*), whose evil nature contains some elements of good. Scott addressed this problem himself, stating that no matter how hard he had tried to do otherwise, his rogues emerged as heroes. More accurately, the rogues had more life and depth than did the heroes.

NATURE

Scott's ballads and verse tales are not, however, anchored to the issues of characterization, to the conflicts between good and evil, or even to the differences between heroes and villains. Virtually obliterating the shallowness of those characters, the poet's almost passionate love for the beauties of nature infuses practically every poem. In that sense, and within the context of his abilities to communicate that love to a relatively large and varied reading audience, Scott may indeed be identified with the early Romantic poets. Traditionally, his sophisticated English readership perceived Scotland—especially the Highlands—as a physical and intellectual wilderness; at best, readers of that day recalled only the Gothic descriptions of James Macpherson's Ossianic poems or the Addisonian sketches of the essayist Henry Mackenzie. Then, with *The Lay of the Last Minstrel*, *Marmion*, and *The Lady of the Lake*, Scott revealed the culture of his native land, and "Cold diffidence, and age's frost,/ In the full tide of my song were lost." He carried his readers on his poetic back "Across the furzy hills of Braid," through "all the hill with yellow grain," and over "To eastern Lodon's fertile plain"; through Scott's lines, his readers far to the south undertook a vicarious trek into a land that had been virtually shut off from their imaginations.

In addition to satisfying the imaginative needs of his Romantic-age readers, Scott conscientiously guided them through an almost microscopic study of physical nature, as if he were conducting a tour: going over each scene, textbook in hand, noting the various species of plants and shrubs, stones and rocks, surveying "each naked precipice,/ Sable ravine, and dark abyss" to uncover "Some touch of Nature's genial glow." For example, in the description of Lake Coriskin (in *The Lord of the Isles*), the landscape portrait captures the warmth of nature and the poet's feeling for color: In addition to the genial glow of Nature, "green mosses grow" atop Benmore, while "health-bells bud in deep Glencoe"—all of which serves up a sharp contrast to the "Black waves, bare crags, and banks of stone" that constitute the "bleakest" side of the mountain. Again, in depicting

Edinburgh and the camp in *Marmion*, the poet directs his audience to the "rose on breezes thin" that clash headlong with "Saint Giles's mingling din" as he strives to document the specifics of the distance (topographical and imaginative) "from the summit to the plain."

CRITICAL ASSESSMENTS

Critical response to Scott's poetry has ranged from kindness to indifference. Perhaps the fairest assessment of his poetry is Scott's own. He never aspired to equal Wordsworth or Coleridge or Byron; he wanted only to enjoy life and literature (indeed, even in that order), disclaiming everything beyond the love of Scotland and its traditions. That love obviously led him to poetry, as it did to prose fiction, to biography, to history, and to scholarly editing and collecting. When he finished with one of those aspects of the good, intellectual life, he simply went on to something else. Literary history must be prepared to accept Scott on his own terms and on that middle ground.

OTHER MAJOR WORKS

LONG FICTION: *Waverley: Or, 'Tis Sixty Years Since*, 1814; *Guy Mannering*, 1815; *The Antiquary*, 1816; *The Black Dwarf*, 1816; *Old Mortality*, 1816; *Rob Roy*, 1817; *The Heart of Midlothian*, 1818; *The Bride of Lammermoor*, 1819; *Ivanhoe*, 1819; *A Legend of Montrose*, 1819; *The Abbot*, 1820; *The Monastery*, 1820; *Kenilworth*, 1821; *The Pirate*, 1821; *The Fortunes of Nigel*, 1822; *Peveril of the Peak*, 1823; *Quentin Durward*, 1823; *St. Ronan's Well*, 1823; *Redgauntlet*, 1824; *The Betrothed*, 1825; *The Talisman*, 1825; *Woodstock*, 1826; *The Fair Maid of Perth*, 1828; *Anne of Geierstein*, 1829; *Castle Dangerous*, 1831; *Count Robert of Paris*, 1831; *The Siege of Malta*, 1976.

SHORT FICTION: "Wandering Willie's Tale," 1824; *Chronicles of the Canongate*, 1827 (2 volumes); "Death of the Laird's Jock," 1828; "My Aunt Margaret's Mirror," 1828; "The Tapestried Chamber," 1828.

PLAYS: *Halidon Hill*, pb. 1822; *Macduff's Cross*, pb. 1823; *The House of Aspen*, pb. 1829; *Auchindrane: Or, The Ayrshire Tragedy*, pr., pb. 1830; *The Doom of Devorgoil*, pb. 1830.

NONFICTION: *The Life and Works of John Dryden*, 1808; *The Life of Jonathan Swift*, 1814; *Lives of the Novelists*, 1825; *The Life of Napoleon Buonaparte: Emperor of the French, with a Preliminary View of the French Revolution*, 1827; *Religious Discourses by a Layman*, 1828; *Tales of a Grandfather*, 1828-1830 (12 volumes); *The History of Scotland*, 1829-1830; *Letters on Demonology and Witchcraft*, 1830; *The Journal of Sir Walter Scott*, 1890.

TRANSLATIONS: *"The Chase," and "William and Helen": Two Ballads from the German of Gottfried Augustus Bürger*, 1796; *Goetz of Berlichingen, with the Iron Hand*, 1799 (of Johann Wolfgang von Goethe).

EDITED TEXTS: *Minstrelsy of the Scottish Border*, 1802-1803 (3 volumes); *A Collec-*

tion of Scarce and Valuable Tracts, 1809-1815 (13 volumes); *Chronological Notes of Scottish Affairs from the Diary of Lord Fountainhall,* 1822.

BIBLIOGRAPHY

Bold, Alan, ed. *Sir Walter Scott: The Long-Forgotten Melody.* London: Vision Press, 1983. Nine essays cover such subjects in Scott's works as the image of Scotland, politics, and folk tradition and draw on Scott's poetry for illustration. The essay by Iain Crichton Smith, "Poetry in Scott's Narrative Verse," shows appreciation for the art of the poetry. Includes endnotes and an index.

Crawford, Thomas. *Scott.* Rev. ed. Edinburgh: Scottish Academic Press, 1982. A revision and elaboration of Crawford's widely acclaimed study of Scott. Examines Scott's work as a poet, balladist, and novelist.

Goslee, Nancy Moore. *Scott the Rhymer.* Lexington: University Press of Kentucky, 1988. Aiming to restore Scott as a poet, this book analyzes in detail his major poems. A discussion of *The Lay of the Last Minstrel* is followed by examinations of the long poems from *Marmion* to *Harold the Dauntless.* These poems are affirmations of romance within self-reflexive frames of irony. Contains ample notes and an index.

Lauber, John. *Sir Walter Scott.* Boston: Twayne, 1989. A good starting point for a study of Scott. The first three chapters provide an overview of Scott's career; the rest provide discussions of the novels. Includes a chronology and a select bibliography.

Lincoln, Andrew. *Walter Scott and Modernity.* Edinburgh: Edinburgh University Press, 2007. Lincoln examines Scott's use of the past to explore issues in the modern world. He analyzes both widely read poems and Scott's better-known novels.

Mitchell, Jerome. *Scott, Chaucer, and Medieval Romance: A Study in Sir Walter Scott's Indebtedness to the Literature of the Middle Ages.* Lexington: University Press of Kentucky, 1987. Describes the influences of Geoffrey Chaucer and medieval romances at work in Scott's narrative poetry, early novels, middle novels written during his financial collapse, and novels of the darkly declining years. The style and structure of the novels are analyzed before a conclusion is drawn. Augmented by preface, notes, and an index.

Scott, Sir Walter. *The Journal of Sir Walter Scott.* Edited by W. E. K. Anderson. Edinburgh: Canongate, 1998. Scott's journals offer invaluable biographical insights into his life and work. Includes bibliographical references and index.

Sutherland, John. *The Life of Walter Scott.* Cambridge, Mass.: Blackwell, 1995. A narrative account that penetrates into the darker areas of Scott's life. The value of Scott's writing today as much as in his heyday is justified by Sutherland's account.

Todd, William B., and Ann Bowden. *Sir Walter Scott: A Bibliographical History, 1796-1832.* New Castle, Del.: Oak Knoll Press, 1998. Lists variant editions of the verse as well as the fiction, and casts light on Scott's occupations as advocate, sheriff, antiquarian, biographer, editor, historian, and reviewer.

Tulloch, Graham. *The Language of Walter Scott: A Study of His Scottish and Period Language*. London: Andre Deutsch, 1980. In eight chapters and two appendices, Tulloch examines Scott's use of Scotch-English in his poetry and fiction. The special features of the language are analyzed in terms of vocabulary, grammar, and spelling. Scott's reading is also examined as a source of his language materials. Includes a bibliography and an index.

Samuel J. Rogal

PERCY BYSSHE SHELLEY

Born: Field Place, near Horsham, Sussex, England; August 4, 1792
Died: At sea off Viareggio, Lucca (now in Italy); July 8, 1822

PRINCIPAL POETRY
Original Poetry by Victor and Cazire, 1810 (with Elizabeth Shelley)
Posthumous Fragments of Margaret Nicholson, 1810
Queen Mab: A Philosophical Poem, 1813, 1816 (as *The Daemon of the World*)
Alastor: Or, The Spirit of Solitude, and Other Poems, 1816
Mont Blanc, 1817
The Revolt of Islam, 1818
Rosalind and Helen: A Modern Eclogue, with Other Poems, 1819
Letter to Maria Gisborne, 1820
Adonais: An Elegy on the Death of John Keats, 1821
Epipsychidion, 1821
Posthumous Poems of Percy Bysshe Shelley, 1824 (includes *Prince Athanase*,
    Julian and Maddalo: A Conversation, *The Witch of Atlas*, *The Triumph of Life*,
    The Cyclops, and *Charles the First*)
The Mask of Anarchy, 1832
Peter Bell the Third, 1839
The Poetical Works of Percy Bysshe Shelley, 1839
The Wandering Jew, 1887
The Complete Poetical Works of Shelley, 1904 (Thomas Hutchinson, editor)
The Esdaile Notebook: A Volume of Early Poems, 1964 (K. N. Cameron, editor)

OTHER LITERARY FORMS

Except for *A Defence of Poetry* (1840), Percy Bysshe Shelley's essays are not classics of English prose, but they have influenced writers as diverse as George Bernard Shaw, H. G. Wells, and Bertrand Russell, and they are useful as glosses on the poetry. "On Love," for example, introduces Shelley's concept of the "antitype," the perfect mate, uniquely suited to one's intellect, imagination, and sensory needs, a "soul within our soul," but purged of all one finds unsatisfactory within oneself. Love is defined as the attraction to the antitype. Shelley describes this longing for a mirror image of perfection:

> If we reason, we would be understood; if we imagine, we would that the airy children of our brain were born anew within another's; if we feel, we would that another's nerves should vibrate to our own, that the beams of their eyes should kindle at once and mix and melt into our own, that lips of motionless ice should not reply to lips quivering and burning with the heart's best blood. This is Love.

Percy Bysshe Shelley
(Library of Congress)

Love, as the attraction toward refined idealism, figures as well in Shelley's theory of the formative power of poetry.

In *A Defence of Poetry*, he argues that "the great secret of morals is Love." Through identification with the "beautiful which exists in thought, action, or person, not our own," one becomes moral through the process of empathizing. Love is thus an act of the sympathetic imagination. Because poetry, and literature in general, enhances and exercises the ability to empathize, it is an agent of tremendous potential for the moral regeneration of humankind. It goes without saying that the poet thus has a high office in the government of morality; he is Shelley's "unacknowledged legislator." By this phrase, Shelley did not primarily mean that poets are unacknowledged for the good they do, but rather that they themselves were not and could not be aware of the power of their beauty. Shelley's poet is not in control of his power, for, in the language of his great metaphor of the creative process,

> the mind in creation is as a fading coal which some invisible influence, like an inconstant wind, awakens to transitory brightness: this power arises from within, like the colour of a flower which fades and changes as it is developed, and the conscious portions of our natures are unprophetic either of its approach or its departure.

Hence, poets do not control their inspiration—in fact, when writing begins, the most intense phase of inspiration has already passed; they express more than they understand; they feel less than they inspire; they are "the influence which is moved not, but moves. Poets are the unacknowledged legislators of the World."

ACHIEVEMENTS

One of the six greatest English Romantic poets, Percy Bysshe Shelley is arguably the most versatile stylist among all English poets. His genius for versification enabled him to employ an astonishing variety of stanzaic patterns and poetic forms with equal facility. He has two basic styles, however—the sublime or rhapsodic, heard in such poems as *Alastor*, "Hymn to Intellectual Beauty," *Prometheus Unbound: A Lyrical Drama in Four Acts* (pb. 1820), and *Adonais*; and the urbane or conversational style, found in poems such as *Julian and Maddalo, Letter to Maria Gisborne*, and *Epipsychidion*. In this latter mode, especially in the standard pentameter line with couplets, Shelley grew increasingly conservative prosodically, achieving a control almost neoclassical in balance and poise. Lyrical, unremitting intensity, however, is the defining quality of Shelley's verse.

BIOGRAPHY

In *Great Expectations* (1860-1861), Charles Dickens has the convict Magwitch put his life's story, as he says, into a mouthful of English—in and out of jail, in and out of jail, in and out of jail. Percy Bysshe Shelley's life falls into a similar pattern—in and out of love, in and out of love, in and out of love. Shelley admitted as much in a letter to John Gisborne, written the year he was to drown in a boating accident, and expressive of a truth he discovered too late: "I think one is always in love with something or other; the error, and I confess it is not easy for spirits cased in flesh and blood to avoid it, consists in seeking in a mortal image the likeness of what is perhaps eternal." At the age of twenty-nine, Shelley was still looking for his antitype; he believed he had found her, at last, in a nineteen-year-old Italian girl imprisoned in a nunnery, and had written one of his greatest poems, *Epipsychidion*, in celebration, typically disregarding the impact the poem would have on his wife Mary. Mary, however, had been party to a similar emotional event five years earlier when Shelley had abandoned his first wife, Harriet Westbrook Shelley, then pregnant with his second child, to elope with Mary. Both times Shelley speculated that the women could live with him, together, in harmony—the first combination, wife Harriet as sister, lover Mary as wife; the second combination, as stated metaphorically in *Epipsychidion*, wife Mary as Moon, Teresa Viviani as Sun to Shelley's Earth, with a comet, Claire Claremont, Mary's half-sister, zooming into their "azure heaven" as she willed.

One of Shelley's great biographers, Kenneth Neill Cameron, says that Shelley was rather ahead of his time, at least ahead of today's liberal divorce laws, but most readers still find the facts of Shelley's love-life disturbing. His vision of love is wonderful; his idealism that sought to change the world through love and poetry is wonderful; the reality of that vision and idealism translated into life was a disaster. Shelley knew it and this awareness caused him to seek self-destruction.

His intense fits of love aside, Shelley could be the most thoughtful and loving of men. He was selfless, generous to a fault, a brilliant radical devoted to saving the world and just as passionately devoted to the pursuit of metaphysical truth. Edward John Trelawny provides a description of Shelley in his study, German folio open, dictionary in hand (Shelley always read literature in the original—Greek, Latin, Spanish, Italian, German—so that he could be sensitive to the style and linguistic nuances of the art), at 10 A.M., and the identical picture at 6 P.M., Shelley having hardly moved, forgetting he had not eaten, looking tired and pale. "Well," Trelawny said, "have you found it?," referring to some truth Shelley sought. "Shutting the book and going to the window," Shelley replied, "'No, I have lost it': with a deep sigh: 'I have lost a day.'"

Shelley was born into a family of landed gentry. His father, Timothy, was a member of Parliament and his grandfather Bysshe Shelley was a very wealthy landowner. Shelley studied at Eton, where he rebelled against the hazing system; fell madly in love with a cousin, Harriet Grove; attended Oxford, briefly, until his expulsion for printing a pamphlet defending atheism; and completed his teenage years by eloping with sixteen-year-old Harriet Westbrook, the daughter of a wealthy merchant. Harriet and Shelley had two children, Ianthe and Charles, the latter born after Shelley had left Harriet to elope with Mary Godwin, the sixteen-year-old child of Mary Wollstonecraft, author of *A Vindication of the Rights of Woman* (1792), and William Godwin, author of *The Inquiry Concerning Political Justice and Its Influence on General Virtue and Happiness* (1793). After Harriet committed suicide by drowning, probably because of her pregnancy with another man's child, Shelley married Mary. The couple lived in England for a while, but left for Italy to protect Shelley's health and to escape the group of friends, including William Godwin, who had come to depend on Shelley for financial support.

In Italy, they settled near Lord Byron, who had fled England for his own personal reasons—a divorce and a child allegedly by his half-sister. Mary and Shelley had two children, Clara and William. When Clara died from an illness exacerbated by the traveling that Shelley forced on his family in Italy, the love-light seemed to wane in the Shelleys' marriage. The following year, 1819, Shelley's son died, and even greater despondency descended on them. Shelley was also disheartened by his ineffectiveness as a poet—no popularity, no audience, no hope of saving the world through his poetry. In *Adonais*, his eulogy for John Keats, Shelley tempts himself to put the things of this world aside, to die. On July 8, 1822, Shelley and Edward Williams set sail from Leghorn, too late in the afternoon considering their destination and with a storm pending. They drowned in the brief tempest. Several weeks later, the two bodies were discovered on separate lonely beaches. In Shelley's pockets were a book of Sophocles and Keats's latest volume of poems, opened as if he had been reading. Byron, Trelawny, Leigh Hunt, and some Italian health officials cremated the bodies, Hellenic style, on the beach. Trelawny claims that Shelley's heart would not burn, or at least did not burn, and that he salvaged it from the ashes. Shelley, who likened the poet to fire and who prominently used the image of releasing one's fate to the stream, thus lived and died the myth of his poetry.

ANALYSIS

Percy Bysshe Shelley mutedly noted in his preface to *Prometheus Unbound* that he had "what a Scotch philosopher terms, 'a passion for reforming the world.'" One might think that this would have endeared his work at least to the reading public left of center and to later readers who value the reforming spirit in humankind. Yet Shelley was almost able to name his readers, they were so few, and today, of the six major poets who dominate the canon of British Romanticism—William Blake, William Wordsworth, Samuel Taylor Coleridge, Byron, Keats, and Shelley—it is still Shelley who remains the least popular. For one reason or another, and though Shelley will always have a cadre of eloquent apologists, dedicated scholars, and brilliant explicators, he is usually out of favor with a significant group of readers. He has been criticized for bad thinking, for bad writing, and for bad living. Devaluations of his thought and poetry have largely been overcome, but this last—especially when made by sensitive feminist readers who find his narcissistic theory of love stupidly, if not heartlessly, destructive to the women in his life—is difficult to refute, if one grants its relevance to his art.

Shelley's theme of self-destructiveness leads to his poetry's most brilliant moments, but perhaps the weakness in Shelley's use of the antitype motif is that it fails to recognize even the possibility that the mate—the woman—exists in her own right, and that her likeness to the fiction of the poet's imagination might not be the best or safest evidence of her worth. In Lord Byron's *Manfred* (1817), the concept of the antitype is also used, but Byron is critical of the theme from the woman's point of view—Manfred has destroyed his lover, Astarte, with this dangerously egotistical love and madly strives to win her forgiveness. Shelley seems incapable of such a critique of his most important theme; therein may lie the weakness in his work. Except in this respect, Shelley was not in the least simpleminded concerning the problem of reforming the world according to his standards. Shelley desired more than the world could ever offer; he knew it, but he could not stop trying to close the gap between the ideal and the real, the vision and the fact. So powerful is his honesty that tension pervades his poetry, idealism playing against skepticism, irony hedging assertion. He ardently believed that humans were perfectible, if they would only will it. At its most optimistic, his poetry seeks to arouse the reader's will to strive for perfection; at its most pessimistic, it is the poet's private struggle with the desire to escape through death.

JULIAN AND MADDALO

One might take a poem of balanced opposites as a synecdochic introduction to Shelley's thought and art. *Julian and Maddalo* presents the issues, the imagery that typically embodies them, and the quest to dissolve division in nature, society, and personal life. The conversants in this urbane, sophisticated debate are Julian, a thin disguise for Shelley, and Maddalo, or Lord Byron. Julian, the preface suggests, is the idealist, "passionately attached to those philosophical notions which assert the power of man over his own mind, and the immense improvements of which, by the extinction of certain moral superstitions, human society may be yet susceptible." Maddalo is the card-carrying cynic, and the tragedy from Julian's point of view is that Maddalo is one of the few who might be capable of changing the world, if he would only will it. It is Maddalo's weakness to be proud; he does not think the world worth the effort. A maniac also enters the poem as a character who was destroyed through unrequited love. Finally, Maddalo's little daughter is the ever-present, romantic image of humankind's potential.

The poem opens with a vision of harmony. Julian and Maddalo have been riding along the Lido of Venice, a waste of a beach, at sundown, and Julian responds to the correspondence he senses between the inner and outer worlds:

> I love all waste
> And solitary places; where we taste
> The pleasure of believing what we see
> Is boundless, as we wish our souls to be:
> And such was this wide ocean, and this shore
> More barren than its billows.

Later, Maddalo will offer a constricted image of the soul, but for now, Shelley allows his better half to continue. Disagreeing with earlier Romantic work of Wordsworth and Coleridge, which argued for the sufficiency of humankind's relationship with nature, Julian/Shelley adds a companion to the landscape experience: "and yet more/ Than all, with a remembered friend I love/ To ride as then I rode." The friends are in perfect accord with each other as well as with nature. As they gallop along the beach, the wind brings the "living spray" into their faces, the blue heavens open, "stripped to their depths," and the waves send forth a "sound like delight . . ./ Harmonizing with solitude," carrying into their hearts "aereal merriment." The personal relationship is as perfect: "the swift thought,/ Winging itself with laughter, lingered not,/ But flew from brain to brain." As they turn homeward, however, division enters the poem, beginning with a discussion on "God, freewill and destiny:/ Of all that earth has been or yet may be." Julian takes the brighter side, Maddalo, the darker. Shelley represents the argument metaphorically as two perceptions of landscape. Julian first offers a perception of the dissolution of the landscape's natural boundaries created by the light of the setting sun; Maddalo then counters with a brilliant image of the constricted soul and the madding passions, the bell of the insane asylum.

Julian first calls attention to the division between East and West, earth and sky. The Alps are a "heaven-sustaining bulwark reared/ Between the East and West"; only "half the sky/ Was roofed with clouds of rich emblazonry"; the sun pauses in a "rent" between the clouds; the hills are separate like a "clump of peaked isles." Then quite dramatically light begins to do its work of transformation:

> as if the Earth and Sea had been
> Dissolved into one lake of fire were seen
> Those mountains towering as from waves of flame
> Around the vaporous sun, from where there came
> The inmost purple spirit of light, and made
> Their very peaks transparent.

This diffusion of water with fire, earth with air, air with fire, and water with earth, completed in the fleeting intensity of the Sun's pause, becomes a vision of hope for human reconciliation through love. The Sun's light is love and just as it can dissolve the perception of landscape boundaries so can the emotion dissolve boundaries in personal life and society. Nature teaches a lesson; even the city becomes a divine illusion, "Its temples and its palaces did seem/ Like fabrics of enchantment piled to Heaven."

Maddalo, however, is not taken by the vision. He insists on observing the sunset from a "better station." Between them and the Sun is now imagined the madhouse, "A windowless, deformed and dreary pile," its bell tolling "In strong and black relief" for the maniacs to begin their evening prayers. Looking at his image of the bell and the asylum, Maddalo interprets:

> And such . . . is our mortality
> And this must be the emblem and the sign
> Of what should be eternal and divine—
> And like that black and dreary bell, the soul,
> Hung in a heaven-illumined tower, must toll
> Our thoughts and our desires to meet below
> Round the rent heart and pray—as madmen do
> For what? they know not,—till the night of death
> As sunset that strange vision, severeth
> Our memory from itself, and us from all
> We sought and yet were baffled!

If Byron literally spoke these lines, they are among the best lines of poetry he ever composed. The soul is no beach stretching to the horizon; it is finite, and dreary, and obfuscating. It provokes the heart with its spirituality to strive for the infinite in complete bewilderment, till death closes the quest. There is nothing eternal and divine; it is simply mortality at odds with itself. In the twilight, the "black bell became invisible" and the enchanted city "huddled in gloom," its ships, towers, palaces—emblems of commerce, church, and government—faded into the absurdity of night.

The following day, Julian argues that

> it is our will
> That . . . enchains us to permitted ill—
> We might be otherwise—we might be all
> We dream of . . .
> Where is the love, beauty and truth we seek
> But in our mind? and if we were not weak
> Should we be less in deed than in desire?

Maddalo counters that such human weakness is incurable, that no matter how strong an argument Julian can make to prove the perfectibility of humankind, empirical evidence and experience will undermine it. Maddalo adduces as evidence the case of a maniac, who was like Julian an idealist but has been destroyed by unrequited love. Their visit to the maniac's cell in the asylum whose bell they had heard the preceding night reveals a man of rent heart, musing disjointedly and pathetically on his suffering. Still in love, he refuses to commit suicide because he does not want his former lover to feel responsible for his death. Julian feels that if he had the opportunity to befriend the man, he might save him, but the strength of Maddalo's argument has been felt. After many years, Julian returns to Maddalo's castle and learns from his grown daughter that the maniac's lover returned and he recovered; then, however, they separated once more. At Julian's entreaty, she reveals the whole story, but out of bitterness toward the world he refuses to disclose the resolution (as Shelley refuses to disclose it to his readers): "the cold world shall not know," concludes the poem. The debate has not resolved the issue. The maniac's recovery, although temporary, indicates that love is indeed the force that Julian has maintained, if one can sustain the will to love. Thus the poem returns to its starting point: Clearly one can will to love, or, at least, act as if one loved, but constancy is the problem, as the maniac's lover indicates.

ALASTOR

The same tensions that animate *Julian and Maddalo* inform Shelley's first major poem, *Alastor*. The poet-persona of *Alastor* begins as a happy youth. He seeks knowledge and truth from philosophy, nature, history, and travel, and experiences moments of high inspiration, as when, standing amidst the ruins of the cradle of civilization, "meaning on his vacant mind/ Flashed like strong inspiration, and he saw/ The thrilling secrets of the birth of time." On his quest, he has been cared for by an Arab maiden, who brings food to him from her own plate and watches him dream innocently throughout the night, till to her father's tent she creeps "Wildered, and wan, and panting," but he does not recognize her love for him. Then, one night after leaving her locale, he has "a dream of hopes that never yet/ Had flushed his cheek." He dreams of his antitype, the perfect female of intellect, imagination, and sense to match his own. She speaks in low solemn tones of knowledge, truth, virtue, liberty; she next breathes the "permeating fire" of her pure mind in a song of passionate poetry; then, in the most erotic passage one will find in the Romantic canon, they join in sexual climax. She arises and the dreamer sees

> by the warm light of their own life
> Her glowing limbs beneath the sinuous veil
> Of woven wind, her outspread arms now bare,
> Her dark locks floating in the breath of night,
> Her beamy bending eyes, her parted lips
> Outstretched, and pale, and quivering eagerly.

He receives her, "yielding to the irresistible joy,/ With frantic gesture and short breathless cry," folding his frame in "her dissolving arms." At the moment of climax, "blackness veiled his dizzy eyes, and night/ Involved and swallowed up the vision; sleep,/ Like a dark flood suspended in its course,/ Rolled back its impulse on his vacant brain."

One would wish to sleep forever to have such dreams, for how can such a dream be fulfilled? The world, which was once so beautiful to the poet, now appears vacant when he awakens. Cryptically, the narrator tells us that "The spirit of sweet human love has sent/ A vision to the sleep of him who spurned/ Her choicest gifts." Was the Arab maiden one of those gifts, or was she merely the catalyst of an awakening sexuality? Regardless, he now "eagerly pursues/ Beyond the realms of dream that fleeting shade," knowing that the realm beyond dream is most likely death. He moves madly through society and nature more to burn out than to seek a likeness of the veiled maid. When he tires or seeks infrequent nourishment, an image of the maid's eyes forces him on. In a passage that underscores the narcissism of his quest, the reflection of his own eyes in a fountain where he drinks provokes her shadowy presence.

He moves on, following a stream to its unknown source, for he has dimly perceived an analogue between "What oozy cavern or what wandering cloud" contain its waters and what mysterious source his own thoughts and visions may have. He finally stops in a virginal nook above the perilous mountain landscape and prepares to die. He is "at peace, and faintly smiling" as the crescent moon sets on his life: "His last sight/ Was the great moon," which as it declines finally shows only the tips of its crescent:

> the alternate gasp
> Of his faint respiration scarce did stir
> The stagnate night:—till the minutest ray
> Was quenched, the pulse yet lingered in his heart.
> It paused—it fluttered.

The moon sets, and he dies. Why does his heart pause and flutter? Is he duped by the moon's tips appearing to be eyes, or does he smile faintly because he is aware of the irony? Or does he move from irony to the excitement of belief at the moment before final truth? The reader cannot know, but the poem's narrator finds little hope for the world when "some surpassing Spirit,/ Whose light adorned the world around it" dies an untimely death not with "sobs or groans,/ The passionate tumult of a clinging hope;/ But pale despair and cold tranquillity."

As he moved like a phantom through the landscape, the poet of *Alastor* recognized that nature provided a condition like love for its animate and inanimate beings—swans floating in pairs, "Ivy clasp[ing]/ The fissured stones with its entwining arms"—but that he belonged outside the circle. Shelley could not maintain the romantic myth that, as Coleridge wrote in "This Limetree Bower My Prison," "Nature ne'er deserts the wise and pure," or, as Wordsworth wrote in "Lines Composed a Few Miles Above Tintern Abbey," "In nature and the language of the sense,/ [is] the anchor of my purest thoughts, the nurse,/ The guide, the guardian of my heart, and soul/ Of all my moral being." Shelley did write in his essay "On Love" that one seeks correspondence with nature when one is denied human love; he paraphrased an unknown source to the effect that, if one were in a desert, "he would love some cypress." As is evident in *Julian and Maddalo* and *Alastor*, Shelley preferred human companionship, because there is a force impelling the physical world that is antithetical to love. Shelley called this force Necessity, or physical determinism. *Mont Blanc* provides its principal image.

Mont Blanc

In what becomes a showdown of sorts between mind and matter, imagination and necessity, Shelley begins *Mont Blanc* by recognizing that mind shares with matter a significant feature. The sense impressions that flow through the mind's stream of thought are impelled by a force as mysterious as that which drives the river from its home in the clouds down the mountain's ravine. Is it the same force? Critics have struggled with this problem, for Shelley did not make the matter very clear, or perhaps it is as clear as possible without being reductive of a difficult metaphysical question. On one hand, Shelley imagines the Power as residing above the world of mutability, "Remote, serene, and inaccessible," but not without profound effect on the world below. The Power's image is the mountain's summit, which none can see but which all can feel in the form of the forces it releases that destroy and preserve, its glaciers and its rivers. Its position is amoral, perfectly nonanthropomorphic. The glaciers wreak their havoc, "The dwelling-place/ Of insects, beasts, and birds" their spoil. "The race of man," too, "flies far in dread; his work and dwelling/ Vanished, like smoke before the tempest's stream." On the other hand, majestic rivers, such as the Arve of Mont Blanc, derive from the same source and are "The breath and blood of distant lands." Can the mind of humankind be a manifestation of such a power? This is the question to which the poem leads, but just as Shelley offers the answer in the final stanza, he undermines it.

Addressing the mountain he says, "The secret strength of things/ Which governs thought, and to the infinite dome/ of heaven is as a law, inhabits thee!" While thought may be governed by a psychological determinism, Shelley seems to imply a distinction between causally determined thought and the products of imagination—poetry and value. He stresses that "Mont Blanc yet gleams on high," above the vicissitudes of our world, where "In the calm darkness of the moonless nights,/ In the lone glare of day, the snows descend/ Upon that Mountain, none beholds them there," and without fanfare he begins describing, valuing, and symbolizing what he has just indicated none behold:

> Winds contend
> Silently there, and heap the snow with breath
> Rapid and strong, but silently! Its home
> The voiceless lightning in these solitudes
> Keeps innocently, and like vapour broods
> Over the snow.

The winds pile the snow for the coming glacier with the quality of "breath," because, while the glacier will bring death, its next state of being as river will bring life—"The breath and blood of distant lands." Likewise emphasizing the absent force of mind that now interprets and values the cold causality of the mountain's secret summit is the acknowledgment that all this is happening "Silently . . ./. . . but silently!" No ears, no sound; no perceiver, no value. The poem concludes: "And what were thou, and earth, and stars, and sea,/ If to the human mind's imaginings/ Silence and solitude were vacancy?"

Something in the human mind renders value, recognizes or makes meaning for this universe, or decides there is no meaning. These are acts of ultimate power; the rest is a "dull round," as the human mind itself may enact when it refuses to transcend the path of association with its power to create, to vision, and to will. Shelley does not make this case as forcefully as it is presented here, however; he concludes with a question, not the strong declarative the reader might wish. The imagining undermines the assertion of "The secret strength of things"; the surmise of the conclusion undermines the imagining. This ambivalence does not derive from some precious sense of caution, but from Shelley's genuine uncertainty.

PROMETHEUS UNBOUND

Shelley's belief in the power of love was unequivocal, however, and *Prometheus Unbound* reveals on a mythic scale the transformation that will occur when love rather than fear and hatred binds relationships among nations and humankind. *Prometheus Unbound* is a psychological drama that, along with other works of the Romantic period, asserts the power of mind in transforming the world. The French Revolution having failed to rid France of despotism, British writers sought to fulfill by individual transformation the apocalyptic hopes it had aroused. The logic was simple: If the mind and heart of the reader could be changed, the world would be changed. Thus Wordsworth, the major poet of the period, writes at the height of his optimism: "Paradise, and groves/ Elysian, . . ./ . . . why should they be/ A history only of departed things" (Prospectus to *The Recluse*). The hope of the Romantics was not naïve, but rather a variation of an eternal hope to improve the world.

Shelley's promise was that if humanity could just will to love, everything wonderful would follow. Thus, Prometheus, the mythic champion of humankind, chained to a rock in the Indian Caucasus for three thousand sleepless years, finds that he no longer hates the tyrant, Jupiter, and as a consequence, the universe swells with the love, the growth, and the energy of springtime.

Ironically, Prometheus's transformation begins, not more than fifty-five lines into the first act, as he dwells on the satisfaction he will feel when Jupiter is dethroned and made to kiss "the blood/ From [Prometheus's] pale feet," which could then trample him, except that he would disdain Jupiter too much to do so. Then he says: "Disdain? Ah no! I pity thee," for the suffering Jupiter will endure at his demise, and his pity leads to grief: "I speak in grief,/ Not exultation, for I hate no more,/ As then, ere misery made me wise." There is a significant relationship between Jupiter's power and Prometheus's hatred, Jupiter's demise and Prometheus's love: Though he has been the hero of humankind, Prometheus has been responsible for the tyranny of the universe, because he empowered Jupiter with his hate—in fact, willed the inflictions of Jupiter on humankind. When he transcends his hatred to love, Jupiter inevitably falls. It is the dialectic of the master and the slave; the slave's willed obeisance gives the master his power. Prometheus recalls his curse, which began the reign of Jupiter, and the reader begins to understand one half of the dialectic.

On a literal level, perhaps it appears foolish that the sufferer could hold power over the oppressor, as Prometheus claims, but, if one considers the action on the psychological level, where Shelley intended the battle to be fought and won, one can understand that a mind indulging in hatred blights the potential joy of life. At some level, Prometheus understands this, and retracts his curse, yet he must still undergo a test from the furies (perhaps representing his historical consciousness), which brings to his sight the truth of humankind's condition. The Reign of Terror of the French Revolution, the rejection and murder of Christ, the general wave of personal violence and horror, are all summoned to reveal this darkest truth: "those who endure/ Deep wrongs for man, and scorn and chains, but heap/ Thousand-fold torment on themselves and him." The plight of humankind is absurdly tragic: "The good want power, but to weep barren tears./ The powerful goodness want: worse need for them./ The wise want love, and those who love want wisdom;/ And all best things are thus confused to ill."

Prometheus's response to this futility is: "Thy words are like a cloud of winged snakes/ And yet, I pity those they torture not." "Thou pitiest them?" the fury cries: "I speak no more," and vanishes defeated. Prometheus's love has endured. From this moment on, the action of the play moves forward, as if on its own pattern of necessity, to overthrow Jupiter and rejuvenate humankind. As love trickles down through the universe and the society of humankind, there are "thrones . . . kingless," men walking together without fawning or trampling, all "Scepterless, free, uncircumscribed." Though still subject to chance, death, and mutability, ruling over them like slaves, man is free, liberated consciousness, "The King/ Over himself." The "mind-forg'd manacles," to quote William Blake's "London," are sundered. The mind of man is now "an Ocean/ Of clear emotion/ A heaven of serene and mighty motion."

Yet, as wildly joyous and supremely optimistic as *Prometheus Unbound* is, the reader is warned at the close that even this mythic bliss cannot remain unguarded. Should the world fall again into its tyranny, the morality that will reincarnate her beauty, freedom, and joy again must be this:

> To suffer woes which Hope thinks infinite;
> To forgive wrongs darker than Death or Night;
> To defy Power which seems Omnipotent;
> To love, and bear; to hope, till Hope creates
> From its own wreck the thing it contemplates;
> Neither to change nor falter nor repent:
> This . . . is to be
> Good, great and joyous, beautiful and free;
> This is alone Life, Joy, Empire and Victory.

Prometheus Unbound is a difficult reading experience, a highly pitched lyric extended over four acts, without tonal relief, but it is essential reading for the student of Shelley and the Romantic period.

Part of Shelley's vision in *Prometheus Unbound* is that man would be passionate, "yet free from guilt or pain/ Which were, for his will made, or suffered them," and that women would be

> gentle, radiant forms
> From custom's evil taint exempt and pure;
> Speaking the wisdom once they could not think,
> Looking emotions once they feared to feel
> And changed to all which once they dared not be.

EPIPSYCHIDION

Many might find Shelley a prophet of modern morality, or immorality, depending on point of view, but it is certain that even the most liberal in the nineteenth century could not quite live this ideal, not even Shelley's handpicked women. In *Epipsychidion*, however, he allows himself a pure fantasy of relational perfection that celebrates his discovery, at last, of his antitype. The chief skepticism of the poem is not that he might be excessive in his rapture, but rather that language is not capable of adequately expressing his rapture, its object being perfection. The poem opens with a rhapsodic invocation without parallel in English literature, and struggles throughout with its diction to aggregate images and symbols that might invoke a rhetoric of infinity. Shelley has found the veiled maid of *Alastor*: "I never thought before my death to see/ Youth's vision thus made perfect. Emily,/ I love thee; . . . Ah me!/ I am not thine: I am a part of *thee*."

This perfect woman was Teresa Viviani, the teenage daughter of the governor of Pisa, who had confined her in a nunnery. The Shelleys became interested in her plight and this lovely victim of paternal tyranny inflamed Shelley's soul. He imagines how perfect it would be if Emily/Teresa could join him and Mary in a ménage à trois, for he has never been one of the "great sect,/ Whose doctrine is, that each one should select/ Out of the crowd a mistress or a friend,/ And all the rest, though fair and wise, commend/ To cold oblivion," though the moral code might demand such behavior. "True Love in this differs from gold and clay,/ That to divide is not to take away." Thus, if Mary would be the Moon—"The cold chaste Moon . . ./ Who makes all beautiful on which she smiles,/ . . ./ And warms not but illumines"—Emily would be the Sun and together they would form those spheres of influence "who rule this passive Earth,/ This world of love, this *me*." Finally, however, he and Emily both fly out of orbit, leaving the moon behind, to dwell in a paradisal isle.

Language cannot deal with the infinite limits of this vision: "The winged words on which my soul would pierce/ Into the height of love's rare Universe,/ Are chains of lead around its flight of fire.—/ I pant, I sink, I tremble, I expire!" Sympathetic readers of Shelley wince at these moments; his detractors triumph. Even Shelley was a bit embarrassed by the emotion of this poem, because the woman it celebrated finally married a boor. Shelley wrote to John Gisborne: "The 'Epipsychidion' I cannot look at." Mary Shelley also had a difficult time looking at it; *Epipsychidion* is the only poem in her excellent edition of Shelley's poems on which she does not comment.

"HYMN TO INTELLECTUAL BEAUTY"

Shelley often wore his heart on his sleeve for daws to peck at, to paraphrase William Shakespeare's Iago, especially in the great series of poems representing himself as the *poète maudit*, the suffering poet vainly striving to save those who reject him. "Hymn to Intellectual Beauty," "Ode to the West Wind," and *Adonais* constitute the constellation and farthest reaches of this personal myth. Of course there is a great deal of vanity involved. One perceives that the world is not perfect; one attempts to save it and fails, thereby proving that the world really is bad, even worse than one thought. One then strives harder, becoming more assured that one is needed and that one's work is essential, rejection feeding vanity in a wicked, self-defeating cycle. Throughout, one retains one's heroic self-image.

In "Hymn to Intellectual Beauty," Shelley describes the dynamics of his dedication to poetry. While on a youthful search for truth, in much the manner of the poet of *Alastor*, he calls on the "poisonous names with which our youth is fed," God, ghosts and heaven, without success; he sees nothing, he hears nothing that responds to his Metaphysical anxieties in a direct way. He experiences something, however, that profoundly moves him. As he muses deeply "on the lot/ Of life" within the context of nature's springtime regeneration, "Sudden, thy shadow fell on me;/ I shrieked, and clasped my hands in ecstasy." The shadow is that of the spirit of beauty, an inexpressible something that transiently brings value to life—life's only value—by evoking in the receiver, its guest, a pulse of spiritual joy. If it could be a permanent experience, "Man were immortal, and omnipotent." The poet says that his life has been dedicated to creating a medium for evoking this spiritual condition. He vows that he will dedicate his "powers/ To thee and thine—have I not kept the vow?" he asks the spirit. His hope has been that if others could be given the experience of spiritual ecstasy, the world would be reborn. The time he has spent in reading, thinking, writing—those hours know, he says, that joy never

> illumed my brow
> Unlinked with hope that thou wouldst free
> This world from its dark slavery,
> That thou—O awful Loveliness,
> Wouldst give whate'er these words cannot express.

In seeking to suggest this evanescent condition, Shelley creates several of the most alluring similes in English, such as, in the fourth stanza: "Thou—that to human thought art nourishment,/ Like darkness to a dying flame!" As the mind is a fading coal, so the darkness intensified makes thought appear brighter, thereby nourishing its waning condition so that it does not appear to be waning at all. The loveliness of verse makes the mind seem as full of beauty and intensity as the moment of inspiration had promised. The poem's opening lines, however, are the ultimate of Shelleyan perfection: "The awful shadow of some unseen Power/ Floats though unseen amongst us!" It is "Like clouds in starlight widely spread,—/ Like memory of music fled,—/ Like aught that for its grace may be/ Dear, and yet dearer for its mystery." These lines are Shelley in his power, for no other poet has so effectively failed to express the inexpressible and thereby succeeded in his attempt to evoke it. While Shelley was curiously winning the battle of expression, however, he was losing the war.

"ODE TO THE WEST WIND"

Unlike the modern age, which conceded, in the words of W. H. Auden, that "poetry makes nothing happen," the Romantic and Victorian periods permitted their artists to believe that they could and ought to be effectual. Several seemed to be: Wordsworth, Charles Dickens, Alfred, Lord Tennyson, and Robert Browning had enormous moral influence. Shelley did not; in fact, Matthew Arnold, the great social and literary critic of

Victorian England, likened Shelley to an "ineffectual angel, beating in the void his luminous wings in vain." In 1819, at the age of twenty-seven, Shelley wrote his most perfect poem on his ineffectuality. "Ode to the West Wind" is a prayer for power to further the vision of *Prometheus Unbound* in nineteenth century England and Europe, by a poet who has been battered with failure.

In its five terza rima sonnet stanzas, which describe the autumn of earth, sky, sea, and poet—the elements of earth, air, water, and fire—Shelley's impassioned ode takes the literal cycle of the seasons through metaphorical transformations to approach an answer to the question: "If rebirth happens in nature, can it happen in society, with my verse, like the west wind, as the catalyst of the transition from near death to new life?" The first and last stanzas are illustrative of the metaphorical union the poet seeks with the regenerative wind. Stanza 1 presents the west wind in its dual function of destroying and preserving, driving dead leaves "like ghosts from an enchanter fleeing," and blowing seeds to "their dark wintry bed" where they will "lie cold and low,/ Each like a corpse within its grave, until/ [the wind of spring] shall blow/ Her clarion o'er the dreaming earth" to awaken the seeds to life. Of course, the dead leaves have the function of preserving the seed beds.

In the final stanza, the poet prays that his "dead thoughts" might be driven "over the universe/ Like withered leaves to quicken a new birth!" His seeds are his words, and because he is the equivalent of fire, his words are likened to ashes and sparks—some merely functional, some inspirational—that are now dormant in the waning hearth that is his life. Thus, if his verse could be sufficiently empowered by spirit, like a wind, he might produce a conflagration through the blowing about of ashes and sparks. As the spring of stanza 1 had her clarion, his verse will be "to unawakened Earth/ The trumpet of a prophecy." "O Wind," he closes, "If Winter comes, can Spring be far behind?" Clearly, if those leaves of stanza 1—"Yellow, and black, and pale, and hectic red,/ Pestilence-stricken multitudes"—which have been accurately interpreted as the suffering races of humankind, and those leaves of stanza 5—the poet's "dead thoughts"—can both be set afire by the spark of the poet's verse, both may rise from the ashes to new life. The final question, however, is threatening to the dream, for though it is certain that spring follows winter in nature, it is not at all certain that if total spiritual darkness covers humankind, a springtime of recovery will follow.

In stanza 4 of "Ode to the West Wind," Shelley represents himself as praying to the wind "in my sore need": "Oh! lift me as a wave, a leaf, a cloud!/ I fall upon the thorns of life! I bleed!/ A heavy weight of hours has chained and bowed/ One too like thee: tameless, and swift, and proud." He finally shed the weight of hours to join, not the wind, for that is to be bound still in the world of process, change, and dying hopes, but a poet of his generation who preceded him into the realm "where the eternal are." His elegy for John Keats, *Adonais*, signaled the final shift of his quest from social and personal visions of resurrected worlds and discovered antitypes to transcendence of human life and care.

ADONAIS

Shelley believed that Keats had been mortally wounded by a scurrilous review of his early work, *Endymion: A Poetic Romance* (1818). "The savage criticism," he says in his Preface to *Adonais*, "produced the most violent effect on his susceptible mind; the agitation thus originated ended in the rupture of a blood-vessel in the lungs; a rapid consumption ensued, and the succeeding acknowledgments . . . of the true greatness of his powers, were ineffectual to heal the wound thus wantonly inflicted." This is not casebook medicine, but it does say something about the doctor who provides such an empathic diagnosis. Shelley self-consciously identified with Keats's early rejection and sought as well to identify with his early death.

Through the first thirty-seven stanzas of the poem, Shelley's narrator mourns Adonais's untimely death, culminating with the fancy of Shelley's image visiting the tomb in homage to a dead fellow poet. The group of mourning poets stands aside to smile "through their tears" at this maudlin creature "Who in another's fate now wept his own." The muse, Urania, among the mourners for one of her most gifted, asks him his name; his response is to make "bare his branded and ensanguined brow,/ Which was like Cain's or Christ's." Then, in a moment of intense self-consciousness, Shelley disrupts this indulgent self-projection to criticize with truth—"Oh! that it should be so!" He is no important, mythical sufferer; though it has been his dream to be one, the comparison will not hold. Shortly, the poem moves to the second phase of its development, the realization that the living must not mourn for Adonais, who has "awakened from the dream of life," but for themselves: "*We* decay/ Like corpses in a charnel; fear and grief/ Convulse us and consume us day by day,/ And cold hopes swarm like worms within our living clay."

The second movement concludes with a pivotal question: "What Adonais is, why fear we to become?" The poem's third movement, stanzas 52-55, becomes darkly suicidal, but triumphant in its grasping of a new direction, a new vision. Life is imaged as a "dome of many-coloured glass" which "Stains the white radiance of Eternity,/ Until Death tramples it to fragments." Beyond Life is the Platonic "One," the blinding light of truth which humankind knows only from its shadows manifested in material form. "Die," the poet challenges, "If thou wouldst be with that which thou dost seek!" The beauties of natural, human, and aesthetic forms are "weak/ The glory they transfuse with fitting truth to speak." The challenge then becomes personalized as the poet addresses his heart, the image of his mortality and emotional life: "Why linger, why turn back, why shrink, my Heart?" Its hopes are gone, its love is gone, "what still is dear/ Attracts to crush, repels to make thee wither." The sky smiles, the wind whispers the invitation of Adonais: "oh, hasten thither,/ No more let Life divide what Death can join together." He feels the source of the fire he has represented as a poet, beaming, "Consuming the last clouds of cold mortality." Finally, the poem's concluding stanza aggregates the principal imagery of Shelley's major poetry to illustrate that throughout his work an undercurrent has been moving to this moment of poetic self-annihilation:

The West Wind descends to blow; as in *Alastor*, the "spirit's bark is driven,/ . . . far from the trembling throng/ Whose sails were never to the tempest given"; the earth and skies, in contrast with the vision of *Julian and Maddalo*, are "riven" to accept the poet, rather than fused to involve him with a romantic vision of earth; he is now "borne darkly, fearfully, afar:/ Whilst burning through the inmost veil of Heaven,/ The soul of Adonais, like a star,/ Beacons from the abode where the Eternal are." The vision was sortly to descend to fact with Shelley's death by drowning.

Shelley admitted to a "passion for reforming the world." He sought an aesthetic medium that would inspire the will of man to close the gap between vision and reality. Shelley's art and thought are unique in the extremes that they bring to English literature; indeed, their fragile loveliness represents the hope and despondency possible only in an age that fervently believed in the infinite potential of man. He was a child of his age, and succeeding generations and imaginations will always need to be challenged by his visions.

OTHER MAJOR WORKS

LONG FICTION: *St. Irvyne: Or, The Rosicrucian*, 1810; *Zastrozzi: A Romance*, 1810.

PLAYS: *The Cenci: A Tragedy in Five Acts*, pb. 1819; *Oedipus Tyrannus: Or, Swellfoot the Tyrant*, pb. 1820; *Prometheus Unbound: A Lyrical Drama in Four Acts*, pb. 1820; *Hellas: A Lyrical Drama*, pb. 1822; *Charles the First*, pb. 1824 (fragment).

NONFICTION: *The Necessity of Atheism*, 1811 (with Thomas Jefferson Hogg); *A Letter to Lord Ellenborough*, 1812; *An Address to the Irish People*, 1812; *Declaration of Rights*, 1812; *Proposals for an Association of. . . Philanthropists*, 1812; *A Refutation of Deism, in a Dialogue*, 1814; *A Proposal for Putting Reform to the Vote Throughout the Kingdom*, 1817; *History of a Six Weeks' Tour Through a Part of France, Switzerland, Germany, and Holland*, 1817 (with Mary Shelley); *An Address to the People on the Death of the Princess Charlotte*, 1817?; *A Defence of Poetry*, 1840; *Essays, Letters from Abroad, Translations, and Fragments*, 1840; *Shelley Memorials*, 1859; *Shelley's Prose in the Bodleian Manuscripts*, 1910; *Note Books of Shelley*, 1911; *A Philosophical View of Reform*, 1920; *The Letters of Percy Bysshe Shelley*, 1964 (2 volumes; Frederick L. Jones, editor).

TRANSLATIONS: *The Cyclops*, 1824 (of Euripides' play); *Ion*, 1840 (of Plato's dialogue); "The Banquet Translated from Plato," 1931 (of Plato's dialogue *Symposium*).

MISCELLANEOUS: *The Complete Works of Percy Bysshe Shelley*, 1926-1930 (10 volumes; Roger Ingpen and Walter E. Peck, editors); *Shelley's Poetry and Prose: Authoritative Texts and Criticism*, 1977 (Donald H. Reiman and Sharon B. Powers, editors).

BIBLIOGRAPHY

Bieri, James. *Percy Bysshe Shelley: A Biography*. 2 vols. Newark: University of Delaware Press, 2004-2005. A well-reviewed valuable addition to Shelley scholarship.

Examines the poet's life through analysis of his cultural, literary, personal and romantic contexts. Includes bibliography and index.

Bloom, Harold, ed. *Percy Bysshe Shelley*. New York: Chelsea House, 1985. An excellent selection of some of the most important works on Shelley published since 1950. Bloom's introduction, an overview of Shelley's poetry, is highly recommended.

Blumberg, Jane. *Byron and the Shelleys: The Story of a Friendship*. London: Collins & Brown, 1992. Blumberg describes the friendship among Lord Byron and the Shelleys. Bibliography and index.

Cronin, Richard. *Shelley's Poetic Thoughts*. New York: St. Martin's Press, 1981. An incisive study of Shelley's thought within his poems and his manner of handling language. Cronin scrutinizes poetic forms as they manage realism and fantasy, elegy and dream. Contains notes and an index.

Duff, David. *Romance and Revolution: Shelley and the Politics of a Genre*. New York: Cambridge University Press, 1994. Duff examines Romanticism and politics in the work of Shelley. Bibliography and index.

Everest, Kelvin, ed. *Percy Bysshe Shelley: Bicentenary Essays*. Cambridge, England: D. S. Brewer, 1992. A collection of biographical and critical essays on the life and works of Shelley. Includes bibliographical references.

Frosch, Thomas R. *Shelley and the Romantic Imagination: A Psychological Study*. Newark: University of Delaware Press, 2007. This volume offers detailed analysis of a few of Shelley's major works. Readers are given insight into the possible meaning behind his themes and characterizations and the personal reasons that Shelley's may have had for using them.

Hamilton, Paul. *Percy Bysshe Shelley*. Tavistock, England: Northcote House/British Council, 2000. Hamilton's biography provides the story of Shelley's life and criticism and interpretation of his works.

Höhne, Horst. *In Pursuit of Love: The Short and Troublesome Life and Work of Percy Bysshe Shelley*. New York: Peter Lang, 2000. A biography of Shelley offering insights into his life and work. Includes bibliographical references and index.

Holmes, Richard. *Shelley: The Pursuit*. New York: E. P. Dutton, 1975. This major biography presents Shelley as a sinister and sometimes cruel artist of immense talent. Holmes claims new answers to questions about Shelley's Welsh experiences and about his paternity of a child born in Naples. Critical readings of Shelley's writings are less valuable than their biographical context. Contains illustrations, bibliography, notes, and an index.

Lewis, Linda M. *The Promethean Politics of Milton, Blake, and Shelley*. Columbia: University of Missouri Press, 1992. Lewis examines the Greek myth of Prometheus in Shelley's *Prometheus Unbound*, John Milton's *Paradise Lost*, and the works of William Blake. Bibliography and index.

Morton, Timothy, ed. *The Cambridge Companion to Shelley*. New York: Cambridge

University Press, 2006. This collection of essays by international scholars examines Shelley, lending much of its attention to lesser-known areas of his writing, including drama, prose, and translations. The essays are organized thematically and are divided into three sections, focusing on his life, his writing, and the role he played in the culture and politics of his time. All the essays are previously unpublished and offer new perspectives on Shelley's writing and his role in the literary canon.

Simpson, Michael. *Closet Performances: Political Exhibition and Prohibition in the Dramas of Byron and Shelley*. Stanford, Calif.: Stanford University Press, 1998. Simpson examines the role of politics and censorship in the plays of Lord Byron and Shelley. Bibliography and index.

Sperry, Stuart M. *Shelley's Major Verse: The Narrative and Dramatic Poetry*. Cambridge, Mass.: Harvard University Press, 1988. This excellent study of *Queen Mab*, *Alastor*, *The Revolt of Islam*, *Prometheus Unbound*, *The Cenci*, *The Witch of Atlas*, *Epipsychidion*, and *The Triumph of Life* attempts to synthesize philosophical, psychological, and biographical approaches to Shelley.

Wasserman, Earl R. *Shelley: A Critical Reading*. Baltimore: The Johns Hopkins University Press, 1971. Wasserman's massive, detailed readings of virtually all Shelley's major poems have been extremely influential. Wasserman emphasizes Shelley's metaphysical skepticism and discusses his conceptions of existence, selfhood, reality, causation, and their relation to transcendence. Some of the readings are very dense and may be intimidating for the beginning student, but no serious student of Shelley can ignore them.

Wheatley, Kim. *Shelley and His Readers: Beyond Paranoid Politics*. Columbia: University of Missouri Press, 1999. Examines Shelley's reception in major British periodicals and the poet's idealistic passion for reforming the world.

Wroe, Ann. *Being Shelley*. Bloomington: Indiana University Press, 2007. This biography focuses on the themes and images that were present throughout Shelley's life and works. Wroe examines his poetry, notes, books, and letters to reveal the links between his life and writing.

Richard E. Matlak

ROBERT SOUTHEY

Born: Bristol, England; August 12, 1774
Died: Greta Hall, Keswick, England; March 21, 1843

OTHER LITERARY FORMS

The collected prose works of Robert Southey (SOW-thee, also SUHTH-ee) comprise almost forty volumes, ranging from literary criticism to biography, from fiction to translations. *Letters from England by Don Manuel Espriella* (1807) is a satiric commentary on everyday life in contemporary England, while *Sir Thomas More* (1829) reveals Southey again examining society, this time by way of conversations between the spirit of the departed More and Montesimos (Southey himself). His so-called novel, the seven-volume *The Doctor* (1834-1847), concerns Dr. Daniel Dove of Doncaster and his horse Nobs; as a fantasy and a commentary on life, the excruciatingly lengthy piece reminds one of Laurence Sterne's *Tristram Shandy* (1759-1767)—without the artistic qualities of that remarkable work of fiction. Hidden within chapter 129 of Southey's effort lies the first-known telling of the nursery classic "The Three Bears."

Life of Nelson (1813) and *Life of Wesley and the Rise and Progress of Methodism* (1820) head the list of Southey's biographical studies. Others of note include *A Summary of the Life of Arthur, Duke of Wellington* (1816); the *Life of John, Duke of Marlborough* (1822); *Lives of the British Admirals* (1833-1840); and *The Life of the Rev. Andrew Bell* (1844, one volume only), the Scottish-born educationist who founded the National Society for the Education of the Poor. Southey's historical writings include the *History of Brazil* (1810-1819), *The History of Europe* (1810-1813), and the *History of the Peninsular War* (1823-1832). In 1812, Southey published *The Origin, Nature, and Object of the New System of Education*. This was followed by *The Book of the Church* (1824), *Vindiciae Ecclesiae Anglicanae* (1826), and *Essays Moral and Political* (1832).

Southey was also an editor and translator. Among his edited works are *The Annual Anthology* (1799-1800), *The Works of Chatterton* (1803, with Joseph Cottle), *Palmerin of England* (1807), Isaac Watts's *Horae Lyricae* (1834), and *The Works of William Cowper* (1835-1837). Southey's notable translations include Jacques Necker's *On the French Revolution* (1797), Vasco Lobeira's *Amadis de Gaul* (1805), the *Chronicle of the Cid* (1808), Abbe Don Ignatius Molina's *The Geographical, Natural, and Civil History of Chili* (1808), and *Memoria Sobre a Litteratura Portugueza* (1809).

ACHIEVEMENTS

During his lifetime, Robert Southey enjoyed moments of popularity and success; there were even those among his contemporaries who believed that he ranked with the best of his nation's poets. He outlived Samuel Taylor Coleridge, Sir Walter Scott, Charles Lamb, William Hazlitt, Lord Byron, Percy Bysshe Shelley, and John Keats, yet rarely does one find mention of his name in a discussion of the significant figures and forces that shaped British Romanticism in the first part of the nineteenth century. Although Southey is deep in the shadows of William Wordsworth and Coleridge, appearing in literary histories only as their mediocre associate, his poetry deserves a careful reading, especially that written before 1801. This early work reveals an extremely high degree of versatility, not always appreciated by those who study only the first rank of nineteenth century British Romantics. The simplicity and directness of language found in Southey's early ballads and short narratives echo Wordsworth's *Lyrical Ballads* (1798), but the pieces succeed because the poet could rise above pure imitation. He could also write irregular odes and heroic epistles that demonstrated his knowledge of the Augustan Age, he knew how to create sublime imagery with the aid of biblical themes, and he could plunge downward to concoct playful exercises with pigs and gooseberry pies. He was adept in a variety of poetic forms: the elegy, the sonnet, the sapphic, the ballad, the metrical tale.

The content of Southey's poems is as varied as the form. While at Balliol College, Oxford, during the period of his enthusiasm for republicanism, he wrote a dramatic poem on Wat Tyler, the leader of the peasant revolt of 1381, while four years later, his piece on the first duke of Marlborough's victory at Blenheim (August, 1704) during the War of the Spanish Succession graphically underscored the poet's sentiments on the futility of war—"But what good came of it at last?" In what seemed a radical shift of poetical gears, Southey rode hard and fast on the waves of the Gothic horror narrative in "God's Judgment on a Wicked Bishop" (1799), in which he adapted the legendary story of a tenth century German bishop who was attacked and then devoured by a pack of rats. At the outset of the nineteenth century, he turned to a series of epic poems—*Thalaba the Destroyer* and *The Curse of Kehama* being two examples—that placed him alongside his contemporaries in the Romantic quest for glamour and the grandeur of distant places and even more distant times.

Southey's greatest weakness may have been his inability to recognize his own limitations as a poet. He remained unaware of what he could do best. He took his role as poet laureate of England far too seriously—especially in view of the fact that the honor came only because Sir Walter Scott refused to accept it. Not only did he exercise poor political and critical judgment by attacking Byron, but he also wrote, in 1821, the unnecessarily lengthy *A Vision of Judgement*, in which he attempted to transport the recently departed King George III into heaven. Byron, of course, replied in the preface to his similarly titled poem (*The Vision of Judgment*, 1822), "If Mr. Southey had not rushed in where he had no business, and where he never was before," paraphrasing Alexander Pope's *An Essay on Criticism* (1711), "the following poem would not have been written." Southey never appreciated his skill as a writer of shorter and less ambitious poems wherein, for example, he could calmly reflect on his personal love of good books in his own large library, as in "My Days Among the Dead Are Past." Perhaps, also, he never realized the extent to which he could display his talent with language, as in the onomatopoetic and highly animated "The Cataract of Ladore." Interestingly enough, when Southey could isolate himself from the perils and problems of a large, ugly world, he achieved considerable maturity as a poet. Unfortunately, the periods of imaginative seclusion were both irregular and inconsistent.

BIOGRAPHY

Although born at Bristol, the son of Robert Southey and Margaret Hill Southey, Robert Southey spent most of his first fourteen years at Bath, in the company of his mother's half-sister, Miss Elizabeth Tyler. Biographers describe Tyler as a lady endowed with strong personal attractions, ambitious ideas, an imperious temper, and a significantly large library. The last-mentioned asset allowed young Southey early introductions to dramatic literature, classical poetry, and the epics of Edmund Spenser. Thus, his entrance into Westminster School in April, 1788—after shorter terms at small schools in Corston and Bristol—found him well prepared to pursue learning. Nevertheless, he demonstrated little interest in subjects outside the narrow limits of his own idiosyncratic reading tastes: ceremony, ritual, and world mythology and religion. Four years later, the school authorities expelled him for his published essays against Westminster's system of corporal punishment, specifically the flogging of students by their masters for trivial offenses. Through the efforts of his maternal uncle, the Reverend Herbert Hill, Southey gained entrance to Balliol College, Oxford (after first having been refused admission by Christ Church because of the Westminster School incident). The significant events during his undergraduate term proved to be friendships formed with Samuel Taylor Coleridge and Robert Lovell. The three determined to emigrate to the banks of the Susquehanna River in the United States, there to embark on a scheme of an ideal life of unitarianism and pantisocracy (a Utopian community in which all members would rule equally). Interestingly enough, the relationship acquired even stronger ties (which would eventually cost Southey considerable money and labor) when the friends married the three daughters of the widow of Stephen Fricker, an unsuccessful sugar-pan merchant at Westbury. Southey's marriage to Edith Fricker occurred in November, 1795.

When Elizabeth Tyler heard of her nephew's proposal to leave England, she evicted him from her house. By that time, Southey had embarked on several literary projects, and, fortunately, a young publisher, Joseph Cottle, came to his aid and purchased the first of his epic poems, *Joan of Arc*. Moreover, his uncle, Herbert Hill, invited him to visit Lisbon, resulting in *Letters in Spain and Portugal* (1808) and *Madoc*. After returning to London, he began to study the law, but soon abandoned that exercise (as he had turned from divinity and medicine at Oxford) and once more focused his attention on poetry. Seeking seclusion, Southey moved first to Westbury, then to Burton (in Hampshire), producing additional ballads and eclogues and working hard on his *History of Brazil*. In April, 1800, serious illness forced him to seek the temperate climate of Portugal, where he remained for a year, completing *Thalaba the Destroyer* and continuing to plod along with the Brazilian history. Back in England, he settled first at Keswick, then moved to Dublin as secretary to the chancellor of the Irish exchequer, Isaac Corry. He then moved to Bristol, but the death of his mother and infant daughter drove him away from his birthplace. In 1803, partly to satisfy his wife, Southey and his family took up residence at Greta Hall, Keswick; there, practically under the same roof as his brother-in-law Coleridge, he made his home for the remainder of his life.

Work and activity at Keswick brought Southey into close association with Wordsworth and, more important, provided the motivation to produce his most ambitious poetic works. Financial pressures (particularly the support of Coleridge's family in addition to his own), however, forced him to forsake poetry temporarily for more lucrative prose projects, which he churned out in significant quantity between 1803 and 1832. At

Greta Hall, he amassed a library in excess of fourteen thousand volumes, including works that he eventually edited and translated. Between 1808 and 1839, he edited and contributed to the *Quarterly Review*, the result of his association with Sir Walter Scott. That relationship proved to be most advantageous to Southey's literary career, for although Scott could not arrange to secure for his friend the post of historiographer royal, he did, in 1813, transfer the offer to be poet laureate from himself to Southey. To his credit, the latter accepted the honor only on condition that he would not be forced to write birthday odes to the sovereign or to members of the royal family. Unfortunately, however, he did manage to get into trouble with Byron and others of the liberally inclined Romantic poets when he wrote *A Vision of Judgement* and seemingly challenged liberal opinion. Despite squabbles with his contemporaries, his reputation remained high, as witnessed by offers to edit the *Times* of London and to serve as librarian of the Advocates' Library, Edinburgh—both of which he declined.

In November, 1837, Edith Southey passed away—for years she had been failing mentally. The poet-essayist himself, according to contemporary accounts, had by this time become afflicted with softening of the brain, manifested by an obvious indifference to everyone and everything except his beloved books. Suddenly, near the end of his sixty-fourth year, Southey married (on June 4, 1839) Caroline Ann Bowles, a poet and hymnodist with whom he had maintained a close correspondence for more than twenty years. When the couple returned from their wedding tour, Southey's condition worsened; he passed gradually from insensibility to external matters into a complete trance and died on March 21, 1843. The poet laureate was buried in Crosthwaite churchyard, and friends placed memorials in Westminster Abbey and Bristol Cathedral.

ANALYSIS

Robert Southey's poetical career proved, indeed, to have been a struggle: His desire to create from impulse and inspiration came into conflict with his duty to earn money from his pen. During his early period, he wrote a large number of ballads and metrical tales for the *Morning Post* at the then-going rate of one guinea a week. When he republished those in book form, money again became the principal motive, as it did once more in 1807 when he had to support Coleridge's family as well as his own. At that time, he announced that, if necessary, he would take on more reviews and articles for the magazines and would write additional verses for the newspapers. Thus, judgment and analysis of his poetry must balance what Southey wanted to do with what he had to do. Throughout his professional life, he tried desperately to preserve the time for literary labors worthy of his talent; as long as that division existed, he could perform his hackwork without fear of humiliation or sacrifice. Unfortunately, time and energy eventually failed him, and his poems—both serious and popular—became less salable; after 1820, he saw himself as more historian than poet.

In 1837, two years prior to the illness that would eventually incapacitate him,

Southey prepared the last collected edition of his poems to be published during his lifetime. That task provided an opportunity for the poet to survey his own work, to rank as well as to analyze. Thus, concerning the narrative poems, he thought *Joan of Arc*, written when he was nineteen, to have the least merit, although the piece did constitute the first stage of his poetic development. *Thalaba the Destroyer*, published five years afterward, allowed Southey to achieve poetic maturity, to set aside the law of nature and permit his poetic fancy to wander freely. For that reason, he chose not to control the rhythmic structure of his blank verse; rather, the lines of that poem follow a spontaneous melody, dividing themselves into varying lengths. In addition, the poet tended to interrupt the ordinary iambic cadence with a sudden trochaic or dactylic movement: for example, "Lo! underneath the broadleaved sycamore/ With lids half closed he lies,/ Dreaming of days to come."

RELIGIOUS EPICS

While a schoolboy at Westminster, Southey had formed the idea of a long poem, epic in form and content, based on each of the important religions (he considered them to be mythologies) of the world. For Islam (then called Mohammedanism), he eventually wrote *Thalaba the Destroyer*; *The Curse of Kehama*, published in 1810, focused on Hinduism. In the latter poem, he again allowed his fancy and his imagery to range freely, seemingly unconcerned with the orthodox notions and sympathies of the vast majority of his readers. For whatever the reasons, however, in *The Curse of Kehama* Southey returned to rhyme; more accurately, he attempted to compromise between the rambling blank verse of *Thalaba the Destroyer* and the symmetry of the traditional English epic form. *Madoc* had been begun before he set to work on *The Curse of Kehama*, but Southey, believing the former to have been his most significant poem, set it aside until he could devote his full attention to it. Finally published in 1805, *Madoc* evidences a pleasing melody and an easy, fluent, and graceful narrative diction. Unfortunately, it met with the least favorable reception of all his long poems.

RODERICK, THE LAST OF THE GOTHS

The failure of *Madoc* did not deter Southey from his grand epic design. In *Roderick, the Last of the Goths*, he produced a long narrative poem that succeeded because the versification and theme managed to complement each other. Relying on the issue of subjugation and underlining it with moral grandeur and tragedy, the poet easily held the interest of his contemporary readers. He began with a single and momentary sin of the passions by an otherwise consistently virtuous monarch and proceeded to unravel the consequences: the slaughter of Christians by Moors in a battle lasting eight days; the king's escape after the battle and his deep remorse and self-inflicted penance of a long and solitary hermitage while others thought that he had been slain; the king's dream, in which his mother appears with instructions to deliver his country from the Moors; and the departure and eventual encounter with the sole survivor of a massacre, who tells the king of the tragedy and inspires him to both personal and patriotic revenge. Southey demonstrated, in *Roderick, the Last of the Goths*, his ability to sustain a narrative while at the same time developing a character, a hero, through a series of meaningful and related adventures: Roderick, in the guise of a priest, passes through the country, meets old friends, and is recognized only by his dog. Finally, the king leads his forces in triumph over the Moors, after which he disappears.

Southey achieved effective rhythm to complement the narrative of Roderick's adventures by taking full advantage of proper names derived from Spanish and from various Moorish and Gothic dialects. He sought diversity of both rhythm and language, knowing well how John Milton, for example, had underscored the substance of his theme in the opening book of *Paradise Lost* (1667, 1674) with his roll call of Satan's evil host. Thus, in a single passage of twenty-six lines from book 4, the poet relies on the effect of a dozen or so proper names to vary his rhythm, as

> Skirting the heights of *Aguiar*, he reached
> That consecrated pile amid the wild
> Which sainted *Fructuoso* in his zeal
> Reared to *St. Felix, on Visionia*'s banks.

Further, Southey reinforced his narrative with heavy descriptions of natural scenery, furnishing rhetorical respites from the action and the passion of events. He viewed such pauses as essential to the long narrative poem, particularly when they followed long episodes of emotional strain or exaltation. From a positive point of view, the descriptive respites filled the imagination with the sights and the sounds of the beauties of nature, allowing the long narrative poem to serve as a true work of creative art. Southey made such attempts in all his long poems, but he reached the highest levels of perfection in *Roderick, the Last of the Goths*.

"ODE, WRITTEN DURING THE NEGOTIATIONS WITH BUONAPARTE, IN JANUARY 1814"

Although Southey's occasional poetry includes his weakest efforts, there are rare moments of eloquence when the poet is able to give free rein to his emotions. Consider, for example, his "Ode, Written during the Negotiations with Buonaparte, in January 1814." Southey truly detested the diminutive emperor of the French, and he attacked his subject on moral grounds, as well as on the obvious political and patriotic levels. His passions were further aroused by the sight of those individuals who worshiped what they believed to have been the wonders of Napoleon's political and military successes. The poet saw the emperor only as a mean tyrant: "And ne'er was earth with verier tyrant curst,/ Bold man and bad,/ Remorseless, godless, full of fraud and lies"; for those personal and political crimes, demanded Southey, Napoleon must pay with his life.

"FUNERAL ODE ON THE DEATH OF THE PRINCESS CHARLOTTE"

Another of Southey's occasional poems, the "Funeral Ode on the Death of the Princess Charlotte," should be mentioned because its lines are as sensitive and serene as those on Napoleon are harsh and bitter. The poet gazes about the burial grounds at Windsor, where, "in thy sacred shade/ Is the Flower of Brunswick laid!" Then, further surveying the scene, he comments on others lying there—Henry, Edward, Elizabeth, Ann Seymour, and Mary Stuart. Nevertheless, the piece serves as more than a roll call of history, for Southey loses sight of neither his subject nor the tragedy of Charlotte's passing: "Never more lamented guest/ Was in Windsor laid to rest."

LEGACY

In the final analysis, Southey must be seen as a nineteenth century child of the Augustan Age who contributed little to the poetry of Romanticism. Confusion arises when literary historians too quickly connect him with Wordsworth and Coleridge, forgetting, perhaps, that the relationship existed on a personal rather than an artistic level. Artistically and intellectually, Southey had almost nothing in common with the major figures among the first generation of British Romantic poets. He waited until practically the end of his literary life—in the preface to the 1837-1838 edition of his *Poetical Works*—before setting forth what amounted to his poetical and intellectual declaration of independence from the new literature of pre-Victorian England. Southey chose to spend a lifetime with his books, rather than in the company of men; he would retire to a life of literary pursuit, "communing with my own heart, and taking that course which upon mature consideration seemed best to myself."

Southey further maintained that he had no need for the new schools of poetry, for he had learned poetry from the masters, confirmed it in his youth, and exemplified it in his own writing. Indeed, few would deny Professor Renwick's assertion that "No poet since Dryden wrote such pure clean English so consistently." Unfortunately, unlike his contemporaries who set and then followed new trends, Southey seemed more inclined to practice and develop the craft of poetry rather than its art. He never really learned (either in or out of school) that poetry had to come from sources other than labor and learning. Nevertheless, he possessed an ardent and genial piety, a moral strength, a poetic power of depth and variety, and an ability to develop a range of literary forms and interests. In those respects, he deserved the name and the honor of poet laureate.

OTHER MAJOR WORKS

LONG FICTION: *The Doctor*, 1834-1847 (7 volumes).

PLAY: *The Fall of Robespierre*, pb. 1794 (with Samuel Taylor Coleridge).

NONFICTION: *Letters from England by Don Manuel Espriella*, 1807; *Letters in Spain and Portugal*, 1808; *The History of Europe*, 1810-1813; *History of Brazil*, 1810-1819; *The Origin, Nature, and Object of the New System of Education*, 1812; *Life of Nelson*,

1813; *A Summary of the Life of Arthur, Duke of Wellington*, 1816; *Life of Wesley and the Rise and Progress of Methodism*, 1820; *History of the Expedition of Orsua and Crimes of Aguirre*, 1821; *Life of John, Duke of Marlborough*, 1822; *History of the Peninsular War*, 1823-1832; *The Book of the Church*, 1824; *Vindiciae Ecclesiae Anglicanae*, 1826; *Sir Thomas More*, 1829; *Essays Moral and Political*, 1832; *Lives of the British Admirals*, 1833-1840; *The Life of the Rev. Andrew Bell*, 1844.

TRANSLATIONS: *On the French Revolution*, 1797 (of Jacques Necker); *Amadis de Gaul*, 1805 (of Vasco Lobeira); *Chronicle of the Cid*, 1808 (of *Crónica del famoso cavallero Cid Ruy Diaz Campeador*, *La crónica de España*, and *Poema del Cid*); *The Geographical, Natural, and Civil History of Chili*, 1808 (of Abbe Don Ignatius Molina); *Memoria Sobre a Litteratura Portugueza*, 1809.

EDITED TEXTS: *The Annual Anthology*, 1700-1800; *The Works of Chatterton*, 1803 (with Joseph Cottle); *Palmerin of England*, 1807; *Horae Lyricae*, 1834 (by Isaac Watts); *The Works of William Cowper*, 1835-1837.

BIBLIOGRAPHY

Bernhardt-Kabisch, Ernest. *Robert Southey*. Boston: Twayne, 1977. A study of *Joan of Arc* follows a sketch of Southey's early life. Chapter 3 assesses his personality and lyrical poetry. The central chapters analyze his epics and the verse of his laureate years. The last chapter is a survey of Southey's prose. Contains chronology, notes, select bibliography, and index.

Bolton, Carol. *Writing the Empire: Robert Southey and Romantic Colonialism*. London: Pickering & Chatto, 2007. The author places Southey's writings, including his epic poetry, within their historical context to argue that Southey's views created a moral imperialism that shaped Victorian values.

Carnall, Geoffrey. *Robert Southey and His Age: The Development of a Conservative Mind*. Oxford, England: Clarendon Press, 1960. Part 1 focuses on Southey as Jacobin, devoted to radical reform and democracy. Part 2 analyzes Southey as Tory, advocating strong government and conservativism. Finally, the question of whether Southey should be called an apostate is examined. Supplemented by illustrations, two appendixes, and an index.

Curry, Kenneth. *Southey*. London: Routledge & Kegan Paul, 1975. Reviews Southey's life, prose, and poetry. Includes bibliography and index.

Pratt, Lynda, ed. *Robert Southey and the Contexts of English Romanticism*. Burlington, Vt.: Ashgate, 2006. A specially commissioned collection of essays on Southey that examine the links between the writer and English Romanticism. The essays focus on culture, politics, and history, although many deal with his writings, including his poetry.

Simmons, Jack. *Southey*. 1945. Reprint. Port Washington, N.Y.: Kennikat Press, 1968. A substantial biography of modest length, this book details Southey's education, his friendship with Samuel Taylor Coleridge, and his sojourn in Portugal. His fame leads to political controversies, and his declining years begin with the death of his daughter Isabel. Contains illustrations, a note on the Southey family, a list of Southey's works, notes, and an index.

Smith, Christopher J. P. *A Quest for Home: Reading Robert Southey*. Liverpool, England: Liverpool University Press, 1997. A historical and critical study of the works of Southey. Includes bibliographical references and index.

Speck, W. A. *Robert Southey: Man of Letters*. New Haven, Conn.: Yale University Press, 2006. This biography of the poet discusses his poetry but also establishes Southey as more than a poet: as essayist, reviewer, historian, biographer, and novelist. Includes bibliography and index.

Storey, Mark. *Robert Southey: A Life*. New York: Oxford University Press, 1997. Storey tells the fascinating story of a complex and contradictory man, the mirror of his age, and provides a different perspective on familiar events and figures of the Romantic period.

Samuel J. Rogal

WILLIAM WORDSWORTH

Born: Cockermouth, Cumberland, England; April 7, 1770
Died: Rydal Mount, Westmorland, England; April 23, 1850

<small>PRINCIPAL POETRY</small>
Descriptive Sketches, 1793
An Evening Walk, 1793
Lyrical Ballads, 1798 (with Samuel Taylor Coleridge)
Lyrical Ballads, with Other Poems, 1800 (with Coleridge, includes Preface)
Poems in Two Volumes, 1807
The Excursion, 1814
Poems, 1815
The White Doe of Rylstone, 1815
Peter Bell, 1819
The Waggoner, 1819
The River Duddon, 1820
Ecclesiastical Sketches, 1822
Poems Chiefly of Early and Late Years, 1842
The Prelude: Or, The Growth of a Poet's Mind, 1850
The Recluse, 1888
Poetical Works, 1940-1949 (5 volumes; Ernest de Selincourt and Helen Darbishire, editors)

<small>OTHER LITERARY FORMS</small>

In addition to his poetry, William Wordsworth's preface to the second edition of his *Lyrical Ballads* is the single most important manifesto of the Romantic position in English, defining his ideas of the primary laws of nature, the working of the imagination, the process of association of ideas, and the balance of passion and restraint in human conduct.

<small>ACHIEVEMENTS</small>

William Wordsworth was one of the leading English Romantic poets. Along with William Blake, Samuel Taylor Coleridge, Lord Byron, Percy Bysshe Shelley, and John Keats, Wordsworth created a major revolution in ideology and poetic style around 1800. The Romantic writers rebelled against the neoclassical position exemplified in the works of Alexander Pope (1688-1744) and Samuel Johnson (1709-1784). Although all such broad generalizations should be viewed with suspicion, it is generally said that the neoclassical writers valued restraint and discipline, whereas the Romantic poets fa-

William Wordsworth
(Library of Congress)

vored individual genius and hoped to follow nature freely. Wordsworth's poetry praises the value of the simple individual, the child, the helpless, the working class, and the natural man. Such sentiments were explosive in the age of the French Revolution, when Wordsworth was young. He helped to define the attitudes that fostered the spread of democracy, of more humane treatment of the downtrodden, and of respect for nature.

BIOGRAPHY

The northwestern corner of England, which contains the counties of Northumberland and Westmorland, is both mountainous and inaccessible. The cliffs are not as high as those in Switzerland, but they are rugged, and the land is settled mainly by shepherds and by isolated farmers. The valleys have long, narrow, picturesque lakes, and so the region is called the English Lake District. William Wordsworth was born and lived much of his life among these lakes. Many of the English Romantic writers are sometimes called lake poets because of their association with this area. Wordsworth was born in 1770 in the small town of Cockermouth in Cumberland. Although he later wrote about the lower classes, his own family was middle class, and the poet never actually worked with his hands to make his living. His father was a lawyer who managed the affairs of the earl of Lonsdale. The poet had three brothers (Richard, John, and Christopher) and a sister (Dorothy). For the first nine years of his life, the family inhabited a comfortable house near the Derwent River. William attended Anne Birkett's school in the little town of Penrith, where Mary Hutchinson, whom he married in 1802, was also a student. His mother died when he was seven. The two brothers, William and Richard, then boarded at the house of Ann Tyson while attending grammar school in the village of Hawkshead.

Apparently this arrangement was a kindly one, and the boy spent much time happily roaming the nearby fields and hills. He also profited from the teaching of his schoolmaster William Taylor, who encouraged him to write poetry. In 1783, his father died and the family inheritance was tied up in litigation for some twenty years. Only after the death of the earl of Lonsdale in 1802 was Wordsworth able to profit from his father's estate. With the help of relatives, he matriculated at St. John's College, Cambridge University. Although he did not earn distinction as a student, those years were fertile times for learning.

While he was a student at St. John's, between 1787 and 1791, the French Revolution broke out across the English Channel. During his summer vacation of 1790, Wordsworth and his college friend, Robert Jones, went on a walking tour across France and Switzerland to Italy. The young students were much impressed by the popular revolution and the spirit of democracy in France at that time. Wordsworth took his degree at St. John's in January, 1791, but had no definite plans for his future. The following November, he went again to revolution-torn France with the idea of learning the French language well enough to earn his living as a tutor. Passing through Paris, he settled at Blois in the Loire Valley. There he made friends with Captain Michael Beaupuy and became deeply involved in French Republican thought. There, too, he fell in love with Annette Vallon, who was some four years older than the young poet. Vallon and Wordsworth had an illegitimate daughter, Caroline, but Wordsworth returned to England alone in December, 1792, probably to try to arrange his financial affairs. In February, 1793, war broke out between France and England so that Wordsworth was not able to see his baby and her mother again until the Treaty of Amiens in 1802 made it possible for him to visit them. His daughter was then ten years old.

In 1793, Wordsworth must have been a very unhappy young man: His deepest sympathies were on the side of France and democracy, but his own country was at war against his French friends such as Captain Michael Beaupuy; he was separated from Annette and his baby, and his English family associates looked on his conduct as scandalous; the earl of Lonsdale refused to settle his father's financial claims, so the young man was without funds and had no way to earn a living, even though he held a bachelor's degree from a prestigious university. Under these conditions, he moved in politically radical circles, becoming friendly with William Godwin, Mary Wollstonecraft, and Thomas Paine. In 1793, he published his first books of poetry, *An Evening Walk* and *Descriptive Sketches*.

Wordsworth and his younger sister, Dorothy, were close friends. In 1795, the poet benefited from a small legacy to settle with her at Racedown Cottage in Dorset, where they were visited by Mary Hutchinson and Samuel Taylor Coleridge. In 1797, they moved to Alfoxden, near Nether Stowey in Somerset, to be near Coleridge's home. Here a period of intense creativity occurred: Dorothy began her journal in 1798 while Wordsworth and Coleridge collaborated on *Lyrical Ballads*. A walking trip with Dorothy along the Wye River resulted in 1798 in "Lines Composed a Few Miles Above Tintern Abbey." That fall, Coleridge, Dorothy, and Wordsworth went to study in Germany. Dorothy and the poet spent most of their time in Goslar, where apparently he began to write *The Prelude*, his major autobiographical work which he left unfinished at his death. Returning from Germany, he and Dorothy settled in Dove Cottage in the Lake District. In 1800, he completed "Michael" and saw the second edition of *Lyrical Ballads* published. With the end of hostilities in 1802, Wordsworth visited Vallon and their daughter in France, arranging to make an annual child-support payment. Upon his return to England, he married Mary Hutchinson. During that year, he composed "Ode: Intimations of Immortality from Recollections of Early Childhood."

In 1805, his brother John was drowned at sea. Wordsworth often looked on nature as a kindly force, but the death of his brother in a shipwreck may have been a powerful contribution to his darkening vision of nature as he grew older. In 1805, he had a completed draft of *The Prelude* ready for Coleridge to read, although he was never satisfied with the work as a whole and rewrote it extensively later. It is sometimes said that when Wordsworth was a "bad" man, fathering an illegitimate child, consorting with revolutionaries and drug addicts, and roaming the countryside with no useful occupation, he wrote "good" poetry. When he became a "good" man, respectably married and gainfully employed, he began to write "bad" poetry. It is true that, although he wrote prolifically until his death, not much of his work after about 1807 is considered remarkable. In 1813, he accepted the position of distributor of stamps for Westmorland County, the kind of governmental support he probably would have scorned when he was younger. His fame as a writer, however, grew steadily. In 1842 when his last volume, *Poems Chiefly of Early and Late Years*, was published, he accepted a government pension of three hundred pounds sterling per annum, a considerable sum. The next year, he succeeded Robert Southey as poet laureate of England. He died April 23, 1850, at Rydal Mount in his beloved Lake District.

ANALYSIS

When the volume of poetry called the *Lyrical Ballads* of 1798 was published in a second edition (1800), William Wordsworth wrote a prose preface for the book that is the single most important statement of Romantic ideology. It provides a useful introduction to his poetry.

LYRICAL BALLADS

Wordsworth's preface to *Lyrical Ballads* displays the idea of primitivism as the basis of the Romantic position. Primitivism is the belief that there is some primary, intrinsically good "state of nature" from which adult, educated, civilized humankind has fallen into a false or wicked state of existence. When Jean-Jacques Rousseau began *The Social Contract* (1762) with the assertion that "Man was born free, and yet we see him everywhere in chains," he concisely expressed the primitivist point of view. The American and French revolutions were both predicated on Romantic primitivism, the idea that humanity was once naturally free, but that corrupt kings, churches, and social customs held it enslaved. The Romantic typically sees rebellion and breaking free from false restraint to regain a state of nature as highly desirable; Wordsworth's preface shows him deeply committed to this revolutionary ideology. He says that he is going to take the subjects of his poems from "humble and rustic life" because in that condition humankind is "less under restraint" and the "elementary feelings" of life exist in a state of simplicity.

Many writers feel that serious literature can be written only about great and powerful men, such as kings and generals. Some writers apparently believe that wounding a king is tragic, while beating a slave is merely funny. Wordsworth's preface firmly rejects such ideas. He turns to simple, common, poor people as the topic of his poetry because they are nearer a "state of nature" than the powerful, educated, and sophisticated men who have been corrupted by false customs of society. Many writers feel that they must live in the centers of civilization, London or Paris, for example, to be conversant with new ideas and the latest fashions. Wordsworth turns away from the cities to the rural scene. He himself lived in the remote Lake District most of his life, and he wrote about simple shepherds, farmers, and villagers. He explains that he chooses for his topics

> humble and rustic life . . . because, in that condition, the essential passions of the heart find a
> better soil in which they can attain their maturity, are less under restraint, and speak a plainer
> and more emphatic language; because in that condition of life our elementary feelings coex-
> ist in a state of greater simplicity, and consequently may be more accurately contemplated.

He sees a correspondence between the unspoiled nature of humankind and the naturalness of the environment. Romantic ideology of this sort underlies much of the contemporary environmentalist movement: the feeling that humans ought to be in harmony with their environment, that nature is beneficent, that people ought to live simply so that the essential part of their human nature may conform to the grand pattern of nature balanced in the whole universe.

The use of the words "passion" and "restraint" in Wordsworth's quotation above is significant. English neoclassical writers such as Alexander Pope tended to be suspicious of human passions, arguing that anger and lust lead people into error unless such passions are restrained by right reason. For Pope, it is necessary to exercise the restraint of reason over passion for people to be morally good. "Restraint" is good; "passion" bad. Wordsworth reverses this set of values. Humans' natural primitive feelings are the source of goodness and morality; the false restraints of custom and education are what lead people astray from their natural goodness. In his preface, Wordsworth seems to be following the line of thought developed by Anthony Ashley-Cooper, the third earl of Shaftesbury (1671-1713) in his *An Inquiry Concerning Virtue or Merit* (1709). Shaftesbury asks his readers to imagine a "creature who, wanting reason and being unable to reflect, has notwithstanding many good qualities and affections,—as love to his kind, courage, gratitude or pity." Shaftesbury probably is thinking of creatures such as a faithful dog or a child too young to reason well. In such cases, one would have to say that the creature shows good qualities, even though he or she lacks reasoning power. For Shaftesbury, then, to reason means merely to recognize the already existing good impulses or feelings naturally arising in such a creature. Morality arises from natural feeling, evidently present in creatures with little reasoning power.

Wordsworth's preface is heavily influenced by Shaftesbury's argument. He turns to simple characters for his poems because they exhibit the natural, primary, unspoiled states of feeling that are the ultimate basis of morality. Wordsworth's characters are sentimental heroes, chosen because their feelings are unspoiled by restraints of education and reason: children, simple shepherds and villagers, the old Cumberland Beggar, Alice Fell, and so on. While William Shakespeare often puts a nobleman at the center of his plays and relegates the poor people to the role of rustic clowns, Wordsworth takes the feelings of the poor as the most precious subject of serious literature.

The preface displays two kinds of primitivism. Social primitivism is the belief that humankind's state of nature is good and that it is possible to imagine a social setting in which humans' naturally good impulses will flourish. Social primitivism leads to the celebration of the "noble savage," perhaps an American Indian or a Black African tribesman, who is supposed to be morally superior to the sophisticated European who has been corrupted by the false restraints of his own society. Social primitivism was, of course, one of the driving forces behind the French Revolution. The lower classes rose up against the repression of politically powerful kings and destroyed laws and restraints so that their natural goodness could flourish. Unfortunately, the French Revolution did not produce a morally perfect new human being once the corrupt restraints had been destroyed. Instead, the French Revolution produced the Reign of Terror, the rise of Napoleon to military dictatorship, and the French wars of aggression against relatively democratic states such as the Swiss Republic. With unspeakable shock, Wordsworth and the other Romantics saw the theory of social primitivism fail in France. The decline of Wordsworth's poetic power as he grew older is often explained in part as the result of his disillusionment with revolutionary France.

A second kind of primitivism in the preface is psychological. Psychological primitivism is the belief that there is some level in the mind that is primary, more certain than everyday consciousness. In the preface, Wordsworth says that humble life displays "the primary laws of our nature; chiefly, as far as the manner in which we associate ideas." Here Wordsworth refers to a very important Romantic idea, associational psychology, which developed from the tradition of British empirical philosophy—from John Locke's *Essay Concerning Human Understanding* (1690), David Hume's *Enquiry Concerning Human Understanding* (1748), and especially David Hartley's *Observations on Man* (1749).

When Wordsworth speaks in the preface to the *Lyrical Ballads* about tracing in his poems the "manner in which we associate ideas," he is endorsing the line of thought of the associational psychologists. Poems trace the process by which the mind works. They help people to understand the origins of their own feelings about what is good and bad by demonstrating the way impressions from nature strike the mind and by showing how the mind associates these simple experiences, forming complex attitudes about what proper conduct is, what fidelity and love are, what the good and the true are. In *The Prelude*, one of Wordsworth's main motives is to trace the history of the development of his own mind from its most elementary feelings through the process of association of ideas until his imagination constructs his complex, adult consciousness.

Wordsworth's preface to the second edition of *Lyrical Ballads* set out a series of ideas that are central to the revolutionary Romantic movement, including both social and psychological primitivism, the state of nature, the "noble savage," the sentimental hero, the power of the imagination, and the association of ideas. These concepts are basic to understanding his poetry.

"LINES COMPOSED A FEW MILES ABOVE TINTERN ABBEY"

Wordsworth's "Lines Composed a Few Miles Above Tintern Abbey" (hereafter called simply "Tintern Abbey") was composed on July 13, 1798, and published that same year. It is one of the best-known works of the English Romantic movement. Its poetic form is blank verse, unrhymed iambic pentameter, in the tradition of John Milton's *Paradise Lost* (1667, 1674). In reading any poem, it is important to define its dramatic situation and to consider the text as if it were a scene from a play or drama and determine who is speaking, to whom, and under what circumstances. Wordsworth is very precise in telling the reader when and where these lines are spoken. Tintern Abbey exists, and the poet Wordsworth really visited it during a tour on July 13, 1798. Because the poem is set at a real point in history rather than once upon a time, and in a real place rather than in a kingdom far away, it is said to exhibit "topographic realism." The speaker of the poem reveals that this is his second visit to this spot; he had been there five years earlier. At line 23, he reveals that he has been away from this pleasant place for a long time and, at lines 50-56, that while he was away in the "fretful stir" of the world he was unhappy. When he was depressed, his thoughts turned to his memory of this natural scene, and he felt comforted. Now, as the poem begins, he has come again to this beautiful site with his beloved younger sister, whom he names directly at line 121. The dramatic situation involves a speaker, or persona, who tells the reader his thoughts and feelings as if he were addressing his younger sister, who is "on stage" as his dramatic audience. Although the poem is autobiographical, so that the speaker resembles Wordsworth himself and the sister resembles Dorothy Wordsworth, it is better to think of the speaker and his listener as two invented characters in a little play. When William Shakespeare's Hamlet speaks to Ophelia in his play, the audience knows that Hamlet is not the same as Shakespeare although he surely must express some of Shakespeare's feelings and ideas. So, too, the reader imagines that the speaker in "Tintern Abbey" speaks for Wordsworth, but is not exactly the same as the poet himself.

The poem displays many of the ideas stated in the preface to the *Lyrical Ballads*. It begins with a description of a remote rural scene, rather than speaking about the latest news from London. In this rustic setting, the speaker discovers some essential truths about himself. The first twenty-two lines describe the natural scene: the cliffs, orchards, and farms. This is a romantic return to nature, the search for the beautiful and permanent forms that incorporate primitive human goodness. The speaker not only describes the scene, but also tells the reader how it generates feelings and sensations in him. In lines 23-56, the speaker says that his memory of this pure, natural place had been of comfort to him when he was far away. Lines 66-90 trace the speaker's memory of his process of growing up: When he first came among these hills as a boy, he was like a wild animal. He was filled with feelings of joy or fear by wild nature. As a boy, nature was to him "a feeling and a love" that required no thought on his part. That childish harmony with nature is now lost. His childish "aching joys" and "dizzy raptures" are "gone by." As he fell away from his unthinking harmony with nature, his power of thought developed. This power is "abundant recompense" for the childish joys of "thoughtless youth." Now he understands nature in a new way. He hears in nature "The still sad music of humanity." At line 95, he explains that his intellect grasps the purpose and direction of nature, whereas his childish experience was more intense and joyous but incomplete. Now, as an adult, he returns to this natural scene and understands what he had only felt as a child, that nature is the source of moral goodness, "the nurse, the guide, the guardian of my heart, and soul of all my moral being."

At line 110, he turns to his younger sister and sees in her wild eyes his own natural state of mind in childhood. He foresees that she will go through the same loss that he experienced. She too will grow up and lose her unthinking harmony with the natural and the wild. He takes comfort in the hope that nature will protect her, as it has helped him, and in the knowledge that the memory of this visit will be with her when she is far away in future years. Their experience of this pastoral landscape is therefore dear to the speaker for its own sake, and also because he has shared it with his sister. He has come back from the adult world and glimpsed primitive natural goodness both in the scene and in his sister.

The poem employs social and psychological primitivism. The rural scene is an imagined state of primitive nature where human goodness can exist in the child, like Adam in the garden of Eden before the Fall of Man. The poem shows how the primitive feelings of the boy are generated by the forms of nature and then form more and more complex ideas until his whole adult sense of good and bad, right and wrong, can be traced back to his elementary childish experiences of nature. Reason is not what makes beauty or goodness possible; natural feelings are the origin of the good and the beautiful. Reason merely recognizes what the child knows directly from his feelings.

Critics of Wordsworth point out that the "natural" scene described in the opening lines is, in fact, not at all "natural." Nature in this scene has been tamed by man into orchards, hedged fields, and cottage farms. What, critics ask, would Wordsworth have written if he had imagined nature as the struggling jungle in the Congo where individual plants and animals fight for survival in their environmental niche and whole species are brought to extinction by the force of nature "red in tooth and claw"? If Wordsworth's idea of nature is not true, then his idea of human nature will likewise be false. While he expects the French Revolution to lead to a state of nature in joy and harmony, in fact it led to the Reign of Terror and the bloodshed of the Napoleonic wars. Critics of Romantic ideology argue that when the Romantics imagine nature as a "kindly nurse," they unthinkingly accept a false anthropomorphism. Nature is not like a kindly human being; it is an indifferent or neutral force. They charge that Wordsworth projects his own feelings into the natural scene, and thus his view of the human condition becomes dangerously confused.

"MICHAEL"

"Michael: A Pastoral Poem" was composed between October 11 and December 9, 1800, and published that same year. It is typical of Wordsworth's poetry about humble and rustic characters in which the sentiments or feelings of human beings in a state of nature are of central importance. The poem is written in blank verse, unrhymed iambic pentameter, again the meter employed in Milton's *Paradise Lost*. Milton's poem explores the biblical story of the fall of Adam from the Garden of Eden. Michael's destruction in Wordsworth's poem shows a general similarity to the tragedy of Adam in *Paradise Lost*. Both Michael and Adam begin in a natural paradise where they are happy and good. Evil creeps into each garden, and through the weakness of a beloved family member, both Adam and Michael fall from happiness to misery.

The poem "Michael" has two parts: the narrative frame and the tale of Michael. The frame occupies lines 1-39 and lines 475 to the end, the beginning and ending of the text. It relates the circumstances under which the story of Michael is told. The tale occupies lines 40-475, the central part of the text, and it tells the history of the shepherd Michael; his wife, Isabel; and their son Luke. The frame of the poem occurs in the fictive present time, about 1800, whereas the tale occurs a generation earlier. The disintegration of Michael's family and the destruction of their cottage has already happened years before the poem begins. The frame establishes that the poem is set in the English Lake District and introduces the reader to the "I-persona" or speaker of the poem. He tells the story of Michael and knows the geography and history of the district. A "You-character" who does not know the region is the dramatic audience addressed by the "I-persona." In the frame, "I" tells "You" that there is a hidden valley up in the mountains. In that valley, there is a pile of rocks, which would hardly be noticed by a stranger; but there is a story behind that heap of stones. "I" then tells "You" the story of the shepherd Michael.

Michael is one of the humble and rustic characters whose feelings are exemplary of the natural or primitive state of human beings. He has lived all his life in the mountains, in communion with nature, and his own nature has been shaped by his natural environment. He is a good and kindly man. He has a wife, Isabel, and a child of his old age named Luke. The family works from morning until far into the night, tending their sheep and spinning wool. They live in a cottage far up on the mountainside, and they have a lamp that burns late every evening as they sit at their work. They have become proverbial in the valley for their industry, so that their cottage has become known as the cottage of the evening star because its window glimmers steadily every night. These simple, hardworking people are "neither gay perhaps, nor cheerful, yet with objects and with hopes, living a life of eager industry." The boy is Michael's delight. From his birth, the old man had helped to tend the child and, as Luke grew, his father worked with him always at his side. He made him a perfect shepherd's staff and gave it to his son as a gift. Now the boy has reached his eighteenth year and the "old man's heart seemed born again" with hope and happiness in his son.

Unfortunately, Michael suffers a reversal of his good fortune, for news comes that a distant relative has suffered an unforeseen business failure, and Michael has to pay a grievous penalty "in surety for his brother's son." The old man is sorely troubled. He cannot bear to sell his land. He suggests that Luke should go from the family for a time to work in the city and earn enough to pay the forfeiture. Before his beloved son leaves, Michael takes him to a place on the farm where he has collected a heap of stones. He tells Luke that he plans to build a new sheepfold there and asks Luke to lay the cornerstone. This will be a covenant or solemn agreement between the father and son: The boy will work in the city, and meanwhile the father will build a new barn so that it will be there for the boy's return. Weeping, the boy puts the first stone in place and leaves the next day for his work far away. At first, the old couple get a good report about his work, but after a time Luke "in the dissolute city gave himself to evil courses; ignomiy and shame fell on him, so that he was driven at last to seek a hiding-place beyond the sea." After the loss of his son, Michael still goes to the dell where the pile of building stones lies, but he often simply sits the whole day merely staring at them, until he dies. Some three years later, Isabel also dies, and the land is sold to a stranger. The cottage of the evening star is torn down and nothing remains of the poor family's hopes except the straggling pile of stones that are the remains of the still unfinished sheepfold. This is the story that the "I-persona," who knows the district, tells to the "You-audience," who is unacquainted with the local history and geography.

The poem "Michael" embodies the ideas proposed in Wordsworth's preface to the *Lyrical Ballads*. He takes a family of simple, rural people as the main characters in a tragedy. Michael is a sentimental hero whose unspoiled contact with nature has refined his human nature and made him a good man. Nature has imprinted experiences on his mind that his imagination has built into more and more complex feelings about what is right and wrong. The dissolute city, on the other hand, is confusing, and there Luke goes astray. From the city and the world of banking and finance, the grievous forfeiture intrudes into the rural valley where Michael was living in a state of nature, like a noble savage or like Adam before his fall.

The poem argues that nature is not a neutral commodity to be bought and sold. It is man's home. It embodies values. The poem demands that the reader consider nature as a living force and demonstrates that once one knows the story of Luke, one never again can look on a pile of rocks in the mountains as worthless. That pile of rocks was a solemn promise of father and son. It signified a whole way of life, now lost. It was gathered for a human purpose, and one must regret that the covenant was broken and the sheepfold never completed. Likewise, all nature is a covenant, an environment, filled with human promise and capable of guiding human feelings in a pure, simple, dignified, and moral way. The function of poetry (like the "I-persona's" story of Michael) is to make the reader see that nature is not neutral. The "I-persona" attaches the history of Michael to what otherwise might be merely a pile of rocks and so makes the "You-audience" feel differently about that place. Likewise, the poem as a whole makes the reader feel differently about nature.

"Tintern Abbey" and "Michael" both explore the important question of how human moral nature develops. What makes humans good, virtuous, or proper? If, as the preface argues, people are morally best when most natural, uncorrupted by false custom and education, then the normal process of growing up in the modern world must be a kind of falling away from natural grace.

"ODE: INTIMATIONS OF IMMORTALITY FROM RECOLLECTIONS OF EARLY CHILDHOOD"

Wordsworth's "Ode: Intimations of Immortality from Recollections of Early Childhood" (hereafter called "Ode: Intimations of Immortality") is also concerned with the process of growing up and its ethical and emotional consequences. The poem is written in eleven stanzas of irregular length, composed of lines of varying length with line-end rhyme. The core of the poem is stanza 5, beginning "Our birth is but a sleep and a forgetting." Here the poet discusses three stages of growth: the infant, the boy, and the man. The infant at birth comes from God, and at the moment when life begins the infant is still close to its divine origin. For this reason, the newborn infant is not utterly naked or forgetful, "but trailing clouds of glory do we come from God." The infant is near to divinity; "Heaven lies about us in our infancy," but each day leads it farther and farther from its initial, completely natural state. As consciousness awakens, "Shades of the prison house begin to close upon the growing boy." In other words, the natural feelings of the infant begin to become constrained as man falls into consciousness. A boy is still near to nature, but each day he travels farther from the initial source of his natural joy and goodness. The youth is like a priest who travels away from his Eastern holy land, each day farther from the origin of his faith, but still carrying with him the memory of the holy places. When a man is fully grown, he senses that the natural joy of childish union with nature dies away, leaving him only the drab ordinary "light of common day" unilluminated by inspiration. This process of movement from the unthinking infant in communion with nature, through the stage of youth filled with joy and natural inspiration, to the drab adult is summarized in stanza 7, from the "child among his new-born blisses" as he or she grows up playing a series of roles "down to palsied Age."

The poem as a whole rehearses this progression from natural infant to adulthood. Stanzas 1 and 2 tell how the speaker as a child saw nature as glorious and exciting. "There was a time when meadow, grove, and stream . . . to me did seem apparelled in celestial light." Now the speaker is grown up and the heavenly light of the natural world has lost its glory. Even so, in stanza 3, his sadness at his lost childhood joys is changed to joy when he sees springtime and thinks of shepherd boys. Springtime demonstrates the eternal rebirth of the world, when everything is refreshed and begins to grow naturally again. The shepherd boys shouting in the springtime are doubly blessed, for they are rural characters, and moreover, they are young, near the fountainhead of birth. In stanza 4, the adult speaker can look on the springtime or on rural children and feel happy again because they signify the experience he has had of natural joy. Even though, as he says in stanza 10, "nothing can bring back the hour of splendour in the grass, of glory in the flower," the adult can understand with his "philosophic mind" the overall design of the natural world and grasp that it is good.

THE PRELUDE

The Prelude is Wordsworth's longest and probably his most important work. It is an autobiographical portrait of the artist as a young man. He was never satisfied with the work and repeatedly rewrote and revised it, leaving it uncompleted at his death. He had a fairly refined draft in 1805-1806 for his friend Coleridge to read, and the version he left at his death in 1850 is, of course, the chronologically final version. In between the 1805 and 1850 versions, there are numerous drafts and sketches, some of them of the whole poem, while others are short passages or merely a few lines. When a reader speaks of Wordsworth's *The Prelude*, therefore, he is referring not so much to a single text as to a shifting, dynamic set of sometimes contradictory texts and fragments. The best edition of *The Prelude* is by Ernest de Selincourt, second edition revised by Helen Darbishire (Oxford University Press, 1959), which provides on facing pages the 1805-1806 text and the 1850 text. The reader can open the de Selincourt/Darbishire edition and see side by side the earliest and the latest version of every passage, while the editors' annotations indicate all significant intermediate steps.

The 1805 version is divided into thirteen books, while the 1850 version has fourteen. Book 1, "Introduction, Childhood and Schooltime," rehearses how the poet undertook to write this work. He reviews the topics treated in famous epic poems, in Milton's *Paradise Lost*, Edmund Spenser's *The Faerie Queene* (1590, 1596), and other works. He concludes that the proper subject for his poem should be the process of his own development. He therefore begins at line 305 of the 1805 version to relate his earliest experiences, following the ideas explored above in "Tintern Abbey" and his "Ode: Intimations of Immortality." He traces the earliest impressions on his mind, which is like the tabula rasa of the associational psychologists. "Fair seed-time had my soul, and I grew up/ Foster'd alike by beauty and by fear." He tells of his childhood in the lakes and mountains, of stealing birds from other hunters' traps, of scaling cliffs, and especially a famous episode concerning a stolen boat. At line 372, he tells how he once stole a boat and rowed at night out onto a lake. As he rowed away from the shore facing the stern of the boat, it appeared that a dark mountain rose up in his line of vision as if in pursuit. He was struck with fear and returned with feelings of guilt to the shore. Experiences like this "trace/ How Nature by extrinsic passion first peopled my mind." In other words, impressions of nature, associated with pleasure and pain, provide the basic ideas that the imagination of the poet uses to create more and more complex attitudes until he arrives at his adult view of the world. The process described in the stolen boat episode is sometimes called the "discipline of fear."

Book 2 concerns "School-Time." It corresponds to the three stages of life outlined in "Ode: Intimations of Immortality": infant, youth, and adult. As in "Tintern Abbey," in *The Prelude*, book 2, Wordsworth explains that his early experiences of nature sustained him when he grew older and felt a falling off of the infant's joyful harmony with the created universe. Book 3 deals with his "Residence at Cambridge University," which is like a dream world to the youth from the rural lakes: "I was a Dreamer, they the dream; I roamed/ Delighted through the motley spectacle." He talks of his reading and his activities as a student at St. John's College, concluding that his story so far has been indeed a heroic argument, as important as the stories of the ancient epics, tracing the development of his mind up to an eminence, a high point of his experience.

Book 4 recounts his summer vacation after his first year of college, as he returns to the mountains and lakes of his youth, a situation comparable to the return of the persona in "Tintern Abbey" to the rural scene he had previously known. He notes the "inner falling-off" or loss of joy and innocence that seems to accompany growing up. Yet at line 344, he tells of a vision of the sun rising as he walked homeward after a night of gaiety and mirth at a country dance, which caused him to consider himself a "dedicated spirit," someone who has a sacred duty to write poetry. Later in this book, he recounts his meeting with a tattered soldier returned from military service in the tropics and how he helped him find shelter in a cottage nearby. Book 5 is simply titled "Books" and examines the role of literature in the poet's development. This book contains the famous passage, beginning at line 389, "There was a boy, ye knew him well, ye Cliffs/ And Islands of Winander." There was a youth among the cliffs of the Lake District who could whistle so that the owls would answer him. Once when he was calling to them the cliffs echoed so that he was struck with surprise and wonder. This boy died while he was yet a child and the poet has stood "Mute—looking at the grave in which he lies." Another recollection concerns the appearance of a drowned man's body from the lake.

Book 6, "Cambridge and the Alps," treats his second year at college and the following summer's walking tour of France and Switzerland. When the poet first arrived at Calais, it was the anniversary of the French Revolution's federal day. The young man finds the revolutionary spirit with "benevolence and blessedness/ spread like a fragrance everywhere, like Spring/ that leaves no corner of the land untouched." Frenchmen welcome the young Englishman as brothers in the struggle for freedom and liberty and they join in a common celebration. The Alps were a formidable barrier in the nineteenth century, seeming to separate the Germanic culture of northern Europe from the Mediterranean. Crossing the Alps meant passing from one culture to a totally different one. Ironically, the poet records his errant climb, lost in the fog and mist, as he approached Italy, so that the English travelers cross the Alps without even knowing what they had done. Perhaps the crossing of the Alps unaware is like his observation of the French Revolution. The poet *sees* more than he *understands*. Book 7 treats of the poet's residence in London. As one would expect, the city is unnatural and filled with all kinds of deformed and perverted customs, epitomized at the Bartholomew Fair, "a hell/ For eyes and ears! what anarchy and din/ Barbarian and infernal! 'tis a dream/ Monstrous in colour, motion, shape, sight, sound."

Book 8, "Retrospect—Love of Nature Leading to a Love of Mankind," is in contrast to book 7. Opposed to the blank confusion of the city, book 8 returns to the peaceful, decent rural scenes of the Lake District. It contrasts a wholesome country fair with the freak shows of London. Nature's primitive gift to the shepherds is beauty and harmony, which the poet first experienced there. Such "noble savages," primitive men educated by nature alone, are celebrated as truly heroic.

Book 9 tells of the poet's second visit to France and residence in the Loire Valley. It suppresses, however, all the real biographical details concerning Wordsworth's affair with Annette Vallon and his illegitimate daughter. As he passes through Paris, the poet sees "the revolutionary power/ Toss like a ship at anchor, rock'd by storms." He arrives at his more permanent home in the Loire Valley and makes friends with a group of French military officers there. One day as he wanders with his new friends in the countryside, he comes across a hunger-bitten peasant girl, so downtrodden that she resembles the cattle she is tending. His French companion comments, "'Tis against *that* which we are fighting," against the brutalization of humankind by the monarchical system. In later versions, at the conclusion of this book, Wordsworth inserts the story of "Vaudracour and Julia." This love story seems to stand in place of Wordsworth's real-life encounter with Vallon. Book 10 continues his discussion of his visit to France, including a second visit to Paris while the Reign of Terror is in full cry and the denunciation of Maximilien Robespierre takes place. This book also traces his return to England and the declaration of war by England against France, which caused the young Wordsworth deep grief. The French Revolution was probably the most important political event in the poet's life. His initial hopes for the French cause were overshadowed by the outrages of the Reign of Terror. His beloved England, on the other hand, joined in armed opposition to the cause of liberty. In the numerous reworkings of this part of his autobiography, Wordsworth steadily became more conservative in his opinions as he grew older. Book 10 in the 1805 text is split into books 10 and 11 in the 1850 version. In this section, he explains that at the beginning of the French Revolution, "Bliss was it in that dawn to be alive,/ But to be young was very heaven." Yet the course of the revolution, running first to despotic terror and ending with the rise of Napoleon, brought Wordsworth to a state of discouragement and desolation.

Book 11 in the 1805 text (book 12 in the 1850 version) considers how one may rise from spiritual desolation: Having lost the innocent joy of primitive youth and having lost faith in the political aims of the French Revolution, where can the soul be restored? At line 74, the poet tells how "strangely he did war against himself," but nature has a powerful restorative force. At line 258, he enters the famous "Spots of time" argument, in which he maintains that there are remembered experiences that "with distinct preeminence retain/ A vivifying Virtue" so that they can nourish one's depleted spirits. Much as in "Tintern Abbey," a remembered experience of nature can excite the imagination to produce a fresh vitality. Book 12 in the 1805 version (book 13 in the 1850) begins with a summary of nature's power to shape man's imagination and taste:

> From nature doth emotion come, and moods
> of calmness equally are nature's gift,
> This is her glory; these two attributes
> Are sister horns that constitute her strength.

The concluding book tells of the poet's vision on Mount Snowdon in Wales. On the lonely mountain, under the full moon, a sea of mist shrouds all the countryside except the highest peaks. The wanderer looks over the scene and has a sense of the presence of divinity. Nature has such a sublime aspect "That men, least sensitive, see, hear, perceive,/ And cannot choose but feel" the intimation of divine power. In this way, Nature feeds the imagination, and a love of nature leads to a sense of humankind's place in the created universe and a love for all humankind. The poem ends with an address to the poet's friend Coleridge about their mutual struggle to keep faith as true prophets of nature.

It is often said that Wordsworth's *The Prelude*, written in Miltonic blank verse, is the Romantic epic comparable to *Paradise Lost* of Milton. Other critics point to a similarity between *The Prelude* and the bildungsroman, or novel of development. *The Prelude* is subtitled "The Growth of a Poet's Mind" and bears considerable resemblance to such classic stories as Stendhal's *The Red and the Black* (1830), in which the author traces the development of the hero, Julien Sorel, as he grows up. Finally, most readers find an important pastoral element in *The Prelude*. The "pastoral" occurs whenever an author and an audience belonging to a privileged and sophisticated society imagine a more simple life and admire it. For example, sophisticated courtiers might imagine the life of simple shepherds and shepherdesses to be very attractive compared to their own round of courtly duties. They would then imagine a pastoral world in which shepherdesses with frilly bows on their shepherds' crooks and dainty fruits to eat would dally in the shade by fountains on some peaceful mountainside. Such a vision is termed pastoral because it contrasts unfavorably the life of the real author and audience with the imagined life of a shepherd. *The Prelude* makes such pastoral contrasts frequently: for example, in the depiction of rural shepherds in the Lake District compared with urban workers; in the comparison of the life of a simple child with that of the adult; and in the comparison of the working classes of France and England with their masters. The pastoral elements in *The Prelude* are a natural consequence of the primitivism in the poem's ideology.

Wordsworth is one of the recognized giants of English literature, and his importance is nearly equal to Milton's or Shakespeare's. Even so, his work has been the subject of sharp controversy from its first publication until the present. William Hazlitt in his *Lectures on the English Poets* (1818) argues that Wordsworth is afflicted with a false optimism and that his idea of nature is merely a reflection of the human observer's feelings. Aldous Huxley in "Wordsworth in the Tropics" in *Holy Face and Other Essays* (1929) attacks the unnaturalness of Wordsworth's view of nature. John Stuart Mill's *Autobiography* (1873), on the other hand, discusses the restorative power of Romantic poetry and the capacity of Wordsworth to relieve the sterility of a too "scientific" orientation. Later critics have continued the controversy.

The apparent decline of Wordsworth's poetic powers in his later years has occasioned much debate. Was he disillusioned with the course of the French Revolution so that he could no longer bear to praise humankind's primitive nature? Was he so filled with remorse over his affair with Annette Vallon that his inspiration failed? Was he a living demonstration of his own theory of the development of man from infant, to boyhood, to adult: that as man grows older he becomes more and more remote from the primitive feelings of the infant who comes into this world trailing clouds of glory, so that old men can never be effective poets? In any case, the young Wordsworth writing in the 1790's and the first decade of the nineteenth century was a voice calling out that life can be joyful and meaningful, that humankind's nature is good, and that people are not alone in an alien world, but in their proper home.

OTHER MAJOR WORKS

NONFICTION: *The Prose Works of William Wordsworth*, 1876; *Letters of William and Dorothy Wordsworth*, 1935-1939 (6 volumes; Ernest de Selincourt, editor).

BIBLIOGRAPHY

Barker, Juliet. *Wordsworth: A Life*. New York: Viking, 2002. This biography traces Wordsworth's life over eight decades, shedding light on his relationship with his family, his early poetic career, and his politics.

Bloom, Harold, ed. *William Wordsworth*. New York: Chelsea House, 2009. A collection of critical essays on Wordsworth, with an introduction by Bloom.

Bromwich, David. *Disowned by Memory: Wordsworth's Poetry of the 1790's*. Chicago: University of Chicago Press, 1998. Bromwich connects the accidents of Wordsworth's life with the originality of his works, tracking the impulses that turned him to poetry after the death of his parents and during his years as an enthusiastic disciple of the French Revolution.

Gill, Stephen. *William Wordsworth: A Life*. New York: Oxford University Press, 1989. This first biography of Wordsworth since 1965 makes full use of information that came to light after that time, including the 1977 discovery of Wordsworth's family letters as well as more recent research on his boyhood in Hawkshead and his radical period in London.

_____, ed. *The Cambridge Companion to Wordsworth*. New York: Cambridge University Press, 2003. The fifteen essays in this compilation provide excellent introductions to Wordsworth's works.

Johnston, Kenneth R. *The Hidden Wordsworth: Poet, Lover, Rebel, Spy*. New York: W. W. Norton, 1998. A thoroughgoing reexamination of the poet's life that places him far more firmly in the tradition of liberal Romanticism than previous twentieth century critics or even his own contemporaries might have thought.

Liu, Yü. *Poetics and Politics: The Revolutions of Wordsworth*. New York: Peter Lang, 1999. Liu focuses on the poetry of Wordsworth in the late 1790's and the early 1800's. In the context of Wordsworth's crisis of belief, this study shows how his poetic innovations constituted his daring revaluation of his political commitment.

Simpson, David. *Wordsworth, Commodification, and Social Concern: The Poetics of Modernity*. New York: Cambridge University Press, 2009. A discussion of Wordsworth and his works that looks at how his political and philosophical views affected his writings.

Sisman, Adam. *The Friendship: Wordsworth and Coleridge*. New York: Viking, 2007.

An intimate examination of Wordsworth and Samuel Taylor Coleridge's friendship and its deterioration.

Worthen, John. *The Gang: Coleridge, the Hutchinsons, and the Wordsworths in 1802.* New Haven, Conn.: Yale University Press, 2001. Worthen describes the relationships among Samuel Taylor Coleridge and his wife, Sarah; William Wordsworth and his sister, Dorothy; and the Hutchinson sisters, Mary and Sara.

Todd K. Bender

CHECKLIST FOR EXPLICATING A POEM

A. Before reading the poem, the reader should:
1. Notice its form and length.
2. Consider the title, determining, if possible, whether it might function as an allusion, symbol, or poetic image.
3. Notice the date of composition or publication, and identify the general era of the poet.

B. The poem should be read intuitively and emotionally and be allowed to "happen" as much as possible.

C. In order to establish the rhythmic flow, the poem should be reread. A note should be made as to where the irregular spots (if any) are located.

II. Explicating the Poem

A. *Dramatic situation.* Studying the poem line by line helps the reader discover the dramatic situation. All elements of the dramatic situation are interrelated and should be viewed as reflecting and affecting one another. The dramatic situation serves a particular function in the poem, adding realism, surrealism, or absurdity; drawing attention to certain parts of the poem; and changing to reinforce other aspects of the poem. All points should be considered. The following questions are particularly helpful to ask in determining dramatic situation:
1. What, if any, is the narrative action in the poem?
2. How many personae appear in the poem? What part do they take in the action?
3. What is the relationship between characters?
4. What is the setting (time and location) of the poem?

B. *Point of view.* An understanding of the poem's point of view is a major step toward comprehending the poet's intended meaning. The reader should ask:
1. Who is the speaker? Is he or she addressing someone else or the reader?
2. Is the narrator able to understand or see everything happening to him or her, or does the reader know things that the narrator does not?
3. Is the narrator reliable?
4. Do point of view and dramatic situation seem consistent? If not, the inconsistencies may provide clues to the poem's meaning.

C. *Images and metaphors*. Images and metaphors are often the most intricately crafted vehicles of the poem for relaying the poet's message. Realizing that the images and metaphors work in harmony with the dramatic situation and point of view will help the reader to see the poem as a whole, rather than as disassociated elements.

1. The reader should identify the concrete images (that is, those that are formed from objects that can be touched, smelled, seen, felt, or tasted). Is the image projected by the poet consistent with the physical object?
2. If the image is abstract, or so different from natural imagery that it cannot be associated with a real object, then what are the properties of the image?
3. To what extent is the reader asked to form his or her own images?
4. Is any image repeated in the poem? If so, how has it been changed? Is there a controlling image?
5. Are any images compared to each other? Do they reinforce one another?
6. Is there any difference between the way the reader perceives the image and the way the narrator sees it?
7. What seems to be the narrator's or persona's attitude toward the image?

D. *Words*. Every substantial word in a poem may have more than one intended meaning, as used by the author. Because of this, the reader should look up many of these words in the dictionary and:

1. Note all definitions that have the slightest connection with the poem.
2. Note any changes in syntactical patterns in the poem.
3. In particular, note those words that could possibly function as symbols or allusions, and refer to any appropriate sources for further information.

E. *Meter, rhyme, structure, and tone*. In scanning the poem, all elements of prosody should be noted by the reader. These elements are often used by a poet to manipulate the reader's emotions, and therefore they should be examined closely to arrive at the poet's specific intention.

1. Does the basic meter follow a traditional pattern such as those found in nursery rhymes or folk songs?
2. Are there any variations in the base meter? Such changes or substitutions are important thematically and should be identified.
3. Are the rhyme schemes traditional or innovative, and what might their form mean to the poem?
4. What devices has the poet used to create sound patterns (such as assonance and alliteration)?
5. Is the stanza form a traditional or innovative one?
6. If the poem is composed of verse paragraphs rather than stanzas, how do they affect the progression of the poem?

7. After examining the above elements, is the resultant tone of the poem casual or formal, pleasant, harsh, emotional, authoritative?

F. *Historical context.* The reader should attempt to place the poem into historical context, checking on events at the time of composition. Archaic language, expressions, images, or symbols should also be looked up.

G. *Themes and motifs.* By seeing the poem as a composite of emotion, intellect, craftsmanship, and tradition, the reader should be able to determine the themes and motifs (smaller recurring ideas) presented in the work. He or she should ask the following questions to help pinpoint these main ideas:
   1. Is the poet trying to advocate social, moral, or religious change?
   2. Does the poet seem sure of his or her position?
   3. Does the poem appeal primarily to the emotions, to the intellect, or to both?
   4. Is the poem relying on any particular devices for effect (such as imagery, allusion, paradox, hyperbole, or irony)?

BIBLIOGRAPHY

GENERAL REFERENCE SOURCES

BIOGRAPHICAL SOURCES

Cyclopedia of World Authors. 4th rev. ed. 5 vols. Pasadena, Calif.: Salem Press, 2003.

International Who's Who in Poetry and Poets' Encyclopaedia. Cambridge, England: International Biographical Centre, 1993.

CRITICISM

Brooks, Cleanth, and Robert Penn Warren. *Understanding Poetry.* 4th ed. Reprint. Fort Worth, Tex.: Heinle & Heinle, 2003.

Day, Gary. *Literary Criticism: A New History.* Edinburgh, Scotland: Edinburgh University Press, 2008.

Draper, James P., ed. *World Literature Criticism 1500 to the Present: A Selection of Major Authors from Gale's Literary Criticism Series.* 6 vols. Detroit: Gale Research, 1992.

Habib, M. A. R. *A History of Literary Criticism: From Plato to the Present.* Malden, Mass.: Wiley-Blackwell, 2005.

Jason, Philip K., ed. *Masterplots II: Poetry Series, Revised Edition.* 8 vols. Pasadena, Calif.: Salem Press, 2002.

Lodge, David, and Nigel Wood. *Modern Criticism and Theory.* 3d ed. New York: Longman, 2008.

Magill, Frank N., ed. *Magill's Bibliography of Literary Criticism.* 4 vols. Englewood Cliffs, N.J.: Salem Press, 1979.

MLA International Bibliography. New York: Modern Language Association of America, 1922- .

Nineteenth-Century Literature Criticism. Detroit: Gale Research, 1981- .

Vedder, Polly, ed. *World Literature Criticism Supplement: A Selection of Major Authors from Gale's Literary Criticism Series.* 2 vols. Detroit: Gale Research, 1997.

Young, Robyn V., ed. *Poetry Criticism: Excerpts from Criticism of the Works of the Most Significant and Widely Studied Poets of World Literature.* 29 vols. Detroit: Gale Research, 1991.

POETRY DICTIONARIES AND HANDBOOKS

Carey, Gary, and Mary Ellen Snodgrass. *A Multicultural Dictionary of Literary Terms.* Jefferson, N.C.: McFarland, 1999.

Deutsch, Babette. *Poetry Handbook: A Dictionary of Terms.* 4th ed. New York: Funk & Wagnalls, 1974.

Drury, John. *The Poetry Dictionary.* Cincinnati, Ohio: Story Press, 1995.

Kinzie, Mary. *A Poet's Guide to Poetry.* Chicago: University of Chicago Press, 1999.

Lennard, John. *The Poetry Handbook: A Guide to Reading Poetry for Pleasure and Practical Criticism.* New York: Oxford University Press, 1996.

Matterson, Stephen, and Darryl Jones. *Studying Poetry.* New York: Oxford University Press, 2000.

Packard, William. *The Poet's Dictionary: A Handbook of Prosody and Poetic Devices.* New York: Harper & Row, 1989.

Preminger, Alex, et al., eds. *The New Princeton Encyclopedia of Poetry and Poetics.* 3d rev. ed. Princeton, N.J.: Princeton University Press, 1993.

Shipley, Joseph Twadell, ed. *Dictionary of World Literary Terms, Forms, Technique, Criticism.* Rev. ed. Boston: George Allen and Unwin, 1979.

INDEXES OF PRIMARY WORKS

Frankovich, Nicholas, ed. *The Columbia Granger's Index to Poetry in Anthologies.* 11th ed. New York: Columbia University Press, 1997.

_____. *The Columbia Granger's Index to Poetry in Collected and Selected Works.* New York: Columbia University Press, 1997.

Guy, Patricia. *A Women's Poetry Index.* Phoenix, Ariz.: Oryx Press, 1985.

Hazen, Edith P., ed. *Columbia Granger's Index to Poetry.* 10th ed. New York: Columbia University Press, 1994.

Hoffman, Herbert H., and Rita Ludwig Hoffman, comps. *International Index to Recorded Poetry.* New York: H. W. Wilson, 1983.

Kline, Victoria. *Last Lines: An Index to the Last Lines of Poetry.* 2 vols. Vol. 1, *Last Line Index, Title Index*; Vol. 2, *Author Index, Keyword Index.* New York: Facts On File, 1991.

Poem Finder. Great Neck, N.Y.: Roth, 2000.

POETICS, POETIC FORMS, AND GENRES

Attridge, Derek. *Poetic Rhythm: An Introduction.* New York: Cambridge University Press, 1995.

Brogan, T. V. F. *Verseform: A Comparative Bibliography.* Baltimore: Johns Hopkins University Press, 1989.

Fussell, Paul. *Poetic Meter and Poetic Form.* Rev. ed. New York: McGraw-Hill, 1979.

Hollander, John. *Rhyme's Reason.* 3d ed. New Haven, Conn.: Yale University Press, 2001.

Jackson, Guida M. *Traditional Epics: A Literary Companion.* New York: Oxford University Press, 1995.

Padgett, Ron, ed. *The Teachers and Writers Handbook of Poetic Forms.* 2d ed. New York: Teachers & Writers Collaborative, 2000.

Pinsky, Robert. *The Sounds of Poetry: A Brief Guide.* New York: Farrar, Straus and Giroux, 1998.

Preminger, Alex, and T. V. F. Brogan, eds. *New Princeton Encyclopedia of Poetry and Poetics.* 3d ed. Princeton, N.J.: Princeton University Press, 1993.

Spiller, Michael R. G. *The Sonnet Sequence: A Study of Its Strategies.* Studies in Literary Themes and Genres 13. New York: Twayne, 1997.

Turco, Lewis. *The New Book of Forms: A Handbook of Poetics.* Hanover, N.H.: University Press of New England, 1986.

Williams, Miller. *Patterns of Poetry: An Encyclopedia of Forms.* Baton Rouge: Louisiana State University Press, 1986.

ROMANTIC POETRY

Appleby, Carol. *German Romantic Poetry: Goethe, Novalis, Heine, Hölderlin.* Maidstone, Kent, England: Crescent Moon, 2008.

Greenfield, John R., ed. *British Romantic Poets, 1789-1832: First Series.* Dictionary of Literary Biography 93. Detroit: Gale Research, 1990.

_____, ed. *British Romantic Poets, 1789-1832: Second Series.* Dictionary of Literary Biography 96. Detroit: Gale Research, 1990.

Hanak, Miroslav John. *A Guide to Romantic Poetry in Germany.* New York: Peter Lang, 1987.

Hardin, James, and Christoph E. Schweitzer, eds. *German Writers in the Age of Goethe, Sturm und Drang to Classicism.* Dictionary of Literary Biography 94. Detroit: Gale Research, 1990.

_____. *German Writers in the Age of Goethe, 1789-1832.* Dictionary of Literary Biography 90. Detroit: Gale Research, 1989.

Jackson, J. R. de J. *Poetry of the Romantic Period.* Vol. 4 in *The Routledge History of English Poetry.* Boston: Routledge & Kegan Paul, 1980.

_____. *Romantic Poetry by Women: A Bibliography, 1770-1835.* Oxford: Clarendon-Oxford University Press, 1993.

Jordan, Frank, ed. *The English Romantic Poets: A Review of Research and Criticism.* 4th ed. New York: MLA, 1985.

McLane, Maureen N., and James Chandler, eds. *The Cambridge Companion to British Romantic Poetry.* New York: Cambridge University Press, 2008.

Martinez, Nancy C., Joseph G. R. Martinez, and Erland Anderson. *Restoration-Romantic.* Vol. 3 in *Guide to British Poetry Explication.* Boston: G. K. Hall, 1991.

O'Neill, Michael, and Charles Mahoney, eds. *Romantic Poetry: An Annotated Anthology.* Malden, Mass.: Wiley-Blackwell, 2008.

Reiman, Donald H. *English Romantic Poetry, 1800-1835: A Guide to Information*

Sources. American Literature, English Literature, and World Literature in English: An Information Guide Series 27. Detroit: Gale Research, 1979.

Roberts, Adam. *Romantic and Victorian Long Poems: A Guide*. Brookfield, Vt.: Ashgate, 1999.

Rydel, Christine A., ed. *Russian Literature in the Age of Pushkin and Gogol: Poetry and Drama*. Dictionary of Literary Biography 205. Detroit: Gale Group, 1999.

GUIDE TO ONLINE RESOURCES

WEB SITES

The following sites were visited by the editors of Salem Press in 2010. Because URLs frequently change, the accuracy of these addresses cannot be guaranteed; however, long-standing sites, such as those of colleges and universities, national organizations, and government agencies, generally maintain links when their sites are moved.

The Cambridge History of English and American Literature
http://www.bartleby.com/cambridge

This site provides an exhaustive examination of the development of all forms of literature in Great Britain and the United States. The multivolume set on which this site is based was published in 1907-1921 but remains a relevant, classic work. It offers "a wide selection of writing on orators, humorists, poets, newspaper columnists, religious leaders, economists, Native Americans, song writers, and even non-English writing, such as Yiddish and Creole."

LiteraryHistory.com
http://www.literaryhistory.com

This site is an excellent source of academic, scholarly, and critical literature about eighteenth, nineteenth, and twentieth century American and English writers. It provides numerous pages about specific eras and genres, including individual pages for eighteenth, nineteenth, and twentieth century literature and for African American and postcolonial literatures. These pages contain alphabetical lists of authors that link to articles, reviews, overviews, excerpts of works, teaching guides, podcasts, and other materials.

Literary Resources on the Net
http://andromeda.rutgers.edu/~jlynch/Lit

Jack Lynch of Rutgers University maintains this extensive collection of links to Web sites that are useful to researchers, including numerous sites about American and English literature. This collection is a good place to begin online research about poetry, as it links to other sites with broad ranges of literary topics. The site is organized chronologically, with separate pages about the Middle Ages, the Renaissance, the eighteenth century, the Romantic and Victorian eras, and twentieth century British and Irish literature. It also has separate pages providing links to Web sites about American literature and to women's literature and feminism.

LitWeb

http://litweb.net

LitWeb provides biographies of hundreds of world authors throughout history that can be accessed through an alphabetical listing. The pages about each writer contain a list of his or her works, suggestions for further reading, and illustrations. The site also offers information about past and present winners of major literary prizes.

Poet's Corner

http://theotherpages.org/poems

The Poet's Corner, one of the oldest text resources on the Web, provides access to about seven thousand works of poetry by several hundred different poets from around the world. Indexes are arranged and searchable by title, name of poet, or subject. The site also offers its own resources, including Faces of the Poets—a gallery of portraits—and Lives of the Poets—a growing collection of biographies.

Representative Poetry Online

http://rpo.library.utoronto.ca

This award-winning resource site, maintained by Ian Lancashire of the Department of English at the University of Toronto in Canada, has several thousand English-language poems by hundreds of poets. The collection is searchable by poet's name, title of work, first line of a poem, and keyword. The site also includes a time line, a glossary, essays, an extensive bibliography, and countless links organized by country and by subject.

Western European Studies

http://wess.lib.byu.edu

The Western European Studies Section of the Association of College and Research Libraries maintains this collection of resources useful to students of Western European history and culture. It also is a good place to find information about non-English-language literature. The site includes separate pages about the literatures and languages of the Netherlands, France, Germany, Iberia, Italy, and Scandinavia, in which users can find links to electronic texts, association Web sites, journals, and other materials, the majority of which are written in the languages of the respective countries.

Electronic databases usually do not have their own URLs. Instead, public, college, and university libraries subscribe to these databases, provide links to them on their Web sites, and make them available to library card holders or other specified patrons. Readers can visit library Web sites or ask reference librarians to check on availability.

Canadian Literary Centre

Produced by EBSCO, the Canadian Literary Centre database contains full-text content from ECW Press, a Toronto-based publisher, including the titles in the publisher's Canadian fiction studies, Canadian biography, and Canadian writers and their works series, *ECW's Biographical Guide to Canadian Novelists*, and *George Woodcock's Introduction to Canadian Fiction*. Author biographies, essays and literary criticism, and book reviews are among the database's offerings.

Literary Reference Center

EBSCO's Literary Reference Center (LRC) is a comprehensive full-text database designed primarily to help high school and undergraduate students in English and the humanities with homework and research assignments about literature. The database contains massive amounts of information from reference works, books, literary journals, and other materials, including more than 31,000 plot summaries, synopses, and overviews of literary works; almost 100,000 essays and articles of literary criticism; about 140,000 author biographies; more than 605,000 book reviews; and more than 5,200 author interviews. It also contains the entire contents of Salem Press's MagillOnLiterature Plus. Users can retrieve information by browsing a list of authors' names or titles of literary works; they can also use an advanced search engine to access information by numerous categories, including author name, gender, cultural identity, national identity, and the years in which he or she lived, or by literary title, character, locale, genre, and publication date. The Literary Reference Center also features a literary-historical time line, an encyclopedia of literature, and a glossary of literary terms.

MagillOnLiterature Plus

MagillOnLiterature Plus is a comprehensive, integrated literature database produced by Salem Press and available on the EBSCOhost platform. The database contains the full text of essays in Salem's many literature-related reference works, including *Masterplots, Cyclopedia of World Authors, Cyclopedia of Literary Characters, Cyclopedia of Literary Places, Critical Survey of Poetry, Critical Survey of Long Fiction, Critical Survey of Short Fiction, World Philosophers and Their Works, Magill's Literary Annual*, and *Magill's Book Reviews*. Among its contents are articles on more than 35,000 literary works and more than 8,500 poets, writers, dramatists, essayists, and philosophers; more than 1,000 images; and a glossary of more than 1,300 literary terms. The biographical essays include lists of authors' works and secondary bibliographies, and hundreds of overview essays examine and discuss literary genres, time periods, and national literatures.

Rebecca Kuzins
Updated by Desiree Dreeuws

GEOGRAPHICAL INDEX

CATEGORY INDEX

SUBJECT INDEX